NO AR

S0-ADG-908

Teenage
Motherhood

Carolyn Simpson

THE ROSEN PUBLISHING GROUP, INC./NEW YORK

Published in 1992, 1998 by The Rosen Publishing Group, Inc.
29 East 21st Street, New York, NY 10010

Revised Edition 1998

Cover photo by Seth Dinnerman

Library of Congress Cataloging-in-Publication Data

Simpson, Carolyn.
    Coping with teenage motherhood / Carolyn Simpson.
      p.   cm.
    Includes bibliographical references and index.
    Summary: Provides information and advice on how to cope as a teenage mother before and after the baby is born.
    ISBN 0-8239-2569-2
    1. Teenage mothers—United States—Life skills guides—Juvenile literature. [1. Teenage mothers. 2. Pregnancy.]
I. Title.
HQ759.4.S568   1992
306.85'6—dc20   92-8168
                                                       CIP
                                                        AC

Manufactured in the United States of America

ABOUT THE AUTHOR ◇

Carolyn Simpson teaches psychology at Tulsa Community College and is a therapist at the Family Mental Health Center in Tulsa, Oklahoma. She has worked in the mental health field since 1973, principally as a clinical social worker. She also taught and counseled in an alternative high school program originally designed for pregnant and parenting teens in Bridgton, Maine.

Ms. Simpson received a bachelor's degree from Colby College, Waterville, Maine, and a master's degree in Human Relations from the University of Oklahoma. She has written several books on health-related issues and careers. They include *Coping with an Unplanned Pregnancy* and *Coping with Asthma*.

The author lives with her husband, their three children, and their dogs, Lion and Wolf, on the outskirts of Tulsa.

Acknowledgments

Many people have helped me prepare this book. I am profoundly grateful to the Planned Parenthood organization of Tulsa for its information and willingness to answer my questions; to MEND—the Crisis Pregnancy Center of Broken Arrow, Oklahoma, for its help; and especially to the teens at the Margaret Hudson School of Tulsa, who shared so much advice. Thanks to Jan Figart, the executive director of this innovative and tremendously successful school, for her time and helpfulness.

And to my friends Becky, Shelly, Lisa, and Lisa, who shared their thoughts and experiences with me: my special thanks.

Contents

	Introduction	1
1	Facing Pregnancy	2
2	Finding a Support System	12
3	Things to Expect During Pregnancy	21
4	Providing for the Baby	36
5	Preparing for Labor and Delivery	45
6	Following the Birth	60
7	Dealing with a New Baby	69
8	Suddenly Being a Mother	77
9	Taking Care of Your Own Needs	84
10	Birth Control Options	91
11	As Your Child Grows	100
12	How Do I Know I'm Doing Okay?	110
	Glossary	117
	Where to Go for Help	119
	For Further Reading	121
	Index	123

Introduction

This book has two purposes. The first is to *educate* you about the unfolding process of pregnancy, birth, and the raising of a child.

But more than that, it is intended to show you that there are many ways to face the experience, and that when something bad happens (maybe your parents throw you out or your boyfriend dumps you), there are still alternatives. If your family can't support you (emotionally or financially), there are agencies that can help. If you can't afford prenatal care, there are resources open to you. If you discover that your infant isn't the sweet little doll you expected, there are people and books to help you learn to cope.

I don't pretend to know the answers to every situation, but I have a wealth of experience myself (having had four children); and many pregnant and parenting teens from the Margaret Hudson School shared their experiences and advice with me.

This book will help you familiarize yourself with all the facets of pregnancy, birth, and early childrearing. Read the books listed in the For Further Reading section if you want to explore certain subjects in greater depth. At the end of each chapter I've included "Advice from Teen Moms," comments that parenting teens gave me to pass on to you. More than anything else, these girls wanted me to tell you, "Don't give up! It WILL get better."

CHAPTER 1

Facing Pregnancy

Many teen pregnancies happen by accident. Although teens have sex, many do not believe they will become pregnant. Because of this, many teens who become pregnant are not prepared to face the reality of pregnancy. According to Advocates for Youth, almost 3,000 teenage girls become pregnant each day, and about 1 million teens become pregnant every year. Teens need to recognize the signals their bodies are sending to them about a possible pregnancy. By finding out as soon as possible, they have many options available to them. If, however, they ignore the signs, many of the options will no longer be available to them.

Usually, the first clue to pregnancy is a late menstrual period or a slight amount of bleeding about the time your period was due. Some girls complain that their breasts "tingle"; it's a feeling that usually indicates your period is about to start, but it doesn't start. Your breasts simply go on feeling tingly and sensitive.

Even if you haven't noticed that your period is overdue or experienced any breast sensations, there are other signs. Nausea and vomiting are common symptoms of early pregnancy. Some people wake up feeling queasy; some stay queasy all day; some feel queasy only at mealtimes. Unfortunately, some teens convince themselves that they feel sick because they're nervous, under a lot of stress, or catching the flu. If the nausea is accompanied by a need to go to the bathroom more frequently, they may tell themselves they have a bladder infection, which itself is reason enough to see a doctor.

If you even suspect you're pregnant (and *any unprotected act of intercourse* can lead to pregnancy), find out for sure immediately. Pretending that the symptoms mean something else or ignoring them won't make the pregnancy go away. Simply not wanting to be pregnant won't make it go away either. Finding out early—verifying the pregnancy—gives you options and the opportunity to seek early prenatal care, which will result in a better pregnancy and a healthier baby.

Pregnancy Tests

So how do you find out for sure whether you're pregnant? You can check it out in a variety of ways. To check it out in secrecy, you can buy one of the home pregnancy tests available in drugstores or supermarkets. They cost from $6 to $17, depending on the brand and whether the kit contains one or two tests. The good things about these kits are that you can use them without anyone else knowing, they're more accurate than in the past, and they can be used as early as two or three days after your period was due.

The tests have easy-to-follow directions. All you have to do is check your results. Best of all, the results show up in three minutes. If you have any questions, most kits have a toll-free number printed on their package, so you can consult with someone (in privacy) about your results.

The problems with home pregnancy tests are that if you take the test in private you may not have a support person to help you *deal* with the news, and that the test results are sometimes inaccurate. It is always wise to confirm a positive result with a physician whenever possible. If you want someone available to give you advice, your best bet is to go to a clinic that offers pregnancy testing and follow-up care. You can find these clinics in the Yellow Pages of your phone book under Birth Control or Pregnancy Counseling or Family Planning. The services are almost always free, and you can often get the result in a matter of minutes. If you are pregnant, you can talk to a professional about your options.

If you don't mind going to your family physician and you can afford it, that is another option. The nurse will probably test your urine and your blood. The doctor may then give you a physical exam. If it's just a couple of days after your period was due, you may only be given a blood test. The result from a blood test is more dependable than a urine test, especially early in the pregnancy.

Each method—seeing your doctor, going to a clinic, or using a test kit at home—has its advantages and disadvantages. What matters is that you decide to *use one of them.* The longer you wait to confirm your pregnancy, the fewer options you have available.

Once you find out that you're pregnant, it may take some time to digest the news. The sooner you accept the fact that you are indeed pregnant, the sooner you can start preparing for the event. Tests *can* be wrong, but if you've taken more than one, and they have come back positive—then learn to accept the fact and move on.

Coping with Feelings

Accepting the fact that you're pregnant means dealing with an assortment of emotions. Perhaps you'll be shocked that "it could happen to me!"; perhaps you'll be angry at yourself—or at the guy—for not being more careful. Perhaps you'll wonder how this will change your life. You may be angry, confused, and depressed. "What am I going to do now?" You may be scared. "What are my parents going to say?" "How can I tell them?" Then again, you may be excited and pleased in some ways. To some people, having a baby signifies adulthood. It proves that someone must have found you desirable, and that might bring a smile to your face. The reality of actually having created a life probably won't sink in right away.

First of all, accept all of your feelings. It's okay to be angry, distressed, and depressed. It's okay even to wish you weren't pregnant. Talk to a counselor who can help you deal with your feelings, and then forgive yourself. Forgive your boyfriend, too. Carrying around anger and resentment for the next nine months will be a waste of your time.

Next, consider your circumstances and set some goals. Do you want to marry the father of the baby? Does he want to marry you? Is that practical, or are you both too young and inexperienced to handle the responsibilities that come with marriage? Is your partner someone with whom you want to spend the next fifty years or so, because that's how long a marriage can last. If you can't envision living with this guy or you suspect he won't remain faithful to you (or you won't remain faithful to him) for the duration, then consider other possibilities. Getting pregnant may have been a mistake, but don't make it worse by marrying someone you don't really love. Young people do much of their growing and changing in their early twenties, so you two may become very different people in the next five to ten years.

There are other options to consider. You may decide to be a single parent, with help from the father. Abortion may be an option if it is morally acceptable to you. Adoption is an option that may allow you some control as to where your baby ends up.

Breaking the News

First, tell the father. After all, it's his baby too. He has rights and responsibilities to the baby as well. Sit down with him and calmly discuss your options. You will want or need his financial support.

Telling your parents can be very hard. I know one girl who didn't tell her parents until she was almost eight months pregnant because she feared their reaction. I kept wondering what was going to happen when the baby came. Was she going to murmur, "Oh, by the way, I'm having a baby now"? The longer you put off telling them, the harder it will be. Get it over with. Pick a time when neither you nor they will be distracted. In other words, don't blurt out the news as they're hustling off to work in the morning. You might wait until the evening dishes are done and your parents are relaxing, maybe with the newspaper or a book. Mention that you have something important to discuss with them. Since you will probably be nervous, have your first few words memorized. Tell them that you're pregnant and how you're feeling about it. Because most parents have certain expectations for their children, they may initially be upset. Your parents may also need time to think about the situation. Give them time and let them express their feelings, as long as they aren't abusive to you, and if you want their help, consider your options together. Will you remain with them and raise the baby at home? Will you place the baby for adoption?, etc. After the initial shock has worn off, chances are your parents will handle the news better than you think.

If you are afraid to tell your parents, talk to a counselor first to decide how best to approach them. The people at family planning clinics are usually willing to help a teenager tell her parents. No matter how much you fear your parents' anger or resentment, take this step and continue to set goals.

Prenatal Care

The urgency about confirming your pregnancy and telling the appropriate people rests in the importance of getting prenatal care as early as possible. Tests need to be done to identify any health problems you may have and to pinpoint any possible risks attached to the pregnancy. Failure to obtain prompt prenatal care can lead to birth complications, a premature baby, or a low-weight baby. If money is a problem (as it is for a majority of teenagers), consider a family planning clinic, the city health department, or Planned Parenthood (a nationwide network of family planning clinics designed to help low-income people). At Planned Parenthood, the doctors will treat you at a reduced charge, depending on your financial need.

What to Expect on Your First Appointment

Your first appointment with your doctor is very important. It is during this appointment that your doctor will gather all the necessary information to determine if you will have a normal and healthy pregnancy. The doctor will ask about your personal and family history to determine if the baby is at risk for inherited diseases. The doctor will also conduct a physical exam, which will include a pelvic examination and a blood pressure reading, as well as check your height and weight. Blood and urine samples will be taken and examined. The doctor will assess your current overall health. The doctor will also discuss general guidelines for a healthy baby, such as diet, exercise, the need to avoid using drugs and alcohol, and other dangers to be aware of. This is generally the time to ask questions and discuss your concerns.

You will need to see your doctor every three to four weeks up to the seventh month of pregnancy. During the eighth month, you will need to see your doctor every two weeks, and in the ninth month of pregnancy, you will see your doctor weekly.

Ultrasound is a common test done during pregnancy. A jelly is smeared on your stomach. A device called a transducer is moved around the stomach. This device sends out sound waves, which are used to create a picture of the fetus. This test is used to check if the fetus is developing normally as well as to confirm the stage of your pregnancy.

Continuing School

Along with considering your relationship with your parents, consider how your pregnancy will affect your ability to finish school. When I was a teenager, it was understood that if a girl became pregnant she dropped out of school. Nowadays, it is understood that the worst thing a teenager can do is abandon her education. Education is often what gives people opportunities to a better future. To give up your education and stay home waiting for the baby to be born is a grave mistake. Wonderful programs are available (which we will explore in the next chapter) that can enable you to continue to go to school and to learn valuable information about your pregnancy and about parenting skills.

School may seem like one more burden that you don't want to deal with. You may be afraid that other students will gossip behind your back about your pregnancy. And how will you be able to concentrate when your life is changing so drastically? But think carefully about what will happen if you quit school.

If you drop out of school, how will you support yourself and your child if your parents stop supporting you or if the father neglects his responsibilities? How will your decision affect the rest of your life? Will you be able to find a job that pays well and doesn't require a high school diploma? How will you be able to take care of your child on a minimum-wage job, provided that you can find someone to baby-sit while you're working? Typically, a minimum-wage job does not support a family. You will need to prepare for a career, and the best way to do that is to stay in school.

There are solutions to almost every problem. There are separate schools for pregnant and parenting teens and places where you can bond with other teenagers who are in similar circumstances. There are schools where you can learn about proper nutrition and stress reduction while you are pregnant. By continuing your education in these special programs, you will end up a better parent. You will be able to provide a better future for your child.

Changes in the Welfare System

Many changes have recently taken place in the welfare system. In 1996, Congress passed welfare reform that greatly affected the aid available to teenage parents. In the past, many single teenage mothers received welfare from a program called Aid to Families with Dependent Children (AFDC). All mothers, including teenagers, who met the eligibility requirements were able to receive cash assistance from AFDC. But AFDC has been eliminated and replaced with a new program called Temporary Assistance to Needy Families (TANF).

TANF places new eligibility restrictions on minor parents. Under new requirements, single mothers under the age of eighteen will not receive federally funded cash aid unless they live with a parent, legal guardian, another adult relative, or another approved adult-supervised arrangement. If a mother is under eighteen years of age and has not received a high school diploma or equivalency degree, she has to attend school in order to receive aid. There is also a new lifetime limit of five years for receiving TANF.

Some states may have even stricter restrictions on welfare than the federal laws. Because programs and rules will differ from state to state, it's important to speak to social services in your state to determine what kind of public assistance is available to you. For more information about the welfare policy in your state, look in your local Yellow Pages under Social and Human Services. It will list people and organizations that can help you.

Advice from Teen Moms

1. "Be open with the father about the pregnancy. Don't keep it a secret from people close to you."

2. "Don't expect it to be easy; it won't be."
3. "Just because you're pregnant doesn't mean you have to marry. If you're not sure you want kids, there is always adoption. It is much better to place a child in love and security than to keep it in unstable conditions."
4. "Don't look down on yourself."
5. "Get medical care as soon as you become pregnant."
6. "Continue with your life. Finish school."

CHAPTER 2

Finding a Support System

F acing teenage parenthood can be scary. You have barely finished being a child yourself. All of a sudden, you have to face the responsibility of taking care of a baby. But teens need to realize that they don't have to handle these responsibilities alone. There are many people who can help. By building a support network of people, such as your parents, the father of your child, relatives, or friends, you can get help during and after your pregnancy to ease your burden. These people will also be able to help you cope with problems you may experience.

You'll first want to consider how supportive the father of your baby is going to be. Is he someone you want to help you emotionally through the pregnancy? Would you want him with you during delivery? Is he supportive and dependable? No matter what your current relationship with the father is, he is obligated by law to support his child until the child reaches maturity (legally defined as age eighteen). You may not want your boyfriend's emotional support, but his financial support will definitely help you. Remember, the pregnancy is probably going to be a shock to him, so give him time to adjust.

Let him be upset (as long as he isn't hurting you), and then wait for him to calm down. Whether or not you and he continue a relationship, he will always have an obligation to this child. If he's a guy who can also respond to your changing needs, and you can depend on him, you are indeed fortunate. He'll have to grow up during this pregnancy, just as you will. If he isn't emotionally supportive, however, you can't force it. You can expect financial support, but you can't make him love you or the child or accept what has happened to his life.

People on Your Side

Next, consider for a moment who else is on your side. What about your parents? Think of them as your primary allies. Even if they aren't able to help financially, they can assist you in decision-making and help you find the right agencies to lend you financial support. Many girls have told me that their parents were upset when they first heard about the unplanned pregnancy, but nonetheless came around, especially as it became obvious how much their help was needed.

Your parents can help you in lots of ways. For one thing, it's a relief just to be able to share your unexpected news. Using your energy to plan for the baby is certainly better than using it to guard a "secret." If you're willing to listen to your parents, they may help prepare you for your upcoming role: what you'll need to buy for a new baby, the medical care he or she will need, how to cope when the baby doesn't sleep through the night.

If your parents are financially secure, they might help with the basic necessities for the baby that you may not be able to afford. Even when parents seem to have trouble making ends meet, they may make a budget to fit the baby's needs.

Parents can give you moral support while you're dealing with the pregnancy, they can give you financial support, and they can give you a sense of being nurtured yourself— that is, if they're emotionally and financially able to do so. Some parents are not.

What do you do if your parents are not willing or able to help you? Consider your relationship with the father of the baby. Is he someone with whom you'll maintain a relationship, even if you don't marry? If so, how support- ive can *his* parents be? Perhaps they'll want to be in- volved with their grandchild and are in a better position than your parents to lend financial support. Should your parents kick you out (as has happened to some girls), con- sider living with your boyfriend's parents or looking to community service agencies for help.

How Friends Can Help

Friends can be a good source of help during this time. They can help you stay grounded. While you are stressing about how the baby will change your life, you can call up a friend and catch up on the latest gossip at school. This can be a valuable stress release method. Through this, you realize there is still a world beyond pregnancy and moth- erhood, and every second of your life does not have to revolve around the baby.

But you may also find that the common interests you share with your friends may disappear during and after your pregnancy. Your priorities have changed; you are worrying about your pregnancy and how your life will change because of the baby. Your friends, however, are probably still worrying about school, dating, and parties. Because of these differences, you may find that you and some friends may drift apart. You may want to find some new friends who understand your concerns or even share the same concerns.

Some girls find these friends in YWCA support groups or school parenting programs. The girls in these programs and groups probably share your circumstances. You may have an easier time talking to them about your concerns and fears. However, this does not mean your old friends can't or won't understand your problems. Good friends are those who support you no matter what the circumstances.

Professional Care

When you need professional advice, look to your doctors and nurses and the support people who are providing pre-natal care. If you go to a clinic, you may find yourself with a rotating shift of doctors. That makes it hard to establish a relationship with your primary-care physician. Not all clinics operate that way, however. You may have appointments with one specific doctor, but he or she may not be the one who helps with your delivery. If you have a different doctor with each appointment, try to establish rapport with the nurses. You need to feel comfortable with those who are taking care of you so that you'll feel free to ask about whatever is bothering you. Remember, you're entitled to be taken seriously and to be treated with respect.

Doctors like to have patients ask questions or voice complaints. It's hard for them to guess how a patient is feeling. Don't assume that because of your age, your questions or complaints won't be taken seriously. Asking questions about your condition and about labor and your ability to get through it will enable you to cope better with problems that you may face in the future.

Other Sources of Support

It's harder to deal with your pregnancy when you have little or no family support, but other sources of support are available. Many community service agencies will provide you with financial resources and prenatal care, or at least help you obtain them. Some may even provide child care or help you find a job. As mentioned in chapter 1, most family planning clinics offer free pregnancy testing. Family planning clinics offer referral services, which means they can point you in the right direction if they can't help you with what you need. They can help you find a support group for pregnant teenagers; they can help you find a childbirth class to join; they can help you find lodging and the financial resources to pay for it.

Some clinics have emergency supplies of baby food and can lend you baby furniture, baby products, and maternity clothing. All the teenager has to do is show need and promise to return the things borrowed. Later on, these same support personnel can help with birth-control information and filing for welfare assistance.

The advantage of developing a relationship with someone at a clinic is that you have another human being willing to walk you through one of the most confusing times in your life. The staff member, who often has a background in counseling or health education, can provide short-term counseling or refer you to another professional should you need more intensive treatment for an emotional problem. He or she can offer you concrete resources, not merely advice. After the baby comes, you can continue, at some clinics, to receive baby-care education and birth control information.

Most agencies prefer to work with teenagers who have told their parents about the pregnancy. If this is difficult for you, they'll help you break the news. However, if you don't want your parents to find out right away, ask about the clinic's policy before you involve yourself.

Planned Parenthood in most cases offers pregnancy testing, birth control information, and a prenatal clinic with a sliding-scale fee (which means you pay what you can afford to pay—determined by them). Sometimes these clinics work with hospitals so that you see your doctor for prenatal visits at the clinic, and the same doctor delivers your baby in the hospital.

As was mentioned earlier, you can find family planning clinics in the Yellow Pages of your phone book under Birth Control, Family Planning, and Pregnancy Counseling. Planned Parenthood will be listed in the white pages if there's one in your area.

Your city health department is an inexpensive alternative to family planning clinics, but the waiting list for treatment is usually long, and the care provided is less private.

Support from the School System

Whether you believe it or not, your school can be a helpful part of your support network. We have already discussed the importance of staying in school during your

pregnancy. This does not mean you have to stay in a traditional school that may not meet your needs. There are
many alternative schools that can help pregnant and parenting teens with their education as well as take into consideration their circumstances.

Some programs allow the pregnant teenager to continue attending class with her peers, and they provide
health and parenting classes so that she'll be better
prepared for parenthood. When the baby comes, she can
resume her classes and leave her infant in the capable
hands of day-care workers in the school. For some
girls, the idea of never leaving their old school and
friends is appealing, but for others it is intimidating. "I
didn't want to hang around a place where everyone
was staring at me all the time," one girl said. "And I sure
didn't want to try to squeeze myself into those desks,
or have my water break in class, or something equally
embarrassing."

There are also programs that take the teen out of
the traditional setting and place her in a separate facility.
The teenager is surrounded by other pregnant and parenting teenagers, and the day-care facility is right at the
school so the girls can be close to their babies. These programs help the teens learn to be good parents as well as
good students. They learn from their teachers, counselors,
and school nurses how to take care of themselves and
their babies. More than that, the staff and students
become close to one another, with the adults serving as
mentors and giving the girls hugs and support that
they might not be getting anywhere else. The teens I
talked with in some of the programs actually looked
forward to school each day. They discovered that school
gave them more than education: It gave them back their
self-esteem.

"Self-Support"

Last, but far from least, *you* are your own best support. First of all, take care of yourself. Taking care of yourself benefits the baby as much as it does you. The baby receives its nourishment from you; what goes into you goes to the baby. This may be hard, especially if you crave foods, such as potato chips, that aren't good for the baby.

Doctors will prescribe vitamins for you, but vitamins are *supplements* to balanced meals, not replacements for them. You need to eat vegetables, fruits, proteins, and dairy products. In fact, as a teenager, you need to increase your protein intake and drink an extra glass of milk each day.

If you're taking an iron supplement (as most doctors will prescribe) and even if you're not, you may get constipated. Some girls turn to laxatives for relief. This can be dangerous, particularly as you approach labor. Instead, eat more green, leafy vegetables and fresh fruit. Drink eight to ten glasses of water each day. You probably think you hit the bathroom enough as it is, but the water cleanses your system. If you have a real problem with constipation, try a natural-fiber preparation, such as Metamucil or Fiberall.

More words of wisdom: Limit your fat intake, lay off the junk food, and watch out for artificial sweeteners. We don't know enough about how artificial sweeteners can affect your fetus, so better to play it safe than sorry.

Advice from Teen Moms

1. "By all means, don't drop out of school."
2. "Become involved with support groups and/or

church activities. Sometimes they provide assistance at times of need."

3. "When you're pregnant, take care of yourself and eat right."

CHAPTER 3

Things to Expect During Pregnancy

T his chapter will cover most of the physical side effects of pregnancy, as well as possible emotional changes. Don't feel that you have to experience all of them in order to be "normal." No pregnancy is the same. There are ways to lessen the symptoms that bother you most, but in many circumstances it's a matter of simply hanging in there for the next several months. There are things you should avoid when you're pregnant, and this chapter will discuss many of them. We will also hear from other teen moms about the best and worst parts of pregnancy for them.

Nausea

The first physical symptom you'll probably notice when you are pregnant is nausea. Many women get a queasy stomach early in pregnancy; some spend a part of each day vomiting. Nausea doesn't indicate anything good or bad about your pregnancy, nor does it indicate the sex of the baby. Some people get sick; others don't. Doctors say it probably has to do with hormones. The increased level of hormones that sustain your pregnancy make many women feel nauseated. Theoretically, the nausea and vomiting last only three months, but some women report feeling sick for the duration of their pregnancy.

If you do get sick at the beginning of pregnancy, take heart. There are things you can do. If you get sick upon rising in the morning (the typical time for nausea to set in), keep some crackers on your nightstand. Start nibbling the crackers before you even lift your head off the pillow. Eat several small meals throughout the day. Some women find eating solid protein, such as meat or cheese, just before going to bed helps stave off morning sickness. Consult your doctor or nurse if you simply can't keep food down. Remember, the baby receives nourishment from you, and if you're not getting anything substantial, neither is he or she. Drink lots of fluids. You don't want to dehydrate yourself. Popsicles are good, and frozen fruit juice bars have some nutritional value too. Ginger ale or a cola can also ease feelings of nausea. The nausea should pass in three months. Keep looking ahead.

One last thought: Don't *expect* to get sick. Not all women do.

Fatigue

You'll probably start feeling more tired than usual, and as your pregnancy progresses you'll even want to take naps to get through the day. Resting more doesn't mean you're wimping out. You need your rest for several reasons. First, you're sustaining a life inside you; your heart has to work harder, and your body is expending a great deal of energy in helping the fetus become fully developed. Second, you need to conserve some of your energy for labor. Third, toward the end of pregnancy you'll have more trouble sleeping at night. Fourth, as the pregnancy progresses, you will be carrying more and more weight, often as much as twenty-five to thirty-five pounds. If you're tired, sleep. If you can't stretch out, at least put your feet up.

When your belly starts ballooning, it'll be hard to sleep in any position. Doctors suggest lying on your side, with a pillow propped between your legs for comfort. Don't lie flat on your back; that puts more strain on your insides.

In the beginning of your pregnancy, you may need to urinate more frequently because your bladder rests on your uterus. Because your uterus is expanding, it puts pressure on your bladder. During the fifth, sixth, and seventh months, you will have probably become used to going to the bathroom every hour or so. In the last stages of pregnancy, you'll again feel like you're going to the bathroom a lot. By then, your enlarged uterus is pushing on your bladder so much that it can't hold its full capacity; you may even leak some urine if you laugh too hard, sneeze, or drink too much. You can't change that, but you can be prepared for it. Wear panty shields and always locate the bathrooms as soon as you arrive somewhere.

The Pregnant Belly

Naturally, your belly is going to expand during your pregnancy. It doesn't happen overnight. You'll first notice your clothes feeling tighter and the waistbands having no give. Not many people can afford several seasons of maternity clothes. So adjust your buttons and wear over-sized shirts.

Leggings are a good choice early on because they expand more than regular pants. Soon enough, the day will come when your belly refuses to fit into your pants. Most maternity clothes are flexible, and you can wear it in your fourth month through your ninth month.

Don't panic when your waist disappears, and the shape of your body changes! If you eat right, you should be able to regain your shape quite easily after your pregnancy. If you do have trouble, consult with your physician about how to reach your ideal weight.

Weight Gain

Try not to worry about weight gain too much during your pregnancy. Just as each pregnancy varies, the weight gain also differs from woman to woman. Sometimes this weight gain depends on the size of the woman. If you eat healthily and do moderate exercises, such as walking and swimming, you will have nothing to worry about. You should consult your doctor before beginning an exercise program, especially if you were not physically active before your pregnancy. If your obstetrician thinks you are gaining too much weight, he or she will let you know and will review your eating habits. Gaining too much weight can complicate your pregnancy, and it will also be harder to lose that weight after the birth of the baby.

Most obstetricians recommend an average weight gain of twenty-four pounds, although acceptable weight gain can be as little as twenty pounds and as much as thirty-five pounds or even more. About twenty pounds of your weight gain are the result of the baby: the average baby weighs about seven and a half pounds; your placenta and membranes weigh about two pounds; amniotic fluid weighs about two pounds; your expanded uterus increases in weight by about three pounds; and your breasts become about two pounds heavier. Also, the body produces about four pounds of extra blood and other fluids.

You will probably feel more hungry than usual, but that does not mean you're supposed to double your intake of food because you're eating for two. An average pregnant woman needs to consume between 2,000 to 2,400 calories a day. This number can increase depending on how active you are. The weight gain only comes off easily afterward if you've eaten sensibly during the pregnancy.

Other Symptoms

You may encounter some other symptoms that are the result of being pregnant—like hemorrhoids. Hemorrhoids occur when the veins around the anus become swollen and may bleed due to constipation or straining during bowel movements. Hemorrhoids can be avoided by eating plenty of fresh fruits and vegetables. You can also try natural fiber preparations.

Doctors see more bladder infections in pregnant women. This may be a sign of not drinking enough fluids. Remember to drink a lot of water and fruit juices.

You'll probably experience an increase in vaginal discharges. There is no need to be concerned unless there is a strong, unpleasant odor or excessive amount of discharge, which may signal an infection. Toward the end of your pregnancy, your vaginal canal will produce lubrication for the baby. Wearing panty shields may help you deal with the discomfort.

Some pregnant women experience sinus trouble, nosebleeds, and headaches. You should always ask your doctor before taking a medication because it could affect the baby.

Your skin will become itchy because it's drier and is stretching. Just apply body lotion regularly. Avoid long, hot baths. Stretch marks? If you get them (and not all women do), keep applying lotion to them. The marks across your abdomen, breasts, and legs will fade into pearly white lines after the baby is born. Having stretch marks does not mean that you didn't take care of yourself or that you gained too much weight too fast. Some people have more elastic skin than others. About all you can do is keep the skin lubricated.

You may experience leg cramps, particularly at night. They can be very painful. You may find relief by changing your position or by taking a warm bath. Tell your doctor if it happens often or lasts more than a few minutes.

You may feel dizzy when you stand up or get up in the morning. Remember, your heart is working overtime to take care of you and the fetus, so you need to rest more. Getting up alters your blood pressure; hence, you may feel dizzy. Try doing everything at a slower pace. It helps.

Another symptom of pregnancy is gas. Your stomach will churn, and your bowels will rumble. Because your intestines are being pushed out of shape by your uterus, they have a harder time moving food along quietly. Before you take an over-the-counter drug for gas, check with your doctor.

Some women develop something called "the mask of pregnancy." It's a dark patch over part of your face, which eventually subsides after childbirth. You may also get a dark brown line down the middle of your abdomen. That too disappears a few weeks or months after delivery.

Toward the end of pregnancy you may start feeling breathless as your uterus pushes against your diaphragm. Sometimes you can feel the baby's foot in your rib cage or kicking you in other unpleasant ways.

You may notice other things about your pregnancy that I haven't mentioned. It doesn't mean that your pregnancy is abnormal, nor does it mean that it's not a problem. Anything that bothers you is worth mentioning to your doctor and nurse. The following paragraphs discuss symptoms that require *immediate* attention.

Symptoms Requiring Immediate Medical Care

Vaginal bleeding can have a variety of causes. Not all bleeding is dangerous. Sometimes it occurs after sexual intercourse. Some women bleed for a couple of months into their pregnancy around the time when they are supposed to have their period. But any amount of steady or heavy bleeding should be reported to your doctor. It could be a sign of placental problems.

Placenta previa is a condition in which the placenta is not located high enough in the uterus, but is instead partly or completely over the cervix. This can be dangerous especially toward the end of the pregnancy when the cervix begins to expand. This expansion can tear the placenta. Bleeding will occur from the vagina from this tear. This bleeding can be dangerous and even deadly to the fetus. A cesarean section is performed to prevent further bleeding.

Premature rupture of membranes is another serious condition. The membranes that surround the fetus usually rupture just before or during labor, but they can rupture weeks or months before the due date. This is dangerous, especially if they rupture in the middle of your pregnancy (when the baby is unable to survive outside the womb) because there is a risk that labor will begin. If you feel a sudden gush or a continual flow from your vagina, contact your doctor immediately.

Any swelling (particularly any sudden swelling) in the limbs should be reported to your physician.

Continuous vomiting should be reported.

Sex During Pregnancy and STDs

Pregnancy does not mean an end to sex. You can have sexual relations all the way up to delivery, although some physicians tell patients to refrain from intercourse in the final month of pregnancy. But you must be certain of your partner's sexual history. You can't tell by looking at a person whether he has a sexually transmitted disease (STD), or even AIDS, an STD with no cure. If you engage in unprotected sex (just because you're already pregnant), you may contract an STD and pass it to your baby, endangering his or her health.

What STDs should you worry about? Genital herpes, for one. It's a common enough infection, but it can't be cured, only treated. You don't get rid of herpes; it merely goes into remission from time to time. If you know you have herpes, tell your doctor. He or she will do weekly tests in your last month of pregnancy to determine whether the herpes virus in your vagina is active or in remission. If you have an active case of herpes when you go into labor, you'll need to have a cesarean section to avoid passing the infection to the baby as it moves through the birth canal. Otherwise, your child may be born blind.

Chlamydia is the most common STD in the United States today. The only symptom may be an increase in vaginal discharge. Chlamydia can be passed to the baby in the birth canal, resulting in eye infection, pneumonia, and stomach and intestinal problems. Chlamydia is easily treated with erythromycin, a drug that is not known to be harmful to the fetus.

Women are tested for gonorrhea during prenatal care. However, you can catch gonorrhea even though you are pregnant, and 98 percent of women show no symptoms. Gonorrhea can be passed from the mother to the baby in the birth canal. Gonorrhea may damage the baby's eyes.

If you have reason to believe you've been exposed to HIV, the virus that causes AIDS, tell the doctor immediately. Get yourself tested; some doctors ask you to have an HIV test anyway when you're pregnant.

AIDS has no cure so far. If you are HIV-positive, there's a strong chance your baby will be born HIV-positive.

Emotional Aspects of Pregnancy

Sometimes it is more difficult to deal with the emotional aspects of being pregnant. The emotional ups and downs are a reflection of your raging hormones, your attitude toward the event, and how much support you have. Being upset doesn't mean that you're a bad person or that you reject the pregnancy. Anyone is bound to feel stressed by such an important event. You will experience many feelings during your pregnancy.

Some people feel only joy and happiness during pregnancy. Every discomfort is welcomed because it reminds the woman that she's actually having a baby, or she may be excited because she will be a mother soon. She will have a cuddly little baby to love and who'll love her back. If you have a positive attitude, it will make all the difficult aspects of being pregnant easier to handle.

But for the majority of women (teens and adults alike), pregnancy is a time when feelings change often. One minute you're happy, the next minute you're worried. One day you're proud of your shape, the next day you're embarrassed. One day you appreciate your boyfriend's or your husband's concern, the next day you feel as if he takes no interest in you.

Accept all your feelings, even the negative ones. Pregnancy is hard work. Being upset and angry at your circumstances isn't unusual and doesn't mean you're hurting the baby. Hating the difficulties of pregnancy doesn't mean you hate the child you've created.

You may be scared about the actual process of childbirth. We're all scared of the unknown. You will feel better if you have a support system in place: people who will listen to your fears and complaints, who will give you comfort and assurance that you'll do just fine.

Some fears may be lessened by talking with others, such as nurses, counselors, doctors, friends, and other pregnant women, about the process of birth and what options you will have for pain relief. The more you know ahead of time, the less you have to fear.

You may feel more dependent than usual on your boyfriend, husband, or parents because of your fears. Accept it for now; you'll revert to your usual, more independent nature after the baby is born, and you've started feeling comfortable about being a parent.

You may worry whether the baby is going to be okay. Staying healthy yourself will help to ensure a healthy baby. Share your concerns with your health care providers. They'll talk over your concerns with you. Read books on pregnancy, delivery, and baby care. This will help relieve many of your fears.

You'll no doubt be excited when you first feel the baby move. The baby is always moving, but you'll become aware of the fluttery feelings around the fifth or sixth month. At first it may feel like indigestion or bubbles bursting inside you. You may even get used to the sensations and miss them after delivery.

Alcohol and Other Drugs

It's important to stay healthy, not only to make the delivery easier for you, but also to help ensure that you will have a healthy baby. Whatever you eat crosses the placenta to the baby. That's why you need to stay away from drugs and alcohol. Even if you drink only a small amount of beer or wine, the fetus ends up with the same proportion in his or her body. Your liver can process the alcohol out of your system, but the fetus's immature liver is not capable of doing so. Babies whose mothers drank alcohol while pregnant can be born with fetal alcohol syndrome. Fetal alcohol syndrome results in neurological problems that damage the intelligence, motor abilities, coordination, and judgment of the fetus. A baby born with fetal alcohol syndrome will suffer its disabling effects for the rest of his or her life.

The U.S. Food and Drug Administration states, "Presently, there is no known safe level of alcohol consumption below which no risk is present." That means that no one knows how much alcohol one can drink without permanently damaging the baby. Why take any risk at all?

Drug abuse can lead to low-birthweight babies. It can cause premature separation of the placenta, resulting in a stillbirth and the possibility of the mother bleeding to death. In 38 percent of pregnancies in which the mother abuses drugs, miscarriage results. A large number go into premature labor. It doesn't matter which drug you abuse; they all carry consequences. Crack cocaine can lead to addiction for both the mother and child. Because it is smoked, crack cocaine reaches the brain faster and in greater quantity than cocaine that is sniffed. Crack causes an increase in blood pressure. Remember, your heart is already working doubly hard to maintain a normal pregnancy. The stress from drug-induced high blood pressure compounds that.

Use of cocaine during pregnancy can lead to respiratory and kidney disease in the fetus. The baby may be born underweight and lack muscle coordination. He or she may be addicted to the drug and go through withdrawal. Cocaine-exposed babies often have severe developmental and behavioral problems.

Researchers have discovered that infants whose parents are drug users are at a higher risk for sudden infant death syndrome (SIDS).

SIDS causes a baby to die suddenly without any apparent reason. SIDS usually occurs when the infant is two or three months old.

Parents with infants who are at a higher risk for SIDS, because one or both parents have abused drugs, can monitor their infants to prevent this tragedy. They need to be trained in CPR (cardiopulmonary resuscitation) and in proper usage of monitoring equipment.

If you are addicted to drugs or alcohol, get help immediately. This will help both you and your baby. Get into a substance-abuse program. If you are using alcohol or other drugs while pregnant, get help immediately. This will help both you and your baby. If you suspect you are addicted, try to find a substance-abuse treatment program. Women who are chemically dependent need help themselves, and until they get it and remain clean and sober, they are unable to provide the care their children need. If you can't take care of your baby, there's a chance that you will lose your child. If you don't know of a drug-abuse program in your area, call (800) 662-HELP. This is a free call for referral to a drug-treatment program and is operated by the National Institute on Drug Abuse.

Dangers of Smoking

Smoking can also damage the health of your fetus during pregnancy. Cigarettes contain 4,000 chemicals that will cross the placenta. When you inhale a cigarette, the baby receives less oxygen. If you smoke regularly, the fetus can suffer from low birth weight, or be born premature or stillborn. Like other drugs, smoking is addictive, and you may need help in quitting. There are many products available in drug stores without a prescription that can help you quit. However, you should ask your doctor before using these products.

Secondhand Smoke

Secondhand smoke also presents a health threat to those who inhale it. Because of this threat, many states have laws restricting smoking in public places. If you inhale secondhand smoke, your fetus will also be exposed to it. Sidestream smoke, the smoke that comes directly from a burning cigarette, contains even higher amounts of dangerous chemicals, such as tar, nicotine, carbon monoxide, and ammonia.

Once your baby is born, he or she can still be harmed by cigarette smoke. Children under one year of age who are exposed to secondhand smoke have an increased chance of developing respiratory illnesses.

Other Dangers

Other dangers in the environment include smog and lead paint. If you live in an older place, don't scrape the paint or refinish the furniture while you're pregnant. And don't go near others who are doing it either. Don't expose yourself to harmful fumes, such as cleaning fluid, glue, or pesticides. Wash all vegetables and fruits carefully. Avoid aerosol products; switch to pump containers.

Toxoplasmosis is an infection caused by a parasite carried by mice. Mice pass this parasite to other animals, such as cats and cows, via their fecal matter. If the mother becomes infected by this during her pregnancy, the parasite will cross the placenta and infect the baby as well. Infected babies can be born with severe eye and central nervous system damage. Women can avoid toxoplasmosis by cooking all meat thoroughly and by not handling or changing cat litter.

Advice from Teen Moms

"Stay away from drugs. They may make you feel better when things are going bad, but all that does is repress the feelings until a later date. Not only that, it's a waste of money."

The best thing about being pregnant was . . .

- "knowing the wonderful time I'll have with my child."
- "that very second when he got here."
- "having my boyfriend there."
- "getting attention."
- "having a baby that I can love."
- "not having a period."
- "when it was over."
- "feeling like I was loved."
- "at the end, getting a beautiful child."

- "feeling the baby move and the anticipation of seeing your baby."

The worst thing about being pregnant was . . .

- "starting to dislike foods I used to love and eating foods that I used to hate."
- "being so fat."
- "the many mood changes."
- "feeling fat and ugly and that I'll never have this kid."
- "gaining almost eighty pounds."
- "not being able to fit into any of my clothes."
- "always feeling sick and tired and dizzy."
- "always being in a grouchy mood."
- "not being able to smoke or have as much coffee as I wanted."
- "getting sick."
- "feeling miserable all the time."
- "being scared of what's to come and not being able to get a part-time job."

CHAPTER 4

Providing for the Baby

Most first-time parents know very little about how much money it will cost to feed, clothe, and care for this new little baby. And teens who've never been on their own usually know little about providing for themselves. So in this chapter we'll look at the costs involved in preparing for the baby, as well as the considerations for housing and support. If you think your situation is beyond hope, cheer up. There are always solutions; you just have to find them.

Before thinking about how you're going to buy all that basic baby equipment, you need to know how you're going to live and feed yourself first. Maybe your parents will flatly tell you that you can't live with them and expect their support. Maybe your home life is so chaotic that you wouldn't want to live under their roof even if they offered it. But more than likely, you'll stay with your parents.

Living at Home

Living with your parents can be good for two reasons: One, you don't have to pay room and board, and two, you have some ready-made company and baby-sitters. Once the baby comes, you'll have to sit down with your folks and decide just what everyone's role will be. If you want them to be the baby's grandparents, don't expect them to take on parental responsibilities as well. It is your job to change the diapers, orchestrate the feedings, and arrange for sitters. It isn't particularly rewarding work, and it's certainly not the fun part of raising a child, but it is important and has to be done. Don't assume that your mother is always available and willing to watch the baby so you can go out with your friends.

Then again, if you do not take responsibility for the baby, your parents may have to take over for you. If you abdicate your mothering role to them, don't complain when the baby looks to them as parents. If you count on them to provide the day-to-day care of the baby, don't complain when they provide the discipline too.

Whose Support?

Perhaps you just don't want to be dependent on your parents any longer. Or maybe you think it'll be easier to live on your own, making the rules and enforcing them as you choose.

But living on your own is not necessarily easier. You have to find a decent place to live, and decent places cost money. How will you afford such a place? You cannot receive cash aid from welfare if you're under eighteen unless you live with your parents or another adult. If you have a job, who will take care of your baby when you're working? Can you find or afford a baby-sitter? Does your job pay enough to support both you and the baby? Remember, new welfare laws have a lifetime limit of five years for receiving welfare.

Even if you're over eighteen and can move out on your own, there are other things to consider. How will you support yourself? Will you struggle on your own, or will you find a roommate? Will that roommate be someone equally responsible, or someone who is just looking to get away from home? If you move in with your boyfriend, will he quit school to get a job? Will he support you? Should you marry him now, wait until you see what kind of father he'll be, or live apart so you can separate more easily if the time comes?

The Baby's Father

Getting along with your boyfriend (whether you make him your husband or not) is hard work. It will be hard for a guy to understand your needs right now. Your boyfriend may be preoccupied with his upcoming responsibilities. He may be angry at having to give up or postpone some things for the baby (maybe his dream of a career or travel), or angry at himself for not being more careful. If he's honest, he may admit to jealousy over the attention you're getting. He may be struggling with fears about being a good father.

Keep the communication lines open with your boyfriend or spouse. In the beginning, the pregnancy may be more important to you than to him, mostly because it will be apparent only to you. The father can't readily *see* that you're carrying a baby. The baby is not a physical reality to him at this point. Around the time you're more comfortable with yourself (in the second trimester), the father will start to see for himself that you're pregnant. Then he may start being extra careful with you—although by that time you won't feel so fragile. After all, you've felt this pregnancy for three whole months already.

Sharing your feelings, fears, and hopes with him will make the experience more significant to him. But also listen to him and encourage him to talk about his feelings. When people listen to each other without passing judgment, they validate each other. You'll be saying to each other, "How you're feeling right now is important to me."

Teens who have been emancipated (declared an adult by the courts) have the option of living on their own. There are, however, difficulties involved with living alone so consider this as a last resort.

It is hard to support yourself on your own, and it is hard to be the only person responsible for a baby twenty-four hours a day. In addition, it's lonely. Are you afraid of the dark? Do you have trouble staying off the telephone when you're all by yourself? How will you even furnish the place? Before making this decision, think carefully about what your decision to move out will entail and if you can live on your own.

Needs and Wants for the Baby

Now let's look at what the baby will need. If you can't afford to buy all the basics new—and not many teenage parents can—there are other ways to get them.

First of all, learn how to draw up a budget, and then stay within it. One of the hardest things for anyone to learn is how to live within a budget. Figure out how much money will come in regularly and decide what things (rent, utilities, food) must be paid for first. Allocate the remaining money wisely. Ask a capable adult (your parents, a counselor, or a teacher) to help you prepare a budget if you have no experience.

Then it is a good idea to draw up a list of wants and needs for the baby. What are the items you want for the baby, and what are the items you *must* have to provide proper care? Take care of the baby's *needs* first, then tackle the *wants* with any leftover money.

What should you buy new? A mattress and an infant car seat as well as small items, such as bottles and pacifiers.

You should purchase a new mattress because they wear out quickly from use. You'll need to have a car seat for when you take your baby home from the hospital. You will not be allowed to take the baby home in a car without a car seat. One reason to buy a new car seat is that they are being improved constantly; what was acceptable a year or two ago may no longer be acceptable. Also, the newer ones are easier to use.

You can buy a crib at a secondhand store or garage sale, but make sure the bars of the crib are no more than $2\frac{3}{8}$ inches apart. Many older cribs have bars that are more widely spaced. Disasters have happened when babies have slipped their heads between crib bars and have been unable to get their heads back through the bars. Also make sure the crib is in decent condition.

You'll need a high chair eventually, and you may want a swing, playpen, carriage, and stroller. If you can't afford these items yourself, see if you can borrow them from a friend or relative. Check with family planning clinics about whether they lend baby furniture. Visit garage sales or consignment shops for bargains. Since baby stuff is used only for a few years, most things should be in good condition.

When you or your parents can't afford something, look for it secondhand. Make a list of things you need. Then if a friend decides to give you a baby shower or asks what you need for the baby, you can consult your list. Now is not the time to say, "Oh, get me anything." Do your friend and yourself a favor by being specific. People would rather give you something you need than something they think you need.

Baby Clothes

Besides furniture, what else will the baby need? Depending on whether the baby is born in summer or winter, you can get away with a minimum of baby clothes. You'll need T-shirts and sleepers—lots of them; you'll be surprised how quickly a little teeny baby can soil his or her clothes. You might prefer gowns with drawstrings at the bottom. They allow you to change the baby's diaper more easily than fumbling with zippers and snaps in a sleeper. Have a lightweight jacket on hand and a winter coverup if it's that time of the year. You can borrow or buy these clothes secondhand. The only people you impress with designer labels at this point are your friends. The baby doesn't know the difference.

Have a lot of blankets and sheets on hand. It's amazing how many times you'll have to change the sheets in the first few days and weeks, in addition to the clothes. Bumper pads for the crib are also helpful, to cushion the sides of the crib so the baby doesn't bump his or her head.

Diapers are another essential. There are cloth and disposable diapers. Cloth diapers can be more economically sound because you reuse them. Today's cloth diapers are also more comfortable than those of the past. Velcro covers are used rather than pins and plastic pants, making them safer and more comfortable. Those who do not wish to wash and fold diapers endlessly can opt for a diaper service, but that can be expensive. You throw away the disposable ones, but they are not cheap, whether you opt for the store brand or buy the cute character-printed ones. Buy what you can afford. You can also call the manufacturer's toll-free number. Companies will sometimes send you money-saving coupons to buy more of their product.

It is also useful to buy twenty-five or more cloth diapers to use as burp cloths on your shoulder, to wipe up drool or spit-up, and as all-purpose cloths when you are away from home with the baby.

Toys

What about toys for the baby? For the first couple of months you and your friends will be more intrigued with the toys than the baby will. A mobile, hung well above the crib out of reach, is nice to have, as are gadgets that play lullabies to the baby. Beyond that, the baby won't be very interested. He or she will prefer the sight of your face and the sound of your voice to anything else. Remember, in the beginning the baby will be eating and sleeping, and that's about it.

If you have extra money, or have parents who simply can't resist, buy rattles and other brightly colored shake toys—things that the baby can explore (safely) with his or her mouth and (later on) hands. Make certain that toys are safe for infants, with no parts that will come off, such as button eyes, glued-on parts, ribbons that are simply tied (rather than sewn on), etc. Also, make certain that toys are not painted with toxic paint. If you get stuffed animals, remember your baby's size. Don't dwarf him or her with an animal that appeals to you; get something small. Don't leave things in the crib that can suffocate the baby—no pillows! Babies sleep flat; they don't need pillows.

Pediatrician

Last, though certainly not least, line up a pediatrician for your baby and plan to visit him or her regularly. Often, you can have one recommended to you when you are in the hospital after you have given birth.

You don't go to the doctor only when you think the baby is sick. Your baby will need a check-up at the hospital before going home and when he or she is approximately one month old. Then he or she will also need shots, and make sure you follow instructions about feeding and handling. The baby stays healthy because of regular pediatric appointments. Keep them. If you can't afford a private pediatrician, consider taking your baby to the county health department for visits.

If you don't breast-feed your baby, you'll need to know which formula your doctor recommends. Babies have different needs, and different formulas are available to meet those needs. You can buy formula in powder form or in premixed liquid. This is one place where you cannot skimp on quality. Diluting the formula with water to make it go further destroys its nutritional value. In effect you'll be starving your baby. If you don't breast-feed, plan on spending a bundle of money on formula for at least the first year of your baby's life. If you're low on funds, ask for help from the welfare office, a family planning clinic, or your parents.

Keep revising your list and your budget. Your needs and wants will change periodically, and maybe your assets will grow as well.

Advice from Teen Moms

1. "Make the best life for your child, because you can never go back and change the way you raised your kid."
2. "If you have decent parents, let them help. If not, find help."
3. "Be prepared; your life will change. You must grow up. If you're not ready, let someone else raise the child."

CHAPTER 5

Preparing for Labor and Delivery

L abor and delivery will happen whether you're prepared or not. Eventually this baby is going to be born, and though some women might want to skip this part of the event, that isn't an option.

For some women (teens included), labor is a breeze, lasting a mere couple of hours. But for the majority of women, labor lasts longer and is considerably more painful, especially when it's a first child, than menstrual cramps. Part of what's so scary about it—and so, makes it seem to hurt all the more—is that most teenagers don't know what to expect. Misunderstandings, confusion, and fear all contribute to a more painful experience than necessary. With that in mind, let's see what happens during childbirth and what you can do to make it less painful. Just as all pregnancies are different, so are all labors. This chapter is only meant to familiarize you with the process and with a few of the possible complications.

Childbirth Classes

After you have read this chapter, I suggest you read one of the childbirth books in the For Further Reading section. You can't know too much about labor and delivery. If you can afford it or know of free classes, take a childbirth class, whether you want to have a medicated delivery or not. You don't have to be married to take childbirth classes. Your mother or your best friend can be your support person. I know some teachers who have served as girls' labor coaches. And you're not committing yourself to natural childbirth by just joining the class. Many women (and men, too) simply want to know more about what's coming up.

If you can't take classes, you can still talk to your doctor, nurse, mother, and school counselors about labor and delivery. School counselors may not all be versed in health care procedures, but anyone who has ever gone through labor and delivery will remember it. They can either give you advice or suggest people and books that can.

Practice relaxation techniques ahead of time. Don't wait until your contractions are three minutes apart before you try to remember the techniques you learned in class. If you don't know any relaxation techniques, we'll describe some midway through this chapter.

Pain Medication

Before we look at the process of childbirth, let's consider what kind of medication is available to relieve the pain. Knowing there is relief available makes the experience more manageable for many women.

First are the painkillers (like Demerol) that are used to reduce the pain. The problem is that you can't have enough of the drug to take away *all* of the pain because the medication crosses the placenta, and you don't want the baby to get too much. Talk about this option with your doctor, or with someone who has used it before, if it interests you. I found that no amount of Demerol disguised the pain for me. It still hurt like crazy, and the drug made my brain so fuzzy that I wasn't certain if I'd had the baby or was still in labor. I could tell what was going on around me, but my mind was very foggy, and I kept insisting to the nurses that it was time for my next dose. Sometimes doctors use tranquilizers to relax you, so that you can help more with the delivery.

Regional anesthesia is used to numb parts of your body to pain and does not harm the baby.

An epidural block works by blocking sensation from your waist down. The anesthesiologist inserts a needle into the membranes surrounding the spinal cord in your lower back. A thin tube is then inserted to administer the anesthetic as needed. The good part is that you have no awareness of pain. It's as if the shot took away the pain, and you can actually begin to enjoy the experience. The bad part is that the shot is hard to administer, so a qualified anesthesiologist must be on duty when you need it. Not only that, the shot itself can be painful. The needle is long, and you have to curl up in a fetal position (which is the last thing you feel like doing when you are in labor) so it can be inserted. Sometimes the anesthetic takes effect on only one side of your body, and you end up feeling one-sided contractions. I've had both good and bad experiences with the epidural block. Once I felt as if I were having a baby out of one side of my body. The other time I couldn't believe the relief I felt.

The spinal block is also a shot that eases pain while allowing the woman to stay alert, but it can't be given until birth is expected within a few hours. It stops the pain, but as far as I'm concerned you've done all the work by then. Dilating (when the cervix, the neck of the uterus, opens to allow for the baby to pass through) is what hurts the most. Drawbacks to the spinal block are the accompanying feeling of dead weight, and pain relief that lasts only two to three hours. My legs no longer seemed to belong to me, and I couldn't help push the baby out because I wasn't aware of any sensation to push. With a spinal block, there's a chance of a spinal headache, which can be quite severe.

The combined spinal-epidural block is a new method that combines the spinal and epidural methods. It is usually given when the woman is dilated three to four centimeters. The spinal shot is given, and a small tube is inserted to provide medication when needed. Because this is a relatively new method, it may not be available in all hospitals.

The pudendal block is an anesthetic injected into the vaginal wall to lessen the pain of repairs after delivery. The doctor gives you a quick shot (not particularly painful, though it's all relative to the greater pain of childbirth) to numb the area between the birth canal and the rectum. Sometimes a doctor performs a episiotomy. He or she makes a cut to widen the area for the baby to come out. It isn't as bad as it sounds and helps prevent tearing. Some doctors prefer not to do episiotomies because it requires them to cut into muscle tissues. By contrast, if a tear occurs, no muscle tissue is torn. As a result, a tear generally heals more quickly than would an episiotomy. In addition, some women feel that doctors give the episiotomy whether or not it is necessary. If you do not want an episiotomy, discuss this with your doctor before you go into labor.

Your last resort, one that is reserved for emergencies

and not labor pains, is general anesthesia, in which the anesthesiologist puts you to sleep. At some point during a· painful labor experience you might think "going to sleep" is a good idea, but it's not an option because of risks to the mother. It's only for surgery, such as a cesarean section, which we'll discuss at the end of the chapter.

Labor

Let's go back now and talk about what happens in labor and why teenage pregnancies are considered high-risk situations. Many complications can accompany teen pregnancies. If the adolescent hasn't finished her own growing, her pelvis may be too small for a vaginal delivery. Cesarean delivery (informally called C-section) is always more of a risk because it is major surgery. Teens are often poorly nourished, because they lack either the money or the knowledge to eat better. They don't always seek early prenatal care because they're trying to keep the pregnancy a secret from their parents or they don't know how to pay for it, and part of what makes for an easy delivery is a healthy pregnancy.

What actually happens in labor? The uterus contracts to signal the beginning of the birth process. Every labor is different, but there are usually similar indicators which signal the beginning of labor. One of these signs is the discharge of the mucus plug that sealed the uterus.

Another sign is the rupture of the membranes that surround the amniotic fluid. When this happens you may feel a sudden gush or a steady flow. This rupture can happen at the beginning or later during the labor.

Contractions also indicate the beginning of labor, but not always. Some contractions are a sign of false labor. It is often hard for women to tell the difference between the two. Contractions that occur at regular intervals and with increasing intensity usually mean labor is starting.

The cervix, the neck of the uterus, has been closed during the pregnancy (to keep infection out and the baby in). In the days before delivery, it has begun to shorten and to become thinner. Now it begins gradually to dilate or open up. It will stretch to ten centimeters in width, which is just enough in most instances to allow safe passage of the baby's head, the widest part of the baby.

For some women, the first indication that labor is about to begin may be the loss of the mucus plug that has covered your cervix throughout the pregnancy. You may notice blood or a heavy vaginal discharge. For others, the mucus plug may come out once contractions have already begun.

One word of warning. *Never* try to induce labor on your own. Some girls think they can bring on labor by using laxatives or giving themselves an enema. Some try lifting heavy items or exercising vigorously. All of these things are dangerous, not to mention highly uncomfortable. Your baby will arrive in time. If your labor needs inducing (doctors will typically induce labor if you still haven't given birth more than two weeks past your due date), your doctor can do it.

When you begin to feel contractions, call your doctor. He or she will tell you when to go to the hospital.

Contractions are the way your body pushes the baby out of your uterus, through the cervix, and along the birth canal. They begin gradually, with perhaps one contraction every hour or every half hour. At first, contractions may feel like gas pain or a backache.

As time passes, the contractions become more frequent, until they are about a minute apart. Then, you feel a strong urge to push. The baby is ready to come out.

Contractions are painful. Some people describe them as severe menstrual cramps. But many people find that they are much worse.

As we discussed before, every pregnancy is different, and this means every labor is also different. The intensity of the pain and the duration of the labor are different for every woman. If you do start hurting and are surprised at the intensity of the pain, remember those relaxation techniques you learned in the birthing class. Now is the time to use them. If you don't know any, here are a few suggestions, developed from my first unmedicated childbirth, which lasted twenty-six hours.

1. Have a focal point that you can take to the hospital with you, something that you can focus on to help overcome the pain. If you don't want to look at something, use a person's voice as your focal point.
2. Learn how it feels to relax your body while you are still pregnant. When you start having a contraction during labor, you'll naturally tighten up. If you know how "tension and tightness" feel, you can relax your body, letting go of some of the pain that comes from tension.
   - Tighten your hand into a fist. Hold for five seconds, then relax slowly.
   - Feel your hand go limp and your fist loosen. Wiggle your fingers to ensure that they're completely relaxed.
   - Move on to your arm. Follow the same procedure. Tighten the arm, hold the position for five seconds, and then release.
   - Tighten and relax each part of your body from your head to your toes.

3. During labor, have your support person help you relax when the pain is most intense by encouraging you to visualize specific tranquil scenes, such as a day in the sun at the beach or a cooling mountain breeze. Visualization doesn't require that you've been to these places, just that you can imagine them.

4. When all else fails, focus on your partner's voice. Go beyond the words. Listen to the tone of his or her voice, listen to how it rises and falls. If your partner can't keep anxiety out of his or her voice, focus on something else.

5. Block out everything else. Shut your eyes and listen to your partner's voice or the nurse's voice.

6. The pain will increase and become more frequent, but you can ride it out. Pain medication is always available, and you are not a failure for using it.

Let's look at some of the things that can happen during labor. When you're well into labor, and the doctor says to head for the hospital, what types of procedures will you encounter?

One of the first steps will be to see how dilated your cervix is. A physician will put his or her hand on your cervix to check. This can be very painful.

While many hospitals no longer give enemas routinely, you might want one if you're offered one. Ask your doctor about this in advance so you know what to expect. When you reach the stage where you're pushing the baby out, if your bowels are not empty, the contents will pass out along with the baby.

You'll have your pulse and blood pressure checked and your temperature taken. You may be hooked up to an IV so that liquids can be administered during labor. Dehydration is a complication, so doctors routinely request IVs to prevent it. If you don't want the IV, talk with your doctor about it ahead of time. You won't be in much of a mood to argue about anything in the midst of contractions.

They'll probably hook up an external fetal monitor (a belt around your belly) to keep track of the baby during labor. One drawback to this is that it prevents you from standing up or walking around, both of which may feel much more comfortable than sitting or lying down. Ask your doctor about this beforehand, as well as the nurse in the hospital. Sometimes the nurse will arrange for you to be hooked up to the fetal monitor every few minutes, allowing you to walk or stand in the meantime. The doctor may instead use an internal monitor, a little electrode inserted through your vagina and attached to the baby's scalp to check its heart rate. If you're not hooked up to monitors yet, you'll probably be encouraged to walk around. You may want to pace out of excitement or anxiety—or you may find the idea of walking revolting.

Some hospitals routinely put a urinary catheter on a woman in labor so that if she needs to urinate, the urine will be caught. It is uncomfortable, however, and unnecessary. You can always just tell the nurse that you need to urinate during labor, and he or she will help you to the bathroom.

Stages of Birth

Stage 1 of childbirth includes the whole dilation process of the cervix to a width of ten centimeters, roughly four fingers' width. Contractions occur every five minutes or so down to every two minutes, and they may last a full minute. Take the pains one at a time. Don't think about riding out several hours of them; that will discourage you. In the beginning, up to four centimeters, it won't necessarily seem so bad. I remember telling my nurse, "This isn't so bad. I thought it was supposed to hurt."

"Don't worry, it'll hurt," she advised me.

Transition is the time your cervix is dilating from eight to ten centimeters. This can really hurt. Some women feel anxious, while others are calm. You may feel like vomiting, you may actually vomit, and you may experience uncontrollable shaking and chills. Transition, fortunately, is usually brief—well, compared to the rest of it. If you're still unmedicated, you may find yourself in a very ugly mood. I remember telling my husband I was sick of the whole thing and would he please just take me home! Toward the end you'll feel a pressure on your rectum and swear you need to move your bowels. It will be the baby, who has moved down into the birth canal and whose head is pressing against your rectum.

By this stage you will probably have lost all dignity. I didn't care how obnoxiously I acted to either my husband or the nurse; I was infuriated that they couldn't take this pain away. (In subsequent labors I used medication and did not experience these mood swings—probably because I wasn't hurting.) Anyway, transition is over when you're fully dilated, and there's nothing sweeter than hearing the nurse or doctor announce that you're "complete." They will have been checking your progress, by measuring finger widths in your cervix, throughout your labor. You'll be relieved to have the hand probes end for the moment.

Stage 2 signals pushing and delivery of the baby. It could last as much as an hour or more, although it is often shorter. While some women complain that the pushing hurts, I found the experience a blessed relief after contractions. It took a lot of energy to push and not push when the nurse told me, so maybe I was too busy to realize I was hurting, but I truly did not sense pain. (I got a sore throat, though, from all the heaving I did.) If this stage of labor goes on too long, you'll probably feel worn out, but usually it is a welcome part of delivery because it means the baby is about to be born. If you haven't been moved to the delivery room, you will be now.

When the baby pops out (and that's how it seems), you'll feel immense relief. In a normal delivery the head comes out first, then the shoulders are maneuvered out, and the rest slips out like a fish. The pain is *gone*. There is no residual pain.

Stage 3 consists of the delivery of the placenta. It can be very painful having the doctor press down on your belly or use instruments to extract it. In addition, this is the time that the doctor will stitch any tears in your vaginal wall or tears (or episiotomy) at the opening of your vagina.

Support Person

During this whole process you need a support person to help you stay focused and calm. Whoever is there to help you (whether it's your mother or girlfriend or husband), be sure that person is there for *you*, not to chat with the nurses. Make sure the support person realizes that you may behave badly during labor and say things you don't mean. I threw up on my husband during labor. He just peeled off his sweater and continued to sit by me and talk to me calmly.

The nurse who helps you through labor won't be the nurse you got to know in your doctor's office. He or she is someone who works solely in the labor and delivery room. The experience of your delivery depends to some extent on your relationship to this person. Can you bond with this nurse? Is she responsive to you? Does a shift change occur during your labor so that midway through you get a new nurse? Teens told me they did better in labor if they liked the nurse and were willing to follow his or her advice.

Cesarean Section

What about a C-section? The doctor may consider a C-section, which is removing the baby through an incision in your abdomen, for several reasons. One is if you are in labor for hours without dilating and if artificial stimulation (with pitocin, for example) doesn't help. Another reason is if the baby is in a breech position—with the buttocks presenting first instead of the head—or any other unusual position and can't be turned. It is much more painful and risky to the baby to deal with a breech delivery. You may also have a C-section if you have blood pressure problems or if your water broke more than twenty-four hours earlier.

If during labor you pass meconium-stained water, it means that the baby has had a bowel movement of meconium in utero. He or she is at risk of swallowing the liquid if not delivered immediately. Allowing the baby's lungs to fill with meconium-stained water risks infection and respiratory problems. The monitors can indicate any fetal distress during labor, reflected in a reduced heart rate. If there is distress that cannot be corrected, the doctor will perform an emergency C-section.

When you're going through labor and feeling awful, you might think a C-section would be a lot easier, particularly if you were put to sleep for it. But a C-section is major surgery. Recovery is longer and more painful, and you'll be glad later that you didn't have one.

You may be awake or asleep during a cesarean delivery. If there is time to administer anesthesia, you'll be numbed and left alert to watch (behind draped sheets) the birth of your baby. Your support person will be allowed in the room only if it has been agreed upon in advance, and his or her presence won't interfere with the surgery. If it's an emergency procedure or the epidural block isn't totally effective, you'll be given general anesthesia, which will make you unconscious. Your support person, husband or not, may be barred from surgery under those circumstances. Hospitals and doctors may differ on the matter. The surgery takes about an hour. The baby is delivered in the first fifteen minutes; the rest of the time is spent stitching you up. The incision is usually made horizontally across your lower abdomen, in the pubic hair and out of sight if you later want to wear a bikini. In some situations the cut is made vertically down your belly.

When you awake, assuming you've been knocked out, you'll be surprised that it's over so fast. And at least initially, you'll probably feel more grogginess than pain.

The important thing to remember, however, is that everyone experiences labor differently. Part of the pain comes from our physical builds; part of it comes from the levels of apprehension we feel. Common emotions following delivery can include euphoria or sheer relief. Some people feel energized, some feel proud of their accomplishment, some feel tearful, and some feel happy from all of the attention. You may feel a burst of love for this new baby you worked so hard to have, but then again you may feel too tired to feel anything else.

Bonding

One word about bonding. It does not necessarily come in a great gush with the birth of the baby. Bonding, feeling intense love for the baby, may not happen suddenly at all. It sometimes occurs outside your awareness. One day you just realize how important this new little baby is.

When my first child was born I expected to feel a great outpouring of love for her. Honestly, though, my first feeling was of relief that I was out of pain. I waited for the tremendous feeling of love to wash over me, and I was embarrassed to admit to the nurse that I didn't feel any different. I thought I must be a bad mother because I couldn't identify any feeling for my baby except fondness. It wasn't until days later, when she had to be hospitalized for jaundice and was literally out of my hands for twenty-four hours, that I suffered tremendous emotional pain. Bonding sometimes occurs instantaneously, but more often than not it comes gradually and without fanfare. If you're being an attentive mother, relax. It'll come.

Advice from Teen Moms

1. "When in labor, try not to be fussy with the nurses; listen to them 'cause they're trying to help you, and they wouldn't tell you wrong."
2. "Read about childbirth, and ask questions about being a mother and delivery. Go to classes if possible. Be prepared for what will happen when the baby is born and after."
3. "Labor really hurts!"

4. "Labor was hard, painful but exciting!"
5. "Labor was hard on my back."
6. "What was labor like? Well, it was horrible, and all that kept running through my mind was I'm not going to do that again for a long, long time!"
7. "Labor can be scary and frightening, but it helps to know as much as you can [about] what to expect."
8. "About as much as you can say about labor is that we all survived it."

CHAPTER 6

Following the Birth

Your stay in the hospital varies depending on the type of delivery you had. Federal law sets a minimum stay of forty-eight hours. Check with your doctor, or call your insurance company about their policy. Women who give vaginal births usually stay two to three days while women who deliver by cesarean stay up to a week. After a vaginal delivery you'll spend an hour or so in the recovery room; the father and family members can be with you then, but you may prefer simply to rest. The nurses will be cleaning up your baby, weighing him or her, and settling him or her into the nursery.

Teenagers are usually better than older women at bouncing back from labor and delivery, but many may be surprised to find themselves going home well before they feel like it.

Let's look at what will be happening to you—physically and emotionally. Then we'll get back to the baby.

Physical Aftereffects

The bleeding that follows childbirth (called lochia) will continue for ten days or more. It will fade from bright red at delivery, to a brownish color, and then to yellow, much as your period does in a week's time. Your uterus will continue to contract as it shrinks to close to its former size. The hormone oxytocin is responsible for the painful contractions, and the doctor can give you pain medication if the discomfort gets intense. Every so often a nurse will come by and press on your abdomen. She's helping the uterus contract more, but it's unpleasant nonetheless. Once the staff is content that you're doing okay on your own, they'll stop. They'll be checking your sanitary pad to monitor the bleeding (you don't want to be passing clots), and they may bind your breasts and put an ice pack on them if you don't plan to breast-feed your baby. This may all sound very undignified to you right now, but you'll probably accept it willingly after what you've been through.

I had my first child at a birth center, and the nurse told me I could go home (with the baby) as soon as I urinated without incident. "You mean I have to go to the bathroom today?" I asked. I'd planned to use the bathroom in a few days, but the idea of sitting on a cold toilet at that particular moment was scarier than skydiving. After all that has happened to that part of your body, it's hard to believe your insides won't fall out when you expose them again.

Well, relax. It doesn't hurt to urinate again, except for a quick burning sensation if you've had an episiotomy. Soaking that part of your anatomy in a sitz bath helps the swelling go down and the stinging go away. To avoid infection, take showers rather than baths. The hardest part will be relaxing enough to use the toilet freely. Running water in the sink sometimes reminds your body what it's supposed to be doing.

Milk for the baby usually doesn't come until the third day. In the meantime, if you're nursing your baby, he or she will be getting valuable colostrum (a thin liquid produced in the first day or so after delivery, which contains antibodies a baby needs) from your breasts. When the milk does come in, you'll know it. Your breasts will feel heavy and full; they'll start to tingle as the milk "comes down." You'll actually feel relief as the baby starts nursing, because full breasts hurt. If you do decide to breast-feed (more about that in chapter 7), ask the nurse for help. It's hard to figure out how to hold a wobbly newborn and get the nipple into its mouth at the same time. Don't believe anyone who says it all comes naturally.

If you don't want to breast-feed your baby, be sure to tell your doctor so that he or she can give you medicine to help dry up your breasts. Your breasts will prepare to feed this baby whether or not you plan on exercising the option. Your milk will still come in. The pills will help dry you up, so to speak, but the nurses may bind your breasts tightly to discourage them from engorging. Ice packs will help, because when the milk does come in, your breasts will burn and throb. You'll run a fever and feel extremely tender, but the feeling will subside in a day or two. Don't think you'll escape the burning sensation by breast-feeding instead; you'll encounter it anytime you stop breast-feeding, unless you stop gradually.

In the weeks after delivery you may find yourself sweating more than usual. Nothing is particularly wrong; it just means that your hormone production has dropped, and your body is trying to get back to normal. Menstruation will begin again from eight to twelve weeks after delivery, but don't think that you can't get pregnant because you haven't resumed your periods. You can!

After a C-section, you'll encounter a longer period of adjustment. Because you have had major surgery, you'll stay a few days longer in the hospital so they can monitor you. The nurses will get you up within twenty-four hours. When you first push yourself into a sitting position, you'll probably be shocked at how weak you are. You wouldn't think such a small incision could cause so much discomfort! I speak from experience. After my C-section (with my last child), I swore I was going to lie in bed for the rest of my life. I finally put my feet on the floor; the nurse held me on one side, my husband on the other. I felt as if my abdomen were on fire. It took several days of walking before I was more comfortable. And it took several days more before I could walk without holding on to my belly.

You'll still bleed vaginally with a C-section (the lining of the uterus is sloughing off), but the bleeding will be lighter and of shorter duration.

You'll be more tired after having had a C-section and won't be allowed to lift anything remotely heavy, nor will you feel like it. Climbing stairs will discourage you, and standing will tire you quickly.

As you're recovering in the hospital, you'll hurt mostly from gas. Actually, gas is a good sign; it means that your intestines are working again, moving food along as they're supposed to. The nurses will give you pills to make you pass gas because it relieves the pain.

Depression

Many women feel some degree of depression after the birth of a baby. Some women, especially first time mothers, are confused and frightened by this depression.

Postpartum depression is normal and occurs a few days after the baby's birth. This depression is caused by many factors. The primary reason is that the hormone levels in a woman's body change after the birth.

Many women also feel an emotional letdown after the birth. From the day a woman realizes she is pregnant, her life revolves around her pregnancy. She looks forward to the birth, dreams about it, fears it, and all of a sudden, it is over. She is no longer the center of attention; the baby is. There is suddenly this little person who is totally dependent on her. Many women are daunted by this responsibility.

Another contributing factor to depression is the way a woman feels about her body after the birth. She may feel fat and unattractive, as if she will never regain her old form.

These factors, together with the physical and mental fatigue many women feel after giving birth, are enough to bring many women to a state of depression.

Postpartum depression usually cures itself within a few weeks, but there are ways you can better cope with the depression. Get plenty of rest and get as much sleep as you can. You body has been through a lot, and it needs time to recuperate. Trying to get uninterrupted sleep with a new baby in the house can be difficult. A supportive partner or your family can be quite helpful in this situation.

Try not to accomplish too much too soon. If there is laundry to be done or dishes sitting in the sink, let them wait. Trying to tackle all your responsibilities and chores while trying to take care of an infant soon after giving birth will only add to your depression. Wait until you have regained your strength and take on these responsibilities one by one instead of trying to do everything all at once.

If your depression becomes chronic and does not go away a few weeks after giving birth, or if you feel severely depressed, you may require medical attention. If you find yourself in a deep depression, and you feel like you don't have the strength or energy to get out of bed and take care of your baby, call your doctor or school nurse or ask a family member for help. If your condition is caused by a hormone imbalance, there is medication that can restore your hormone balance. A counselor can also help you get over your depression.

Depression is like nausea in early pregnancy—it does not affect all women. Do not sit around expecting to get depressed. You may be so busy and happy being a mother that depression never becomes a problem.

Possible Problems for the Baby

Now, let's talk about the baby. You can keep your baby with you in your hospital room or have him or her brought in from the nursery whenever you want. But what if there are complications?

Premature Birth

Babies who are born prematurely (before thirty-eight weeks) tend to be hospitalized longer, depending on how premature they are. The earlier they are born, the more underdeveloped their lungs and major organs will be. Preemies run the risk of developing respiratory problems and infections. If their lungs are not fully developed, monitors may be used to check and assist their breathing. If your baby is premature you'll see all kinds of equipment surrounding him or her. The doctor may order your baby to be put into an incubator to regulate his or her body temperature. All infants wear little caps to protect their heads from heat loss.

A premature baby may develop jaundice because the liver cannot filter out the pigment bilirubin, which is produced by the breakdown of excessive red blood cells not needed after birth. The bilirubin builds up to a dangerous level, turning the baby a yellowish color. The doctor will put such a baby in an incubator under fluorescent lights, which converts the bilirubin so the body can excrete it more easily.

Premature babies cry more frequently, but more quietly, than full-term babies. They are more easily startled, are smaller, and seem more fragile. You may feel angry and cheated about your baby's condition. You may not feel sure you can take care of him or her properly. You may feel guilty, blaming the baby's condition on something you did or didn't do while you were pregnant. All of these feelings are normal, but you need to talk about them. Your friends and family may be willing to listen, but you also need to express your concerns and fears to professionals who can help you. Your baby may have to stay longer in the hospital, and it's frightening and heartbreaking to leave the hospital that first time without your new baby. Your baby needs your love and attention. He or she will learn your voice and your scent; hang in there. When your baby is healthy enough to be released, the doctor will tell you what to do and what to expect.

Fetal Alcohol Syndrome

Fetal alcohol syndrome, or FAS, is a condition a baby is born with because his or her mother drank alcohol during her pregnancy. A baby born with FAS will have an odd-looking face; will experience behavioral problems, such as hyperactivity; and will have a hard time learning to read, write, and interact with other people. In addition to this, FAS babies will also suffer physical consequences, such as trouble with their hearts, lungs, kidneys, or other parts of their bodies.

To protect your health and the health of your baby, do not drink alcohol if you are pregnant. Even if you have only a couple of drinks here and there, you are endangering the life of your baby. No one knows how much alcohol is too much. Even a small amount of alcohol can hurt your baby. Don't take the risk.

Babies require a lot of attention and love. This means you have the responsibility of keeping your baby healthy, safe, and happy. Babies born with FAS will require a lot more attention. Sometimes, no matter what you do, it is impossible to calm down a baby with FAS. It's hard enough for most teenagers to cope with the responsibilities of raising a healthy child—don't increase those responsibilities by drinking.

Drugs and Pregnancy

If you use drugs during your pregnancy, your baby will also be affected. He or she may be born addicted to the drug you used during your pregnancy. You can damage the health of your baby. Your baby may shake a lot, develop lung infections easily, and may have problems breathing.

If your baby has drug-related problems, seek professional help. He or she may require special care. If you are still abusing alcohol or drugs, you need to seek help to overcome your addiction, or you will risk hurting or losing your baby.

AIDS and Pregnancy

If you are HIV-positive or have AIDS, the virus can be passed to your baby. One out of every three babies born to HIV-infected women remains HIV-positive and usually dies before his or her fifth birthday.

*   *   *

Pregnancy and giving birth can be frightening, especially if you are not prepared for it. You may be frightened of the pain involved in giving birth, be worried about your ability to take care of the baby, or be worried about the baby's health. Just remember that pregnancy and birth are perfectly natural, and no matter how scared you are of doing something wrong, you will do fine. If you are healthy and take care of yourself and do not abuse drugs or alcohol during your pregnancy, chances are your baby will be born healthy.

Advice from Teen Moms

"Being a mother isn't just holding the cute little baby all the time. It's a lot of responsibility."

CHAPTER 7

Dealing with a New Baby

I f you are a first-time mother, you may be anxious about and fearful of how you will take care of your baby once you leave the hospital. While in the hospital, you have a staff of doctors and nurses to answer your questions about the baby or take care of the baby when he or she cries. But when you get the baby home, you and your boyfriend or husband will be responsible for all of the baby's needs. If the baby cries or seems unhappy, *you* will need to find the solution. In this chapter, we will look at some of the problems you may encounter in caring for your new baby.

Colic

Colic is a problem that affects newborns. It usually ends by the third month. When a baby has colic, this means that he or she is suffering from attacks of abdominal pain. The baby responds to this pain by crying, sometimes for hours on end. Nothing seems to be able to stop the crying;

changing the diaper, feeding, picking him or her up— nothing works. The baby's face becomes flushed, the legs drawn up toward the abdomen, and his or her hands and feet may be cold. You may begin to worry that something may be seriously wrong with your baby, but colic is not dangerous to the baby. However, it can be upsetting to parents to have a baby who will not stop crying.

A baby with colic will usually cry after a feeding because the abdominal pain occurs in the intestines. No one is sure why some babies suffer from colic while others do not. One possible cause is the foods that breast-feeding mothers eat. Foods with a high carbohydrate content may cause excessive fermentation in the infant's intestines. The air swallowed by the infant during feeding can be another cause.

While time will eventually cure colic, there are other methods that may stop an infant from crying. If your baby is crying, first check the obvious reasons. Is he or she hungry or does his or her diaper need to be changed? Sometimes babies cry because they want love and attention. Picking up these babies, rocking or walking them, or even singing to them will often stop the crying. If none of these methods work, your baby may have colic.

One method to try is picking up your baby and laying him or her across your lap, abdomen down, and massaging the back. You can also try placing a hot water bottle on the abdomen to relieve some of the pain. However, you need to be very careful that the water bottle is not too hot, because it can burn the baby. Test it by holding it against the inside of your wrist. If it is uncomfortable, it is definitely too hot for your baby's stomach.

Try to distract the baby by appealing to one of its senses. If the room is dark, brighten it or vice-versa. However, don't try everything at once.

A colicky baby will stop crying after having a bowel movement or passing gas. These relieve pain in the intestines. If your baby is colicky, it's very important to burp him or her after every feeding. This will prevent air from going into the intestines.

If none of these methods work, and your baby will not stop crying, and there are no signs of sickness, do not be afraid to let the baby cry for a bit. Some babies will just cry themselves to sleep.

If you are at your wit's end, call your physician and ask for help. You can ask the father to take over or call a friend or relative to come over and relieve you for a bit. If you are so frustrated that you feel that you may harm your baby, get help immediately. Call an abuse hot line if no one is immediately available to take over. You can permanently damage a baby by shaking or hitting it. You can easily kill a baby in one fleeting moment of anger. Take a deep breath, count to ten; relieve that anger and frustration some other way without harming your baby.

Sleep

All newborns are supposed to sleep between sixteen and seventeen hours the first few days. As the weeks go by, your baby will stay awake longer. Newborns awaken every few hours (usually not more than three) to eat, whether you are breast- or bottle-feeding; they cannot eat enough at one time to stay full for longer than that. If anyone develops a sleep disturbance at this point, it will be you, not the baby. You (or someone) has to get up throughout the night to feed the baby. Some babies start sleeping through the night at as early as two months old; others take longer. Some sleep through the night from the beginning. It doesn't mean you're a better or worse mother for having a baby who sleeps a lot. Just be prepared to give up a regular sleep pattern yourself, and get some help when needed.

FEEDING

One of the most important things you have to decide soon after the birth of your baby is the method of feeding. Should you breast- or bottle-feed? There is no right or wrong decision. You simply need to decide which is a more convenient method, depending on your schedule and what you think is best for you and your baby. Let's look at the pros and cons of breast- and bottle-feeding.

Breast-Feeding

Breast milk is best for babies; even makers of baby formula agree. Breast milk is made especially for your baby and contains the correct amount of nutrients as well as antibodies that help your baby fight off infections. In addition, babies who breast-feed are less likely to suffer from constipation, colic, diarrhea, and allergies. Another advantage of breast-feeding is that it is free, which is nice, especially if you're on a budget. Breast-feeding also offers advantages to the mother: Breast-feeding burns about 500 calories daily, and the baby's sucking causes the uterus to shrink back to its normal size. If you breast-feed, you do not have to clean and sterilize bottles or worry about warming them up, which can be difficult if your baby wakes up in the middle of the night crying and demanding to be fed immediately.

Another advantage of breast-feeding is that your body will produce as much milk as your baby needs. If your baby eats a lot and often, your body will produce a larger amount of milk; if your baby eats a little, your body will adjust to produce the right amount of milk needed.

Finally, breast-feeding encourages the bond between mother and child in a very physical manner.

A disadvantage of breast-feeding is that you need to be careful about what you eat. What you eat will also go to your baby via your breast milk. You need to eat well-balanced meals and avoid fatty, spicy, or acidic foods or other foods that may have adverse effects on your baby. This is especially true in the first couple of months. This may not be so simple, especially since you have been watching your diet since you first became pregnant. You cannot eat anything you feel like as long as you are nursing.

Another disadvantage is that with breast-feeding, you cannot measure how much your baby has ingested. The actual process of nursing can also be difficult for the mother and the baby and will take time and practice before you and the baby are comfortable with it.

Bottle-Feeding

Today's bottle-feeding formulas offer babies nutritional, well-balanced meals similar to that of breast milk (although they lack vital antibodies found in breast milk that help babies fight off infections).

Bottle-feeding can also be more convenient because it can be done anywhere. If you need to breast-feed your baby but you are not home, it can be inconvenient to find a private place to nurse. Bottle-feeding is also more convenient if you need to go to school or to work and cannot be there to feed your baby. With bottle-feeding, you can immediately tell how much your baby has eaten. Mothers also do not have to worry about what they eat because it will not affect their babies.

One big disadvantage of bottle-feeding is that you have to buy the formula, which is expensive. But under no circumstances should you dilute your baby's formula to make it go further. This is dangerous because diluting the formula decreases the nutritional value, and your baby can starve to death.

You will also need to make sure the bottle, ring, nipple, and water used to mix the formula (if you use a powdered or concentrated formula) are properly cleaned and sterilized. This can be done with hot water and soap, followed by boiling or by running bottles, rings, and nipples through the hot cycle of a dishwasher. You also need to properly warm up the formula. This is usually done by placing the bottle in a pan filled with hot water. Do not use the microwave to warm formula, because microwaves do not heat the formula evenly. It can create hot spots which can burn the baby's mouth. However inconvenient this may sound, it will seem more so if your baby wakes up crying to be fed in the middle of the night. You will need to sterilize the bottle and warm up the formula while trying to calm your baby down.

Both breast- and bottle-feeding provide your baby with the proper nutrition he or she needs. The method you choose largely depends on your lifestyle. No matter what method you use, remember that feeding your baby can be a special and rewarding experience. Most newborns spend the first few weeks of their lives either sleeping or eating. Since there is not much opportunity to know your newborn while he or she is sleeping, feeding is the best time to get to know your baby better. You and the father can use this time to bond with your baby and become more familiar with each other. To make the most of this time, try the following tips:

- Try to find a quiet and comfortable place to nurse. This can sometimes be difficult with the busy schedules that most people have, but don't try to juggle another task while feeding. Relax and concentrate only on your baby.
- Change the baby's diaper before feeding so that he or she can fall asleep after eating (as some babies will) without interruption.
- Most importantly, make sure your feeding positions allow you to make eye contact with your baby.

We have only mentioned some of the things you can expect when dealing with a baby. There are many other things you will have to deal with as you learn more about the newest addition to your family. Try not to worry too much about whether you're doing something right or wrong, unless you lose control of your temper and fear you may abuse your baby. Remember that your baby loves you. Even if you make a few mistakes in the beginning, your baby will not notice and will not love you less for them. There is no code of strict rules to follow for raising a baby. Common sense is often your best guide. If you have specific questions or concerns, there are people who can help. Your doctor, school nurse, family members, and other relatives will be glad to help you. Just relax and enjoy this special time with your baby.

Advice from Teen Moms

1. "Read books and talk to other parents so you'll know what to expect from the different stages of child development."
2. "Don't give up; it gets a lot easier."
3. "Don't blame the child. YOU did this, not the child. You have to take responsibility."
4. "Realize that you can never go back to how your life used to be."

The hardest thing to get used to was . . .

- "how much responsibility I had."
- "waiting on the baby hand and foot; having to guess what was wrong with him because he couldn't tell me."
- "not being able to come and go as I did before."
- "old friends not understanding the meaning of responsibility, so it was almost impossible to do things with them."
- "getting up at all hours during the night."
- "the crying."

CHAPTER 8

Suddenly Being a Mother

L earning to stay at home can be an unappealing aspect of motherhood. All of a sudden, you have this new little person to take care of, and the responsibilities *never go away*! It never ceases to amaze me that I went to the hospital one afternoon and came back the next day with an infant. One day I was just a woman; the next day I was a mother!

No matter what your earlier teen years were like, those days are over now. If you were carefree, stopping home every so often for family meals, you're not going to be so carefree anymore. A baby needs his or her meals on time every day, and you're responsible for providing them. If you once partied every weekend, you're not going to have the energy to do that anymore. Many teens think that being pregnant is exciting and makes them grown up. But once you have the baby, the excitement may fade in the face of all that responsibility. You're suddenly a mother, and you may not feel prepared.

What's Expected of You

Whether or not you're still excited about being a mother, let's look at your new responsibilities and the baby's needs. Once again, if you know what to expect, you may feel more comfortable.

When I had my first child, I wasn't sure what I would do with her once I got her home. I wasn't sure how to hold her, and she was so fragile-looking that I was almost afraid to touch her. When my husband and I got her home, we turned up the thermostat to about 80 degrees, thinking she needed to be warmer. We bundled her in blankets because it was winter, and we sat around, sweltering ourselves, watching her sleep. Fortunately, our pediatrician caught on and told us to turn down the thermostat. The baby doesn't need a room temperature warmer than 70 degrees, and he or she doesn't need to be buried under layers of blankets. That was my first lesson; I made many more mistakes. We all can use some well-worn advice when we're first-time parents, no matter what our ages.

One disillusioning thing you'll discover right away is that babies are very self-centered. At first all they know is their own needs: food, a dry diaper, a soothing environment, a warm body to hold them. They are not separate enough to realize that they can give anything back, or that you'd even expect it.

Any baby needs love, attention, food, and stimulation. Fortunately, he or she doesn't always know if we're doing something wrong and won't penalize us for being new at the job.

The baby also needs proper medical attention. You may have a number of questions about how to care for a newborn. For instance, the umbilical cord dries up and drops off between twelve to fifteen days. In the meantime, it's just there, getting in the way when you're changing the diaper. You have to cleanse and disinfect the cord carefully to avoid infection.

You should also know CPR and the Heimlich maneuver (used to dislodge items from the throat of someone who is choking) in case of medical emergencies involving your child.

Keep all regular doctor appointments for the baby. In the beginning you'll probably have as many appointments for a well baby as you would for one who is sick. Babies stay healthy because they're seeing a doctor. The doctor will want to know if your baby is eating enough, gaining weight, and moving about at the scheduled time. Your doctor will know all the shots the baby needs and when to give them. If money is a problem, you can see a doctor at the county health department, but if you can cover the baby on your or your parents' insurance policy, choose a private physician. It's good to develop a rapport with your doctor so that if the baby gets sick during the night, you'll have someone to call.

You may feel better having the baby sleep in your room (or you may have no other option), but babies can make a lot of noise when they sleep. At first, it's nice to have the baby so near, but very soon you'll notice all the little noises, and they may keep you awake. I started sleeping better once I moved our baby out of our room, although it took me a while to trust that she was breathing okay in the other room. Excessive worrying won't keep the baby any safer, but it will deplete your energy, leading to fatigue and a short temper.

There are things you can do to ensure a safe environment for your baby. First of all, buy some of those inexpensive electrical outlet covers and close up all of your outlets. It doesn't matter that your infant can't even turn over yet, let alone crawl around on the floor to get into trouble. Do it right from the start; then you don't have to worry about it when he or she is old enough or mobile enough to get into things. Never leave a pillow in a baby's crib, since a baby can suffocate under one.

For the same reason, never leave a baby unattended on a waterbed or on a couch where he or she can suffocate under the cushions.

Also, bind the cords of window blinds so they are out of reach of a curious baby. Don't let the baby have toys that can come apart or that have dangling strings. A baby can strangle on them in a matter of minutes. Babies explore their world through their mouths, so assume that anything your baby can reach will go into his or her mouth.

If you have items that are breakable or have small, swallowable parts, put them out of sight. Like the electrical outlets, you never know when your baby is old enough to get into them. Get into the habit of storing dangerous or valuable items out of sight. Attach latches or closures to cabinet doors to prevent babies from opening them.

Smoking around a baby is dangerous for two reasons. One, you run the risk of dropping ashes on the baby. Two, and more important, studies have shown that secondhand smoke leads to an increase in respiratory infections in children. If you stop, you'll be saving your baby's health as well as your own—and a lot of money. Also ask others not to smoke around your child.

As you've probably guessed, adjusting to a baby requires an awful lot of sacrifices. You lose regular sleep, you can't go out much, and you never have enough money. Raising a baby is hard work.

Help with Your Baby

You're not a bad person if you resent the baby's demands on you. If you're shouldering most of the responsibilities yourself, it's understandable. If you're jealous that the father doesn't have as much to do as you or isn't as tied down, that's normal too. Nonetheless, it's not okay to fly off the handle, blame the baby, or neglect the baby simply because you feel like it. At such times you need some help, not just advice.

If you get along with your family and they're reliable, consider calling them first. Perhaps they'll take the baby for a few hours, allowing you to get out for a while. You aren't a hero for staying with your baby twenty-four hours a day. Smart people take breaks. The advantages of using family members are that you know them, and you usually don't have to pay them. The disadvantages lie in your wearing out your welcome from calling on them too much, and the opportunity it gives them for over-involvement and taking over.

If you have been abused by someone in the family, don't for a moment think the person has reformed without treatment and wouldn't bother your baby. Many abused women have told me that their abusers began to abuse their children when the opportunity presented itself. People who molest children *do not grow out of it*. Keep your baby safe, as you wish someone had done for you. Remember, babies can't tell you if something is wrong. They can only cry, so it's up to you to figure out any problem, from ear infection to trauma. Better to leave your family out of it, if there's any risk of trouble.

Aside from your parents, who else is there? What about the baby's father? If you've married him, he's right there and fully capable of doing "his share." Talk with him about how you're feeling. If you two can't help each other with the baby care, your marriage is already on a bad footing. Raising a baby is not "woman's work." Two parents are needed for the job. If you're fighting over it, talk to a school counselor or a mental health professional. There are clinics that don't cost a fortune. Look in the Yellow Pages.

Even if you didn't marry the father, he can be involved in taking care of the baby. If you trust him and believe he is responsible enough to take care of a baby, talk to him about it. He is legally responsible for providing financial support, but he may also be able to provide emotional support. He is the father, and he has and deserves the right to be part of the baby's life. The baby deserves it too. But don't just give him the baby and expect him to know what to do. It is best to invite him over and let him watch and learn how you take care of the baby. He may be nervous and afraid of accidentally hurting the baby, just as you were when you first started, but gradually he will learn. Once you both are comfortable with leaving the baby alone with him, you will find it's nice to have the father be a part of your baby's life. It's always good to have another person to depend on when you're trying to raise a baby on your own.

If you're in a school program (whether traditional high school or an alternative program), consider asking a teacher or counselor for advice. Teachers are usually flattered to be asked questions because it means you consider them important and knowledgeable. If you need advice, or only a pat on the back, look up your teacher or counselor after class. A teacher or a counselor or an adult from your church can be a mentor for you.

If you find yourself so frustrated that you want to hurt your child, call the abuse hot line listed in your phone book. If no number is identified as a hot line, call the emergency room of any hospital; they can tell you what to do if they can't help you themselves. Calling Parents Anonymous or an abuse hot line won't "get you in trouble." Your child's welfare is at stake, and if you call someone to keep yourself from hurting the child out of anger or frustration, you'll be better off. The counselor can talk you through your anger and suggest ways to cool off or get help.

Take some parenting classes to learn more about baby care in the various stages of development. Your school may offer free classes; if not, check out the YWCA, a family planning clinic, your hospital, or your church. Some classes charge a fee, but you might get it waived in cases of financial need. Many excellent courses are free. You can't know too much about parenting. If you can't find a class, take out some books from the library and read up on baby care. Not knowing all about parenting doesn't mean you're a bad mother. Recognize that you aren't going to know everything and that you can ask questions and do some reading to find answers.

Advice from Teen Moms

1. "Learn how to take care of your baby."
2. "Don't blame your child for keeping you away from things you want."
3. "You need to get away from the child once in a while."

CHAPTER ◇ 9

Taking Care of Your Own Needs

S o far, we've looked at problems you might encounter after you've brought the baby home. We've looked at the baby's needs and how you can best provide for them. It's natural to feel both pride and resentment about your new baby. In this chapter, let's just consider *you*. At some point, you may begin wondering, "When is there time for *me*?"

When you're taking care of a baby, particularly a newborn, you won't have enough time for everyone, including yourself. The baby's needs will take up most of your time. If you're married or involved in a steady relationship, you will have to make time for your partner as well as for yourself.

This can be a test of your marriage. In order for a marriage to be successful, a couple must spend time with each other. With a new baby, this can be difficult. Both of you may be so tired from working and taking care of the baby that you don't have the time or the energy to talk to each other or to enjoy each other's company. You may spend hours together, but if that time is spent taking care of the baby, your love life may disappear after a while. Your baby may be very important to both of you, but he or she shouldn't take up all of your time. You and your husband shouldn't drift apart because of the baby. You need to spend quality time with each other if the marriage is going to last.

See if you can leave the baby with your parents or other relatives for a few hours a week. If you can afford it, hire a baby-sitter. You can also note the time your baby sleeps consistently and plan to use that time to get reacquainted with each other. It's important to share your feelings with and talk to each other. Keep the lines of communication open. This is vital if your marriage is going to work. If you can talk to each other, you will have a better chance of working through any problems that may come up in the future.

Resuming Sex

Eventually, you'll start thinking of having sex again. Sexual feelings don't go away just because you're a mother. And childbirth isn't always so painful or remembered to be so painful that sex is shelved for long. Doctors routinely suggest that you wait six weeks before engaging in sex, in order for the episiotomy (if you had one) to heal and to limit the risk of infection. Will sexual intercourse hurt when you resume? Not usually. You'll probably feel apprehensive because you'll expect it to hurt, and you might be uncomfortable if the episiotomy site hasn't completely healed. You may worry that you'll be all stretched inside after having had a baby pass through your birth canal. The vagina is surprisingly resilient; you won't be all stretched, and you might be even tighter if the doctor stitched you up afterward. Your only real concern should be avoiding another unplanned pregnancy.

Sex is a good way to reconnect with your husband, but adjust your expectations for the first few times. You don't have to see stars, but likewise you don't want to engage in sex halfheartedly, always with your ear to the baby's room.

Don't spend time worrying whether you're still attractive to your husband, or whether others are more so. If you take an interest in your husband and your love life, he'll more than likely reciprocate your attention.

Pressing for Marriage

If your current boyfriend is your baby's father, you may have mixed feelings about not being married to him. Did *he* not want to marry you, or did *you* reject him? Are you waiting for him to "shape up"? One girl I know got pregnant a second time, hoping that if she had a boy this time her boyfriend would agree to marry her. She ended up with two children under the age of two and a part-time boyfriend who eventually left her and moved in with someone else.

Before you try to orchestrate a hasty marriage, consider some things. Does he show a sincere interest in the baby, or is he simply proud of his accomplishment? Does he resent the attention you show the baby, or is he willing to share you? Does he expect the relationship to continue as before and you to be available to party at all hours? Is he abusive? Statistics show that boyfriends who beat their girlfriends will beat their wives, too. And if he beats you, what makes you think he won't hurt the baby? Abusive people don't typically make exceptions. Assess your answers to these questions and decide whether or not marriage to the father is the right thing to do for you and the baby.

The father is legally responsible to support his child. If he doesn't, contact the Department of Human Services.

Dating Again

If your pregnancy was not the product of a steady relationship, and you're not even in touch with the baby's father, at some point you'll start dating again. How does a person date when she's taking care of a baby and can't go anywhere without him or her?

First of all, you can date and take the baby along, though that doesn't give you any time alone with your date. Or you can ask a willing family member to watch the baby so that you can go out. You might consider asking your date over for dinner; you can be alone once the baby falls asleep. Of course, you'll want the guy to like your child, but don't expect him to act like a father to your child, at least in the beginning. You won't be able to enjoy yourself with a person if you're constantly sizing him up for fatherhood. Besides, he'll probably sense what you're doing and may feel uncomfortable.

Unfortunately, it is also true that boyfriends sometime abuse their girlfriends' children, especially if they are asked to baby-sit them. For your sake and for your baby's sake, be careful about whom you choose to date.

You're entitled to date; you're entitled to have some fun without the baby always being there. But you can't shirk your responsibilities as a mother to pursue your pleasures. Line up a sitter or a reliable friend to stay with the baby.

Think of Yourself

In order to be able to nurture someone else, you have to nurture yourself. If you're giving 98 percent to your baby and 2 percent to your boyfriend or spouse, there's nothing left for you. Soon enough you will feel resentment about the situation. You won't have the energy or the inclination to take care of anyone else. That's why it's so important to do things for yourself during this time.

Nurture your own growth. If you dropped out of school to have the baby, get back into some program after you have your baby. Many schools have alternative classes for pregnant and parenting teens. Work on your GED so that you can complete your high school requirements. Consider a vocational class or a work/training school program. By learning a trade or a skill and furthering your education, you can support yourself and the baby. Knowing that you will be able to support yourself and your baby will help build your self-confidence. School counselors want you to finish your education, so they will do what it takes to help you. Call them. Many places have day-care services right on the premises; you wouldn't have to find a sitter, and you wouldn't be separated from the baby for the whole six hours. Career training is also an incentive to get off government support. Being a responsible adult can help you make a good life for your child.

If you have finished school and are simply taking a break to raise the baby, develop some hobbies. Even if you have support for the rest of your life, you'll need to do something with your spare time. Your baby will not always need your undivided attention. What will you do when your baby grows older and no longer turns to you for his or her every need?

Try to have a night out with your friends occasionally. You need them to remind you that you're not just a mother. Believe me, after a few weeks of diapers and bottles you'll jump at the chance to be "free" for a night.

What You've Lost

Spending time with your friends may remind you of all that you're missing out on. There *are* losses connected with raising a child. Most notably, you've lost your freedom to come and go as you please. You cannot make decisions without considering that new little person who shares your life. You've also lost your own childhood; from now on you have to act like a grown-up. Some people think they'll get to relive their childhood when they have a baby, but more often than not what happens is that they realize all the things they've missed. You can't go back and recreate your own childhood; you have to go forward and provide for your baby's childhood. You may be sad that your pregnancy interrupted your plans to travel or to go to college. You're missing out on opportunities that others may have.

However, having a baby doesn't mean you've been cut off from the rest of the world. There are many things you can do to bring a sense of fulfillment to your life. Make some new friends through school, church, or a parenting program. Find an outlet for your energy other than immersing yourself completely in the baby. Find out what makes you special; what are your talents? Give something back to your community. Volunteer at the children's library. Brush up on your social skills. Remember, when this baby starts school you're going to be dealing with teachers all over again but from a different vantage point.

There is no doubt that having a baby will change your whole life. But having a baby doesn't and shouldn't mean you should stop pursuing your goals and dreams. It just means you have to make certain adjustments to reach those goals. As you become more and more immersed in your baby's needs, remember your own needs and realize that, as important as your baby is to you, he or she isn't your whole life. You need to take time to take care of your own needs.

Advice from Teen Moms

"Once a day or night, find time to do something for yourself—whether it's painting your nails or relaxing in a bubble bath—just something you enjoy *for yourself*."

CHAPTER 10

Birth Control Options

Birth control is an important issue that you must consider after the birth of your baby. You now realize that taking care of one baby can be overwhelming; imagine how difficult it would be if you suddenly had two babies to take care of.

Some women are under the false impression that since they have just given birth, or are breast-feeding, or their periods have not started again, they cannot become pregnant. Your body is capable of becoming pregnant again even if you are nursing or your period has not started. Any unprotected act of sexual intercourse can lead to pregnancy. Use a reliable form of birth control.

This chapter will discuss the many birth control options available, as well as how the birth control you used before may need to be changed because of your pregnancy. You can also discuss birth control options with your doctor during your postpartum examination, which usually takes place six weeks after the birth of your baby.

The Pill

The birth control pill is almost 100 percent effective when used properly. The pill must be taken every day, without fail, or its effectiveness will decrease.

The pill is made from two synthetic hormones, estrogen and progesterone. These hormones can also be found naturally in the body. Birth control pills keep the ovaries from releasing eggs. Without the release of eggs, there is practically no chance for pregnancy.

The pill is used by more than 17.5 million women in the United States and is safe, but there are a few side effects involved. These side effects can include weight gain, breast tenderness, bloating, and irregular bleeding or spotting. The pill can also cause nausea, which should go away after a while. The weight gain should only last for a little while, too.

The risk to your health with the pill is very small. There is a rare but serious danger of developing blood clots. A tiny barrier can form in the vein or arteries, stopping the flow of blood. Blood clots can cause heart attacks or strokes. The pill has also been known to cause high blood pressure in a small number of women. The risks of taking the pill increase if the woman smokes.

But the pill also has certain advantages. For some women, it reduces or stops painful cramps and reduces menstrual flow, as well as reduces the number of days of menstruation.

The pill must be prescribed by a doctor and costs about $12 to $15 a month, depending on the brand you use. There are clinics that may be able to provide the pills to you at a discount price.

However, it is important to realize that the pill will not protect you from sexually transmitted diseases (STDs), such as gonorrhea, chlamydia, or HIV. If you are unsure of your partner's sexual history, use a condom. A condom can help protect you against STDs.

If you are breast-feeding and are interested in using birth control pills, speak to your doctor about it. The hormones in the pills may be passed to your baby via your breast milk. The low level of hormones found in today's pills poses no real danger to babies, but it is safer to check with your doctor. The pill may also reduce the level of milk production in the mother, but this is usually temporary.

Depo Provera Injection

Many women prefer having an injection of Depo Provera once every three months to taking a pill every day. The shot, given intramuscularly in the buttocks or upper arm, is almost as effective in preventing pregnancy as female sterilization. Your doctor can explain this injection to you.

The shot is given every thirteen weeks. It's given only during the first five days of your menstrual period or within five days following childbirth if you're not breast-feeding. Otherwise, it is given six weeks after childbirth. If you miss getting your injection on time, your doctor will want to determine that you are not pregnant before giving you another shot.

Women who have had breast cancer, unexplained vaginal bleeding, or liver disease are not candidates for this method of birth control. Some women who use this method complain of a change in their menstrual cycle. Some say they bleed more than usual; most women find they bleed less. It may take as long as a year to regain fertility after a woman stops the injections.

While this method is great for those who don't want the daily hassle of taking a pill, it does nothing to protect against sexually transmitted diseases, including HIV.

Implants

Norplant is another method of birth control used by women. It is 99.5 percent effective. Norplant consists of six match-size tubes of synthetic hormone similar to progesterone that a doctor inserts into the patient's upper arm. Its effectiveness lasts about five years. At the end of the five years, the doctor will remove the tubes. However, a doctor can remove the implants anytime the woman wishes. They do not have to remain in place for five years. Unlike with the Depo Provera injection, a woman can get pregnant immediately once the implants are removed.

With Norplant, you don't have to worry about taking a pill every day. For forgetful people, that can be a plus. If the tubes are properly implanted, you won't even notice they are there.

But there are drawbacks. It may cost several hundred dollars to have a doctor implant and later remove the tubes, but sometimes the cost is subsidized. Doctors are better at implanting them now, but some can still make an unsightly mess of your arm if they're not familiar with the process. In addition, removing the implants can be painful and can scar your arm. Some women complain of irregular periods, headaches, and mood changes among other side effects. Many women prefer the implants over the Depo Provera injections, but the greatest disadvantage is that the implants offer no protection against sexually transmitted diseases. If you are unsure of your partner's sexual history, use a condom.

If you want to know more about this birth control option, ask your doctor.

The Diaphragm

Some women prefer to use the diaphragm, which is a circular rubber cap inserted into the vagina and fitted over the cervix to block sperm from entering the cervix (the entrance to the uterus). You have to be fitted for a diaphragm by a doctor. After giving birth, some women find they need a larger diaphragm than the one they used before the birth. Bring your old diaphragm to your postpartum examination so your doctor can check whether it still fits. If you rely on this method, you have to use it *every* time you have sex, even if you think the time is "safe." You must insert the diaphragm before engaging in sex. You must leave the diaphragm in place for six hours after sex. If you take it out immediately, enough sperm are left in your vagina to progress into your uterus.

Use a spermicide with the diaphragm to increase its effectiveness. Nonoxynol-9 is the most effective spermicide now on the market. Although not as effective as condoms, it is also effective in lessening the risk of STDs. Some women find it abrasive, causing itchiness and rashes. If you think you're allergic to this ingredient, talk to your doctor about another spermicide you can use in its place.

Take good care of your diaphragm. Check it periodically for tears. Don't use petroleum jelly as a lubricant with your diaphragm; the petroleum will damage the rubber. If you need additional lubrication, use K-Y jelly.

A diaphragm needs to be positioned in a certain way. Make sure you know how to insert it before you leave your doctor's office. Don't leave the office until you're sure you can properly insert it on your own.

Does the diaphragm interfere with sex? Can your partner feel it? If positioned correctly, the diaphragm does not interfere with sex. If he knows you have a diaphragm in place, he'll probably eventually recognize its feel. But it won't be an unpleasant sensation if you have it in right.

Another disadvantage of the diaphragm is that you have to be comfortable with your body to use it. If you're squeamish about using tampons, you probably won't like the diaphragm. And if you don't like it, you probably won't use it.

The Condom

Another method of birth control is the condom, which is also the only method capable of protecting yourself against STDs and AIDS. Notice I didn't say that it *prevents* them. At the moment, it is only safe to say that it's capable of doing so. Condoms can break or slip off. A condom is not a 100 percent effective means of birth control, although you can increase its effectiveness if you use spermicide with it. There is now a female condom available, although its failure rate is higher than the male condom.

Condoms come in different sizes and textures. If you decide to use the condom, get in the habit of requiring your partner to put it on before there is *any* penile insertion. Make the act of donning a condom a part of your lovemaking. Remember, petroleum jelly causes deterioration of rubber, so don't endanger your condoms by using petroleum jelly with them.

Your partner must withdraw his penis as soon as he

ejaculates. Leaving it inside you may permit the condom to slip off. To prevent pregnancy, as well as STDs, you don't want *any* seminal fluid coming in contact with your vagina.

Condoms are relatively cheap, and they can be purchased in any drugstore, grocery store, or gas-station rest room. If you're more concerned with birth control than your boyfriend is, *you* buy the condoms. But don't carry them around in your purse or rely on one that your boyfriend has had in his back pocket all week. Heat weakens condoms, causing them to break.

Ideally, men should be responsible enough to provide birth control, but the reality is that you, the woman, get pregnant. Therefore, you should always take precautions, whether or not you think your partner should share the responsibility. If you're embarrassed to go to the store and buy a package of condoms, consider how you'll feel if you're back there buying a pregnancy test.

There are other methods of birth control, but the methods mentioned here are the most reliable and the safest for teens. Other methods not mentioned may not be reliable or suitable for teenagers. However, the most reliable method to prevent pregnancy and STDs is abstinence.

I talked about sexually transmitted diseases in chapter 3 in discussing the complications of pregnancy, specifically herpes, gonorrhea, and chlamydia. Usually, women don't show many symptoms of these diseases (except with an active case of herpes), so they don't have them treated. Untreated STDs can render you sterile and can make you very ill. If you're already pregnant, they can hurt your baby during delivery. STDs are serious, and the number of cases of these diseases is on the rise because many teenagers do not take proper precautions against them.

AIDS

AIDS is an STD with no cure. Many people have died of AIDS-related complications. Although recent medical developments can slow the disease and prolong life, no cure has been found.

AIDS is caused by the human immunodeficiency virus (HIV). When this virus enters the body, it attacks the immune system. It is the immune system that protects us against foreign invaders, such as bacteria and viruses. Without the immune system, the body is left defenseless against infections. HIV does not kill, it just leaves the body vulnerable to other infections. These infections may be harmless to healthy individuals but can kill people who are HIV-positive. Two such infections are Kaposi's sarcoma, a skin cancer, and Pneumocystis carinii, a form of pneumonia, a lung infection.

Teenagers are in great danger of contracting AIDS. According to the Center for Disease Control and Prevention, teenagers now make up 20 percent of the number of people infected with HIV. Many teenagers believe they are going to live forever and that nothing will happen to them. They don't believe that AIDS can affect them, so many do not take steps to protect themselves. HIV is passed in bodily fluids, such as blood, semen, and vaginal fluids. It can be passed in one *single* contact, and once the virus enters the body, nothing can stop it.

Because of the deadliness of this disease, there is a lot of fear surrounding AIDS. Some people believe that only certain groups of people get it, such as homosexuals or drug users, but AIDS shows no prejudice in picking its victims. AIDS affects everyone. Women, men, children, homosexuals, and heterosexuals can all contract the disease. The only defense we have against this disease is knowledge. You need to be aware of how this disease is spread and avoid those activities. If you are going to have sex, make sure you know your partner's sexual history and use a condom.

Advice from Teen Moms

1. "Be careful when having sex."
2. "Use birth control if you choose to have sex."
3. "Use a condom."
4. "Just because you haven't gotten pregnant doesn't mean you don't have to use birth control."
5. "If you wish to have sex, use birth control."
6. "Don't get pregnant again during your teen years."
7. "Don't get pregnant again until you are old enough to have a good job and are mature enough to handle the responsibilities."

CHAPTER 11

As Your Child Grows

E ven though it feels at first as if you'll be tied down for the rest of your life, soon enough your baby grows up. As your child grows, he or she will begin to need you less. Many mothers cherish the moments when their babies need them completely because this time is over quickly.

Let's talk a little about your child's changing needs. Children all face the same developmental tasks, but they do not develop at the same rate. Most first-time mothers worry that their child is not developing on schedule and fear that something must be wrong. Probably nothing is wrong; the child is just developing at his or her own pace. You can't will your child to reach all the developmental milestones on *your* timetable. So it's not always useful to compare notes with your friends about your child's progress.

Following are some stages that children go through, but don't be concerned if your child is a month or two or even more behind in reaching these stages. If you have any concerns, ask your pediatrician. All children start out seeing themselves as the center of the universe. Babies explore their world through their senses, primarily their mouth. At first everything, no matter how gross it appears, goes into their mouth. They suck on the thing; they chew on it; and often, to our disgust, they swallow it. You might try exploring your house from your baby's perspective sometime. Crawl around on your hands and knees, and check out what's in his or her line of vision and within reach.

Getting Around

In the beginning, babies are aware of their primary caregiver, usually their mother. They know not only your face but your scent, and they prefer it to all others. They prefer looking at faces and bright colors, bold contrasts, or bold black-and-white designs. Remember that when you buy baby toys.

Babies usually learn first to roll over from stomach to back. The first time it happens is usually an accident, but the child readily seeks to repeat the experience if it doesn't totally startle him or her. Then the baby learns a harder task: to roll from the back onto the stomach. Babies sit up at about six months. They crawl around on their bellies before making it up onto their knees. Then, before they can actually propel themselves forward on their knees, they get stuck moving their torso back and forth while their knees remain firmly on the floor. They rock back and forth until one day they suddenly take off. Crawling is a complicated process, believe it or not although not all children crawl; some go directly to walking. Children may pull themselves up into a standing, hanging-on position at around eight months old. Next they walk around holding on to things (even unstable things, so be alert). Finally, they walk on their own at anywhere from nine to fourteen months. Walking at an early age does not necessarily mean they are smarter. All it may mean is that they have better motor development. Usually, if a child excels in one thing, he or she is a little slower in another.

Verbal Communication

The age at which children begin to communicate verbally is different from child to child. When babies are first born, they do little in the way of communicating besides crying. At one month, the baby begins to make throaty sounds. By the time the baby reaches four to six months, he or she will be at the babbling stage. He or she will laugh, gurgle, sigh, and have the ability to vocalize pleasure or displeasure. Between the seventh and ninth months, your baby will be able to produce as many as twelve different sounds, as well as use different vowels. It is at this time that the baby will be able to say "mama" or "dada," and even recognize his or her own name. Between the tenth and twelfth month of life, the babbling will slowly turn into actual words, and he or she will be able to understand simple requests and names.

Developmental Problems

I know from experience that it's easy to get caught up in worries that your child is not normal. Usually, I tell mothers to calm down and quit scrutinizing everything their child does or doesn't do. However, mothers should be advocates for their children and should be willing to consider when things are not quite right with them. Sometimes the doctor, who sees the child for a few minutes at most in the examination room, fails to notice a developmental problem. If you see behavior you think is strange and the doctor doesn't mention it, bring it to his or her attention. If the doctor thinks it's nothing, no harm done. If it is significant, you've saved a lot of time for both the doctor and your child.

As a rule, though, kids develop according to their own inner timetable. Babies cut teeth as early as three months or as late as one year and older. Usually, the early teethers are the first ones to lose their baby teeth (by the age of five). Cutting teeth early means nothing unless you're breast-feeding and getting bitten regularly.

Developing Beyond Infancy

After the infant stage of experiencing their world through their mouths, children go through a concrete stage of thinking in which everything is taken literally. If you say to a three-year-old, "Oh, I'm just not myself today," he or she might respond quite seriously, "Then who are you?" If you pour the same amount of juice into glasses for two kids, but one glass is tall and skinny and the other short and fat, the kid with the tall glass will think he's gotten more juice. Realizing that kids think this way may help you deal with their behavior at times.

At about seven (and remember, this isn't a hard and fast rule), kids develop more abstract thinking and can understand much more. The timing of this stage is why your child may not be ready to read before seven or can add and subtract only by using counters or coins.

If you want to stay on top of your child's stages of development, I suggest you pick up a good baby-care book. Don't drive yourself and your child crazy by comparing notes with every mother who has a child your child's age. Children *do not* develop at the same rate. Have an idea about what takes place when, but don't expect your child to comply.

Enjoy these years with your baby. Keep a journal of cute comments your toddler makes or funny things he or she does. Once the baby is off and running, you can look back over those earlier times and remember. Take a lot of pictures, and have pictures taken of you and the baby together. If you don't have a camera (or a good enough one), keep it in mind for a shower gift or a birthday gift. Just as you can't spoil a newborn, you can never take too many pictures. Your baby will change dramatically from month to month, and without pictures it's easy to forget how he or she looked as a baby.

Children's Moral Development

Just as children develop physically and intellectually in stages, they develop morally in stages. Very young children behave in order to avoid punishment. But they can't reason at this early stage, and they often haven't developed the ability to empathize with anyone else. So, appealing to your child's sense of decency and fairness doesn't work at first. That's why it takes so long for them to learn to share. The solution is to model the behavior you want to see in them, and continue to reward their compliance.

A Mother's Feelings

How will you feel about your child as he or she grows? Sometimes it depends on your circumstances. If you're having trouble providing for yourself and your baby or your baby is always sick, you may feel more negative than positive emotions. All mothers experience both kinds of feelings. Sometimes you'll be amazed by how bright your child is. Then you may be angry that this smart boy or girl does such bad things. You'll no doubt feel alternately overprotective and too indulgent. You'll wish your child was older, and you'll wish he or she was a baby again.

You'll have a lot of different feelings for this child, and you'll continue to feel all these conflicting emotions forever. You never stop being a mother! The one thing you'll have in common with other mothers is that you'll think about your child constantly. For many years, your life will be tightly bound up with your child's, even if it's not with the child's father.

Day Care

If you go back into the workforce, what will you do with your child? There may be government-sponsored organizations or private organizations that may be able to provide child care or help with the expenses involved. Check with your county health department or family planning clinic for specific details.

You may wonder how you're supposed to find a "good" day-care center for your child. First of all, you'll want a licensed facility. Your school counselor or a social worker should have a list of licensed homes. Visit the centers to check the environment. What is the ratio of children to staff? If it's greater than eight to one (or twelve to one in an older age group), your child will not get much individual attention. Problems may go unnoticed. What is the atmosphere? Do the teachers and administrators welcome your interest, or do they try to steer you away from certain areas or allow you to visit only at set times? How do they treat you? Do they listen to you and take your concerns seriously? How do they relate to your child? Do they try to push him or her into activities, or are they flexible, letting him or her come to them? Do they seem knowledgeable, or do they act as if they know *everything*?

Make a list of questions you want to ask so that nothing goes unanswered. Try not to be intimidated by those in positions of authority. Remember, you're hiring them to care for your child. You want to feel good about your decision.

Is the center in a good location? Is it on a busy street? Is it clean? What are the toys like? Think of what's important for your child, and then check out a variety of day-care centers.

Once you have found a center that you and your child both like, always accompany your child, no matter how old he or she gets to be, to the classroom. Some places have a drive-through front entrance, and you're told to stay in the car while the staff walks your child inside. Nonetheless, you need to know what's going on in the center, and you want to convey to your child that he or she is worth your taking the time to go in with him or her. Your child will probably feel anxious about your leaving at first, particularly if he or she is older than eight months, which is the age when most kids experience "stranger anxiety" and worry about having you out of sight. It may break your heart to leave your child crying, but try to remember that he or she needs some independence, and you're leaving him or her in capable hands.

Learn to recognize signs of abuse, sexual as well as physical. If you find any strange bruises on your child when you pick him or her up, call them to the teacher's attention. Evaluate the explanation. If your child suddenly starts talking too precociously about sex (seeming to know things that he or she shouldn't know), be concerned. If your child seems terrified of the center after having liked it, be concerned. If he or she starts having nightmares or fears going to bed, be concerned. Children regress, revert to more babyish behavior, when they are stressed. This is a warning sign that something is bothering him or her. It may be only because you have another child or a new boyfriend or your routine is disrupted. But it may be because your child is being abused. If you see an increase in aggressive behavior, try to find the reason. In all of the above examples, it is reasonable to suspect abuse, but there can be more than one explanation.

Will your child become more attached to his or her day-care worker than to you? Children do become attached to their caregivers, and that's well and good in most cases. You want them to like the people they spend a great part of their waking hours with. *You, however, will never be replaced!* Your child may adore a teacher, but you are still his or her mother, and he or she will always love you.

The Possibility of Abuse

As your child grows and asserts more independence, you might respond by trying to use control. Ironically, the more you seek to control, the more some children resist. Sometimes your efforts may become abusive. You might hit the child or use threats. You might decide you don't like your child when it's really his or her behavior you hate or the circumstances you find yourself in. Neglecting your child by leaving him or her alone at home or by not providing regular, nutritious meals or a decent bedtime is abuse. Children suffer enormously from emotional abuse, just as they do from physical batterings.

If you find yourself resorting to name-calling or put-downs; if you find yourself wanting to hurt your child; if you constantly think of running away from your child, call an abuse hot line (listed in the front of your phone book) or tell your nurse, doctor, or a trusted adult friend or family member. The point is to get help for yourself. Sometimes, people who were abused as children become abusers themselves. That's why treatment is so important. If you can stop the cycle of abuse now, your child need not grow up to repeat the harsh treatment to his or her children.

A Lifelong Commitment

Raising a child is a lifelong commitment. It is not something you do halfheartedly. Your child will need your love, support, and protection for all of your life. As your child grows older, his or her needs will change, and you will have to meet those changing needs. Even when your child is old enough take care of many of his or her own needs, your job will not end. No parent will argue with you that it's hard work, but along with all that responsibility comes an innocent loving new person who will bring more joy to your life than you ever thought possible. Take it one day at a time. Trying to raise a child when you have barely finished being one yourself can be difficult. Don't become too obsessed about what you have done wrong or could have done better. All that matters is that you love, protect, and support your child. No parent is perfect, and your child will love you no less despite your imperfections. Enjoy and cherish the time you spend with your child.

Advice from Teen Moms

1. "Let your baby grow up. Don't try to keep him or her a baby forever."

2. "Keep a scrapbook, a journal, a photo album full of pictures—or all three—to remember this time."
3. "You never repeat that first time. Even if you do it again."

CHAPTER 12

How Do I Know I'm Doing Okay?

How will you know if you're doing a good job raising your child? Give yourself a quick test; read over the following questions and decide for yourself. Then read the suggestions on baby basics to have on hand, whom to call with problems, and ways to discipline your child.

Am I Able to Meet My Baby's Needs?

1. Can I afford infant formula without diluting it to stretch it out?
2. Do I keep all doctor appointments, no matter how costly or inconvenient?
3. Do I show my baby love through my time and attention?
4. Have I sought to make his or her living environment as safe as possible?

5. Do I know CPR techniques and the Heimlich maneuver for children?

6. Do I know how to take my baby's temperature (rectally and in the armpit)?

7. Do I refrain from smoking in my home and ask others not to smoke around the baby?

8. Have I borrowed or bought all necessary baby equipment? (See list of baby basics at the end of the chapter.)

9. Do I have someone to turn to when I need help with the baby?

10. Am I free to call him or her at any hour of the day or night?

11. Can I control my temper when the baby "acts up"?

12. Is there a pattern of abuse in my family, and can I speak up on my baby's behalf, if necessary?

Am I Able to Meet My Own Needs?

1. Do I have a life apart from motherhood?

2. Do I have hobbies that I still work on?

3. Do I see friends without the baby?

4. Have I set some positive short-term goals?

5. Have I finished school, or am I working toward my diploma?

6. Can I name things for which my baby would be proud of me?

7. Can I support myself and the baby?

8. Do I know how to seek financial assistance?

9. Do I take an interest in my appearance?

10. Do I stay informed of current events and community news?

11. Can I do all these things and provide for the baby at the same time?

Can I Find Fulfillment in a Relationship?

1. Have I reconciled the relationship with my baby's father?
2. Is he supporting me?
3. Do I have time to give to a relationship *and* to the baby?
4. Do I know what birth control options I have?
5. Do I take precautions against AIDS and other STDs?
6. Do I believe those diseases can affect *me*?
7. Am I able to feel complete without a boyfriend or husband?
8. Do I enjoy being with a guy even if I'm not going out on an expensive date?
9. Do I treat myself with respect and expect others to do so?
10. Am I proud of my accomplishments?

If you can answer yes to the last two questions, you've already learned a lot. You *should* be proud, because teenage motherhood is no small undertaking.

Things to Have on Hand for the Baby

diapers (six dozen cloth diapers, diaper pins, plastic pants, and a diaper pail, or two packages of newborn disposable diapers and one dozen cloth diapers for multipurpose use)

T-shirts or "onesies" (ten to twelve)

drawstring nightgowns (three to six)

one-piece rompers (three to six)

sleepers (three to six)

sweater
lightweight jacket } depending on the season
snowsuit coverall

receiving blankets (four)

baby blankets (four)

crib sheets (three to five) (You only need the fitted
   bottom sheet.)

bumper pad (to tie around the edges of the crib)

mattress

mattress pad

formula (if not breast-feeding)

baby bottles with infant-size nipples (one dozen)

bottle brush

rectal thermometer and K-Y jelly

nasal suction bulb (may come free in hospital
   newborn package)

baby lotion

A & D ointment or petroleum jelly

diaper rash cream

infant Tylenol drops (*never* give an infant or child as-
   pirin; it could lead to Reyes Syndrome, a life-
   threatening condition)

car seat

stroller

crib

humidifier

playpen

high chair

books on child care and breast-feeding

laundry detergent formulated to not irritate a baby's skin, such as Dreft

Optional

portable crib

baby carrier

mobile

rattles

baby swing

rocking chair (for you as well as a baby-sized one)

small tub for baths

bathtub seat for a baby who can sit up by himself or herself (*never* leave a baby unattended in water)

baby towels with hoods

washcloths

tapes of recorded sounds or lullabies

nightlight

assorted baby books

WHAT TO DO ABOUT PROBLEMS

Call Your *Family* When . . .

- you need a baby-sitter
- you don't know how to give your baby a bath, pin a diaper, etc.
- you're not sure how to dress your baby for the day
- you need another hand
- you've run out of diapers or formula
- you want to come visit for dinner
- you want someone to talk to
- your baby first turns over on his or her own, smiles the first smile, etc.

Call Your Doctor When . . .

- your baby runs a fever (above 100°) for more than an hour
- your baby coughs and gasps for breath (after you've determined nothing is obstructing the airway)
- your infant refuses to eat for six to eight hours
- your infant is vomiting forcefully or continuously
- your infant has nonstop diarrhea with frequent, watery stools, which can lead to dehydration
- your child's behavior seems unusual (too listless or agitated)
- your baby appears dehydrated: urinates less, is drowsy, feverish, or has a very dry nose, lips, and cheeks
- your baby has a persistent cough
- your infant has a significant change in the color or consistency of bowel movements compared to his or her established pattern

- your baby cries for more than an hour straight and cannot be comforted
- your newborn has a yellow color (check the whites of the eyes)
- your baby has a seizure
- you suspect physical or sexual abuse (have found bruises or injuries on the baby), or have intentionally hurt your baby yourself. Worry about your guilt and possible punishment later. Get the baby to the doctor or hospital fast

Suggested Methods of Discipline

- *Be a good role model.* Children learn first by observing the people close to them. What is *your* behavior saying to them?
- *Encourage good behavior by rewarding the good and ignoring the bad* (as long as the bad isn't dangerous). Use positive reinforcement (praise and rewards) and negative reinforcement (removal of privileges).
- *Associate your child's name with praise, not reprimands.*
- Remember that discipline is not punishment. Instead, it is a way in which parents help their children develop self-control and through which they pass on their values. It is a way of expressing love. Read books that help you figure out effective ways of disciplining your child.

Glossary

bilirubin Pigment produced by the breakdown of red blood cells no longer needed after birth that causes the skin to turn yellow.

colostrum A thin liquid that contains antibodies needed by a baby and is produced by the mother's breasts the first day or so after delivery.

epidural An anesthetizing shot given at three to four centimeter dilation to ease labor pains.

episiotomy Incision from vagina toward the anus, usually performed during childbirth to prevent tearing of the vagina.

fetal alcohol syndrome Term used to describe the physical and psychological problems a baby may have because his or her mother drank alcohol during her pregnancy.

fetus A baby during the first stages of its development in the uterus.

general anesthesia Medication that temporarily renders a person unconscious.

obstetrician A doctor who specializes in the branch of medicine dealing with childbirth.

placenta The structure developed on the wall of the uterus in approximately the third month of pregnancy that enables the mother to provide nourishment and oxygen to the baby and eliminates waste products.

placenta previa Dangerous condition in late pregnancy in which the placenta is located partially or completely over the cervix.

postpartum After the birth.

premature rupture When the membranes that surround the fetus rupture prematurely.

prenatal Before the birth.

spinal block An anesthetizing shot given just before birth or in preparation for a cesarean.

sudden infant death syndrome (SIDS) When an infant suddenly dies without apparent cause.

ultrasound A test done during pregnancy to determine the stage of pregnancy and to check the development of the fetus.

Where to Go for Help

Domestic Violence Hot Line
(800) 942-6906
(800) 942-6908 (En Español)

National Organization of Single Mothers
P.O. Box 68
Midland, NC 28107-0068
(704) 888-5063

Parents Anonymous
(909) 621-6184

Planned Parenthood Federation of America
810 Seventh Avenue
New York, NY 10019
(212) 541-7800
Web site: http://www.ppfa.org/ppfa/
e-mail: communications@ppfa.org.

Single Parent Resource Center, Inc.
31 East 28th Street
New York, NY 10016
(212) 951-7030

Welfare Warriors
2711 West Michigan Avenue
Milwaukee, WI 53208
(414) 342-6662

Other resources for help:

United Way
Contact your local office for referrals to support services

YMCA/YWCA
Contact your local branch for support services

In Canada

Planned Parenthood Federation of Canada
1 Nicholas Street, Suite 430
Ottawa, ONT, K1N 7B7
(613) 241-4474

For Further Reading

Beyer, Kay. *Coping with Teen Parenting*. Rev. ed, New York: The Rosen Publishing Group, 1995.

The Columbia University College of Physicians and Surgeons Complete Guide to Early Child Care. New York: Crown Publishers, 1990.

Edeiken, Louise, and Johanna Antar. *Now that You're Pregnant*. New York: Collier Books, 1992.

Eisenberg, Arlene. *What to Expect When You're Expecting*. Rev. ed, New York: Workman Publishers, 1991.

Eisenberg, Arlene, Heidi Murkoff, and Sandee Hathaway. *What to Expect: The First Year*. New York: Workman Publishers, 1988.

Fields, Denise and Alan Fields. *Baby Bargain*. Boulder, Co.: Windsor Peak Press, 1994.

Flamm, Bruce. *Birth After Cesarean: The Medical Facts*. New York: Simon and Schuster, 1992.

Hess, Abbot Mary, Elise Anne Hunt. *Eating for Two: The Complete Guide to Nutrition During Pregnancy*. New York: Macmillan, 1992.

Hyde, O. Margaret, and Elizabeth H. Forsyth. *AIDS: What Does it Mean to You?* New York: Walker and Company, 1995.

Kitzinger, Sheila. *The Year After Childbirth*. New York: Simon and Schuster, 1996.

The Philadelphia Child Guidance Center and Jack Maguire. *Your Child's Emotional Health: The Early Years*. New York: Macmillan, 1995.

Russell, Keith and Jennifer Niebyl. *Eastman's Expectant Mother*. Boston: Little, Brown and Company, 1989.

Samuels, Mike, Dr., and Nancy Samuels. *The Well Pregnancy Book*. New York: Simon and Schuster, 1986.
Sears, William and Martha Sears. *The Birth Book*. Boston: Little, Brown and Company, 1994.

Index

A

abortion, 6
abuse, 71, 81, 82–83, 86, 87,
   106–108
   hot lines, 71, 82–83, 108
adoption, 6, 11
aerosols, 34
AIDS (acquired
   immunodeficiency
   syndrome), 28, 29, 68, 96,
   98–99
   and pregnancy, 68
Aid to Families with
   Dependent children
   (AFDC), 10
alcohol and drugs
   addictions, 32, 67
   avoidance of during
   pregnancy, 8, 31–32, 34
   effects on unborn baby,
   31–32, 66–67
   treatment programs, 32
anesthesia
   general, 48–49, 57
   regional, 47–48

B

babies
   care of, 69–76, 78–80
   effect on marriage, 84–85
   feeding, 72–75
   household safety for, 79–80
   material required for, 39–43,
   112–114
bilirubin, 66
birth, stages of, 53–55
birth control, 16, 91–99
bladder infections, 3, 25
bleeding following childbirth
   (lochia), 61
bonding with a newborn baby,
   58, 73, 75
bottle-feeding, 73–74
breast-feeding, 43, 62, 70,
   72–73, 74
breast milk, 62, 72, 73
breech birth, 56
burping babies, 71

C

cardiopulmonary resuscitation
   (CPR), 32, 79
car seats, 40
catheter, urinary, 53
cesarean section (c-section),
   27, 28, 49, 56–57, 63
childbirth classes, 16, 46
child development, 100–109

in abstract thinking, 103
  moral, 104
  problems in, 102–103
  rates of, 100, 102, 103–104
chlamydia, 28, 93
clothing
  baby, 41–42, 113
  maternity, 24
colic, 69–71
  and breast-feeding, 70
colostrum, 62
condoms, 93, 96–97, 99
constipation, 19
contractions, 49–51, 61
crack cocaine, 32
cribs, 40

D
dating, 87
day care, 18, 105–107
  centers, 105–106
Demerol, 46–47
Depo-Provera injection, 93–94
depression, 5, 63–65
diapers, types of, 41–42
diaphragms, 95–96
dilation, cervical, 52, 53, 54
discipline and punishment of
  children, 104, 116
dizziness, 26

E
education, importance of, 9,
  88
enemas, 52
epidural block, 47
episiotomy, 48, 55, 85

F
family planning clinics, 7, 15,
  16–17, 40
fatigue, 22–23, 63, 64, 79
fetal alcohol syndrome (FAS),
  31, 66–67
fetal monitors, external, 53
formula, baby, 43, 73, 74
  dangers of diluting, 43,
  74

G
gas, 26, 63
gonorrhea, 29, 93

H
Heimlich maneuver, 79
hemorrhoids, 25
herpes, genital, 28
HIV (human
  immunodeficiency
  virus), 29, 68, 93, 94,
  98–99
hospital stays, 60
hunger, increased, 25

I
incubators, 65
iron supplements, 19

J
jaundice, in newborns, 66

L
labor (and delivery), 45–59
  complications with, 7, 49,
  56–57
  dehydration during, 52–53

emotions associated with, 57–58, 63–64

inducing, 50

physical aftereffects, 61

premature, 33, 65–66

reactions of teenage mothers, 58–59

support person during, 55–56, 57

lead paint, 33

leg cramps, 26

low birth weight, 31, 33

M

marriage, 5–6, 86–87

"the mask of pregnancy," 26

meconium, in delivery, 56

medication during pregnancy, 25

membranes, premature rupture of, 27

menstruation, 2, 62–63

mood shifts, abrupt, 29–30, 54

morning sickness, 21–22

mucus plug, 50

N

natural childbirth, 46

nausea and vomiting, 3, 21–22, 28

Norplant implants, 94

nutrition and diet, 19, 22, 31, 73

O

obstetricians and obstetrics, 7–8

oxytocin, 61

P

pain medication, 46–49

parenting

classes, 83

emotions associated with, 104–105

family support, 81, 115

lifestyle changes, 89–90

responsibilities of new fathers, 81–82, 87

responsibilities of new mothers, 64, 76, 77–83, 110–111

single, 6

pediatricians and pediatrics, 43, 79, 115–116

pill, the, 92–93

pillows and suffocation, 43, 80

placenta previa, 27

Planned Parenthood, 7, 17

preemies, 65–66

pregnancy

counselors and counseling, 4, 5

early signs of, 2, 3

emergency symptoms, 27–28

emotions associated with, 5, 29–30

environmental dangers during, 33–34

father's reaction to, 38–39

financial support, 13–14, 16, 36

friends' support, 14–15

guidelines for a healthy, 8, 19, 31–34, 67

living at home during, 37

living away from home

during, 37–38, 39
negative aspects, 35
parents' support, 13–14, 37
positive aspects, 34–35
responsibilities of the father,
    6, 12–13, 38–39
responsibilities of the
    mother, 37
school support, 17–18
self-support, 19, 37–38, 39
sex during, 28
staying in school during, 8–9
symptoms or side-effects,
    21–34
telling parents about, 6–7,
    17
tests, 3–4
who to tell about, 6–7
working during, 37–38
prenatal care, 7
pudendal block, 48

R
relaxation techniques, 46,
    51–52

S
school and schooling for
    pregnant teens, 9, 18
self-esteem and self-image, 18,
    64, 86
sex
    resumption after childbirth,
        85–86
    unprotected, 28
sexual abstinence, 97
sexually transmitted disease
    (STD), 28–29, 92–93, 94,
    95, 96, 97–99

shots, for babies, 43
skin, dryness and itchiness, 26
sleep and sleeping problems
    in babies, 71–72
    in mothers, 23, 72, 79, 80
smoking
    effects on babies and
        children, 80
    effects on fetuses, 33
spermicides, 95
spinal block, 47–48
spinal-epidural block, 48
stillbirth or miscarriage, 31, 33
"stranger anxiety" in children,
    106
stretch marks, 26
Sudden Infant Death
    Syndrome (SIDS), 32
sweeteners, artificial, 19
swelling of the limbs, 28

T
teen pregnancy
    accidental, 2
    rates of, 2
Temporary Assistance for
    Needy Families (TANF),
    10
transition, 54
toxoplasmosis, 34
toys, baby, 42–43, 80
    safety, 42–43
    toxic paint, avoiding, 43

U
ultrasound, 8
umbilical cord, 78–79
urination
    following childbirth, 61

increased frequency of, 3, 23
uterus, expansion of, 23

V
vaginal bleeding, 27, 63
vaginal discharge, 25
verbal communication, 102

W
walking and crawling, 101–102
weight gain, 23, 24–25
  average during pregnancy,
    24–25
  excessive, 24
welfare, 10, 16, 37–38

THE OTHER WORLD
Issues and Politics
of the Developing World

Third Edition

Joseph N. Weatherby

Randal L. Cruikshanks

Emmit B. Evans, Jr.

Reginald Gooden

Earl D. Hu

Richard Kran

Dianne Long

California Polytechnic State University, San

LONGMAN

An imprint of Addison Wesley Longman, Inc.

New York • Reading, Massachusetts • Menlo Park, California • Harlow, England
Don Mills, Ontario • Sydney • Mexico City • Madrid • Amsterdam

**The Other World: Issues and Politics of
the Developing World, Third Edition**

Longman, 10 Bank Street, White Plains, N.Y. 10606

Associated companies:
Longman Group Ltd., London
Longman Cheshire Pty., Melbourne
Longman Paul Pty., Auckland
Copp Clark Longman Ltd., Toronto

Executive editor: Pamela Gordon
Production editor: Linda Moser
Editorial assistant: Chia Ling
Cover design: David Levy
Production supervisor: Edith Pullman
Compositor: University Graphics

Library of Congress Cataloging-in-Publication Data
The other world : issues and politics of the developing world / Joseph
    N. Weatherby . . . [et al.]. — 3rd ed.
        p.   cm.
    Includes bibliographical references and index.
    ISBN 0-8013-1670-7
    1. Developing countries.   I. Weatherby, Joseph.
    D883.087   1997
    909'.09722—dc20   96-10554
                                                             CIP

1 2 3 4 5 6 7 8 9 10-MA-0099989796

Dedicated to Ann Berry Weatherby, September 6, 1971–September 21, 1994.

"I wonder what she will grow into, and whether she will be lucky or unlucky to have been dragged out of chaos. She ought to have some rare qualities both of mind and body, but these do not always mean happiness or peace."

Sir Winston Churchill on the birth of his daughter, Diana

Contents

Preface   *ix*

Introduction   *xiii*

PART I   GLOBAL ISSUES IN THE OTHER WORLD   **1**

CHAPTER 1 **THE OTHER WORLD**   **3**

Defining the Other World   *4*
The Changing World   *4*
Understanding the Other World   *7*
Characterizing the Other World   *10*
The Plight of Other World Women   *14*
The Dilemma of the Other World   *16*
ISSUES FOR DISCUSSION   *17*
Notes   20
A Student Guide to Useful Reference Materials on the Other World   20
For Further Reading   21

CHAPTER 2 **THE OLD AND THE NEW: COLONIALISM,
NEOCOLONIALISM, AND NATIONALISM**   **22**

Colonialism   *22*
History of Colonialism   *23*

Motives for Colonialism   *26*
The Legacy of Colonialism   *31*
Neocolonialism   *34*
Nationalism   *39*
Summary   *40*
ISSUES FOR DISCUSSION   *41*
Notes   48
For Further Reading   49

CHAPTER 3   DEVELOPMENT   50

Values, Ideologies, and Development   *51*
A History of Development Efforts   *54*
Beyond Ideology: Politics, Power, and Self-interest   *62*
Conclusions   *63*
Summary   *66*
ISSUES FOR DISCUSSION   *66*
Notes   71
For Further Reading   72

CHAPTER 4   CONFLICT RESOLUTION AND THE
            OTHER WORLD   73

Domestic Conflict   *75*
International Conflict   *84*
International Institutions   *89*
Summary and Conclusion   *96*
ISSUES FOR DISCUSSION   *97*
Notes   101
For Further Reading   102

PART II   OTHER WORLD REGIONS   **103**

CHAPTER 5   LATIN AMERICA   105

Geography   *108*
People   *110*
History   *111*
Economics   *116*
Government   *118*

CASE STUDIES   *123*
   Mexico 123, Brazil 126, Cuba 131
Looking Ahead   *135*
FLASHPOINTS   *138*
   *Narcotics Traffic 138, Panama 140, Zapatista Uprising in Chiapas,
   Mexico 141, North American Free-Trade Area 143, Environment 145,
   Haiti 146*
Notes   148
For Further Reading   149

CHAPTER 6   SUB-SAHARAN AFRICA   150

Geography   *151*
People   *152*
History   *157*
The Colonial Experience   *159*
Government   *164*
Economics and Natural Resources   *169*
CASE STUDIES   *172*
   South Africa 172, Rwanda 175, Zimbabwe 177, Angola-Namibia 178
FLASHPOINTS   *179*
   *Africa and AIDS 179, Horn of Africa 180, Africa on the Move 182,
   Nigeria 183, Mozambique 184, Land Mines 185, Zaire 185,
   Environment 186*
Summary   *187*
Notes   188
For Further Reading   188

CHAPTER 7   ASIA   190

Geography   *194*
People   *195*
History and Government   *196*
CASE STUDIES   *200*
   East Asia: China 200, South Asia 205, Southeast Asia 212
FLASHPOINTS   *216*
   *Afghanistan 216, Cambodia 217, China's Borders 217, China's
   Leadership 218, Development versus Environmental Destruction 219,
   India-Pakistan 220, Islamic Fundamentalism 221, North Korea 221,
   Sri Lanka 222, Taiwan 223*
Summary   *224*
Notes   224
For Further Reading   225

CHAPTER 8   THE MIDDLE EAST AND NORTH AFRICA   227

Geography   *231*
People   *237*
Religion   *238*
History   *241*
The Colonial Experience   *244*
Government   *246*
Economics and Natural Resources   *246*
CASE STUDIES ON MIDDLE EASTERN NATIONALISM   *247*
  Turkey 249, Iran 250, Egypt 252, The Arabs 253, Israel 255
Looking Ahead   *257*
FLASHPOINTS   *258*
  *Palestine 258, The Palestinians 259, The Intifada (Uprising) 261,
  Armenia 261, Six New Muslim States 262, Kurdistan 263, The Iraqi
  Disputes 263, Strategic Waterways and Oil Pipelines 265, Cyprus 266,
  OPEC and the Politics of Oil 266, The 1994 Civil War in Yemen 267,
  The Algerian Dispute 267, The Oil Fires of Kuwait: An Environmental
  Disaster of Epic Proportions 268*
Summary   *270*
Notes   270
For Further Reading   272

CHAPTER 9   PROSPECTS FOR THE FUTURE   273

Crossroads 2000: The Other World in the Twenty-first Century   *273*
Decisions 2000   *278*
Toward a New World Order   *282*
New International Relationships   *287*
Conclusion   *291*
Notes   292
For Further Reading   292

Index   295

About the Authors   301

Preface

Much of our perception of the world is from an American perspective. We tend to focus on events in our country, those in other Western nations, and until recently on U.S.–Soviet relations. Yet, despite the military, political, and economic power of the United States, we account for only 5 percent of the world's population. Clearly, most of the world exists outside of our country. Indeed, this Other World has become crucial in understanding the larger world in which we live.

This book aims to help students grasp some of the main dimensions of contemporary global issues in the Third World, which we term the Other World. It is intended to present that part of our world that is considered non-Western in its orientation. To appreciate the Other World in today's international climate, we need to know more about its geography, culture, traditions, and political and historical development.

The Other World is a primer on Third World issues, with an interdisciplinary focus. We make no apology that this book is what it appears to be: a descriptive background to selected world issues. It is descriptive because we emphasize basic information on geography, culture, and political tensions in the Other World. The book targets general education students rather than the specialist. Our position is that these students are better served by a book that emphasizes specific issues, events, and places in a clear, jargon-free way rather than by one written for political science majors and graduate specialists.

We also hope that our analysis will be welcomed by readers who are looking for a supplementary textbook to use in international relations, geography, and comparative government courses in which coverage of the Third World is needed. Our point of view is that with the end of the cold war and the collapse of Soviet power, the focus of world politics has shifted away from an East-West dimension to a North-South dimension.

Two traditional approaches dominate the study of global politics: the comparative approach and the area studies approach. The former addresses the political situation in selected countries with an emphasis on their values, institutions, levels of modernization, and types of governments. A deficiency of this method is that it often fails to provide an overview of the geographical areas in which the separate states are located. However, comparative studies are dominant in the social sciences because of their ability to account for similarities and differences among political communities.

The second approach, area studies, centers on the study of geographic regions. This perspective focuses on a region's general characteristics, including geography, climate, economics, political and social structures, culture, religion, and history. Instead of contrasting the differences among states with dissimilar backgrounds, this method promotes an understanding of the peoples and countries in geographical proximity to one another.

This book combines both perspectives. First, it gives an overview of issues relevant to the understanding of contemporary problems common to the Other World. Second, it provides regional coverage of Latin America, Africa, Asia, and the Middle East and then describes the similarities and differences within these regions. Third, it traces events and issues in selected countries in each region.

All of the chapters have been rewritten to take into account the effects of the end of the cold war and the disintegration of the communist bloc on Other World politics. We have attempted to keep the topics as relevant and up-to-date as possible. Time does not stand still, so we apologize in advance for any illustrations that may have become dated because of the rush of events.

It is our hope that the readers of *The Other World* will gain a new understanding of the major issues that affect much of the world's population. If we are to comprehend the political turmoil in the Middle East or the food crisis in Africa, we need to be aware of the dynamics of life in those regions. Finally, we believe that issues in the Other World do not respect borders and that global interdependence is a fact of life in the late twentieth century.

All of us involved in this book benefited from the comments made by the following reviewers:

Dennis Hart, Western Illinois University

Jimmy Kandeh, University of Richmond

Gerardo L. Munck, University of Illinois at Urbana-Champaign

James Pletcher, Denison University

Nancy Spalding, East Carolina University

Elizabeth Van Wie Davis, Illinois State University

W. Marvin Will, University of Tulsa

Freeman J. Wright, California State University, Fresno

We believe that this text is stronger for their insights. Sherry Couture provided indispensable aid in overcoming the technical difficulties of this project. Others who helped with proofreading and sympathy include A. Norman Cruikshanks, Carol Huff, Mary and Edward Gavin, Mandy Luevano, Hazel Morelan, John Nickerson, Skye Patterson, Ilona Ing, and Jane Weatherby. A special thanks goes to Pam Gordon and Linda Moser, who guided the book through the editorial stages. We also thank our copy editor, Barbara Conner. We are grateful to our colleague, John Culver. Because of the number of coauthors, we each have the luxury of blaming the others for whatever errors remain.

A chapter-by-chapter Test Bank with multiple-choice, true-false, and long- and short-answer questions is available to adopters. To order it, please contact your Longman Higher Education sales consultant or call 1-800-552-2499.

Joseph N. Weatherby

Randal L. Cruikshanks

Emmit B. Evans, Jr.

Reginald Gooden

Earl D. Huff

Richard Kranzdorf

Dianne Long

Introduction

There is nothing more difficult to take in hand, more perilous to conduct, or more uncertain in its success, than to take the lead in the introduction of a new order of things. Because the innovator has for enemies all those who have done well under the old conditions, and lukewarm defenders who may do well under the new.

Niccolò Machiavelli

The Other World is a place of dynamic change. Change is multifaceted: It can be simple or complex, positive or negative, of short- or long-term consequence, welcomed by some, opposed by others, and anticipated or unforeseen, as well as a combination of all of these factors.

Political geographers argue that the international system will soon undergo the most profound change since the modern state system was created. The number of recognized states may even double within the next quarter century. These changes will be the result of trends that are already observable in the Other World. New states are being created as the last colonies become independent. Others are being established as nations break away from already existing states to form additional entities. Finally, new states are also evolving out of the turmoil resulting from both the collapse of the Soviet Union and the end of the cold war. Geographer George Demko succinctly described this process when he observed, "The current changes in the political and economic geography of the world are as significant as what the world went through after the Treaty of Westphalia."[1]

This textbook focuses on the process of change in the Other World. As used here the term *Other World* has a broader meaning than the more commonly used expression *Third World*. The Other World includes both underdeveloped and developed states that because of geography, history, or culture have similar interests and perceptions.

As in the second edition, *The Other World*, Third Edition is divided into two parts. The first part comprises four chapters that address global issues of a general nature, including colonialism, development, and the mechanisms for reducing conflict. Each of these chapters is introductory in nature. They are written for those with little previous exposure to Other World issues. An Issues for Discussion section has been added to each chapter in Part I. It is hoped that these topics raise provocative questions from the perspective of people living in the Other World. The authors have made no attempt to offer solutions to these questions.

The second part presents surveys of the Other World regions involved in change. To make meaningful comparisons, we have organized this part geographically into chapters on Latin America, Africa, Asia, and the Middle East and North Africa. Each regionally focused chapter contains material on geography, people, government, economics, and history. Case studies involving key countries are featured throughout this part. These chapters also contain Flashpoints, which provide background material on issues and conflicts. Each area chapter in the third edition contains a Flashpoint that deals with an environmental issue. The concluding chapter summarizes the main points of earlier chapters and offers a look into the Other World in the century ahead.

Before beginning this study, the reader should recognize that all people make assessments of others that are based on their own cultural biases. For example, we know that a person's color is not a behavioral or cultural characteristic. Nevertheless, because most of the people in the Other World have dark skin and most of the people in the developed world have white skin, cultural and behavioral stereotypes are common. People in the developed world often assume that darker skin is a symbol of backwardness. At the same time, the colonial experience has caused people in the Other World to view white skin as the representation of evil exploitation. If we are to make any headway in understanding others, we must attempt to avoid such stereotypes.

The breadth of subjects covered in these chapters required us to make generalizations, although we have attempted to be specific where possible. At the same time, we hope that we have provided the reader with a useful introduction to the major political issues facing the Other World.

Joseph N. Weatherby

NOTE

1. Robin Wright, "The Outer Limits," *Los Angeles Times*, August 25, 1992, p. H4.

PART I

Global Issues
in the Other World

CHAPTER 1

The Other World

Dianne Long

I am a citizen, not of Athens or Greece, but of the world.
Socrates

Socrates was a man of wide vision and understanding, a "citizen of the world" who knew about the great Babylonian, Assyrian, and Egyptian empires that had dominated "the world" long before his time. But his world included only the Mediterranean regions and the area we now call the Middle East. He would have had little awareness or knowledge of the Far East and the complex civilization of the Zhou dynasty that was in existence during his lifetime. Even if he had some fragments of information about China, it is certain that the Mayan civilization, flourishing on the other side of the world, was totally unknown to him.

Like Socrates, we have all seen the maps and globes that represent our world. But we tend to have limited perspectives based on our small knowledge of much of the world and its peoples. Many of us are not aware that the United States and the former Soviet republics combined make up less than 11 percent of the world's population. One-fifth of the human race is Chinese, 16 percent live in India, and hundreds of millions of others live in states that have only recently gained their independence.

The world's peoples are, for the most part, no longer bound by limited areas as they were during the days of ancient Greece. Rather, over 5 billion people inhabit five massive continents increasingly linked into a "global village" by sophisticated communications and complex social, economic, and political interactions. These linkages bring us in increasing contact with that part of the earth that we know little about—the "Other World."

This chapter will look at Other World definitions and characteristics. Following chapters will consider colonial domination, economic development, and conflict resolution.

DEFINING THE OTHER WORLD

The Other World comprises more than two-thirds of the world's states, the vast majority of which are economically less developed and less industrialized than the Western economies. Although political scientists, economists, and geographers do not always agree about which specific countries make up the *Third World*, the term refers to the countries in Latin America, Africa, Asia, and the Middle East. The shaded areas on the map shown in figure 1.1 identify these regions that various writers refer to as the "have-not," "underdeveloped," "developing," "less developed," "South," "nonindustrialized," or "Third World" countries. These countries encompass more than three-quarters of the world's population, yet our daily references to them tend to include little more than sparse observations about a cultural orientation or a few generalizations about national politics.

The term *Third World* is popular in the Western industrialized community, which refers to itself as the First World and to the former Soviet republics as the Second World. The term *Third World* has historically been employed in reference to those states that are characterized by very limited resources, a chronic inability to overcome the magnitude of the socioeconomic problems they face, and a general sense of hopelessness.

The discussion in this text also includes some developed countries that because of location, history, or culture, are distinct. For example, Kuwait, South Africa, and Israel merit inclusion because of their regional importance and relationships with powerful sponsors outside their areas.

THE CHANGING WORLD

The world of the 1990s is rapidly changing. Western traditions of elections and providing choices in who will govern are fast becoming the choice of peoples in the former Soviet Union and Eastern Europe, some of whom are adapting socialist traditions to Western economic and political institutions. The states of Western Europe are moving even more closely together into an economic entity called the European Union. Germany has reunified into a single state. The republics of the former Soviet Union have moved toward autonomy and freedom from Russian dominance and central control. In some cases, old ethnic rivalries have resulted in conflict and bloodshed as in the Croatia-Serb-Bosnia political crisis.

Many countries in today's world claim to follow a democratic and capitalist model in which concepts of individual rights and free-market assumptions have importance. *Democratic* assumptions include a belief in the equality of political and economic rights possessed by all people in the society. *Capitalism* assumes private ownership of production and trade combined with an unrestricted marketplace. In their extremes, these assumptions include the belief that the market is self-regulating and should be free of government intervention unless it fails. The individual is assumed to maximize self-interest; to own property privately; and to compete with others to achieve efficient production, distribution, and consumption of goods and services. Both economically and politically, the individ-

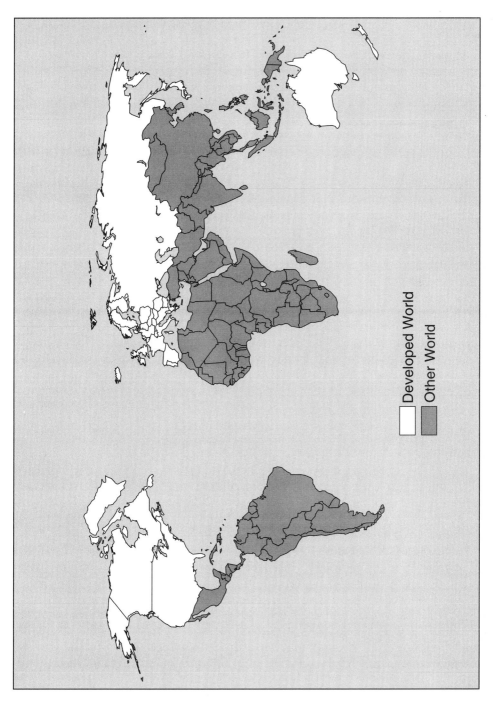

FIGURE 1.1 The Developed World and the Other World

Developed World
Other World

5

ual is important. People are free to own property, start businesses, trade, and make profits with minimal government intervention.

In reality, however, markets fail. And when they do, the people demand government intervention and regulation to ensure that suitable products are available at tolerable prices. In many economies that appear to be capitalist, socialist elements are present to a considerable degree.

Socialist assumptions include the belief that society and markets need to be controlled by government in order to minimize abuses by the powerful and greedy. The society or "collective" holds property for "the common good," and individuals are encouraged to cooperate with one another rather than compete. Economic enterprises such as the mail system, the phone system, the railroads, the health system, the education system, and other elements important to the economic life of a society may be controlled by government. Private ownership of homes and businesses may be tolerated.

A special brand of socialism is called *Marxism*, a doctrine of revolution based on the writings of Karl Marx and Friedrich Engels in which human history is seen as a story of struggle between the exploiting and the exploited classes. In Marxist states, the government plays an especially dominant role in controlling economic affairs. The dismantling of the Russian experiment with Marxism has diminished the appeal of traditional Marxism in the developing world. Examples still exist in North Korea, China, Cuba, and Marxist-led Eastern European states.

In reality, neither the socialist nor the capitalist model seems to produce optimal results. Furthermore, no economy is purely capitalist or socialist. Today, mixed economies prevail. In such economies, there are places where government intervention is deemed appropriate. For example, government often is responsible for national defense and the provision of services to victims of poverty. In other areas private firms provide consumer goods and services. Mixed economic systems require political frameworks that not only encourage markets to develop but also allow regulation when markets fail. They provide opportunities for, as well as safeguards against, private individuals and groups that control communications, transportation, banking, and other vital parts of the political economy.

As ideologies blur and international agreements bring industrial states closer, it is difficult to predict the political and economic changes that will occur. The evolution into a global economy causes changes in the power relationships. These changes may lead to increasing international conflict as nations form regional trading blocs driven by the pursuit of profit rather than by political ideology. Control of labor and raw materials may become the principal source of conflict in the post–cold war era as First World nations and trading blocs compete with one another and as developing nations and masses attempt to resist increasing domination. The 1991 Persian Gulf war indicates the kind of conflict that may characterize the new world order. The Iraqi invasion of Kuwait threatened the supply of oil to, and therefore the economic stability of, the United States, the European Community, and Japan. Although the Soviet Union might have acted to protect Iraqi interests in the cold war, the United States was able to persuade the Soviet Union, and most members of the United Nations (UN), to accept the use of massive military force to end Iraq's occupation of Kuwait. Support for even so odious a dictator as Saddam Hussein among the Arab masses, however, re- vealed common misperceptions of a developing world as sharing political and ideological values. The misunderstanding was compounded by policymakers who failed to understand ethnic rivalries and staggering socioeconomic inequalities— both of which help to explain why Other World countries have little to lose by undertaking aggressive behavior.

UNDERSTANDING THE OTHER WORLD

The consideration of economics, technology, and political structures is important for understanding the world's peoples. Geography is also a significant factor. The view of the Earth from the first *Apollo* spacecraft revealed it as a small marble of three colors: the blue of oceans, the brown of continents, and the changing swirls of white that envelop its climates. The Earth's topographical and geographical features, in continuous dynamic balance with its climates, have influenced much of the destiny of the peoples occupying these fragile lands and traversing its seas. What the *Apollo* photos do not show is the proliferation of national divisions and boundaries.

This discussion of the developing Other World is descriptive and explana- tory. Our approach supports the "diverse dependency" school of thought, which regards the social, political, and economic conditions in various geographic loca- tions within the context of the development of an international advanced econ- omy. It suggests the partial integration of these parts of the world into a global political economy, discussed here as the "global village." In fact, there is *one* world of development, with different states occupying different places in the first, sec- ond, and third sectors of the international political economy.

Modern social systems are considered to be organizationally specialized and interdependent. Much of this specialization occurred in the modern world as a result of the industrial revolution at the turn of the last century, when the factory and the workplace away from home came to symbolize the modern life. More complex and intricate machinery and processes were invented, driving us into a world where computers urge us to act at a faster pace. Today, the spread of tech- nology, especially communications, is accelerating the pace of change.

In 1945, when the UN was founded, 31 of its 51 members, or 61 percent, could have been described as "developing" states. Since then, their number has in- creased to 70 percent of the over 160 members and is still growing (see table 1.1).[1] The entry of so many new states into the UN has shifted the balance of influence and voting power in the General Assembly from Western to non-Western con- trol.

For many new states, the move from colonial status to independence was gained through political and social upheaval. However, as will be discussed in later chapters, ethnic and regional loyalties are still strong and impede the de- velopment of national unity in many of these states.

Today, violent conflict prevails in about 20 different locales in the world and involves millions of people. More than two decades after the U.S. military with-

TABLE 1.1 Roster of the United Nations

The 166 members of the United Nations, with the years in which they became members

Member	Year	Member	Year	Member	Year	Member	Year
Afghanistan	1946	Dominica	1978	Lesotho	1966	Saint Lucia	1979
Albania	1955	Dominican Rep.	1945	Liberia	1945	Saint Vincent and the Grenadines	1980
Algeria	1962	Ecuador	1945	Libya	1955	Samoa (Western)	1976
Angola	1976	Egypt	1945	Lithuania	1991	São Tomé e Principe	1975
Antigua and Barbuda	1981	El Salvador	1945	Luxembourg	1945	Saudi Arabia	1945
Argentina	1945	Equatorial Guinea	1968	Madagascar (Malagasy)	1960	Senegal	1960
Australia	1945	Estonia	1991	Malawi	1964	Seychelles	1976
Austria	1955	Ethiopia	1945	Malaysia	1957	Sierra Leone	1961
Bahamas	1973	Fiji	1970	Maldives	1965	Singapore	1965
Bahrain	1971	Finland	1955	Mali	1960	Solomon Islands	1978
Bangladesh	1974	France	1945	Malta	1964	Somalia	1960
Barbados	1966	Gabon	1960	Marshall Islands	1991	South Africa	1945
Belgium	1945	Gambia	1965	Mauritania	1961	Spain	1955
Belize	1981	Germany, East	1973	Mauritius	1968	Sri Lanka	1955
Benin	1960	Germany, West	1973	Mexico	1945	Sudan	1956
Bhutan	1971	Ghana	1957	Micronesia	1991	Suriname	1975
Bolivia	1945	Greece	1945	Mongolia	1961	Swaziland	1968
Botswana	1966	Grenada	1974	Morocco	1956	Sweden	1946
Brazil	1945	Guatemala	1945	Mozambique	1975		

Country	Year	Country	Year	Country	Year	Country	Year
Brunei	1984	Guinea	1958	Myanmar (Burma)	1948	Syria	1945
Bulgaria	1955	Guinea-Bissau	1974	Namibia	1990	Tanzania	1961
Burkina Faso	1960	Guyana	1966	Nepal	1955	Thailand	1946
Burundi	1962	Haiti	1945	Netherlands	1945	Togo	1960
Byelorussia	1945	Honduras	1945	New Zealand	1945	Trinidad & Tobago	1962
Cambodia	1955	Hungary	1955	Nicaragua	1955	Tunisia	1956
Cameroon	1960	Iceland	1946	Niger	1960	Turkey	1945
Canada	1945	India	1945	Nigeria	1960	Uganda	1962
Cape Verde	1975	Indonesia	1950	Norway	1945	Ukraine	1945
Central Afr. Rep.	1960	Iran	1945	Oman	1971	USSR	1945
Chad	1960	Iraq	1945	Pakistan	1947	United Arab Emirates	1971
Chile	1945	Ireland	1955	Panama	1945	United Kingdom	1945
China	1945	Israel	1949	Papua New Guinea	1975	United States	1945
Colombia	1945	Italy	1955	Paraguay	1945	Uruguay	1945
Comoros	1975	Jamaica	1962	Peru	1945	Vanuatu	1981
Congo	1960	Japan	1956	Philippines	1945	Venezuela	1945
Costa Rica	1945	Jordan	1955	Poland	1945	Vietnam	1977
Côte d'Ivoire	1960	Kenya	1963	Portugal	1955	Yemen	1947
Cuba	1945	Korea, North	1991	Qatar	1971	Yugoslavia	1945
Cyprus	1960	Korea, South	1991	Romania	1955	Zaire	1960
Czechoslovakia	1945	Kuwait	1963	Rwanda	1962	Zambia	1964
Denmark	1945	Laos	1955	Saint Christopher		Zimbabwe	1980
Djibouti	1977	Latvia	1991	& Nevis	1983		

SOURCE: United Nations, 1991.

drawal from Southeast Asia, battles occur in the Vietnam-Kampuchea-Laos area. Tensions also continue between India and Pakistan. The war between Iran and Iraq during the 1980s was one of the more bitter conflicts in recent years, taking more than 1 million lives. And the Iraqi occupation and annexation of Kuwait became a global crisis. Sporadic fighting is endemic among other countries in the Middle East, as well as in the former states of the Soviet Union.

Africa is also a troubled continent, where civil strife exists in almost every country. Diverse ethnic groups divided by language, culture, and ancient rivalries vie for power and its accompanying wealth. Military conflict between Ethiopia and Somalia has continued for years, as has the military and economic disruption in Uganda, Angola, Mozambique, South Africa, Sudan, Somalia, and their respective neighbors. In Latin America, struggles continue in Guatemala, El Salvador, Honduras, Peru, Chile, and Ecuador. UNICEF, the UN agency dedicated to helping the world's young people, held a World Summit for Children in 1990. Leaders of 70 countries addressed the problems of children as both victims of and fighters in war, as well as the brutal exploitation of child labor. The summit's participants reflected on the millions of starving or undernourished children, the millions who receive no formal education, and the many forced to scratch out a living on city streets.

CHARACTERIZING THE OTHER WORLD

The peoples and cultures of the Other World are diverse. Uniformity does not exist. The generalizations below describe common features of some of these countries.

1. Dependence on Western powers
2. Delayed modernization
3. Population explosion
4. Unequal distribution of wealth

In general, then, the Other World faces a wide variety of significant problems. Our task in this book is to outline the major themes and give specific examples.

Dependence on Western Powers

Other World countries share a history of having been colonies of major Western powers. Their economic, and sometimes political, systems are now indirectly controlled through patterns of neocolonialism. Following statehood, emerging countries usually maintain economic and political ties with their former colonial masters, preserving many of the established patterns of commerce, politics, and daily life. Such patterns, however, tend to perpetuate the dependence of the new nation on its former rulers. Political and economic institutions designed to extract resources from the colonies are slightly modified and carried into the postindependence era. These institutions, now occupied by indigenous politicians and

End of Empire: Regimental Plaques on the Khyber Pass, Pakistan
SOURCE: Richard Kranzdorf

business leaders, still primarily serve the interests of the industrial powers. These political and economic elites depend on First World governments and corporations for power and position. Dependency exists in varying degrees. Some are still almost completely dependent on other powers, whereas others are moving away from dependency.

Inflation (rising prices without corresponding increases in goods and services) creates additional hardships. Many peoples not only have low incomes but also find that inflation decreases the value of what little they have. In attempting to support and stabilize economic development, governments have borrowed heavily from Western and Japanese banking institutions. Latin American nations alone owe more than $500 billion to banks in the United States, Western Europe, and Japan.[2] Such debt levels constitute a risk of general economic instability in the entire world.

Delayed Modernization

Most developing states have a shortage of experienced and skilled managers, scientists, and engineers, a situation that is complicated by high illiteracy rates. Moreover, the limited number of technologists usually is isolated in one or two population centers in each country. Industrialized nations have four times as many managers and technicians per capita. Some countries, such as South Korea, now have intensive training programs to assist in the development of exports and industrialization. Many others, however, are unable to mount such training programs. Sometimes they are unable to pay wages appropriate to certain levels of training (e.g., to physicians), so that the danger of a "brain drain" to the higher-paying rich countries always exists.[3]

Management and technological know-how are critical to industrialization and modernization. Because of a lack of capital and appropriate technology, developing countries have difficulty installing and maintaining sanitation systems, energy systems, transportation and communication networks, national security, and government services. The potential for agricultural and industrial progress is curtailed. Even when financial and technical aid is imported in these areas, there is often little capability to maintain systems and provide inventories of replacement parts and equipment. Technological projects depend on efficiency, punctuality, organization, centralization, and productivity, but often these values conflict with those that are culturally dominant in the developing areas of the world. Decentralization, interdependence, favoritism, decision by consensus, and tribal authority and cooperation are usually more highly regarded than industrialized, organizational values. This situation produces conflict.

Displacement of values may bring chaos to previously stable and self-sufficient Asian, African, Middle Eastern, and Latin cultures, leading to serious social and psychological disruptions. It also raises very fundamental ethical questions about meddling in peoples' lives. One thing is certain: once change has been introduced to a developing country, there is no going back.

Population Explosion

Whereas it took 2 million years for the world's population to reach 1 billion, it took only 100 years to reach the second billion. Today, the world's population has reached over 5 billion and is growing still. Each year, 90 to 100 million people are added. If the present rate continues, over 8 billion people will populate the earth by the year 2025. The great majority will live in the Other World, where the population is growing at two to three times the rate of the industrialized world. Some of the dramatic increases are due to better sanitary conditions and medical technology, which have led to improved infant survival and increased longevity.[4]

Birthrates and poverty are closely linked. The larger the family, the less each person's share of the family's resources. The poorer the family, the more likely the adults will find it desirable to add new family members as future caretakers and workers. Societies are dependent on children, adolescents, and young adults to care for the elderly and to support family unit economies. Additionally, in poor families, inadequate nutrition and medical care may lead to low birth weights and infant deaths. The higher the likelihood of early death or disability, the more likely new workers must be born into families to ensure that the work gets done and there are providers for the elderly. However, as young adults move from farms to cities and as drought diminishes food supplies, life hangs on a thread for the children and the elderly left behind in rural areas. In many nations, food production has increased with improvements in farm management and crop techniques. But without an adequate infrastructure to allocate and distribute these in-

Handle with Care: Unexpected Catch of the Day on the
Shores of Lake Tanganyika, Tanzania

SOURCE: Emmit B. Evans, Jr.

creases, more food does not necessarily mean more food on the tables of the bulk
of the population.

The data in table 1.2 show population and poverty in the developing world
by percentage of the world's population. As you can see, the largest percentage
of the population, as well as of the poor, can be found in Asia. Latin America, the
Caribbean, Europe, the Middle East, and North Africa have proportionately fewer
poor people.

Unequal Distribution of Wealth

The most compelling similarity among developing states is the severe poverty of
most of their people, who generally live at a subsistence level. Over half of the
world's population survives on an annual per capita income of $800 or less. Haiti,
for example, is one of the most impoverished countries in the Western

TABLE 1.2 Population and Poverty in the Developing World

	Percent of World Population 1990	Percent of World Poor 1990	Percent of Low and Middle Income 1994
Sub-Saharan Africa	11.1	16.1	12.0
East Asia	40.2	25.0	37.0
South Asia	29.7	46.4	26.0
Europe, Middle East, and North Africa	7.7	5.9	16.0
Latin America and Caribbean	11.2	6.6	10.0

SOURCES: World Bank, *World Development Report 1990* (New York: Oxford University Press, 1991), pp. 126–127. World Bank, *World Development Report 1994* (New York: Oxford University Press, 1995), p. 163.

Hemisphere. Its per capita gross domestic product (GDP) is approximately $350. Poverty can be measured by more than income or per capita GDP, however. In Haiti, almost a third of the population is under 15 years of age, about 80 percent is illiterate, and life expectancy is 53 years. By contrast, the per capita annual income in the United States is over $15,000, 9 out of 10 people are literate, and life expectancy is over 70 years.[5]

The World Bank issued a major study of the world's poor in mid-1990. The report, issued as the World Bank's annual *World Development Report 1990*, claims that some progress toward overall economic growth has occurred since the 1960s. Fewer people are falling below the poverty line in countries like China and Indonesia, and increases in life expectancy have occurred in the Middle East, Asia, and Latin America. These gains have occurred partly because of foreign aid and partly because of the productive use of labor and increased basic social services in education, health care, and family planning for the poor. Still, 1.1 billion people—a fifth of the world's population—have annual incomes of less than $370, the amount at which the World Bank draws its poverty line.[6] People below this limit are deemed unable to have access to adequate food, shelter, and other necessities of life. The World Bank study foresees a decline by nearly a third in the number of the world's poor by the year 2000. Conditions in Africa, however, are expected to run contrary to the worldwide decline in poverty. Africa's share of the world's poor will double, from 16 percent to 32 percent, in this decade.[7] That continent faces intractable problems such as high population growth; weak basic economic infrastructure; and wars that have devastated Liberia, Angola, Namibia, Mozambique, Ethiopia, Somalia, and the Sudan. The study projects that over 43 percent of the population south of the Sahara will live in poverty in 2000.[8]

THE PLIGHT OF OTHER WORLD WOMEN

For several centuries the books written by world travelers have described the strange and interesting peoples of other lands. Their books were not widely read. A generation ago, however, Americans and Europeans experienced a growing flood of interesting magazines, illustrated with pictures of exotically clothed or unclothed people of color going about their daily lives and religious activities in ethnic costumes and settings. The magazines have been paralleled by a profusion of documentary films. All of these visual images have tended to emphasize the unfamiliar. They appear in strong contrast to the usual informative publications that depict white or light-skinned people in Western attire and activities.

The people of the Other World have less opportunity to see the magazines and movies that depict them, but they have more and more opportunity to learn about the Western world and its ways. What can be said about the tensions and clashes that arise in both directions? What observations can be made, especially about women in the cultural minorities?

First, it must be noted that in traditional cultures throughout the Other World, the family has always been the basic social unit. People are born, nurtured, and taught identities, values, and skills within families. Extended clans and larger political organizations are thought of, even by rulers, as "my family." The larger ethnic or national family determines one's place in the world and one's most fundamental loyalties. But today, close families and extended families are being torn by brutal and sudden political changes in the surrounding world. They have lost their protective isolation.

Second, the cohesion of families and clans is being eroded by new patterns, such as the migration of large numbers of adult males to distant cities, mines, oil fields, and other locations of apparent economic and individual opportunity. Most of them hope to provide for the families who are left behind, and they earnestly try to do so. They find, however, that supporting the distant family while also maintaining themselves is more difficult than they had expected. After complications arise as a result of new involvements, effective close communication with the original family is impossible. At the same time, the absence of adult males shifts all of the family and community responsibilities to the women. They and their children also become more vulnerable to cultural conflict and to victimization and abuse.

Third, the new opportunities that have appeared are certain to be attractive to children and youths, who are characteristically not content to maintain traditional ways, but also not well prepared to succeed in the new ways. Western-oriented education becomes very important but also very competitive. Those who succeed are usually the most energetic and assertive, the best and the brightest, but they are unlikely to be willing to return home. Those who remain find that they have greater loads and fewer capable helpers.

Fourth, traditional cultural values are threatened by the intrusion of foreign ideas, customs, and dress. Exposure to Western people, institutions, and media introduce such influences as Christianity, democracy, dating, rock music, denim jeans, and use of alcohol. Such changes are not easily tolerated. Even the veneer of modern dress is not accepted in some cultures. In many areas of Africa and the Middle East, Moslem women on the street continue to cover their hair, and sometimes their faces, as religion and custom dictate. They struggle to maintain their deepest beliefs and their secure patterns. In other places, women become uncertain about ethnic dress—sometimes covering denim jeans or miniskirts—both drawn to new ways and fearful of repercussions from those opposed to their changing status and role in society.

Fifth, Other World women and minorities suffer a higher incidence of health problems, particularly with the breakdown of traditional nutrition and health practices, the continual exposure to unsafe water supplies, lack of adequate sanitation, and exposure to HIV and AIDS. Men who have lived away from home often engage in unsafe sexual behavior. Upon return, they infect their wives, who in turn carry the virus to children in uterus. The spread of the HIV virus and AIDS is of crisis proportion in much of Africa south of the Sahara and in Southeast Asia, where birth control and AIDS prevention are not common practices. The United Nations World Health Organization regularly publishes astounding statistics that show the dramatic spread of these diseases.

Finally, established patterns of subsistence farming and hunting break down and are replaced by new understandings of property and economic structures. Trends toward democratization appear, but they erode such institutions as male-oriented local decision making.

Some trends in democratization are symbolic. For example, the 1979 Convention on Eliminating All Forms of Discrimination Against Women, guaranteeing equal rights to men and women, was signed by 25 countries in sub-Saharan Africa. However, in most Other World countries, patriarchal societies continue to deny women social, legal, political, and economic equity. In practice, access to information on basic human rights and to programs directed toward changing the condition of women is severely restricted.

The United Nations Fourth World Conference on Women and the Non-Governmental Organizations (NGO) Forum on Women convened in Beijing, China, for three weeks of meetings in September 1995 to create a platform for action to improve the status of women. Although over 30,000 activists and politicians addressed the common problems women face, these participants could not fully subscribe to equality between the sexes.

Complicated by changing gender relations, women are caught in the stress of trying to preserve what is necessary for family and cultural life while at the same time clamoring for change. Articulating increased impoverishment and powerlessness, their cry is becoming more shrill at international meetings and global conferences. World leaders find it difficult to ignore pleas for greater participation in political and economic life and a greater say in social policy.

THE DILEMMA OF THE OTHER WORLD

Everywhere, national, cultural, and political systems are shifting in response to complex internal and external pressures and conditions. In the Other World, however, change is occurring at a speed never before seen and in a context of inadequate structures and resources, while leaders express uncertainty about development goals and management strategies for handling chaos.

The world was changing in 1776, when the United States became independent, but it was changing slowly. Events happened and news spread at the speed of sailing ships and a foot's pace. As things changed, the fundamental patterns of rural and city life evolved slowly. However, in the developing world, centuries of change have occurred in only 30 years or less. A person whose grandparents had never traveled more than 10 miles from their birthplace may now be on a jet flight to London or New York. While the father plows with oxen, a brother may be operating a diesel tractor, and a sister may be learning the intricacies of world economies. Countries are being pulled rapidly in one direction or another by contending political, social, and economic forces over which they have little control. Deeply felt religious values and beliefs that gave stability to people's lives in the past are crumbling, to be replaced by new and alien philosophies.

Further, as regional wars flare and military power threatens a region, it is difficult for the world to ignore the impact on stability, world security, and international trade. The 1990s continue to evolve into new patterns of alliances, cooperation, and conflict. These patterns originate out of the human experience and interplay among politics, geography, culture, history, economics, and human behavior. The problems and issues that challenge us are discussed in the chapters that follow.

ISSUES FOR DISCUSSION

1. Will the world population explosion crush us all?

Predictions about population growth have been alarming. Demographers have projected astounding growth rates for the world—particularly for the Other World. Recently, however, they lowered their estimates by 4 billion people. New trends show a global stabilization with a target population of 7.9–9.8 billion people by 2050 instead of the 11.9 billion originally anticipated. What accounts for this lowered projection?[9]

One answer is global conflict, in which thousands die annually across the troubled nations of the world. Yet another is the rise in AIDS- and HIV-related deaths, which are growing dramatically. Casualties also result from the Earth's vulnerability in supporting this number of people.

Social change, such as family planning practices, significantly contributes to slowed population growth. For example, China in the early 1970s had one of the highest population growth rates in the world. At almost 1 billion people— making up one-fifth of the world's population—China introduced a number of family-planning policies. The "later, longer, fewer" campaign of 1972, for example, focused on lowering the birthrate from 6 children for each woman to 1. By 1979, fertility had fallen to 2.7 children, and the one-child policy led to even further reductions, especially in cities.

Social change causes disruption in other areas of life. In China the pattern of one child in cities and two children in rural areas has caused shortages in services for the aged as fewer children are available to care for their parents. Additionally, the preference for male children, the growth in the elderly population, and the fragmentation of the extended family have fractured the society. Are these family-planning policies desirable? Will the carrying capacity of the Earth continue to erode as declining fish, grain harvests, water, and food supplies fail to keep up with growing populations?

2. Will the Other World be able to afford equality regardless of gender and race?

Boutros Boutros-Ghali, secretary-general of the United Nations, noted in his address "An Agenda for Peace—June 1992" that democracy requires respect for human rights and fundamental freedoms—especially for the minorities and the more vulnerable groups in a society, women and children.

Until World War II, international law did not intervene when sovereigns treated their subjects inhumanely. Detention, arbitrary arrest, torture, and execution were commonplace. An international bill of rights—the Universal Declaration—was adopted by the UN in 1946 to promote and protect individuals from government abuse. Nevertheless, sanctions and incentives appear to be discretionary, and abuses are cited in the daily news flashes with little letup. The condition of women and minorities has not improved significantly. But the social stability needed for economic growth demands the empowerment of the poor and the marginalized. If social stability is a requirement of economic growth, will social change be encouraged? And will governments act to improve financial and administrative capacity to protect the weak and prevent the strong from engaging in exploitation?

3. Should the West intervene when abuses occur in the Other World?

It is not easy to generalize about ethnic and religious differences among peoples. Geographic diversity divides people into separate and conflicting ethnic and religious groups, each with its own customs and traditions. Iran, for example, is dominated by the Persians from Parsa, with the Azeri Turks living in the northwest and the Kurds forming a minority along the Turkish and Iraqi border. The Kurds are Sunni Muslims, distinct from the Shia majority. The Arabs live along Iraq's border in Khuzestan Province. And the Baluchi, also Sunni Muslims, live in the southeast and are related to tribes in Afghanistan and Pakistan. Other non-Muslim minorities include Armenians, Jews, Assyrians, and Zoroastrians. The larger society's push to conformity, patriarchal structure, and intolerance of difference fuels contemporary conflicts in the region.

In India and Pakistan, the murder of female babies and young wives has reached epidemic proportions. Poisonings and burnings mask reality: Women have little value and represent financial burdens on families, who must provide wedding gifts (dowries) to shift the financial responsibility elsewhere. In China, some villages have alarmingly few females of marriageable age because of abortions and infant deaths. In some geographic areas of India and China, ethnic cleansing of religious and ethnic minorities is systematically practiced though rarely reported.

Among the Bedouin people of Saudi Arabia, family honor is esteemed. The father is central to the family and society, and both young men and women are expected to obey family wishes. Cultural codes are very important. Marriages are arranged to protect desert wells and to cement relationships between families. Although Bedouins have moved to cities in large numbers, rather than following the nomad life of the desert as they have for centuries, traditional values have changed little. Female honor is valued, and women are excluded from modern production. This exclusion has served to trivialize women's decision-making role and marginalizes their influence within the society.

Since the creation of the United Nations in 1945, over 100 major conflicts have left 20 million dead worldwide, and the United Nations was powerless to intervene because of the 300 vetoes cast in the Security Council. Yet the beginning of the post–cold war era has marked the end of such vetoes, and demands to use the United Nations have accelerated dramatically. Thus, it seems when conflicts arise, nations depend on others to intervene.

As the world clamors for global governance, there are also increasing expressions of nationalism. Other World peoples are requesting sovereignty under ethnic, religious, social, or linguistic identities. This fragmentation of the nation-state system causes a vacuum and threatens economic and social well-being in a geographic area. How can we protect human rights and preserve national autonomy?

4. Can women still prosper when a wage economy is introduced?

Over half of the world's people exist in subsistence economies. To many, the coming of a wage economy and the elimination of subsistence are positive features of modernization. With wages, it is argued, greater possibilities exist for improving family conditions and for trade with other peoples.

However, as men in subsistent societies begin to earn cash wages, they seem reluctant to spend it on the family. At the same time, women continue to have little access to resources. Women often are prevented from owning land, entering into contracts, or engaging in business enterprises. Over time, women's contributions to family survival are discounted not only by wage-earning men in the family but also by government statisticians and economic experts unaccustomed to costing out women's work, including harvesting of forest products, husbanding of food supplies, crafting clothing and household products, and caring for children and elderly family members.

World Bank studies show deterioration in children's nutrition even though wages and purchasing power have increased through development projects. When cash crops are introduced, the disparity between wages and child nutrition worsens. Women work on family cash crop lands instead of in family gardens, which provide food for the table and food to sell at market. As families seek to maximize the use of cash crop lands, deteriorated soils are used for family gardens. Thus, women work harder and at the expense of their families. What should be done to relieve this situation?

*5. At the end of the twentieth century, does the world seem
to be a small or a big place?*

Some see the world as a global village, tied by communication links, international corporations, and trade links that propel ideas and products across oceans to overcome cultural, class, and linguistic barriers. The ability to fax a photo, link up with a friend many time zones away, and extract local currency with a hometown bank card gives the impression that the world is a small place indeed. Jet travel makes almost all parts of the world accessible for tourism and trade. Products like corn flakes and jeans are available in many remote shops worldwide. However, problems also have no boundaries. Pollution, supply shortages, job losses, and crime know no borders.

Yet the diversity of peoples, places, and products seems to be expanding rather than contracting. Cultural expressions distance one group of people from another. Rural infrastructure, that is, bad roads and unreliable communication, makes it difficult to move out of capital cities. The period needed to clear a check at an out-of-town bank introduces a time warp. The availability of medical treatments, educational facilities, and public health regulations to ensure clean water and a safe food supply may be lacking. Do such gaps make the world seem a big place? If impressions vary so greatly, does the world appear small instead?

NOTES

1. Mark S. Hoffman, *The World Almanac and Book of Facts, 1992* (New York: Paros Books, 1992), pp. 828–829.
2. World Bank, *World Development Report 1990* (New York: Oxford University Press, 1991), pp. 126–127.
3. Ibid., pp. 56–73.
4. United Nations Development Programme, *Human Development Report, 1991* (New York: Oxford University Press, 1991), pp. 23–37.
5. World Bank, *World Development Report 1990*, pp. 178–179.
6. Ibid., pp. 5, 178–179.
7. Ibid.
8. Ibid.
9. World Bank, *World Development Report 1994* (New York: Oxford University Press, 1995), p. 163.

A STUDENT GUIDE TO USEFUL REFERENCE
MATERIALS ON THE OTHER WORLD

Most college and university libraries maintain government documents with reports on countries and the issues that concern them. The many reports published by the UN are invaluable, particularly the *Statistical Yearbook* and *Demographic Yearbook*. Some autonomous UN agencies that maintain data on specific issues include the World Health Organization (WHO), the Food and Agriculture

Organization (FAO), the International Monetary Fund (IMF), and the International Fund for Agricultural Development (IFAD).

The *U.S. Statistical Abstract* has data on U.S. aid to foreign states, trade statistics, and other information. The State Department also publishes annually a *Status of the World's Nations*.

Several other useful sources are the *Political Handbook of the World,* ed. Arthur S. Banks (New York: McGraw-Hill, 1995); *The State of the World Atlas,* ed. Michael Kidron and R. Segal (New York: Simon & Schuster, 1990); Charles L. Lewis and Michael C. Hudson, *World Handbook of Political and Social Indicators* (New Haven, Conn.: Yale University Press, 1995); and *DPG Student Atlas of the World* (Guilford, Conn.: Dushkin Publishing Group, 1995).

Also, many countries publish their own statistical abstracts on a regular basis. General information can be obtained in any quality almanac, such as *The World Almanac,* published annually by the Newspaper Enterprise Association (New York). Additional references follow.

FOR FURTHER READING

Almond, Gabriel. *Political Development.* Boston: Little, Brown, 1970.

Ayrton, Pete. *World View 1983.* New York: Pantheon Books, 1983.

Banks, Arthur; Carlip, Vivi; Dewitt, R. Peter, Jr.; and Overstreet, William, eds. *Economic Handbook of the World.* New York: McGraw-Hill, 1981.

Brown, Lester R. *State of the World.* New York: Norton, 1995.

Clapman, Christopher. *Third World Politics: An Introduction.* Madison: University of Wisconsin Press, 1985.

Danziger, James N. *Understanding the Political World: An Introduction to Political Science.* White Plains, N.Y.: Longman, 1991.

Doran, Charles F.; Modelski, George; and Clark, Cal, eds. *North-South Relations: Studies of Dependency Reversal.* New York: Praeger, 1983.

Harrison, Paul. *Inside the Third World.* London: Penguin Books, 1987.

Jackson, John H. *The World Trading System.* Cambridge, Mass.: MIT Press, 1989.

Kurian, George. *Encyclopedia of the Third World.* 3 vols. New York: Facts on File, 1982.

Luitel, S. *Women in Development.* New Delhi: Ratner-Bustak Bhander, 1992.

Plano, Jack C., and Greenberg, Milton. *The American Political Dictionary.* New York: Holt, Rinehart & Winston, 1979.

Sappo, R. K. *Women and Development.* New Delhi: Ashish, 1989.

Sivard, Ruth Leger. *World Military and Social Expenditures.* Leesburg, Va.: World Priorities, 1984.

Smith, T. Alexander. *The Comparative Polity Process.* Santa Barbara, Cal.: ABC-CLIO Information Services, 1975.

Spiegel, Steven L. *At Issue—Politics in the World Arena.* New York: St. Martin's Press, 1991.

Thompson, Mary Anderberg, and Antell, Joan, *The Current History Encyclopedia of Developing Nations.* New York: McGraw-Hill, 1982.

Trainer, Ted. *Developed to Death: Rethinking Third World Development.* London: Merlin Press, 1989.

CHAPTER 2

The Old and the New: Colonialism, Neocolonialism, and Nationalism

Joseph N. Weatherby

Dien Bien Phu was the bell that tolled the twilight of colonialism.
North Vietnamese General Vo Nguyen Giap, on the defeat of the French, 1954

*Washing one's hands of the conflict between the powerful and the powerless means
to side with the powerful.*
Paulo Freire

The West has been involved in colonial activity for almost six centuries. No area of the world has managed to avoid completely being affected by this experience. Places as diverse as Gibraltar and the Falklands are still areas of contention.[1] The dismantling of the major colonial empires held by the Western powers has been one of the key political developments since World War II. The postwar period has also witnessed the rise of both neocolonialism and nationalism as major features of the Other World. This chapter will discuss Western colonialism, neocolonialism, and the Other World's reaction to those events, that is, nationalism.

COLONIALISM

Few subjects in international politics evoke as much emotional reaction as colonialism. Most people have a general idea of what the term means, but attempts to establish a definition agreeable to all are frustrating. It is unnecessary to trace its inconsistent use to determine that its meaning is in the eye of the beholder. However, to avoid confusion, some of the more important aspects of colonialism need to be described.

In earlier times, the term *colonialism* simply described a country's foreign settlements, or colonies. Writers in the complex world of the later twentieth century have used *colonialism* interchangeably with the word *imperialism* to describe the extension of control by one state over another. Used in today's context, both of these terms have an anti-Western bias.

Colonialism and imperialism have slightly different meanings. Colonialism is a relationship in which a group of people located in one country is subject to the authority of the people of another country. This authority can be exercised through direct control by the dominant country, as in the most typical form of colonialism, or through indirect influence, as in neocolonialism. *Neocolonialism* is the process by which rich, powerful, developed states use economic, political, or other informal means to exert pressure on poor, less powerful, underdeveloped states. In both direct colonialism and indirect neocolonialism, the dependent community can be made up of an indigenous people, immigrants, or a combination of the two. Imperialism, however, is the act of acquiring or holding colonies or dependencies. Thus, whereas colonialism describes a relationship between the dominant and the dependent, imperialism is the process of establishing that relationship.

Through the years, the terms *imperialism* and *colonialism* have provoked a wide array of emotional responses. Western countries in the last generation of the Victorian period rationalized that colonialism was a beneficial process that would help to bring a backward Other World into the light of the modern age. Their leaders often argued that the highest calling of society was to extend the benefits of Western civilization to its "black, brown, and yellow brothers" in the rest of the world. In addition, westerners were certain that they were destined by history to act as the trustee for a less fortunate colonial world. It was in this spirit that President William McKinley justified the annexation of the Philippines on the grounds that the United States would bring Christianity to the islands. For many westerners, the term *white man's burden* was both a challenge and an honor.

Today, colonialism no longer implies honor. There is little doubt that the Other World considers it a disparaging word. Using this contemporary tone when speaking of the American and French experience in Vietnam, General Giap said, "The Americans were on the side of the colonialist—the American generals are not very good students of history. Dien Bien Phu paved the way for us to defeat not only the French but later the Americans and now to defend our country against the Chinese."[2]

HISTORY OF COLONIALISM

Many critics charge that colonialism is both a recent development and a result of the expansion of exclusively Western power into the less technically advanced areas of the world. If judged by its definition, it is apparent that colonialism is neither new nor exclusively Western in origin. History abounds with examples of one people exercising control over others. Even the history of Western Europe has been colored by the invasions of Huns, Mongols, and Turks. Most of the world's peoples have been guilty of practicing some form of domination at some time in history.

For almost all of the last 600 years, the West has played the leading role in the colonial drama. In Western colonialism's early stages of development, Portugal and Spain were the major European participants. They were so powerful that in 1494 a papal settlement, the Treaty of Tordesillas, divided the colonial world between them. Under the terms of this agreement, the Portuguese had largely a free hand in Africa, Brazil, and parts of Asia, and the Spanish were free to conquer the rest of the Americas and the Pacific. Soon the colonial fever had spread to the Netherlands, England, and France, each of which carved out great empires of their own in the sixteenth and seventeenth centuries. All of these European actors converged in the Americas, in general, and the Caribbean basin in particular.[3]

Speaking romantically of this period of Christians, conquistadors, and buccaneers, William Lyle Schurz has written,

> The conquest was a thing of superlatives and the men who took part in it were supermen. For never has sheer human will and force of personality accomplished so much through the efforts of so few on so vast a stage. The conquerors not only gave a new world to Castile, their discoveries and conquests resulted in a worldwide social and economic revolution that radically changed the whole pattern of life in Europe and its overseas dependencies.[4]

The first phase of Western colonialism ended in 1781 at Yorktown, Virginia, when American rebels won their independence from the British. At that time, many people in England and other parts of Europe believed that colonies were no longer worth the effort required to hold them. This view was confirmed by the early nineteenth-century withdrawal of the Spanish and French from many areas in Latin America.

Because of perceived needs created by the industrial revolution, colonialism evolved into a new phase during the second half of the nineteenth century. Markets and minerals became the drive that led Europeans to establish new colonies throughout the Other World. During this period, many states attempted to acquire colonies. Although the old imperial powers were in the forefront of the new colonizing activities, they were soon joined by Italy, Germany, Japan, and eventually the United States.

Maps at the end of the nineteenth century showed Britain with an empire that included Hong Kong (1841) in the east, India (1661) in South Asia, and African holdings almost too vast to contemplate. France's empire included Algeria (1830), Tunisia (1881), and Indochina (1884). In the twentieth century, France would acquire Syria (1920), Lebanon (1920), and part of Morocco (1912). Although Spain lost its American empire by 1898, it still maintained modest colonial enclaves in North Africa (1470–1580), West Africa (1860), Fernando Po (1778), and Guinea (1844). Portugal's empire included the ancient enclaves of Macao (1557) and Goa (1510) along with the more profitable colonies of Angola (1484) and Mozambique (1498).

Lesser colonial powers included the Netherlands, Belgium, Germany, Italy, and the United States. The Netherlands controlled the Dutch East Indies (1610–1641). Belgium's king owned the Congo (1884), now called Zaire, until 1908,

A Square in the City of Macao. At one time, only Macao and Canton were open to European trade with China. Macao was established as a Portuguese colony in 1557.

SOURCE: Joe Weatherby

when he ceded the territory to the people of Belgium as a colony. The Italians were established in the horn of Africa (1889), and in this century they carved out an empire in Libya (1911). The Germans held major colonies in southwest Africa (1884), New Guinea (1884), and Tanganyika (1885). The United States acquired the Philippines, Cuba, and Puerto Rico through its victory over Spain in the Spanish-American War of 1898. In this century, the United States leased the Panama Canal Zone (1903), purchased the Virgin Islands (1916), and gained control over the Pacific Trust Territories (1947).

Although few people realized it at the time, traditional colonialism was a dying movement when the twentieth century began. Spain's day in the imperial sun was already over, and the decline of the other powers was soon to follow. As if by apology, even those colonies acquired by Western states in the early years of the century were called "protectorates," a legal fiction, instead of colonies.

When the end finally came to traditional colonialism, it occurred with swift finality. Germany lost its African possessions with its defeat in World War I. Italy and Japan were forced to follow the German example at the end of World War II. In the aftermath of World War II, most of the former possessions of England, France, Belgium, the Netherlands, and the United States won their independence.

The impact of independence on the Other World can best be understood if one considers that these territories included, among others, India and Pakistan (1947), the Dutch East Indies (1949), French North Africa (1956–1962), the Belgian Congo (1960), and the Philippines (1952). Today, only a few quaint anachronisms remain to remind the world of almost 600 years of Western colonial rule (see figure 2.1). Examples of these out-of-the-way places include Lahore, Réunion, Macao, and the Antilles, which are still administered by France, the United Kingdom, Portugal, and the Netherlands.

As an epitaph to this period, it should be pointed out that the peoples subjected to colonial rule in the nineteenth century were both non-Western and non-white. Although this feature of colonialism was not important at the time, it has allowed contemporary critics in the Other World to present their grievances with the West in racial terms.

It is interesting to note that until the invasion of Afghanistan, the former Soviet Union largely escaped criticisms of this type. Even though it contained vast amounts of territory and encompassed millions of people, the Soviet empire was masked by a Marxist ideology to which many in the Other World were sympathetic. To them, the stigma of colonial racism was to be applied only to Western powers. Now that everyone knows how Russians treated non-Russians in the former Soviet republics, it is clear that this position was incorrect. This skepticism was confirmed in 1994 with the brutal Russian invasion of the breakaway Chechen Republic.

MOTIVES FOR COLONIALISM

In view of both the long period and the large number of Western nations involved, it should not be surprising to learn that colonies were established for a variety of reasons. It should also not be surprising to find that many of the stated reasons for establishing colonies were only cover-ups for the real motives. Still, there must have been powerful incentives to induce nations and generations of adventurers to risk hardship and death to establish and hold colonies.

If we look back over the history of this period, we can identify at least five main purposes that led the Western states to establish colonial empires. These motives were neither simultaneously nor universally subscribed to by the participants. Their importance varied by both the Western country involved and the land selected for occupation. However, any list should include the crusading ideal, the economic incentive, the military motive, outlets for surplus population, and the prestige purpose.

Religious and Cultural Motives

Certainly, the desire to spread the Christian faith induced the nations of Western Europe to establish colonies in the Other World. This movement had its birth in the successful reconquest of Spain and Portugal from the Moors in 1492. It was a natural extension of this proselytizing zeal to follow the footsteps of the retreat-

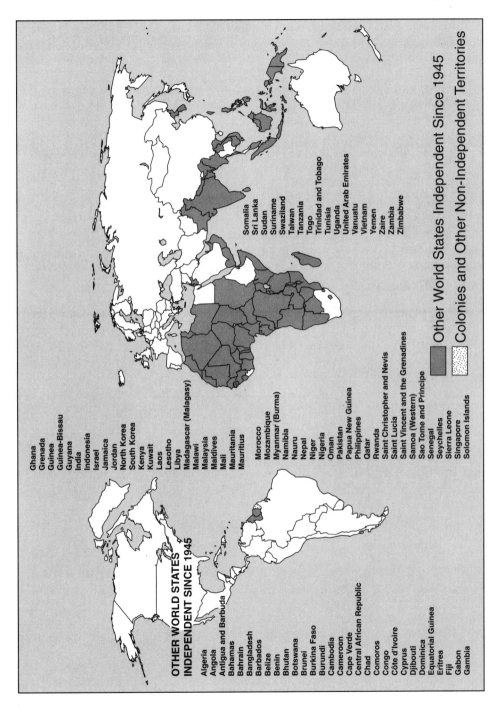

OTHER WORLD STATES INDEPENDENT SINCE 1945

Algeria
Angola
Antigua and Barbuda
Bahamas
Bahrain
Bangladesh
Barbados
Belize
Benin
Bhutan
Botswana
Brunei
Burkina Faso
Burundi
Cambodia
Cameroon
Cape Verde
Central African Republic
Chad
Comoros
Congo
Côte d'Ivoire
Cyprus
Djibouti
Dominica
Equatorial Guinea
Eritrea
Fiji
Gabon
Gambia

Ghana
Grenada
Guinea
Guinea-Bissau
Guyana
India
Indonesia
Israel
Jamaica
Jordan
North Korea
South Korea
Kenya
Kuwait
Laos
Lesotho
Libya
Madagascar (Malagasy)
Malawi
Malaysia
Maldives
Mali
Mauritania
Mauritius

Morocco
Mozambique
Myanmar (Burma)
Namibia
Nauru
Nepal
Niger
Nigeria
Oman
Pakistan
Papua New Guinea
Philippines
Qatar
Rwanda
Saint Christopher and Nevis
Saint Lucia
Saint Vincent and the Grenadines
Samoa (Western)
Sao Tome and Principe
Senegal
Seychelles
Sierra Leone
Singapore
Solomon Islands

Somalia
Sri Lanka
Sudan
Suriname
Swaziland
Taiwan
Tanzania
Togo
Trinidad and Tobago
Tunisia
Uganda
United Arab Emirates
Vanuatu
Vietnam
Yemen
Zaire
Zambia
Zimbabwe

Other World States Independent Since 1945

Colonies and Other Non-Independent Territories

FIGURE 2.1 Countries that Have Received Independence since 1945

27

ing Moors into Africa and from there to conquer a new world in the Americas. For these Iberians, the introduction of Catholicism was as important as the accumulation of resources in their early colonies. At the time when a continent's wealth was to be had in the Americas, the religious crusade was also vigorously pursued. Today, centuries after both the gold and the colonies have disappeared, Latin America's Roman Catholic population, second in size only to Europe's, stands as a legacy to the serious purpose of the religious crusades of Spain and Portugal.

The cultural motivation was also important, affecting both the colonizers and the colonized. One has only to visit former colonies along the North African coast to see the cultural impact of the English, French, Italians, and Spanish, which has survived long after their departure. The Spanish, Portuguese, and French each believed that the highest gift they could bestow was their language, their culture, and their religion. This cultural "gift" was part of their colonial policy until almost the end of their overseas adventure.

The special emphasis on the importation of culture meant that the indigenous culture of the colony was not considered worthy enough to be maintained. In many places, the native culture virtually died out. Modern Egyptians, referring to the French contact with their country in 1798, say with cynicism that the French were in Egypt for only 3 years, but if they had been allowed to stay for 15, Egyptians would "say their prayers in French." Similarly, Muammar al-Qaddafi, the anti-Western leader of Libya, has ruefully remarked, "Any personal action on our part springing from our personality or from our values is cast into doubt, and we ourselves have begun to doubt. That precisely is how colonialism has affected us."[5]

Economic Motives

Religious and cultural colonialism often went hand in hand with economic colonialism. From the very beginning of the Western colonial experience, colonies were seen as a business and the aim was to produce a profit. The desire to become rich was certainly in the mind of almost everyone who dared to tempt fate by joining in any colonial enterprise. Colonies were always used for the profitable import and export of goods by the mother country. In the nineteenth century, economics became the spur that led to the redrawn maps of the Other World.

One might ask if colonies were actually profitable. The answer depends on the time in history, the location, and the conditions in the colony. For example, in the latter part of the eighteenth century, the French colony of St. Dominique, whose economy was based on a slave-powered sugar monopoly, was so lucrative that British claims to vast territories in Canada were considered for possible exchange. Today, almost 200 years after independence, the French have gone; the great plantations are no more; there is a worldwide surplus of sugar; and the same territory, now known as Haiti, is the poorest country in the Western Hemisphere. The boom and bust of this plantation legacy was repeated in Brazil with natural rubber and in other parts of the world with cotton, tobacco, and coffee. At times, colonies held by Belgium in the Congo; the Netherlands in Indonesia; France in Indochina; and Britain in Africa, China, and India were very profitable.

It is easy to summarize some of the reasons that made colonies economically desirable for the mother country: They furnished food, minerals, and even human labor. In return, the mother country supplied the dependent territory with finished products. This arrangement, often monopolistic, gave the mother country's industries preferential trading opportunities unavailable to others. It should be remembered that economic colonialism was not exclusively a one-way street. The countries most successful with their colonies were able to strike a balance between their own desire for economic advantage and the needs of their subject peoples.

Strategic Motives

Following in the footsteps of those who carried the flag for gold and gospel were others who saw the need to protect the mother country's investments. These colonies were established to support more valuable possessions, such as the Spanish occupation of the Caribbean islands to protect and support the mineral-rich colony of New Spain (Mexico). In the nineteenth century Britain adopted a foreign policy based on the establishment of a world empire dependent on control of the seas. To be successful, the British had to establish a string of strategic colonies—including such diverse outposts as Hong Kong, Aden, Malta, Gibraltar, and the Falkland Islands—for defense and for refueling and repairing the fleet. The importance of strategic colonies to the survival of the British Empire was reaffirmed at the beginning of World War II, when Winston Churchill said that if the Spanish had attempted to neutralize Gibraltar he would have been forced to seize the Canary Islands in order to keep the sea lanes to Australia free from German U-boats.[6]

Another type of strategic colony was established to serve as a defense for the mother country itself. The British Crown's 1,000-year association with the Channel Islands, located just off the French coast, has provided a first line of defense against a second Norman Conquest of the home islands. In the same way, much of Spain's North African enclave empire was established to guard against a repetition of the Moorish invasion of the Spanish mainland.

Finally, some strategic colonies were established by nations pursuing a world balance of power. The value of these colonies is understandable only when analyzed in the context of the great-power politics that existed at the time they were established. For example, the nineteenth-century German occupation of the Marshall Islands and Nauru was probably motivated more by international politics than by hopes for economic gain. Certainly, the visit of the German gunboat *Panther* to Agadir in 1911 provoked an Allied fear of German power that led to the Franco-Spanish partition of Morocco in 1912. In that incident, France and Britain invited Spain to occupy northern Morocco to prevent the possible establishment of a German military presence in North Africa, which might upset the balance of power in Europe. It should be clear that the importance of strategic colonies cannot be evaluated by normal standards for other colonies. They may have been costly to hold, as in the case of the Falklands, and their importance lay primarily in their ability to help maintain or safeguard other interests of the mother country.

In many cases, strategic colonies have been the most difficult to deal with in the age of decolonization. Many of them had little or no economic worth. Often they were established and settled by the mother country as territories carved out of another land. In Gibraltar, Ceuta, and the Falklands, the establishment of military bases also involved the expulsion of the indigenous population and resettlement by immigrants considered loyal to the imperial authorities. Today, in the face of Other World pressures for independence, it is questionable which party has the right to make the decision that determines a colony's future. Should it be determined by those who are the territory's current residents or by those who are the descendants of the original inhabitants? The question is more complex than it appears: Spaniards have lived in Ceuta since the fifteenth century, Italian immigrants have inhabited Gibraltar since the beginning of the eighteenth century, and Scots have resided in the Falklands since the early nineteenth century.[7] If one accepts the notion that ancient claims to colonial lands may be pursued in opposition to the present inhabitants, it raises the specter of calls for resettlement in many areas of the world. Yet this is precisely the argument advanced by those who wish to see colonial territorial fates based on historic ties rather than current reality.

Before ending this discussion, we should not overlook those strategic enclaves that were created in uninhabited areas but now have significant populations. In some cases, these people have no wish for separation from the mother country. One example of this type of colony is Hong Kong, which was built on largely uninhabited land obtained from China by the British Crown in the nineteenth century. The local population has grown to over 5 million ethnic Chinese, and they have expressed little desire for a change of status. The pressure to change has come as a nationalistic expression from the People's Republic of China. Should territories such as Hong Kong be returned against their inhabitants' will merely because the land is contiguous? This issue is complex, and the postwar solutions to similar disputes are inconsistent. Usually, the departing Western power can only attempt to arrange the best deal possible for the inhabitants before abandoning the colony. This was the strategy of the British authorities when they agreed that Hong Kong would be returned to China in 1997. For their part, the Chinese promised to let the Hong Kong people maintain internal autonomy for a period of 50 years in a new policy called "one China, two systems." The future is unclear for those residents who were not party to the negotiations but who are destined to live in Hong Kong after 1997.

Finally, it should be noted that over the years many strategic colonies have developed both artificial economies and large populations. If suddenly granted independence or absorbed by surrounding territories, these enclaves and their inhabitants would not be able to survive. The mother countries are often forced to maintain and support them long after the empires they were designed to protect have disappeared. Some of the islands of the Pacific and the Caribbean are examples of this type of misfortune, and many of the flashpoints found throughout this book illustrate the kind of disputes that occur over their fates.

Surplus Population Motive

At different times, the argument that colonies would serve as outlets for a mother country's surplus population has been advanced to justify colonial enterprises. In the past, Britain and France sent convicts, debtors, and other undesirables to Australia and the Americas; and as late as the 1930s, the Japanese talked about relieving their population problem by sending surplus people to Manchuria. Although immigration has often been used as an argument for expansion, it is difficult to find cases in which the exportation of a surplus population was the primary motivation for establishing a colony.

It is easier to find cases in which immigration was used to justify territorial expansion—for example, the nineteenth-century territorial expansion of the United States and Russia. Some critics of Israel's past settlement policy have charged that Jewish immigration into the West Bank of the Jordan was encouraged by the government to justify the expansion of Israel's borders, in much the same way as American and Russian immigration justified the expansion of nineteenth-century borders to the Pacific.

Prestige Motive

Probably the most enigmatic motivation for colonization was the establishment and maintenance of colonies as symbols of greatness. If one looks at the world's remaining colonies, it is evident that many are still held for the purpose of prestige. Spain continues to hold the North African enclaves of Ceuta and Melilla long after the justification for them has ended. These colonies have little economic value, and their existence weakens Spain's own claims to the British-held enclave of Gibraltar. However, to Spain, these small possessions form a link to a glorious overseas tradition. For modern Spaniards, the crusading ideal, the empire, the civil war, and the tradition of military service in Africa far outweigh any political and economic liabilities that these colonies may bring. Because of the rise of anticolonial feelings throughout the Other World, few other powers continue to maintain colonies purely for prestige, although it may partially explain the French role in Martinique and Guadeloupe and the British hold on the Falklands.

THE LEGACY OF COLONIALISM

Most of the Other World has achieved independence during the last 50 years. Since the colonizers inevitably justified their empires with the claim that they were bringing the benefits of Western civilization to a backward world, it is appropriate to assess the results of their efforts.

Ceuta. In Christian hands as early as 1415, this fortress town has been a Spanish possession on the coast of Morocco since 1578. The mountain above Ceuta and the Rock of Gibraltar are called the Pillars of Hercules.

SOURCE: Joe Weatherby

Government

The primary interest of the colonial powers was economic, and the quality of preparation for independence varied. In many places, the British left a class of native civil servants who were prepared to keep the machinery of government running after the British had gone. However, where the evacuation was not amicable or where the mother country's own civil servants had governed, little native expertise existed after independence. This sad state prevailed in many of the colonies of France, Belgium, and Portugal. When Belgium recognized the independence of the Congo in 1960, there were fewer than a dozen university graduates in the country. The highest position held by Patrice Lumumba, the Congolese leader, had been postmaster general.[8] Even under the best of conditions, the bureaucratic transfer from colony to independence was not easy. More often than not, coups, corruption, and dictatorships—not Western-style democracy—were the legacy of colonialism.

Education

One of the claimed benefits of colonialism was access to modern education. Since the beginning of the nineteenth century, Other World students have studied in Europe and America, and Western schools teaching modern science and mathematics have been established throughout the Other World. Unfortunately, the results of Western education have not met initial hopes and expectations. There have been generations of Western-trained elites who are not accepted in the West and who are viewed with suspicion in their own countries. It was said in the nineteenth century that the Ottomans sent their best young people to Paris to learn to become soldiers and engineers. Once they learned French, they read the writings of Hobbes, Locke, and Rousseau instead of artillery manuals. These young people then returned home as "Young Turk" revolutionaries dedicated to the overthrow of the Ottoman Empire. This destabilizing process has been repeated thousands of times in many countries in the last 150 years. For example, many members of the first cabinet established in Iran after the Shah was deposed in 1979 were Western-trained and held Western passports. For years, these leaders had been working from exile in Europe and America for the downfall of the Shah. Many other Western-trained elites have become anti-Western as their education has given them the perspective to see the hypocrisy of Western policies when applied to their own countries. These elites become disenchanted when they realize they would have better spent their time studying the foreign policies of Britain, France, and the United States than utopian Western philosophers. Their disillusionment with the motives of the West has been matched only by their dissatisfaction with conditions at home. Overeducated for the economy, unable to adjust to their own country, and resentful of the West, many of these educated elites have become a major source of instability in the Other World.

Economics

The economies of the Other World are invariably tied to the needs of the developed world. Agriculture in the former colonies is oriented to crops like coffee, tea, and sugar, and industry is oriented to the export of raw materials. For example, after independence from France, the Algerians found that one of their major industries was the cultivation of grapes for wine, a beverage that they were forbidden by their Muslim religion to drink. To compound the problem, the postcolonial French had developed new sources for grapes so there was little market for Algerian wine. The Algerians were forced to destroy many of their vineyards and replant with crops more suited for domestic consumption. The Algerian experience has been repeated as a sad economic fact of postcolonial life throughout much of the Other World.

Health

One of the undeniable legacies of colonialism has been the extension of modern health practices to areas in which they had not been available. Even where the health care needs of the impoverished still overwhelm the available clinics, the situation has improved during the past three decades. Western-initiated improvements in medical care, hygiene, and clean water have dramatically increased life expectancy everywhere in the Other World. The result is that adults are living longer and fewer infants are dying. Unfortunately, these advances have outstripped social practices geared to a more brutal age. The result is a population explosion in the Other World that threatens to destroy any chance for people to enjoy the material gains of the twentieth century. Egypt, which only 100 years ago had no population problem, now has a growth rate that requires an increase in water storage capacity equal to the construction of a new Aswan High Dam every 10 years, just to irrigate enough land to feed its people. With no change in social policy, Other World countries, such as Egypt, are leaking lifeboats, the inhabitants bailing water but doomed ultimately to sink in a sea of humanity. In one way or another, the population explosion, brought on in part by modern health practices, threatens the future of almost every government in the Other World.

Stability

Unlike nations in the West, many states of the Other World have failed to achieve internal unity. The boundaries of most are the result of balance-of-power decisions rather than any desire by Westerners to create states containing the seeds of geographic or cultural unity. The result is a postcolonial world that has few of the economic, social, or political elements generally thought necessary to establish stable governments.

The colonial experience must be judged to have had a generally negative impact on the peoples of the Other World. Although significant material benefits have been inherited from the West, they are offset by the economic, social, and political problems that are the legacy of colonialism.

NEOCOLONIALISM

Today, the great colonial powers of the past no longer occupy the center stage of world affairs. The fate of the world is not determined by traditional colonial powers like Spain, Portugal, Holland, or Belgium. Since colonialism was a primary force in the affairs of nations for nearly six centuries, this question can now be asked: Is colonialism dead or is it merely reappearing in a new form? If traditional colonialism is the only type to be considered, it must be concluded that this era of history has probably come to a close.

The second half of the twentieth century has been characterized by the arrival of almost 100 Other World states on the international scene. This rapid evolution of colonies into sovereign states has led to a situation in which many former colonies now fall under the influence of "new" imperial powers.

The old imperial powers laid the foundations for the Other World as it exists today. They drew the arbitrary boundaries that continue to be a source of conflict. They developed an economic system geared to the provision of needed products for the developed world. They created a leadership caste, which now perpetuates an unfair economic system that exploits the majority for the benefit of the few. The result was the creation of a new colonial system that allows one-fourth of the world to acquire 80 percent of the world's resources.

Fifty years after formal independence, much of the Other World is characterized by hunger, poverty, overpopulation, political instability, and economic dependence. Most of these problems are the legacy of a colonial world that emphasized economic return to the mother country with little regard for the needs of the indigenous inhabitants. Much of the economic, cultural, political, and social institutions of the Other World still serve the interests of the developed world, which is the successor to colonial rule. The economic imbalance between rich and poor, the production of crops for export while children go hungry, and the exportation of bulk raw materials while luxury consumer items are imported are only some of the many problems of the new dependent relationships that have evolved between the developed world and the Other World. As previously stated, the leading colonial powers during the great period of Western expansion were also leaders in world politics. Since World War II, the major neocolonial states have shaped most political events. In the 1990s, the United States, Germany, and Japan play dominant roles in the economic affairs of many Other World states. These neocolonial powers and their older allies, Britain and France, are now the developed world's political leaders. In this context, traditional colonialism is dead, but neocolonialism is very much alive.

What Is Neocolonialism?

Neocolonialism differs from traditional colonialism in at least two respects. First, there is no official acknowledgment of colonial ties because the subordinate government has established legal independence. Unlike traditional colonialism, the control exerted here is indirect. Second, this influence is exercised through the interaction of the dominant nation's banking, business, cultural, and military leaders with the Other World's elites. This process results in relationships that are dependent on the wishes of the dominant power. The political, military, and economic requirements of the controlling state drive the relationship between the two entities, whereas the needs of the subordinate country are of secondary consideration. Today, the Other World has become a dumping ground for consumer goods and military hardware exported from the developed world. Often these imports must be paid for with borrowed funds, which mortgage the future for masses of people in the Other World.

The influence exercised by a dominant power over a dependent state can range from the activities of multinational corporations to the approval of international bank loans. In an interdependent world market, in which the sales of some multinational corporations exceed the GDP of medium-sized states, many Other World nations are particularly vulnerable to outside pressure (see table 2.1). In this environment, externally provoked domestic economic problems can lead to political instability. Other World leaders may be tempted to go along with a neocolonial relationship in order to survive. For instance, when their economy was in trouble in 1994, the Mexican government was forced to make important economic concessions before the United States would guarantee the bank loans considered necessary to stabilize the situation.

In most cases neocolonialism is not driven by malice but by the marketplace. It is not a matter of illegal exploitation but rather a case of the rich, through superior purchasing power, being able to influence Other World economics. This process occurs because the wealthy can outbid the poor for goods and services. The neocolonial relationship is manifested in at least four unequal associations: cultural, political, economic, and military dominance. Taken together, they con-

TABLE 2.1   A 1994 Comparison of the Gross Sales of Six Major American Corporations with the GDP of Selected Other World States

Corporation	Sales in $ Billions	Equals Approximate GDP
General Motors	134	Indonesia
Ford Motor Co.	108	Argentina
IBM	64	Israel
Mobil	57	Malaysia
Philip Morris	51	Philippines
Chrysler	43	Algeria

SOURCE: Adapted from *Fortune* Magazine, *Forbes* Magazine, and the *San Francisco Chronicle*. Gross domestic product is defined as the market value of all goods and services that have been bought for final use during a year. The GDP covers all workers and goods employed within a nation's borders.

stitute a degree of control exercised by the developed world that exceeds anything thought possible during the original fight for independence.

Cultural Domination

Traditional imperial powers proceeded on the assumption that their culture was superior. The Spanish, Portuguese, and French took steps to destroy the indigenous culture of the colonies and to replace it with a culture imported from the mother country. This policy resulted in the total destruction of many societies in the Other World. Although they took a more benign view, even the British spoke of "the lesser breeds." Colonial policies created a westernized upper class throughout the Other World. Two hundred years after independence, Latin American culture is still dominated by Spanish and Portuguese tradition. Thirty years after the French withdrawal from Tunisia, Tunisian elites still speak French. In the 1990s, the upper-class children of the Egyptian revolution talk of London while they play polo and croquet at the British-founded Gazira Club. These Western-oriented elites have become the transmission lines for foreign cultural domination in the Other World.

Radio, television, advertising, newspapers, magazines, and books present a seductive message of Western cultural superiority. From Mexico City to Rabat, from Manila to Lima, young people have been conditioned to want jeans and rock music. This cultural dominance is further reinforced by schools that are often patterned after systems from abroad.

In a society of scarcity, such as exists in much of the Other World, the obsession of the elites to create a native version of Western society has caused scarce resources to be diverted from the country's real needs to serve the interests of the few at the top. This practice leaves the developing nations vulnerable to other forms of neocolonial domination.

Political Domination

Much of the Other World is made up of unstable systems of artificially created states, each of which is fearful of its neighbors and therefore continually preparing for war. Thus many developing states seek the aid of other states to achieve political goals that would be otherwise impossible, making them prime candidates for outside influence.

Other World leaders need financial, technological, and military support from the developed world. To get this help, many are willing to submit to varying degrees of outside political influence, as long as this relationship does not become too visible. Over time, this unequal relationship undermines the popular legitimacy of the government in question, and as a consequence, it forces authorities to continue the arrangement in order to remain in power.

During the cold war, Western intervention in the political affairs of Other World states was rationalized as a necessity in order to "contain communism." In the aftermath of this struggle, foreign interventions will be more difficult to justify. In the 1990s there has been less emphasis on maintaining the balance of power and more concern about securing access to Other World markets, resources, and cheap labor. These post–cold war goals are uncomfortably similar to those of the imperial powers of an earlier age.

Economic Domination

Economic neocolonialism may be pursued as the dominant country's formal policy, or it may occur subtly as the result of informal private activities. For example, whereas Western economic aid is clearly policy-driven, the activities of such great multinational powers as Ford, Standard Oil, and General Electric operate largely outside of the control of both the dominant and dependent countries. On occasion, the dominant government and private corporate policies may coincide, but this is not always the case. Such ambiguity makes the Other World charge that there is always a link between the policies of the neocolonial power and the multinational corporation, but this charge is difficult to prove. Some American corporations have used their foreign operations to frustrate their own government's policies on trade. The bottom-line strategy for multinationals is profit, not foreign policy.

The multinationals advocate free-trade policies that enable them to buy as cheaply as possible and sell for the highest price, regardless of where the market is located. They maintain that a policy of free trade will eventually result in the establishment of a system that will provide the greatest good for the greatest number of people. President Ronald Reagan stated his own support for this approach in a speech made before the board of governors of the World Bank: "My own government is committed to policies of free trade, unrestricted investment, and open capital markets."[9]

No matter the intentions, people in the Other World believe that the economic impact of neocolonialism has a negative effect on their independence. In their eyes, the history of foreign trade has been the promotion of activities that work almost entirely to the advantage of the developed world. Its policy of keeping markets open to free enterprise virtually guarantees that it will continue to maintain a stranglehold on the wealth of the Other World. The rules of the game of trade have been made by the developed world and benefit the developed world. Economic neocolonialism is a legacy of this modern system of trade.

Military Domination

Much of the Other World is politically unstable. To survive in this hostile environment, the weak have had to pursue a policy of nonalignment or seek the protection of a powerful ally. After World War II, the United States and the Soviet Union courted these countries in an effort to structure a favorable balance of power. The result was the creation of military client-state relationships that involved most of the Other World. Since that time, the two superpowers have supplied massive amounts of sophisticated weapons to Other World countries. Weapon availability, parts, and training are all indirect methods for major powers to affect the behavior of their clients. The final outcome of the Falklands war (1982) was influenced by the U.S. spare parts embargo, which denied service to equipment supplied earlier to the Argentine Air Force. Without spare parts, the Argentineans were severely handicapped in both the size and the number of air strikes that they could mount against the British. This deficiency was one factor that ultimately helped to turn the tide of battle in favor of the British forces.

The militaries of the Other World form the life-support system for the arms business in the developed world. Arms sales have been significant sources of income and influence for the United States, the former Soviet Union, South Africa, and a number of states in Europe. President Carter did express concerns about U.S. arms policy, however: "We also need to change our weapons production and weapons sales overseas as a basic foundation for jobs in this country."[10] In the guise of offering a helping hand to friendly nations, developed states are able to tie clients to their arms industry. During the cold war, this policy allowed sophisticated military hardware to fall into the hands of Other World leaders. In many cases, balance-of-power issues took precedence over the consideration of local issues when decisions on arms sales were made. On more than one occasion leaders of selling countries were shocked to find that client states were fighting each other in local conflicts with the weapons that were intended for use in the cold war—for example, the hostilities between India and Pakistan and Iran and Iraq.

The 1990 Iraqi invasion of Kuwait demonstrated the folly of indiscriminate sales of advanced military technology to the Other World. To the surprise and horror of leaders in the developed world, the Iraqis showed that their acquisition of military technology had a level of sophistication that made a military response from the developed world difficult. In the end it took a half million troops and a war to force the modern Iraqi army to leave Kuwait.

Developed nations have found that once their most advanced military technology is in the hands of a foreign leader, they can no longer control its use in the low-intensity conflicts that occur in the Other World. The development of sophisticated arms industries geared to exports by China, Brazil, South Africa, Turkey, Israel, North Korea, and South Korea has introduced a new dimension to this problem. The end of the cold war and the "build down" of the military forces in the United States and the former Soviet Union threatens to cause a "fire sale" of surplus military hardware, further complicating the issue.

In the wake of the 1991 U.S. victory over Iraq in the Persian Gulf, American arms sales to the Other World exploded. The U.S. government was placed in the embarrassing position of condemning Russian arms sales while, at the same time, increasing sales of its own. If the proliferation of exported weapons continues, the developed world's ability to influence low-intensity conflicts through arms sales will be greatly reduced.

In summary, neocolonialism, like traditional colonialism, describes a process in which one people exerts power over another people. In the case of neocolonialism, the subject people are legally independent, so the dominant power's influence is indirect. Because the practice of neocolonialism is now so widespread, it must be considered one of the two major influences on contemporary politics of the Other World. The second is nationalism.

NATIONALISM

Like modern colonialism, nationalism is largely a Western invention. With the rise of the nation-state in Europe during the eighteenth century, Europeans abandoned their traditional loyalties to clan, church, and crown.[11] However, after the American and French revolutions, the situation in Europe changed. No longer were political leaders successfully able to command large followings purely on the basis of divine right, family ties, or papal decrees. For the first time, Europeans started to confer legitimacy on what was to be called the nation-state. This entity would have authority over a group of people, called a nation, who believed that they had a common cultural identity. The sense of identity between the nation and state was strengthened by leaders who emphasized this linkage to reinforce the legitimacy of their rule. Commonly proclaimed symbols of nationhood included racial, linguistic, religious, and historical ties that separated one people from another. In time, the nation's flag, anthem, special days, and other traditions assumed a quasi-religious character that was almost unquestioned. Like the mystics of ancient times, the modern leader who successfully captured these images was able to rule. Today, leaders wrap themselves in the national colors at every opportunity to establish their legitimacy in the minds of the people. Modern nationalism represents the idea that the merger of the nation and the state creates an entity that is more than the sum of its parts. The individual's personal interests are subordinate to the interests of the nation-state. What makes the nation-state different from states of the past is the transference of the people's loyalties, hence legitimacy, to the state instead of to the crown, religion, city, or clan.

Nationalism is based on the notion of exclusivity and, therefore, the superiority of one nation over another. Conversely, one of the features of nationalism is the use of a fear of others to encourage unity. The "foreign devil" is one of the primary motivations for modern nationalism; that is, leaders in both the East and the West portray other leaders as foreign devils to secure popular support for their own policies. The perception of a Saddam Hussein, Muammar al-Qaddafi, Bill Clinton, or Fidel Castro as a foreign devil depends on one's location.

Nationalism in the Other World is part of the legacy of colonialism. As colonial administrators, teachers, soldiers, and missionaries sought to replicate the culture of Europe, they inadvertently planted the seeds of nationalism. Students learning about Magna Carta rights, the French Revolution, and American independence could not avoid drawing parallels between their own situations and the struggles of young Westerners of another age. Nationalism appeared in the hearts and minds of Western-trained elites long before it became the mass movement that it is today. For example, Western-educated intellectuals formulated the beginning of a theory that all Arabs form a single nation. At the time, their purpose was to create unity for a common Arab struggle for independence. Similar nationalists led movements in many Other World locations during the nineteenth and twentieth centuries.

For many years the Marxist-Leninist model was seen by nationalists as an alternative to the Western approach to development, with its neocolonial implications. However, the collapse of the economy in the former Soviet Union has discredited much of this effort in the eyes of many in the Other World. There is doubt about whether the Marxist-Leninist approach will continue to have much influence.

Some nationalists sought to chart a new course between the push-pull approaches of the East and the West. For them, nonalignment was the only way for the individually weak but collectively strong states to avoid the reimposition of colonialism in a new form. During the 1950s, Nkruma in Ghana, Sukarno in Indonesia, and Nasser in Egypt effectively used the East-West rivalry to play off one side against the other. With the end of the cold war, Other World nationalists will have little to bargain with when they are forced to deal with the developed nations. It is questionable whether nonalignment will be a viable policy for them to pursue in the future.

SUMMARY

After nearly 600 years, Western colonialism has come to an end, and over 100 new nations have gained their independence. Born out of the colonial struggle for independence, these new states are engaged in the uneven process of nation building. The traditional symbols of nationalism may not be universally present. Many countries have yet to meet the criteria necessary for a state as it is recognized in the West. Admittedly, these states have artificial and often illogical boundaries and are divided by political ideology and religion. However, they have a common legacy of colonialism, which unites them. This unity is based on the development of a militant nationalism that is anticolonial, antineocolonial, and anti-Western.

If the hostility to the West is to be reduced, the Western policymakers must strive for a new fairness in dealing with the Other World. Fairness needs to be applied to policies on arms sales, trade, and banking. The present neocolonial practices carried out by the West ensure that extreme poverty will be the fate for millions of Other World people. The poor will continue to pay high prices for what they purchase from the West while being paid low wages for what they produce. The perpetuation of this unfair relationship is simply a license for the West to "strip-mine" the Other World for anything that is of value. As long as this situation persists, the West should not be surprised at the hostility, social unrest, and ethnic rivalry coming from the Other World.

ISSUES FOR DISCUSSION

1. Should the Other World be held to the same labor standards advocated in the developed world? The case for hand-tied oriental carpets and the issue of child labor:

For every person living in the United States there are approximately 21,000 people living elsewhere. The majority of these people live at a subsistence level in the Other World. The circumstances of their existence dictate conditions of work that often seem harsh and immoral to Westerners. Is it possible or even fair to hold the Other World states to the same labor standards that have taken 200 years to evolve in the industrialized West?

There is a saying that the wealth of a society can be measured by the age at which the young must go to work. In oriental carpet factories stretching from Morocco across North Africa and South Asia to India and Nepal, the age of children working at the looms is young indeed. Ranging from as young as four to their midteens, thousands of young girls work for up to 14 hours a day in the carpet factories. Fine, hand-tied oriental carpets are produced by children because their hands are considered to be faster and they are more patient in their work than adults.

Oriental carpets are highly praised and find a ready market in the homes and offices of the United States and Europe. Almost all of these carpets are manufactured for export. Few Westerners understand or care to hear about the pain and suffering that is involved in the production of these beautiful, expensive works of art.

Break Time: Child Rug Weavers Taking a
Break in a North African Carpet Factory
SOURCE: Joe Weatherby

The defenders of child labor in the Other World point out that carpet factories and other industries are not unlike the nineteenth-century textile mills and mines that helped to create the wealth of modern Europe and the United States. To them, these harsh conditions are a temporary but necessary part of the development process. Other World businesspersons are outraged when they hear reformers in the West calling for boycotts of their goods simply because they were produced with the help of child labor. They are quick to point out that labor reform is simply another way for the West to restrict competition in a free-market economy. Other World states compete with the only advantage that they have— the willing backs of their young. To them, the old colonial metaphor still applies: After 200 years of playing industrial poker, the West has acquired enough of the economic chips to pronounce the game immoral and demand that the Other World join in a game of contract bridge.

The dilemma for the Other World is clear. The West is attempting to impose its own moral standards on a world that has very different values. In much of the Other World, a child who helps to support a poor family by working at the wheel or the loom is considered to be a good child. In places where the only advantage that industries have over the West is low labor costs, there is no alternative to child labor if the family is to live.

This same story can be repeated in industries that manufacture products destined for Western markets, including sporting goods, textiles, and shoes. Labor organizations in the West have asserted that as many as 100 million children must work in the factories of the Other World for their families to survive.

The developed world may have seen the elimination of the worst excesses of the nineteenth-century England of Charles Dickens. Cripplers may no longer haunt the slums of Cairo looking for children to turn into the beggars described in the stories of Nagib Mafaus. Nevertheless, harsh working conditions for children remain throughout the Other World.

Under the circumstances, should the reader boycott the carpets, textiles, sporting equipment, and shoes manufactured in the Other World because of these labor excesses? To do so will deprive millions of poor people of their only hope for a livelihood. Or should the reader assume that, as has occurred with industrialization in the West, conditions for labor will improve in Other World industries as manufacturing gradually improves the standard of living?

2. Should the Other World be required to adopt the ecological standards of the developed world? Can the Other World achieve a balance between environmental concerns and economic needs?

During the nineteenth century, British industrialists were fond of saying that "where there is muck there is brass," in short, dirt and pollution mean profits. By 1995, the developed world could afford to lead the rest of the planet in expressing concerns about the environment. Leaders from North America and Europe warned of the possibility of an ecological holocaust if drastic changes were not

Pollution. Flowing along the border between Mexico and the United States, the Tijuana River is polluted by the dumping of chemicals from the dozens of *maquiladores*, or small factories, located on the Mexican side of the border. The people in the foreground are waiting for nightfall to slip across the border in the hope of finding work in the United States.

SOURCE: Joe Weatherby

made to improve the environment. Many of their concerns were focused on the environmental problems found in the Other World.

By coupling their aid and foreign trade requirements to environmental policies, developed states were able to transfer their concerns to the Other World. The convention emerging from the UN conference on environment and development was signed by over 180 states. In support of this effort, the United States started to shape bilateral assistance programs in the Other World designed to encourage energy efficiency, renewable energy, and forest management. At the same time, the Europeans called for Other World producers to switch from environmentally unfriendly crops to new strains such as "green" cotton and "green" jute.

Through long-term planning, real progress has been made in improving the environment in parts of the developed world. The United States has dramatically increased the forest lands on the East Coast through replanting projects. In London, the Thames River is now clean enough to support salmon for the first time in hundreds of years. Clearly, the environment can be improved if people have the will and the wealth to make the long-term choices that are necessary. Most of the changes have occurred in the developed world. The question remains, can these environmental successes be repeated in the developing world and, if so, at what price?

People and states are far more vulnerable to the whims of the marketplace in the Other World. Westerners can afford to recycle cans and bottles while, at the same time, consuming millions of trees to supply paper for their Sunday newspapers and disposable diapers. Their wealth allows them to purchase the trees elsewhere or engage in reforestation nearby. Long-term improvements in the environment of the developed world can occur with little personal cost.

Long-term environmental choices are not readily available to much of the Other World. Subsistence farmers engaged in the "slashing and burning" of the rainforest have few choices if their families are to survive. They can continue to farm in the old way to the detriment of the environment. They can leave farming and try to eke out a living in the great slums of cities like Rio de Janeiro, São Paulo, or Mexico City. They can head north to find work as undocumented aliens in the developed world. Like millions trapped in similar situations elsewhere in the Other World, they do not have the luxury to consider long-term alternatives to their day-to-day existence.

Leaders of Other World states also have few long-term alternatives. Their people demand recognizable improvements in living conditions. The leaders must offer hope for a change for the better or face social unrest. In spite of the desire of some to make environmental improvements, rapid development, regardless of the consequences, often seems to be the answer. For example, when Brasilia was established as the new capital of Brazil, it was done to encourage development in the interior, not to preserve the rainforest. Likewise, it may be unreasonable to expect the leaders of other developing states like China, India, and Mexico to place a high priority on environmental protection if it means a substantial delay in economic development. For them the choice is either development or a continuation of neocolonialism.

Try to look at the issue of ecology from the standpoint of the limited choices that people face in the Other World. Already economically subservient to a marketplace dominated by the developed world, what priority should Other World leaders give to the environment at the expense of their own development?

Finally, what should the developed world commit in the way of resources to the improvement of the environment in the Other World? Are people in the developed world willing to make the sacrifices that may be necessary, thereby lowering their standard of living, to free the funds required to improve the environment in the Other World?

3. Is free trade between the developed world and the Other World a good idea? Should the developed world look at the human cost of this kind of trade? The NAFTA treaty is a case in point.

There is general consensus that, in the long run, a free market is beneficial to both the developed world and the Other World. It is believed that competition will eventually cause the best products to be produced at the lowest cost for the consumer. Noncompetitive products will be unable to survive in a free marketplace.

Aristotle, in the Nichomachean ethics, wrote, "There is as much ethics in the equal treatment of unequal cases as in the unequal treatment of equal cases." Nowhere is this paradox more evident than along the border between the United States and Mexico. Called *La Frontera*, this 2,000-mile border is a separate nation separated by an artificial boundary. The people living in this region share an in-

La Frontera. Frontier sign warning California motorists to avoid hitting people illegally crossing the border from Mexico.

SOURCE: Jane Weatherby

terdependence based on family, history, and economics. It is here that a collision of the Other World and the developed world occurs. Here, the sweatshops of the United States and the *maquiladores* in Mexico thrive.

This border is made up of overlapping cultures, economies, and jurisdictions. In Mexico, lax environmental standards and wages as low as four dollars a day have created a new frontier. This process has been aided by the establishment of the border industrial program in 1965, followed by the North American Free Trade Agreement (NAFTA) in 1994. Many U.S. and Japanese companies have relocated south of the border, establishing manufacturing plants called *maquiladores* to produce goods that will be sold in the United States.

Although clearly beneficial to the North American consumer, this practice is costly to many others, both in the loss of jobs and in the destruction of the environment along the border. It has been estimated that the *maquiladores* in Mexico could cost the United States 650,000 jobs within the next three years. At the same time, U.S. residents are filing lawsuits against businesses operating in Mexico for health problems believed to be caused by air pollution drifting across the border.

These developments are also causing social problems in Mexico. Literally thousands of people are moving north in the hope of finding work in the *maquiladores*. This process is overwhelming the social services in Mexico. In one day recently, 20 people in Juarez died from drinking contaminated drinking water.

On the United States side of *La Frontera* live the poorest of America's poor. There, conditions for some people are not much better than in Mexico. It has been estimated that across the border from Juarez, in El Paso, Texas, as many as 75,000 residents may not have running water and sewer systems. Many of these U.S. residents lost their minimum-wage jobs when their employers, taking advantage of NAFTA, moved their manufacturing operations to Mexico. These Americans still

work but now in the hundreds of small sub-minimum-wage sweatshops that pro-
liferate along the border. These businesses operate along the American side in a
lawless atmosphere by subcontracting work for legal manufacturers on both sides
of the border.

Like many places where there is a dramatic collision of wealth and the lack of
it, *La Frontera* is an area of uncertainty and confusion. Does this mean that these people should be sacrificed to further the trading interest of the powerful in the short
term, in the hope that everyone will benefit in the long run? Should the developed
world be concerned that with change there will be winners and losers in tearing
down the trade barriers between the developed world and the Other World?[12]

4. Do Other World states engage in imperialism? If so, is this a different form of imperialism than has existed in the past?

Earlier in this chapter, imperialism was described as the extension of control by
one state over another. Since 1945, over 100 new states have been created from
the ruins of the old empires established by the West. This new world is incredibly complex, making it difficult to generalize about the subject of imperialism.

Are Other World states, who have recently emerged from colonialism, capable of pursuing imperial aims of their own? Most of these states were artificially
created by the colonial powers. Are they now simply engaged in the process of
sorting out their natural boundaries? If so, is this process imperialism?

If imperialism is engaged in by Other World states, it is a more complex
process than the one seen during the period of Western colonialism. This neoimperialism has at least several causes. First, there is the traditional seizure of the
territory of others, as in the cases of China's occupation of Tibet, India's occupation of Hyderabad, Indonesia's invasion of western Iran, Libya's attempt to take
northern Chad, and Iraq's invasions of Iran and Kuwait. All of these incidents
may be described as imperialism in much the same way as was done in the past.

However, other examples of irredentism are more difficult to categorize. Is
there a neoimperialism that includes the acquisition of territory because colonialism created artificial boundaries that fail to correspond to the actual ethnic divisions that exist? The desire for ethnic or tribal hegemony is justified in the seizure
of territory in large parts of the Other World. Depending on one's viewpoint, this
process includes Morocco's occupation of the Spanish Sahara, Somalia's claims to
the Oqaden territory of Ethiopia, and the tribal conflict involving Burundi and
Rwanda.

Defensive imperialism is also a controversial subject. Is a state justified in taking the land of another for purely defensive purposes? Has Israel become a neoimperialist state because of the establishment of the security zone across the southern border of Lebanon? Did the Vietnamese invasion of Cambodia to put down
a hostile regime constitute neoimperialism? Does Syria's occupation of parts of
Lebanon, to deter Israel, qualify it to be called a neoimperialist state?

Finally, are anticolonial liberation movements cases of neoimperialism? If so,
many Other World states are guilty. Some examples of such actions include India's
occupation of the areas on the subcontinent formerly controlled by France, the

seizure of Goa, and the support for separatist movements that led to the establishment of Bangladesh. Argentina attempted to establish control over the Falkland Islands before being defeated by the British. If it were not for the British military commitment to Belize, it might soon be occupied by Guatemala, which has claimed this territory in the past.

Will the complex makeup of Other World states in the 1990s require a more complex definition of imperialism if it is to have any practical meaning? If it exists, how should neoimperialism be defined? Under what circumstances can Other World neoimperialism be justified?

5. Should the United States continue to distribute foreign aid to the Other World?

Perhaps there is no foreign policy program that provokes more controversy and misunderstanding among taxpayers than the foreign aid program. First, people are confused about the amount of the U.S. budget allocated to foreign aid. Most polls indicate that the American people believe that this program takes up as much as 15 percent of the nation's budget. Although the figures are affected by the definition of foreign aid, most estimates place the foreign aid budget at about 1 percent of the national one. Furthermore, although the United States and Japan are the leading contributors in real dollars, the United States ranks near the bottom of the developed world in the percentage of gross national product devoted to this program.

The issue of foreign aid raises more questions than it answers. Not only is there confusion about actual dollar amounts, but there is little agreement about what should be included. What should an aid program accomplish? Who should benefit from foreign aid? Should foreign aid be limited to serving the interest of the donor? Should these programs target only states that are either democratic or promote free-market economics? Is military assistance legitimate foreign aid? Should foreign aid target the poorest states, or should it go to the more developed states: that are in a position to use it effectively? Finally, should aid be given to programs that are morally necessary but economically or politically unproductive?

It may be a surprise to learn that of the approximately $14 billion that the United States sets aside for foreign aid, half is devoted to security or military assistance. The rest of the program is earmarked for economic, humanitarian, and development assistance. However, nearly half of that amount goes to three states: Israel, Egypt, and Russia. This leaves only about $3 billion to be divided among the rest of the Other World.[13] The U.S. example is not unusual. Japan, perhaps the world's largest donor nation, often limits aid to those states that are potential customers.

Another surprising feature of the U.S. foreign aid program concerns the way in which aid is distributed. The richest part of the Other World gets twice as much aid per head as the poorest. Each year, Israelis get about $1,800 per head of U.S. aid, while the poorest aid recipient states receive about $1.[14]

Furthermore, a good bit of aid is really a subsidy for American business and agriculture. Whether it is aerospace, defense, construction, automobiles, or midwestern farmers, many Americans benefit from the foreign aid programs because of the requirement that goods and services must be purchased in the United States. This policy is understandable because to do otherwise would be to ask the American taxpayers to support the products and services of their competitors.

It has been suggested that the taxpayers' desire to help people in real need might be better served if aid money was directed through international organizations such as the World Bank and agencies of the United Nations. Unfortunately, the track record of these organizations has not proved to be much better than that demonstrated by the unilateral programs. On the one hand, critics charge that the World Bank has tended to support huge development projects that have been harmful to the environment. On the other hand, the UN agencies have become so bogged down with short-term missions of peacekeeping and the feeding of refugees that they have had little impact on the long-term improvement of conditions in the Other World.

One of the fastest growing areas of foreign aid is the funneling of money directly through voluntary bodies such as church groups and other nongovernmental organizations. It is argued that these groups are working in ways that have a better chance to get the aid to those who really need it. At this time, this process is still too diverse and new to be evaluated.

The dilemma for the donor states is clear. Foreign aid was modeled after the post–World War II successes of the Marshall Plan in Europe. That plan was intended to jump-start the war-shattered economies of the time. Fifty years later, foreign aid is a vast system, which after the expenditure of $1.4 trillion has failed to improve conditions in the Other World. A recent evaluation of foreign aid programs in 96 countries by the London School of Economics concluded that they had made little impact.

The questions to be considered here are difficult. What should be the purpose of U.S. foreign aid? Should it be an extension of foreign policy? Should American workers be favored in making purchases for foreign aid programs? Finally, how should the United States structure the foreign aid program to ensure that the dollars are most efficiently spent on those who are in need of help?

NOTES

1. For over 100 years, Argentina has claimed the Falkland Islands under the Spanish name Malvinas. In 1982 it fought a war with Britain for control of the islands, which Britain won. Since most maps use the English name, that practice will be followed in this chapter.
2. William Tuohy, "Viet Nam, A Key Battle Reverberates: Dien Bien Phu Recalled," *Los Angeles Times*, May 5, 1984, p. 18.
3. See W. M. Will, "Power, Dependency, and Misperceptions in the Caribbean Basin," in *Crescents of Conflict*, ed. W. M. Will and R. Millett (New York: Praeger, 1985), chap. 2.
4. William Lyle Schurz, *This New World* (New York: Dutton, 1957), p. 112.
5. See Muammar al-Qaddafi, "Third Way," in *Islam in Transition: Muslim Perspectives*, ed. John Donohue and John Esposito (New York: Oxford University Press, 1982), p. 103.

6. Winston S. Churchill, *Their Finest Hour: The Second World War* (Boston: Houghton Mifflin, 1949), p. 519.
7. Lewis M. Alexander, ed., *World Political Patterns* (Chicago: Rand McNally, 1963), p. 262.
8. Daniel Papp, *Contemporary International Relations* (New York: Macmillan, 1984), p. 112.
9. For an explanation of the inequity between the developed world and the Other World, see Ivan Head, "Haves and Have-nots: The Upheaval between North and South," *Foreign Affairs*, 68 (Summer 1989): 71–86.
10. See Jimmy Carter, *New Age Journal*, March/April 1990, pp. 52–54, 132–134.
11. The Treaty of Westphalia (1648), which ended the Thirty Years' War in Europe, is the acknowledged beginning of the modern nation-state.
12. For more information on the industry in *La Frontera*, see Chris K. Raul and Evelyn Iritani, "Asia, Mexico Learn to Work Together," *Los Angeles Times*, May 29, 1995, p. D1.
13. George Moffett, "Foreign Aid on the GOP Chopping Bloc," *Christian Science Monitor*, February 22, 1995, p. 4.
14. "The Question of Foreign Aid," *U.S. News and World Report*, January 30, 1995, p. 32.

FOR FURTHER READING

Berthon, Simon, and Robinson, Andrew. *The Shape of the World: The Mapping and Discovery of the Earth.* New York: Rand McNally, 1991.
Danzinger, James. *Understanding the World: A Comparative Introduction to Political Science.* "The Developing Countries in the Post-Cold War World." Chap 17. New York: Longman, 1996.
The Dorling Kindersley World Reference Atlas. London: Dorling Kindersley, 1994.
Gellner, Ernest. *Nations and Nationalism.* Ithaca, N.Y.: Cornell University Press, 1983.
Ghaliand, Gerard, and Rageau, Jean-Pierre. *Strategic Atlas: A Comparative Geopolitics of the World's Powers.* New York: Harper & Row, 1990.
Harrison, Paul. *Inside the Third World.* "Winner Takes All: Precolonial Societies and Colonialism." Chap. 2. London: Penguin Books, 1987.
JeBlig, H. J. *Human Geography: Culture, Society, and Space.* 4th ed. New York: Wiley, 1993.
Lapping, Brian. *The End of Empire.* New York: St. Martin's Press, 1985.
Poulsen, Thomas. *Nations and States: A Geographic Background to World Affairs.* Englewood Cliffs, N.J.: Prentice Hall, 1995.
Snow, Donald. *Distant Thunder: Third World Conflict and the New International Order.* New York: St. Martin's Press, 1993.
Stokes, Gale. "The Underdeveloped Theory of Nationalism," *World Politics* 31 (October 1978): 150–160.
Trainer, F.E. *Developed to Death: Rethinking Third World Development.* London: Green Print, 1989.

CHAPTER 3

Development

Emmit B. Evans, Jr. and Dianne Long

A growth process that benefits only the wealthiest minority and maintains or even increases the disparities between and within countries is not development.
"The Cocoyoc Declaration"

The idea that international efforts could, or should, be undertaken to build the economies and societies of the Other World is relatively recent. The Western colonial powers used the Americas, Africa, and Asia as sources of raw materials and cheap labor under the systems of mercantilism and capitalism that dominated world economies for 450 years prior to the end of World War II; they saw no reason to "develop" these areas. Other World, or Third World, development first appeared on the international agenda with the winding down of the colonial era and the explosion of newly independent states in the late 1940s.

For many, economic development was part of the logic of political independence. Industrial economies were an integral feature of the Western nation-states that formed the model for most of the new political entities. And for the masses caught up in the torrent of rising expectations released by the promises of independence, a higher standard of living seemed a right that had been won through the struggle for political freedom. For others, building the economies of the new states presented opportunities to establish more effective forms of domination and control through new and more subtle forms of colonialism.

Development has been a dominant feature of Other World economic, political, and social affairs for the past 50 years. Disagreements over how it should be pursued and, indeed, how the concept should even be defined have been the source of ongoing conflicts that have ranged from discussion and debate to terrorism and war. It is consequently difficult to understand the contemporary Other World without an understanding of development. Toward that end, the purposes of this chapter are to consider various definitions based on competing systems of values and beliefs, to survey the history of development efforts, to evaluate the successes and failures of those efforts, and to consider the prospects for development as we approach the twenty-first century.

VALUES, IDEOLOGIES, AND DEVELOPMENT

Attempts to define development in social, economic, or political terms begin on shaky conceptual grounds. Most people think of the concept as an unfolding of events through a succession of states or changes, each of which is preparatory for the next and all of which contribute to some final end. Such efforts are thus exercises in *teleology*, or attempts to explain natural phenomena as being directed toward some final cause or purpose. The assumptions that such ultimate purposes exist and, if they do, that we are intellectually capable of discerning them may be presumptuous from the start.

Human beings are, however, a precocious lot, and doubts about the limits and validity of our knowledge have seldom stopped us from designing grand theories that explain current events in terms of where we are headed. Karl Marx's communist utopia and John Maynard Keynes's capitalist utopia were both built on teleological theories. What people usually do when defining "where we are headed" is to describe that future state in terms of their personal values, or where they would *prefer* for us to go. It is at this point that political values and ideologies (or belief systems) become of crucial importance in defining development.

Development and Conservative Values

A fundamental element in conservative value systems is the belief that one of the keys to human development lies in providing those with special strengths and abilities the *freedom to* pursue their individual interests without constraint. In a dialogue with Socrates reported over 2,300 years ago by Plato in *The Republic*, a Greek sophist named Thrasymachus argued that it is the natural right of the strong to take more than their equal share of what the world has to offer. And the strong are morally justified in designing and operating the institutions of government to pursue their interests, or "might makes right." Over the intervening years, these ideas, which have become known as the Doctrine of Thrasymachus, have provided the rationale for a variety of conservative ideologies that often argue—in social Darwinist, survival-of-the-fittest terms—that protecting the special positions and abilities of those who have risen above the common masses is necessary for the evolution of the human species and the grandeur of humanity.

Capitalism is a contemporary version of the Doctrine of Thrasymachus. One of its basic tenets is that the most secure avenue to development is provided by supply-side economic strategies that encourage and facilitate the accumulation of capital by the able and adept. According to Keynes, in order to develop, societies must pass through a transnational phase in which human greed and avarice are unleashed by the drive for personal profit to propel us through the "tunnel of economic necessity," wherein a concentration of capital in the hands of a few will create an industrial system capable of producing material abundance.

In the Other World, capitalist ideas and ideals have taken the form of "take-off," or modernization, theories, which hold that the surest way to achieve development is to maximize the opportunities for investment by private firms, most of which are located in the industrialized world. The goal is to create a critical mass of concentrated capital that will support the takeoff of Other World economies into sustained economic growth. A more liberal interpretation of this theory adds that the investment of public funds in physical and human infrastructure is a necessary complement to the private market.

In capitalist economic systems, the primary measure of economic progress used throughout the world is the rate of increase in gross domestic product (GDP, formerly GNP, or gross national product), a quantitative measure that represents the total of all goods and services produced by an economy in a year. In Other World countries pursuing takeoff development strategies, increases in GDP indicate that economic output is expanding and that economic development is taking place.

From a conservative perspective, substantial inequality in the distribution of the wealth created by expanding economic output is viewed as natural, just, and necessary. Human beings are viewed as unequal in essence: The poor are poor because of shortcomings *within themselves*, often considered to stem from race, gender, or class. Efforts to improve substantially their lot are not only futile but unjust in that they take from those at the top of society, who have earned their position through their special talents and virtues and whose unencumbered progress is necessary for human evolution. While life is unavoidably harsh for the poor, the capitalist utopia does promise eventual material abundance for all. In the short run, relative economic prosperity for the weaker members of society can best be achieved by the creation of jobs through the concentration of capital into large-scale industries.

Development and Liberal and Radical Values

Those who hold liberal and radical belief systems take a very different view of the nature and degree of differences among people, which lead to very different definitions of the goals of development and how those goals should be pursued. From this perspective, human beings are considered to be equal in essence: While a certain level of inequality is natural in any society because of relatively minor differences in health, intelligence, and emotional balance, the tremendous inequalities that exist within societies and among countries are viewed as primarily the result of shortcomings *within political and economic processes and institutions*. Julius Nyerere, a former president of Tanzania, captures this idea when he writes that

> even when you have an exceptionally intelligent and hard-working millionaire, the difference between his intelligence, his enterprise, his hard work, and those of other members of society cannot possibly be proportionate to the difference between their "rewards." There must be *something wrong in a society* where one man, however hard-working or clever he may be, can acquire as great a "reward" as a thousand of his fellows can acquire between them.[1]

Whereas liberals and radicals agree on the essential equality of human beings, they differ in their solutions to inequality. Liberals advocate peaceful, step-by-step reforms, often based on programs to redistribute wealth from the rich to the poor and to create more equal opportunities for the poor to compete. Radicals believe that, given the resources commanded by world political and economic elites and the manner in which they control existing political and economic institutions, established powers will always be able to keep ahead of and nullify any reform efforts. They argue that justice and equality for all can be achieved only through the overthrow of established political and economic institutions and the rebuilding of individual societies and the international order.

Whether achieved through evolutionary or revolutionary means, definitions of development put forth by liberals and radicals consistently target egalitarian values as the end toward which development should be directed, emphasizing *freedom from* poverty and exploitation, that is, the use of one's resources or labor without fair compensation. Measures of progress include the degree to which nutrition, health, housing, education, and economic security are available equally to all. Such definitions often include the ideal that society should encourage and facilitate the self-fulfillment and self-realization of all. This ideal is central to the utopia envisioned by Marx, where all would share equally in the resources of society and be free to develop their full potential as human beings. More recent examples carry the same theme: A contemporary writer hopes that "development will become a means to serve people";[2] another argues that "development should be a *struggle* to create criteria, goals, and means for self-liberation from misery, inequity, and dependency of all forms."[3]

As the world is becoming increasingly aware of the devastating and threatening global effects of pollution and resource depletion, environmental goals are being merged with egalitarian values to create concepts such as *eco-development,* or balanced social and environmental development. *Sustainable development* is defined as living within the limits of natural systems while ensuring an adequate standard of living for all, meeting the needs of the present without compromising the ability of future generations to meet their own needs.[4]

Such definitions make a sharp distinction between growth and development. *Growth* is defined as things simply getting bigger, or quantitative increases in economic output. In contrast, *development* is defined as things getting better through qualitative changes, which result in improvements in life for all in harmony and balance with nature. Strategies proposed to pursue such change generally emphasize decentralized efforts controlled by local populations to improve life and habitats at the local level. Supporters are encouraged to "think globally and act locally." *Appropriate technology*, or technology that is suitable to particular applications and needs even when more sophisticated technologies are available, is often a part of such strategies.[5] An example might be the use of 10,000 workers with picks and shovels instead of 10 Caterpillar tractors to build a system of levees to control the flooding of small, family agricultural plots, thus supporting small farmers and workers who might otherwise be unemployed and preserving topsoil that would otherwise be washed away.

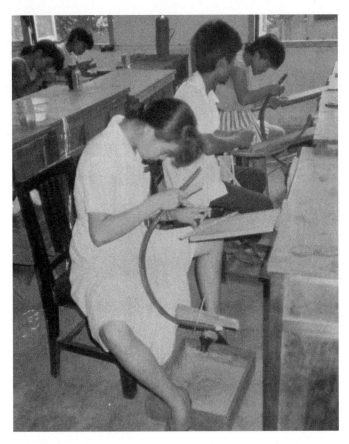

On the Job: Factory Workers Assembling Fans at a Factory in China
SOURCE: Randal Cruikshanks

A HISTORY OF DEVELOPMENT EFFORTS

Competing conservative and liberal or radical value systems gave rise to two different approaches to development after World War II. A few countries, including Cuba, Algeria, Libya, Angola, North Korea, Vietnam, and Cambodia, broke out of the world political and economic order that had been established by the colonial powers and joined the states of the Soviet empire and China to establish development programs ostensibly designed to pursue egalitarian values. With assistance from the major Second World powers, they adopted the ideas and ideals of Marx, Lenin, and Mao to create centralized command economies in which property was communally owned and economic activities were closely orchestrated by socialist and communist party elites.

Most Other World countries remained within the orbit of the old colonial order. With assistance from the Western industrial nations, they adopted development programs grounded in takeoff theory to establish free-market economies guided by capitalist economic policies and practices. Free-market approaches are now coming to dominate most of the world, including the former states of the Soviet bloc and China. To understand the history of development efforts, it is therefore important to explore the ascendancy of the free-market system of international capitalism.

Political Economy and the Ascendancy of International Capitalism

In analyzing political and economic affairs, it is useful to think of politics and economics as closely related, interconnected processes. Before the emergence of classical liberalism from the eighteenth-century writings of John Locke and Adam Smith, politics and economics were in fact studied under the single discipline of *political economy*. The artificial separation of that study into fields of political science and economics has been in large part driven by the assertion that there is no necessary connection between politics and economics. The position is that, under a free-market system, government need only be involved in economic affairs to the extent necessary to provide for defense, protect private property rights, and supply some of the infrastructure for the economy.

Wealth and political power are inseparably linked, however. Governments are integrally involved in the economic affairs of most countries, usually serving the interests of the dominant economic group in society. In communist and fascist systems, governmental and economic institutions are formally fused, and political and economic elites are one and the same. In socialist and capitalist systems, nominal separations between governmental and economic institutions are bridged by informal networks of mutual interests between elites and by "revolving door" mechanisms through which individuals circulate back and forth between institutions. The role of political elites in free-market economies is to maintain conditions within which economic elites have the freedom to pursue their interests with a minimum of interference from other interests in society.

Pause and reflect for a moment on the fundamental connections between political and economic processes apparent in the following standard definitions of politics and economics.

> POLITICS: Who gets what, when, and how
> ECONOMICS: The production, distribution, and use of wealth

The perspective of political economy, which views politics and markets as "in a constant state of mutual interaction,"[6] therefore provides a useful analytical tool.

Immanuel Wallerstein employs the concept of political economy in his study of the system of international capitalism, which he terms the *capitalist world-economy*, which has expanded from its genesis in sixteenth-century Europe to drive much of the politics and economics of the globe today.[7] Tracing that expansion, Wallerstein describes how the pattern of international relations among great world powers ranges on a fluid continuum: At one end, there is an almost even balance among powers of roughly equal strength (a rare and unstable condition); in the middle the powers group into two or more camps, with no side being able to impose its will (the usual state of international affairs); at the other end, a single great power is able to dominate (also a rare and unstable condition). He defines the latter end of the continuum as *hegemony*, or a situation in which one single world power is so dominant that it "can largely impose its rules and its wishes ... in the economic, political, military, diplomatic, and even cultural arenas."[8] Such a condition of hegemony existed when the United Kingdom dominated world affairs from roughly 1815 to 1873 and when the United States came to occupy a similar position of world dominance from 1945 until the early 1970s.

U.S. Hegemony and a New Postwar World Order.   The establishment of a hegemony by the United States at the very same time that programs to develop the Other World were launched had a profound effect on the nature of development efforts and the role and position of Other World states in the international political economy. The United States emerged from World War II as the unchallenged dominant power in the world. It was able to use its power to implement a new world order that was carefully designed to serve its interests and the interests of the other former colonial powers in the capitalist world economy. The foundation for this new order was laid through the Bretton Woods agreements, signed by the Allied powers in 1944.

The Bretton Woods system erected three pillars around which the new order was built. The International Monetary Fund (IMF) was established to further cooperation on monetary matters among the countries of the world. Under IMF guidance, the U.S. dollar became the standard against which the value of other currencies was set, and the United States became the banker for the world. The General Agreement on Tariffs and Trade (GATT) was designed to promote world trade. Periodic trade conferences were scheduled to facilitate negotiations among world trading partners with the goal of maintaining "free" trade through low tariffs on internationally traded goods and services. The International Bank for Reconstruction and Development, or World Bank, which was originally created to facilitate investment in Europe after World War II, turned toward stimulating investment in the Other World.

Early Development Efforts.   With the success of the Marshall Plan to rebuild the economies of Europe and Japan fresh at hand, the Western industrial nations launched a flurry of bilateral and multilateral efforts in the 1960s, which were dubbed the "development decade." The stated intent was to propel Other World economies to a point from which they could take off and achieve self-sustaining growth. John Kenneth Galbraith, a Harvard economics professor who had served as U.S. ambassador to India, published a book in 1964 that aptly described these early development efforts as attempts to copy the institutions and processes of the modern industrial powers. "Development," he observed, "is the faithful imitation of the developed."[9] Galbraith noted three characteristics of these attempts: symbolic modernization, maximized economic growth, and selective growth.

Symbolic modernization gave a developing country the appearance of modernity. Airports and four-lane highways were built, tall buildings were erected, and impressive government offices were constructed. Government leaders flashed the symbols of the industrialized world, as did other segments of society: Men were seen plowing fields with a hand plow but wearing the symbol of modernity—a necktie. No shirt—just a tie: the sign of a Western gentleman.

Efforts to maximize economic growth were directed at increasing economic output as measured by GNP. Growth strategies emphasized large initial capital investments from the World Bank, from private firms located primarily in the industrial nations, and from First World governments, with the goal of establishing industrial bases that could then be expanded. Domestic rates of taxation and savings were set to promote the fastest rate of growth possible.

Some efforts were targeted at building the infrastructure for an industrial society through the strategy of selective growth. A variety of foreign aid programs, many organized under the umbrella of the Development Assistance Committee of the Organization for Economic Cooperation and Development (OECD), were created to address this need. Electric, water, sewer, and communications systems were installed; loans were made to farmers and small businesspersons; and agricultural education and community development activities were initiated. The "green revolution" of the 1960s and 1970s is a good example of a selective growth strategy. Increases in agricultural production were sought to generate funds for industrial expansion through earnings from export crops and to increase the supply of food in Other World countries. Programs were undertaken to encourage the replacement of family-scale farms, which used native seeds, composting, traditional pest-control methods, and hand implements, with large-scale agribusinesses employing hybrid seed strains, fertilizers, pesticides, herbicides, irrigation, and mechanized farm machinery.

Those who conceived of and measured development in terms of increases in economic output were pleased with the results of these early efforts: With some exceptions, development programs were generating dramatic increases in GNP. However, it did not take long for those who had hoped that the development decade would result in a better standard of living for the masses of Other World peoples to realize that the strategies described above were not contributing significantly to that goal. Benefits were accruing primarily to a few, while living conditions for most were not markedly improving; in fact, for some they were actually declining. Along with Galbraith's book, others with titles such as *False Start in Africa*[10] pointed out that the hollow imitation of Western symbols and an emphasis on supply-side economic policies, industrial development, and Western technologies would not result in the kind of economic and social change that would significantly benefit the many. The almost singular emphasis on building an industrial infrastructure and raising GNP meant that basic essentials such as food, housing, and health services were often neglected in favor of exporting minerals and cash crops to earn foreign exchange, much of which was sent back overseas in the form of profits for foreign corporations or spent on importing luxury goods for a burgeoning political and economic elite.

Manpower: A Load of Bricks in Transit to a Construction Site in China
SOURCE: Randal Cruikshanks

A Balance Sheet of Development

We are now in the fourth development decade and thus in a position to evaluate the accomplishments of more than 35 years of sustained development efforts guided by takeoff theory. Advocates of this approach point with satisfaction to statistics that show that Other World GDP per capita has been growing at higher rates than were achieved by the industrial nations in comparable periods of their history, that life expectancy is increasing faster in decades than it did in an entire century in the industrialized world, and that substantial gains have been made in literacy and access to education. Critics point out that while these statistics accurately reflect the fact that conditions have improved in some ways for many and in many ways for some, they hide the true nature of economic processes that have resulted in tremendous disparities within Other World societies and among Other World countries: More than a third are now so poor and economically underdeveloped that they are placed in a special "Fourth World" category in which development seems impossible.

Statistics compiled by the United Nations provide a useful balance sheet of human development progress.[11] Whereas 63 percent of people in the Other World have access to health services, 1.5 billion still lack basic care and do not have safe water and sanitation. Whereas immunization efforts for one-year-olds are saving 1.5 million lives annually, 180 million children under five suffer from malnutrition, and 14 million die each year before reaching their fifth birthday. Whereas income per household head grew 4 percent annually in the 1980s, more than 1 billion people live in extreme poverty, and income is actually declining in large parts of the world. After completing a similar evaluation in which he notes that there were more people living in absolute poverty in 1987 than in 1960, Paul Harrison concludes that

> this balance-sheet can only be read as progress if one abstracts from the human realities. In terms of concrete individual experience, there is a greater absolute quantity of human suffering in the world today than ever before, and all the indications are that it will increase as we approach the millennium. For all the talk and all the action about development, *virtually no progress has been made in the task of eliminating absolute poverty; indeed, there has been gradual regress.*[12]

Harrison's comments parallel those of an Egyptian who once commented that the overall effect of development efforts in Egypt was that more people now lived longer in greater misery.

The links among poverty, security, and population growth are important in understanding this increase in absolute poverty. Poverty and fertility rates are directly related: The higher the degree of poverty in a society, the higher the rate of population increase. The instinct to survive dictates that poor families have more children than wealthier families for very practical economic reasons: Children are a source of security for those living at the margins of survival. More children mean more hands to help with the difficult tasks of eking a living out of a subsistence environment; a working child can contribute to household resources by age 6, and produce more than she or he consumes by age 12. More children increase the probability that one of them might be fortunate enough to secure an education, a rare job, and cash earnings to contribute to the family. More children mean a greater likelihood that someone will be around to help when old age makes it impossible to survive on one's own. High infant and childhood mortality rates mean that the odds of accomplishing all of these objectives are improved by having enough children to replace those who die young.

In transferring much of the wealth of the Other World to the industrialized nations, the forces of colonialism and neocolonialism have substantially contributed to the poverty that is fueling rapid population increases in the Other World. These global shifts in wealth and family security have also contributed to declining fertility rates in the First World. Population policies that address fundamental issues of family security, rather than simply encouraging or enforcing birth control, are the surest way to reduce rates of population growth.

The manner in which the international political economy produces and distributes wealth is well illustrated by the production and distribution of world food resources. If the wheat, rice, and other grains produced throughout the world were distributed equally to all the world's peoples, each individual would receive 3,600 calories per day, well above the average U.S. recommended daily allowances of 2,700 calories for adult males, 2,000 for adult females, and 1,300–3,000 for teenagers. Yet 22 million people die every year from starvation, and 1 billion do not have enough to eat. The typical Western family of four consumes more grain (directly and indirectly in the form of meat) than a poor Indian family of 20.[13]

India, where over a third of the world's hungry people live, is one of the top cash crop exporters in the Other World. The "green revolution" was instrumental in boosting India and a number of other countries to the status of agricultural exporters. However, the benefits of increased agricultural production in those countries have often accrued to those wealthy farmers who could obtain bank loans to purchase the large irrigated farms; mechanized equipment; and expensive seeds, fertilizers, pesticides, and herbicides required for green revolution agriculture. Many poor farmers in these countries have in the process been displaced, driven to marginal dryland plots or the cities, where they are unable to afford the food now produced through expensive farming methods on the lands they once tilled.

Similar consequences have resulted from the acquisition of Other World farmlands by multinational corporations based in the industrialized world. In Brazil, for example, foreign-owned companies, some with holdings in the millions of acres, have displaced Brazilian farmers and shifted the emphasis of agricultural production to export products such as soybeans and beef for fast-food restaurants in the First World. These shifts have created a shortage of black beans, the staple in the diet of Brazil's poor, with a resulting increase in malnutrition.[14]

Brazil provides an especially illustrative example of the balance sheet generated by an economic development process driven by the singular pursuit of increased economic production. In 1964, a military coup established a new government that opened the country to foreign investment by providing an array of attractive incentives and freedoms. In the following ten years, which became known as "the Brazilian economic miracle," the country's GNP tripled, and Brazilian executives became for a time the highest paid in the world. Meanwhile, the real income of 80 percent of the population declined; the production of basic necessities such as food, clothing, and housing remained stagnant; and Brazil's infant mortality rate became the second highest in Latin America. Foreign-owned corporations gained control of 100 percent of Brazil's tire and rubber production, 95 percent of its automobile production, and 80 percent of its television and radio industry (while 60 Brazilian electronics firms were driven out of business or taken over by foreign firms). Surveying these statistics, a group of Catholic bishops and clerics issued a statement on the condition of the Brazilian people in 1975, concluding that

> the Brazilian miracle has resulted in privileges for the wealthy. It has come as a curse upon those who have not asked for it. The rich become always richer and the poor always poorer in this process of economic concentration. Far from being the inevitable result of natural deficiencies, this tragedy is the consequence of international capitalism. Development came to be defined not in terms of the interests of Brazilian society, but in terms of the profits made by foreign corporations and their associates in our country.[15]

Mexico's more recent "economic miracle" repeats the same pattern. By the early 1990s, strong economic growth had resulted in a dramatic concentration of wealth and a widening gap between the rich and the poor: While 92.4 percent of the population earns less than 5,700 U.S. dollars per year, the top of Mexico's socioeconomic hierarchy is now occupied by seven Mexican billionaires, more than in Britain or Saudi Arabia. And the Mexican government has signed a free-trade agreement with the United States and Canada that is encouraging a flood of foreign investment and ownership in the country.

Understanding the Balance Sheet

The preceding balance sheet is not difficult to understand if one considers that the roots of capitalism lie in conservative value systems. Development based on takeoff theory has primarily benefited the strong because it is intended to do so; the accounting system of the capitalist world economy prioritizes individual gain, not egalitarian values. The history of Other World development is consistent with the 400-year trend of capitalism—an ever-increasing concentration of wealth in the hands of a few, much of which is spent on luxury consumption and speculation rather than being reinvested in any industrial infrastructure that might significantly benefit the many in either the short or the long run.

Through an analysis known as *dependency theory*, liberals and radicals in fact argue that, given the position of the Other World in the international political economy, development that would substantially improve the lives of a majority of the Other World's peoples is unlikely to occur at all. They point out that the designation "Third" World is an accurate description of that position: Although there is really only *one* world of political economy, with all the world's states linked in various fashions to the whole, most of the countries of Africa, Asia, and Latin America occupy tertiary positions on the periphery of the dominant political and economic order. Their primary function, as it was under formal colonialism, is to provide raw materials and cheap labor for the industrialized powers. Other World countries are now dominated by structures of neocolonialism that differ little in substance from the colonialism of the past.

From the perspective of dependency theorists, Other World political systems are particularly dependent on the Western industrial powers. Neocolonialism operates through the collusion of Other World political elites, who have been coopted into serving foreign interests. Independence means only that political institutions originally established to facilitate and enforce the extraction of wealth from the Other World are now occupied by African, Asian, and Latin American politicians and bureaucrats instead of by expatriate colonial officials. These new elites serve as "brokers," managing the flow of resources from their countries in return for brokerage fees (or commissions) in the form of foreign aid and other payoffs, which they use to maintain their positions of political control and to build their personal fortunes.

The rule of many Other World political elites in the neocolonial era constitutes a contemporary mercantilism in which national political economies are operated to increase the wealth of the rulers.[16] The widespread corruption, or the use of public office for private gain, that pervades Other World politics is a key factor in explaining why the development programs of many countries have done little to improve the lot of the masses. Much of the political instability endemic to Other World political systems stems from the fact that governments operated openly for private gain (or *kleptocracies*) have very little legitimacy among, or acceptance by, a significant proportion of the population, in neocolonial times as in the past.

Perhaps more difficult to understand is the fact that those countries that have followed communist and socialist development strategies have been only a little more successful in accomplishing egalitarian goals and probably less successful in preserving the natural environment. The inequalities that have developed in these states, although less dramatic than those in the capitalist world, indicate that the tendency of the powerful to serve their self-interests is not unique to capitalism. Economic growth and social inequality is a common pattern, with increases in economic output accompanied by increasing inequality throughout history.[17] The 400-year history of capitalism is an extension of a trend that began 6,000 years ago when humankind first established urban-based civilizations capable of creating wealth in surplus of the resources needed for human survival, a trend accelerated 2,000 years ago when Western civilization emerged in the Greek city-states and legitimized the value of individualistic materialism. While an appreciation of capitalist ideology helps one understand the particular details of the process through which development has come to benefit primarily a few in the capitalist world economy, one must go beyond the level of ideology to the underlying realities of politics, power, and self-interest to understand the universal links between increased economic output and greater inequality.

BEYOND IDEOLOGY: POLITICS, POWER, AND SELF-INTEREST

Politics is commonly defined as the authoritative allocation of scarce values, or who gets what, when, and how. The political process, in other words, determines how those things that people value most (such as survival, wealth, and status) are distributed among a society's, or the world's, peoples. Analysts of the political process have long noted that *power* is the primary factor that determines who gets what, when, and how; an even more concise definition of politics is that it is simply the exercise of power. Power, in turn, is defined as the capacity to control other people's behavior.

There are three types of power: violence, knowledge, and authority. In conflict over the allocation of those things that people value, violence is the most fundamental form of power: Most people place a high premium on avoiding pain and on survival, and the only appeal to the use of violence is violence itself. As Thomas Hobbes observed, when nothing else is turned up, clubs are trumps. However, there are limits on the use of violence to maintain political control: Coercion is expensive, violence tends to escalate, and people will not tolerate rule by violence indefinitely. To maintain their regimes over time, political elites must base their rule more on knowledge and authority.

Most political elites attempt to rule through authority, an institutionalized form of power based on the claim that government has the legitimate right to rule. However, the authority of government ultimately derives from its ability to control the forces of violence in society. *Government* is defined as the institution that has the *enforceable* right to control people's behavior. In determining the allocation of scarce values, laws are actually a form of sublimated violence through which the decisions of government are backed by the ability to enforce dictates with a court system and police and military forces. Governments that last over time also derive much of their power from the control of knowledge. Elites use knowledge power both to control what people know and to create and manipulate images and ideologies that they want people to believe. As noted by Niccolo Machiavelli, the rule of lions must give way to the rule of foxes.

Analysts of the political process have also long noted that self-interest is the driving force, or the engine, of government. Those with political power strive to advance their personal interests, serving broader community interests only to the extent necessary to maintain their positions of control. Closely related is the observation that power corrupts, and that absolute power corrupts absolutely.

The logic of the preceding definitions and observations carries one directly to the conclusion that all governments are *oligarchies*, or political systems controlled by a few to further their self-interests. Governments serve political elites either directly, as in communism and fascism, or indirectly through payoffs derived from serving the interests of economic elites, as in socialism and capitalism. If power determines who gets what and if power corrupts, then there is a natural human tendency for those in control of government to use its institutions and processes for personal gain.

It is on this basis that increases in economic output, in Mesopotamia or ancient Greece or the Other World of the post–World War II era, go primarily to those groups within a society, and to those states within the international political economy, that are able to control the forces of violence and the institutions and policies that determine the distribution of that output. At this level of analysis, ideologies primarily represent efforts by political elites to use knowledge power to convince the public that the government is being operated in the public interest. While ideologies are useful in defining the goals and values that people of various persuasions believe *should* be served by development, they are relatively insignificant in determining political realities. The actual outputs of governments operating with "competing" ideologies are only marginally different; in this context, one can appreciate the observation that while under capitalism man exploits man, under communism it's the other way around.

CONCLUSIONS

The peoples of the Other World face difficult times in the coming years. The internal affairs of many Other World countries are coming increasingly under the direct control of IMF officials, who are imposing *structural adjustment programs* that change domestic spending patterns to make possible repayments on enormous debts owed to First World financial institutions. These changes often include cuts in health, education, and other social service programs. Much of this debt was incurred during the oil shortages of the 1970s and grew with a rise in interest rates in the 1980s. In African countries, this debt typically amounts to five times annual export income. At the end of 1990, Latin American countries had over $423 billion in long-term loans outstanding and had paid out one-fourth of their export receipts in debt repayments, some of which did not even cover interest due. *Privatization programs*, which transfer the control of government services to private, for-profit firms, are further loosening the thin ties that link public resources to public needs.

Power vacuums resulting from the end of the cold war are contributing to spiraling levels of violence in many parts of the Other World. In the decades preceding the fall of the Soviet empire, both the United States and the Soviet Union delivered a substantial portion of their foreign aid in the form of military assistance. Other World dictators who were willing to wave one flag or another as clients in the ideological contest between capitalism and communism, sometimes adroitly playing one side off against the other, amassed enormous military capabilities. With the cold war balance of power now ended, stockpiles of weapons are fueling disastrous conflicts between and within Other World states. This factor played prominently in the 1990 invasion of Kuwait by Iraq and in bloody civil wars and anarchy in Somalia in 1992 and in Rwanda in 1994.[18]

Most of the peoples of the Other World, along with those of the First World and the former Second World, are also threatened by the emergence of a new, transnational world order. Colin Leys defines this new order as one dominated by multinational corporations, regulated by the IMF, and enforced by the awesome power of U.S. military might.[19] Transnationalism represents a new kind of international regime in which the economic interests of multinational actors are coming to supersede the interests and the powers of individual states. National boundaries, and national loyalties, are of little significance in a global economy driven by the ceaseless pursuit of profit. And in a coming age of postindustrial production, the demand (and compensation) for labor is predicted to decline as a transnational elite seeks custom, designer goods made by specialized producers hired at the lowest wage rates possible from a global labor pool, rather than the standardized products of the mass assembly lines that have provided employment to many in the past.

Riccardo Petrella, a futurist for the European Union, describes how the forces of transnationalism are separating all the world's peoples into two classes that cut across national boundaries. Divided into the "fast" and the "slow" on the basis of access to computer and satellite technologies, a global upperclass of the affluent and privileged living in a high-tech archipelago of hyper-developed, walled, and gated city-regions is emerging among a global underclass left to fend for itself in a disintegrating social and environmental wasteland.[20]

The Politics of Change

Those who hold conservative values can find much to be encouraged by in contemporary global trends. Transnationalism heralds a global class apartheid in which the strong are free to pursue their interests unencumbered by any sense of connection with or responsibility to the social commonwealth or the environmental commons. In contrast, those who prefer a different future face tremendous challenges. As noted above, power is the primary factor that determines who gets what, when, and how in the world, and it is power that will ultimately determine whether development processes will continue to be dominated by the goals and values of the capitalist world economy or by alternatives embodied in concepts such as eco-development.

The qualitative changes in societies and in the international political economy necessary to achieve development that would serve egalitarian and environmental values are vast in range and scale. The range of change would have to include political, economic, and social processes and institutions, for all of these aspects of human organization are inseparably linked. Within this web of interconnections, it is impossible to separate economic development from political development or social development; improvements in the economic conditions of the less powerful could be achieved only through parallel improvements in their political and social conditions. The scale of change would have to be fundamental, for the processes and institutions that currently determine the use and allocation of the world's resources are deeply and firmly entrenched. Changes of this extent would require radical transformations in the power relationships that hold these systems together.

As we approach the edge of the twenty-first century, there are signs that the centralized Western power structures that have long dominated our affairs are beginning to crumble under the pressure of converging crises of overpopulation, environmental destruction, resource scarcity, economic discontinuity, and sociopolitical decay. These crises may create opportunities for change in chaos not present in more stable times. As the Chinese have long noted, when there is great disorder under the heavens, the opportunities for change are excellent.

Noting the speed with which we are approaching global limits of social and environmental sustainability, a group of 1,670 leading world scientists recently issued a "warning to humanity," which urged that we have no more than a few decades to reverse trends that are carrying us toward "spirals of environmental decline, poverty and unrest leading to social, economic and environmental collapse."[21] E. F. Schumacher observes that whereas some have challenged the ethic of materialism and argued for different priorities throughout history, "Today, however, this message reaches us not solely from the sages and saints but from the actual course of physical events. It speaks to us in the language of terrorism, genocide, breakdown, pollution, exhaustion."[22] Samuel Huntington hypothesizes a resurgence of Confucian, Japanese, Islamic, Hindu, Slavic-Orthodox, Latin American, and African civilizations against a Western civilization now at the peak of its power and global intrusiveness.[23] And Alvin Toffler argues that we are at one of the greatest turning points in history as breakdown and exhaustion in health, education, transportation, welfare, urban, and ecological systems converge to challenge the centralized power structures that control our societies.[24]

The peaceful revolutions against authoritarian rule that swept the Soviet Union and Eastern Europe at the end of the 1980s provide tantalizing support for these theses, as do mounting signs of institutional collapse and widespread public disenchantment in the Western industrial nations. Significantly, so do democratization and local autonomy movements that are erupting across the Other World, fueled by the irrepressible force of global mass communications.

Changing power relations could provide those who envision development as a way to serve people and to create the means for self-liberation with opportunities in the coming years that seemed impossible in the past. If the information technologies that are elevating knowledge to a position as the dominant source of power were dispersed among the world's masses, the resulting diffusion of power could result in the first true democracies the world has ever known. If the new technologies are controlled by a few, we could be plunged into a new Dark Age of Orwellian proportions. In the coming decades it is likely that those who control knowledge and the technologies of knowledge will also control wealth, violence, and the institutions of government.

As we proceed through a time of pivotal change in human affairs, the individual actions of each of us will count more than at any time in previous years. For we are all participants, whether as consumers, investors, or political activists, in the international political economy that we share with the peoples of the Other World. Our common future depends on our common efforts to build a more sustainable world.

SUMMARY

Other World international relations and domestic affairs have been dominated since the end of World War II by a concern with development. Driven primarily by the capitalist world economy, development programs guided by takeoff theory have resulted in significant increases in GNP/GDP and improvements in the lives of some Other World peoples; they have also contributed to increasing inequality and growing numbers of people living in absolute poverty. Whereas takeoff theorists attribute these problems to the necessities of progress, dependency theorists view them as the result of the exploitation of the Other World by the industrial powers and Other World political elites through structures of neocolonialism. Advocates of both schools ground their positions in political ideologies that express fundamental beliefs and values about the way the world should be.

Powerful world trends in the 1990s indicate that takeoff strategies, now in the form of transnationalism, are likely to continue to prevail as the dominant approach to Other World development, with direct implications for increasing inequality, poverty, and environmental decline and resulting in increasing levels of political, economic, and social instability. Other trends indicate the possibility of changes in power relations that could make possible development designed to promote egalitarian and environmental values. We are living at a pivotal time of convergence in human affairs that will have fundamental consequences for the future of the global community we inhabit with the peoples of the Other World.

ISSUES FOR DISCUSSION

1. Can you refute the Doctrine of Thrasymachus?

The Doctrine of Thrasymachus consists of two reinforcing parts. Part I states that it is the natural right of the strong to take more than their equal share of what the world has to offer. This is a philosophical statement, or one that addresses what is considered to be right and wrong, good and bad. Here Thrasymachus asserts the unbridled right of the strong to take from the weak, drawing on their physical strength, superior intelligence, or any other attribute that would enable them to overpower others. Any means imaginable, including violence and fraud, is morally justified. Part II states that might makes right. Here Thrasymachus addresses how the strong use government to serve their interests by writing and enforcing laws that work to their advantage. The idea that whatever the mighty say is right is right underlies the concept of relative justice—whatever the strong say is just is just, with some laws legitimately applied unequally to different citizens and some laws legitimately applied only to certain groups. For Thrasymachus, justice is whatever is in the interests of the strong.

Liberty, or the freedom to pursue one's interests without constraint, and equality, or freedom from relative poverty and exploitation, are conflicting values; a society cannot encourage one without sacrificing the other. On the one hand, if citizens are free to pursue private interests without constraint, some will invariably take advantage of others, creating greater inequality in society; on the other hand, efforts to build more egalitarian social orders can only be pursued by restraining personal liberty. The ideas expressed in the Doctrine of Thrasymachus are thus among the most significant in the history of political thinking in that they so unequivocally proclaim the value of liberty. They take us to the core of one of the central dilemmas of political organization: Government policies that restrain liberty stifle initiative, whereas policies that encourage liberty result in exploitation. As the basis for the conservative ideas and ideals that provide the foundations of capitalism, takeoff theory, and the ethic of transnationalism, they also take us to the heart of what development should be and can be about.

If Thrasymachus is right, it follows that all governments are oligarchies, or political systems operated by a few to serve their interests. While most claim to have been created by God to serve the people, such claims are part of the fraud perpetuated by elites to hide the fact that government is in fact designed to serve the interests of the strong. If the political institutions that control peoples' behavior to allocate societies' scarce values are operated by a few to serve their interests, it further follows that what we call "civilized" life rests on the exploitation of the weak.

Attempts to refute or support the ideas expressed by Thrasymachus are central to political philosophy. Can you refute the Doctrine of Thrasymachus? If so, how? If not, why not? Consider your response from both normative and empirical perspectives: normative analysis is concerned with what should be, or with moral judgments of right and wrong; empirical analysis is concerned with what is, or the way things are in actual fact.

2. Does inequality always cause political instability?

The ancient Greeks (Plato and Aristotle in particular) believed that to ensure stability in a society, the rich should have no more than five times the wealth of the poorest of the poor. Further, they believed that reproduction should be restricted to hold down population growth, thus avoiding widespread poverty.

Inequality is commonly measured by comparing income levels of the upper one-fifth of the population against those of the bottom one-fifth—the rich against the poor. Will the bottom one-fifth revolt against the highest one-fifth? Worldwide, almost 1 billion people live on less than one dollar a day—most of these in the poorest of the developing countries. Since the 1950s, analyses of relative incomes show that the poor have made little progress. In some countries, only a handful of people can be considered rich; the others live at a mere subsistence level. In many countries of South America and Africa, real per capita income fell dramatically over the last ten years and debt increased.

Industrialization has brought wealth to many Other World countries, particularly Argentina, Brazil, Hong Kong, Mexico, Singapore, South Korea, and Taiwan. Class struggles without broadscale revolution are evident in these places, where the wealth has been concentrated in the top 20 percent of the population.

The largest gap between the rich and the poor is in Brazil, where the top 20 percent earn 33 times more income than the bottom 20 percent. In Mexico, the wealthiest 20 percent earn 20 times more than the poorest. Internationally, the United States ranks between the Philippines and Egypt, with the richest earning 9 times more than the poorest. In most of the industrialized nations, the richest earn 4 or 5 times more, meaning that the United States is decidedly "Other World" in terms of income inequality.

If the ancient Greeks were correct that inequality causes revolution, we should expect more wars and rebellions in the Other World. Indeed, more than 40 wars are being fought today. Excessive aggression and cultural rivalries are often cited as the causes of war; however, underlying these behaviors is often economic deprivation. How can these inequities be resolved? If resolved, would peace and political stability result?

3. What is the impact of new communication technology on future Other World development?

According to takeoff theory, development is centered on economic growth. Economic growth, in turn, rests on harnessing technology to increase productivity. Increases in productivity provide an important measurement in determining the progress of development efforts. Today, the technologies originating in the former Soviet Union and in the Western world are quickly taken up in the Other World. Auto, rail, and air transportation has increased, but not without costs of infrastructure design and pollution. Electrification and nuclear energy projects are undertaken, sometimes at the expense of more critical activities such as the provision of clean water and of land to grow family crops. Medical technologies are newly available, often only for the rich.

However, the growing use of telephones, fax, computer networks, television, and radio has begun to be noticed as implements of economic, social, and political change. Now military upstarts in Mexico can monitor the national army's movements and avoid an ambush. Revolutionaries in Beijing can attract Western sympathy by alerting the world through multimedia coverage of obstacles to a free society. And trade talks can accelerate as leaders communicate by international telephone conversations and Internet conferences.

The availability of fast, relatively cheap, and accessible portable computers together with phone and fax capabilities has the potential of contributing to rapid institutional change—economic, social, and political. Will the industrialized nations continue to exploit less developed nations in this new informational environment? Will technological penetration into the Other World lessen technological dependence and cultural imperialism? Will multinational corporations become more important agents of development than strong nations? What global controls and restrictions will be established to control new technologies?

4. How can you best protect yourself in a transnational world order?

The world orders of colonialism and neocolonialism were generally good to the U.S. middle class. Factories that processed materials drawn from around the world provided high-paying jobs with benefits to generations of workers, spawned a range of support jobs in the professions and the retail and service industries, and provided part of the tax base that built and maintained the country's infrastructure. The new world order of transnationalism is not so kind. Trends toward the specialized production of custom goods by firms with sites around the world, and with loyalty only to corporate profits, mean that U.S. citizens are increasingly competing in a global labor pool for fewer jobs that pay lower wages with few or no benefits.

Over the past 20 years, transnationalism has accounted for the shift of millions of U.S. jobs abroad as multinational firms located in the United States pursue greater profits by saving on labor, plant, and environmental compliance costs. While many of these jobs have been in the garment and automobile assembly industries, they cover the full spectrum of skills and salaries. For example, major U.S.-based computer software companies that pay up to $60,000 per year for top-of-the-line software engineers in Houston can now hire equally well-qualified engineers in China for $6,000 per year; computer-based satellite communications networks make it possible to link employees from around the world in a global virtual worksite, with full and immediate access to any software or hardware tools needed on the job.

The trend toward a hyperaffluent upperclass progressively separated from a growing underclass is well underway in the United States. Two decades of changes in tax, investment, and trade laws have resulted in a greater redistribution of wealth from the middle and lower classes to the rich than at any time in the country's, and probably the world's, history. Steady economic growth has fueled tremendous financial gains for the wealthiest 5 percent of the population while the standard of living of most has declined, despite efforts by mothers entering the workforce to compensate for falling household income. The take-home pay of full-time workers declined by 20 percent over the past 20 years, and the percentage of full-time workers with benefit plans dropped from 84 percent in

1982 to 56 percent in 1995. Of the 20 million jobs created in the United States between 1983 and 1993, 50 percent pay less than $20,000 per year, and 28 percent pay less than $13,000.

The United States is also heavily involved in its own structural adjustment program as public funds that formerly supported public services and infrastructure are being diverted to pay the country's debt. As a part of these readjustments, cuts in public funding for education are resulting in skyrocketing increases in college fees: In California's colleges and universities, fees increased 113 percent between 1990 and 1994. And the average income of the families that send their sons and daughters to college is rising as cuts in financial aid mean that students from lower-income families are unable to attend.

If current trends continue, it is clear that many in today's college-age generation will not be able to enjoy a quality of life as high as that of their parents. For many in the United States and the Other World, transnationalism is likely to mean a declining standard of living.

How can you best protect yourself in a transnational order? Keep in mind that power ultimately determines who gets what in the political process and that the primary sources of power are violence, wealth, and knowledge. What kind of power do you have most access to, and how could you best develop and use it?

5. Do you owe posterity a sustainable world?

It is estimated that the human species has been on the planet for some 4.5 million years. For the bulk of that time, we had little effect on the natural environment, as our hunting and gathering activities caused only slight disturbances in the self-regulating natural ecologies that we inhabited. We began concerted and determined efforts to dominate and control the environment to serve human ends 6,000 years ago with the first urban-based civilizations, and we have since been so successful that our technologies are now overwhelming the natural systems that we evolved with and upon which we depend for our survival. Our impact has become so substantial that we have damaged many of the self-regulating and self-balancing mechanisms that controlled the natural world, creating disturbed ecosystems that can be kept from chaos and collapse only through constant human intervention and manipulation.

Many in the scientific community are now questioning our ability to maintain the necessary balances and equilibriums. The cumulative and long-term effects of pollution, resource depletion, and species and habitat losses seem to be so significantly altering the living world that doubts are being raised about our ability to sustain life as we know it. Unless we dramatically change our stewardship of the earth, it is projected that our environment will become so irretrievably mutilated over the coming decades that future generations will suffer vast misery and eventual extinction.

In response, some ask, "So what? Why should we care? What has posterity ever done for me?" At its extreme, the ethic of transnationalism in fact includes a nihilistic view that the planet is already so overburdened with population and pollution problems that it is beyond saving and that we should therefore live life to the hilt in the time we have remaining. This view provides another rationalization for the short-term greed that is driving the contemporary global economy.

Do you owe posterity a sustainable world? If not, why not? If so, on what is this obligation based? Exactly what are you willing to give up in your current life-style and levels of consumption to make life tolerable and possible for future generations?

NOTES

1. Julius K. Nyerere, *Ujamaa: Essays on Socialism* (Nairobi: Oxford University Press, 1968), pp. 2–3.
2. Charles K. Wilber, ed., *The Political Economy of Development and Underdevelopment* (New York: Random House, 1988), p. 25.
3. James J. Lamb, "The Third World and the Development Debate," *IDOC-North America*, January–February 1973, p. 20.
4. See "The Cocoyoc Declaration," Adopted by Participants in the UNEP/UNCTAD Symposium on Patterns of Resource Use, Environment and Development Strategies, Cocoyoc, Mexico, October 8–12, 1974. Reprinted in *International Organization*, 29, 3 (Summer 1975): 893–901; Lester Brown et al., *State of the World 1991: A Worldwatch Institute Report on Progress toward a Sustainable Society* (New York: Norton, 1991); Jim MacNeill, Pieter Winsemius, and Taizo Yakushiji, *Beyond Interdependence: The Meshing of the World's Economy and the Earth's Ecology* (New York: Oxford University Press, 1991); and World Commission on Environment and Development, *Our Common Future* (New York: Oxford University Press, 1987).
5. See E. F. Schumacher, *Small Is Beautiful: Economics as if People Mattered* (New York: Harper & Row, 1973).
6. Jeffrey A. Freiden and David A. Lake, *International Political Economy: Perspectives on Global Power and Wealth* (New York: St. Martin's Press, 1987), p. 1.
7. Immanuel Wallerstein, "The Three Instances of Hegemony in the History of the Capitalist World-Economy," in *International Political Economy: A Reader*, ed. Kendall W. Stiles and Tsuneo Akaha (New York: HarperCollins, 1991), pp. 427–435.
8. Ibid., p. 428.
9. John Kenneth Galbraith, *Economic Development* (New York: Houghton Mifflin, 1964), p. 3.
10. Rene Dumont, *False Start in Africa* (New York: Praeger, 1969).
11. United Nations Development Programme, *Human Development Report 1991* (New York: Oxford University Press, 1991), pp. 24–25.
12. Paul Harrison, *Inside the Third World: The Anatomy of Poverty* (London: Penguin Books, 1990), pp. 465–466 (emphasis in the original).
13. Ibid., p. 276.
14. *Controlling Interest: The World of the Multinational Corporation* (San Francisco: California Newsreel, 1978).
15. Ibid.
16. Robert H. Jackson and Carl G. Rosberg, "The Political Economy of African Personal Rule," in *Political Development and the New Realism in Sub-Saharan Africa*, ed. David E. Apter and Carl G. Rosberg (Charlottesville: University Press of Virginia, 1994), p. 292.
17. Gerhard E. Lenksi, *Power and Privilege: A Theory of Social Stratification* (New York: McGraw-Hill, 1966).

18. See Robert D. Kaplan, "The Coming Anarchy," *This World*, March 13, 1994, pp. 5–10.
19. Colin Leys, "Learning from the Kenya Debate," in Apter and Rosberg, *Political Development*, p. 227.
20. Riccardo Petrella, "Techno-apartheid for a Global Underclass," *Los Angeles Times*, August 6, 1992, p. D6.
21. Union of Concerned Scientists, *World Scientists' Warning Briefing Book* (Cambridge, Mass.: Union of Concerned Scientists, 1993), p. 4.
22. Schumacher, *Small Is Beautiful*, pp. 293–294.
23. Samuel P. Huntington, "The Clash of Civilizations?" *Foreign Affairs*, 72, 3 (Summer 1993): 22–49.
24. Alvin Toffler, *Powershift: Knowledge, Wealth, and Violence at the Edge of the 21st Century* (New York: Bantam Books, 1990).

FOR FURTHER READING

Apter, David E., and Rosberg, Carl G., eds. *Political Development and the New Realism in Sub-Saharan Africa*. Charlottesville: University Press of Virginia, 1994.

Brown, Lester R., et al. *State of the World 1996: A Worldwatch Institute Report on Progress toward a Sustainable Society*. New York: Norton, 1996.

Clapham, Christopher. *Third World Politics: An Introduction*. Madison: University of Wisconsin Press, 1985.

Harrison, Paul. *Inside the Third World: The Anatomy of Poverty*. London: Penguin Books, 1990.

Lenksi, Gerhard E. *Power and Privilege: A Theory of Social Stratification*. New York: McGraw-Hill, 1966.

MacNeill, Jim, Winsemius, Pieter, and Yakushiji, Taizo. *Beyond Interdependence: The Meshing of the World's Economy and the Earth's Ecology*. New York: Oxford Universiity Press, 1991.

Schumacher, E.F. *Small Is Beautiful: Economics as if People Mattered*. New York: Harper & Row, 1973.

Stiles, Kendall W., and Akaha, Tsuneo, eds. *International Political Economy: A Reader.* New York: HarperCollins, 1991.

Toffler, Alvin. *Powershift: Knowledge, Wealth, and Violence at the Edge of the 21st Century*. New York: Bantam Books, 1990.

Trainer, Ted. *Developed to Death: Rethinking Third World Development*. London: Merlin Press, 1989.

Union of Concerned Scientists. *World Scientists' Warning Briefing Book*. Cambridge, Mass. Union of Concerned Scientists, 1993.

World Commission on Environment and Development. *Our Common Future*. New York: Oxford University Press, 1987.

CHAPTER **4**

Conflict Resolution and the Other World

Randal L. Cruikshanks

> *Considering the circumstances in which the country finds itself, the most conservative thing is to be a revolutionary.*
> Francisco Cambó (Spanish politician, nineteenth century)
>
> *People with appetites for laws or sausages should watch neither being made.*
> Otto von Bismarck (German chancellor, nineteenth century)

Conflict exists everywhere—from playgrounds to the highest levels of government—because individuals, groups, and countries have different goals and interests that collide. Pursuing those goals produces varying degrees of friction, which result in domestic conflict within countries and international conflict between countries. Despite utopian hopes, nothing so far has succeeded in eliminating conflict, leaving the option of trying to control it by political institutions and processes or allowing it to escalate into domestic and international violence.

This chapter examines conflicts involving the Other World and how they are approached. It is intended to serve as a link to the flashpoint sections in chapters 5 through 8 and to the larger problem of conflict resolution at the domestic and international levels. For this discussion several general concepts need to be introduced. First, conflict involves disputes between two or more parties. Second, politics can be viewed as a conflict-resolving process: It involves engagement between two or more contending parties and resolves disputes according to rules and principles. Political conflict involves disputes over power, public policy, and its goals and directions. They are usually resolved by a process of compromise and bargaining. If successful, political solutions produce results that disputants have an interest or stake in supporting. In this process, each side must gain enough of what it wants if the compromise is to work. Rarely can either side get everything it wants.

Sometimes, leaders do not choose political solutions to either domestic or international disputes. Some leaders are unpracticed in or skeptical about the effectiveness of that approach, and others do not want to risk being forced to make an unacceptable compromise on issues of great moral or other importance. For example, traditional leaders may themselves act as arbiters of internal disputes and apply positive or negative sanctions—rewards or punishments. Religious societies may rely on the word of their god or select mediators between god and the people to resolve disputes. Successful political conflict resolution is nonviolent, nonabsolute, and secular. Ideally, participation is available to people of different races, religions, and political persuasions within a state's boundaries. Although this neutral system can work in varying degrees in functioning democracies, its adaptability to traditional societies is still problematic. Iran's retreat to its own culture after the Shah's autocratic attempt to modernize and Westernize the country during the "White Revolution" in the 1970s is a case in point. Iranians, led by fundamentalist Muslims, replaced the Shah's government with one pledged to follow more traditional religious principles.

All countries have political institutions for making public policy. Democracies have some combination of formalized institutions like courts, legislatures, and political parties, each with specialized functions. These institutions have become integral parts of the way in which people think about government and authority—*their* political culture.

History has shown that institutions cannot be readily transplanted intact from one culture to another. Oddly, neither the old colonial powers nor the communists during Soviet expansionism seemed to learn that lesson. In retrospect, it would be just as unlikely for Americans or Russians, with two very different cultures, to incorporate successfully Middle Eastern political principles into their systems as it would be for them to expect the Iranians or the Libyans to adopt theirs. Nevertheless, demands for democracy, freedom, and justice are sweeping the world as never before, whether by minorities in the United States, blacks in South Africa, or political protesters in China. Solving this dilemma country by country will be one of the biggest tasks facing Other World countries as they enter the twenty-first century. It will mean evolving their own political cultures that can support democratic processes tailored to their own values and needs. It will also involve major risks: Democracy is by no means certain to succeed.

For domestic political institutions to resolve conflict effectively, they must be perceived as legitimate and national in scope. Institutions are considered legitimate if most people voluntarily comply with the outcomes of the disputes they mediate; they are national in scope if they affect people equally in the capital cities and in the remotest corners of their furthermost provinces. These are also indexes of a government's authority.

The ability of government institutions to resolve conflict depends on several complex factors. Among the most important are political culture, political institutions, and consensus. *Political culture* consists of citizens' beliefs and attitudes about government, authority, and political participation. *Political institutions* are structures and organizations, both governmental and nongovernmental, involved in making public policy and attempting to resolve conflict. The *political process* is the dynamic that makes them work. *Consensus* is the extent to which there is agreement, at least among the majority, about basic political principles, institutions, and processes. The success of public policy is the result of its public acceptance

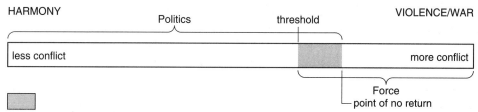

Zone of uncertainty: Intensity of conflict may escalate to violence, but the possibility for deescalation or political resolution remains. Overlap between politics and force in the zone of uncertainty reflects the fact that a conflict can just as easily escalate as deescalate.

FIGURE 4.1 Continuum of Conflict

and compatibility with the prevailing political culture, as well as a government's willingness and ability to enforce it—the law. In the following discussion, the interplay among these four factors will be explored. Bear in mind, however, that the object is not to eliminate conflict, whether domestic or international, but to capture and channel it through political institutions and processes that can resolve it in the form of fair and just policy compromises acceptable to all, or at least most, disputants.

The dynamic of conflict, domestic and international, is illustrated in figure 4.1. Politics can be effective in resolving conflicts that occur anywhere between the "less" end of the continuum and the "threshold." Once the conflict escalates into the "zone of uncertainty," there is just as great a chance that it will escalate beyond the "point of no return" and into violence as there is that it will deescalate into the "political," or nonviolent, zone. If conflict escalates beyond the point of no return, violence and/or war is the usual means of dealing with it. Force is incapable of producing resolution, but a victory by one party can produce at least a temporary end to the violence. Resolutions, however, are possible only if the conflict is deescalated back to the zone of uncertainty or lower. At that point, the politics of bargaining and compromise can become the tools for resolving the conflict in the form of political agreements, laws (domestic), or treaties (international).

DOMESTIC CONFLICT

Most of the Other World is undergoing the process of "development." Any amount of development involves change, and whenever there is change there is likely to be conflict. Usually this conflict occurs between those who favor change, or "modernization," and those who oppose it in the name of protecting traditional values and practices. The disputants typically come from two sources: disgruntled officials from factions in the government itself and those from groups in the population at large.

Government Factionalism

Antigovernment conflict can arise from many sources, have several purposes, and end in serious consequences. In Other World countries, the probability is high that such conflict will be violent because commitment to political resolution is often weak.

Many governments have factions whose allegiance is marginal. In the democratic ideal, competing factions are usually organized into political parties. This arrangement can work because each party agrees to the same rules. In some traditional societies, competing factions often have such divergent outlooks that they are unwilling to work with one another toward some mutually satisfactory compromise. This conflict undercuts the ability of governments to function and reflects the absence of the political consensus so vital to effective conflict resolution. Often, governments are not worthy of support because of corruption, malfeasance, or worse.

Sometimes, antigovernment conflict is the product of struggles among factions in the government with ties to nongovernmental groups that want power and control. These conflicts reflect both deep divisions in a society and the absence of consensus about how that society should be organized. Conflicts also arise between civilian and military leaders in the same government. Typically, military personnel define issues in black-and-white terms, regarding civilian leaders with suspicion or even scorn. Often there is no dependable chain of command subordinating military to civilian political leaders.

Chile is an example of a state where intense internal conflict developed over future domestic and foreign policy. Salvador Allende was elected president in 1970. His foreign policy platform stressed nonalignment in the cold war. Because he favored a socialist domestic policy, his domestic opponents accused him of being pro-Soviet. These policy priorities alarmed both his domestic opponents and Chile's allies, including the United States. In 1973, Allende was murdered in a military takeover with possible U.S. backing, and General Augusto Pinochet was installed as dictator. Pinochet pursued a status quo policy of the pre-Allende establishment. His rule lasted until he was defeated in the first free election in 19 years. He finally stepped down from political if not military leadership, and civilians have taken his place.

In contrast, Nigeria fought a vicious civil war (1967–1970) over which of several ethnic groups would control the government. This conflict tested whether one group could secede because of its second-class status and form a new country, called Biafra. The Biafrans lost. The Nigerian situation is particularly interesting because of its colonial heritage. Like so many Other World countries, Nigeria is not one nation at all but rather a group of nations, or tribes, living within boundaries of an artificial state drawn by the colonial powers. One lesson of Nigeria is that tribal and civil wars are still likely in the absence of viable, legitimate political institutions. As a result, there is no mystery about why military rule prevails in that country and why reforms leading to the possibility of democracy continue to fail.

More recently, a civil war erupted in Bosnia, formerly a republic in what was Yugoslavia. The conflict there escalated to violence in 1991 when Bosnia proclaimed its sovereign independence. That inflamed fears among ethnic, mostly Eastern Orthodox Serbs living in the predominantly Moslem state. With varying degrees of support from the adjacent Serbian Republic, also formerly part of Yugoslavia, the Bosnian Serbs conducted a war of "ethnic cleansing" similar to the ethnic cleansing carried out by the Turks against the Armenians in World War I, Iraq against the Kurds in 1994, and the Hutus and Tutsis against each other in Rwanda during 1994. There was no viable political framework in any of these cases in which the conflict might have been resolved. International institutions were paralyzed with indecision while the global community stood back and watched it happen.

Popular Factionalism

There are some nondemocratic societies whose governments are so unpopular that they are unacceptable arenas for conflict resolution. There, society functions in spite of, not because of, its government. Many parts of the Other World are in this category. When government lacks power as well as legitimacy, conditions are ideal for anarchy and civil war. This condition is most common today in states where traditional institutions have been the customary means for resolving disputes for hundreds of years—where conflict-resolving authority has never been successfully transferred to government institutions. The Republic of the Philippines is a useful example. Besides all its other problems, the government is simply not relevant in many parts of that country.

Alternate Strategies of Domestic Conflict

If a state is evolving "modern" political institutions like courts, legislatures, and political parties, they may be initially inadequate to their conflict-resolving task. Likewise, mature political institutions can be misused by governments to exclude certain elements of the population, as in South Africa before the 1992 election. Figuring out how to approach the resolution of a particular conflict is fundamentally an exercise in strategy. When politics and formal conflict-resolving mechanisms fail or are unavailable, alternate strategies emerge that reflect an escalation of conflict, a breakdown of the political process, and a greater likelihood of violence. These strategies include protests, strikes, civil strife, coups d'état, revolution, and terrorism.[1]

Protests.   Protests are the mildest expression of demands for or against something, although they can easily become riots. The targets of protesters are less likely to be government institutions than the individuals or groups associated with the problem. Price and food riots, frequent in the Other World, are less often directed at government ministries of agriculture than they are at private merchants or government food centers. When protests over Prime Minister Indira Gandhi's reproductive sterilization program degenerated into village riots, local promoters of the program were attacked, not the government itself.

Strikes.   Strikes are a more formal, organized form of protest in which the only sanction available to the strikers is work stoppage. Like protests, strikes result from a breakdown of the political process. They are an attempt to bypass the political process by expressing demands directly to decision makers. In the Other

World, organized workforces are often smaller, less cohesive, and so fragmented that they are barely part of the national economy. For example, it is difficult for subsistence farmers to organize an effective strike even if the law protects such activities. However, there are exceptions, and Bolivia is a case in point. Because its economy is heavily dependent on the mining and production of tin, the Bolivian miners, who have long been organized into unions, can back their demands with realistic threats to strike. Although they have done so from time to time, Bolivian peasant farmers have been less successful because they are more widely dispersed, have more diverse needs, and are hindered by poor communication among themselves. More recently, South Africa's African National Congress (ANC) was able to shock that country's economy with a dramatic strike in July 1992, preceding the election of President Mandela in 1994.

Civil Strife and Civil War. Civil strife and civil war differ only in scope. Always accompanied by violence, the two are common in the Other World. Strife is localized and may consist of ethnic clashes, as in places like Liberia, Nigeria, or Burma. All-out civil war embraces entire countries, as in Angola, El Salvador, Mozambique, Somalia, Bosnia, Rwanda, or Chechnya. Of the kinds of domestic conflict in the Other World, civil strife and revolution have the greatest potential for extensive violence, death, and destruction.

Civil war seems nearly inevitable in a country undergoing the transformational changes associated with development. Though usually domestic in origin, civil wars are vulnerable to external involvement, not least because of the need to obtain weapons abroad. That need, in turn, fosters renewed neocolonial dependency. Internal factions in Other World countries rarely have the leadership, money, or public support to conduct successful military actions against one another. Consequently, there is great pressure on opposing sides to seek outside aid from sympathizing groups and states. During the cold war, the United States, former Soviet Union, and China were frequent patrons, for their own strategic purposes.

The civil wars of Central America expanded into major power confrontations during the cold war. Years of benign neglect spawned domestic insurgencies that begged U.S. and Soviet military assistance to opposing factions. The superpowers were only too anxious to oblige because the region was considered vital to their respective strategic interests. Like the Vietnamese before them, Central Americans lost control of their destinies in an insidious form of neocolonialism that was so common during the cold war and may last well into the new world order.

The Palestinian Intifada, or uprising, in Israeli-occupied territories is an interesting admixture of civil strife and civil war with revolutionary potential. Begun in 1987, the Intifada involved boycotts, strikes, tax protest, and general resistance to what Palestinians considered to be the Israeli occupation of land that is rightfully theirs. Although some violence and even terrorism have been associated with the Intifada, it was much more a popular uprising than a terrorist movement. Perhaps more clearly than any other recent conflict, it represents a predictable result of a situation in which a government refused to acknowledge the grievances of a significant minority. The parallel between that and the South African situation before the 1994 election is both significant and regrettable. Equally significant and commendable is the progress toward peaceful resolution of some of these disputes since 1993 when the Palestine Liberation Organization (PLO) concluded an autonomy agreement with Israel. In South Africa, the people on all sides were able to unite to conduct a peaceful democratic election in 1994 and begin the difficult process of implementing reforms.

Meanwhile, Mexican Indians—Zapatistas—in the southern Mexican state of Chiapas are conducting an uprising of their own. Not only are they protesting their historically harsh treatment by the Mexican government and landowners, but they are also expressing very explicit concerns about the possible effects of NAFTA on their culture, way of life, and environment. Since NAFTA is a manifestation of the growing trend toward global economic liberalization, especially free and unfettered trade, it is not surprising that peoples elsewhere are expressing similar concerns, though so far in a less violent manner.

Coups d'Etat.   *Coup d'état* is a French term used to describe a military takeover of government. Military takeovers strongly imply the use of force, although some are "bloodless" coups. Violent or not, coups are limited, quick, well-planned actions. The violence can be very intense but is usually limited in scope. In some Other World countries, a coup can be unknown to the populace until announced by the new regime. Military governments resulting from coups are often called *juntas*, which is the Spanish word for council. It derives its present meaning from the sad history of military rule in Latin America.

It is important to understand that coups result in the imposition of hierarchical rule inherent to military organizations, instead of an open political process, while leaving the remainder of the system intact. Because there can be an absence of political tradition in the Other World, coups and military rule often seem to opposition forces to be an attractive alternative to the give and take of democ-

Bullet Holes in the Symbol of Peace (Left) and Wreckage of a UN Plane Shot Down While on a Peacekeeping Mission in the Congo (Right)
SOURCE: Emmit B. Evans, Jr.

racy. This is a variation of the so-called "totalitarian temptation"—the temptation by governments to use coercive police powers instead of the slower, "less efficient" democratic process, especially when public order is in jeopardy. Martial law and declarations of a state of emergency are variations on this theme.

Revolution.   It is useful to define revolution as the comprehensive transformation of a system and society. Like coups, revolutions seek to remove and replace political institutions and leaders. Unlike coups, their intent is to eliminate entire political, economic, and social systems and replace them with completely different ones. The two basic kinds of revolution are those initiated by elites and those that arise from the people. Ultimately, revolutions require a combination of both to be successful.[2] They occur when social and political conflict reach such intensity that political differences between factions cannot be negotiated into a compromise, as illustrated in figure 4.1. The Chinese Revolution, which began in 1911, is the best modern example of a revolution initiated and guided by a revolutionary elite. The Mexican Revolution (1910), in contrast, is a good example of a revolution that originated among the people. In the end, neither was completely successful in permanently establishing the entirely new systems intended by the revolutionaries, in no small part because of the staying power of traditional, prerevolutionary institutions and political cultures.

Two other points about revolution need to be mentioned. First, most people think of revolutions as liberal, socialist, or communist. However, they can be guided by any ideology. Some, like Hitler's, are fascist, and others, like Ayatollah Khomeini's, are driven by religious fundamentalism. Second, most revolutions, whatever their ideological orientation, are followed by a period of dictatorial rule. Revolutionaries view dictatorial regimes as the only way to maintain control while political and social systems are being installed. Marx referred to this phenomenon in leftist revolutions as the "dictatorship of the proletariat." The lesson of history is that contrary to Marx's prognostications, dictatorial regimes seldom go away willingly. If a dictatorship disappears, it is most likely to be replaced by another—either of the same persuasion or of the opposite, one supported by counterrevolutionaries. This is another illustration of the attractiveness of coercive solutions to complex problems—the totalitarian temptation. However, the collapse of communism in the former Soviet Union illustrates that there comes a time when dictatorships simply no longer command the power needed to hold a system together that has little popular support.

Terrorism.   Terrorism involves the use or threat of violence, often against innocent people, to "influence political behavior by extranormal means. . . ."[3] It is a strategy of conflict that involves a low risk to perpetrators and a good chance of success. It is inexpensive and it works. Terrorists rely on the intimidating effects of assassinations, random bombings, gassing, or airplane hijackings to accomplish their goals. Though similar in some respects, terrorism is not the same as unconventional warfare, counterinsurgency, or clandestine warfare.

Individuals, groups, and some states use terrorism. The decision to do so is mostly the result of having no other realistic chance to affect political outcomes.

Terrorists are prevented from mounting political efforts that stand any chance of success by lack of access to the political process either at the domestic or at the international level. Some terrorist groups are viewed by themselves and others as having legitimate grievances that unresponsive governments prevent them from articulating. Groups in this category that have used terror from time to time with great effect are several Palestinian factions and the Shining Path (*Sendero Luminoso*) in Peru. Others, such as the drug lords in South America, are more akin to bandits and are supported mostly by people who depend on them for their livelihood. These groups are discussed in part II.

To many, one of the most offensive terrorist practices is seizing and holding hostages. This is an extreme measure employed by groups that are desperate to have their grievances taken seriously. Typically, the hostage takers set some sort of condition, usually ransom, negotiations, or concessions, for the release of the hostages and threaten torture or murder if their terms are not met. One of the most infamous examples was Iran's seizure of 52 hostages at the American Embassy in Teheran in 1979. All of the hostages, held for 444 days, were eventually set free, although there is still some controversy over the extent to which American campaign politics affected the timing of the release. In addition, there is a major problem with placing blame. In the Iranian and subsequent hostage situations, it has been difficult to tell whether the incidents were the result of official state policy or acts committed by uncontrolled groups that happened to be located within that state. These factions may or may not heed the fundamentalist Iranian government, which nevertheless is still held accountable by the United States and other governments. There is evidence that the Iranian government wanted all hostages released sooner but that some Shiites had a more radical agenda of their own.

Bosnian Serbs have introduced the newest and most insidious twist to the taking of hostages. Beginning in 1994, the UN and NATO threatened to use air strikes to protect six so-called Muslim "safe havens." These were places of refuge for Bosnians who were promised protection. In the beginning, the threat of force would elicit requests by the Bosnian Serbs for negotiated truces. Often the truces were violated by them once the threat had passed. Eventually, the Bosnian Serbs realized there was little to no credibility to the threats, so they renewed attacks on the safe havens. As the UN threats of force increased and were taken more seriously, the Serbs held whole villages hostage and in several cases even took United Nations Protection Force (UNPROFOR) personnel hostage. In one extreme case, the Bosnian Serbs threatened to take 33 Ukrainian UN troops hostage if NATO attacked, and the Bosnian Muslims responded that they would do the same if NATO did not attack.

State terrorism, overt and covert, is used by states for their own extralegal purposes. Death squads and assassinations can be an important extrapolitical, if illegitimate, means of accomplishing policy objectives. Death squads, some official and others unofficial, have been used with effect by Brazil, U.S.-backed El Salvador, and South Africa. Assassinations are harder to document, but there is no doubt that many states in and outside the Other World have been guilty of carrying them out. Both are efforts to achieve objectives—such as the elimination of political opposition, including student leaders and newspaper editors—that were not possible by conventional political means.

Why is terrorism used, particularly when it has such a negative connotation? There are a number of answers to that question. The basic answer is that terrorism is usually a symptom of much deeper problems. Individuals, groups, and states use terrorism when, first, a situation is categorically unacceptable and, second, there seems to be no other way they can change it. When the choice is between a totally unacceptable situation or the use of terror for change, the terrorist has little difficulty deciding which to do. Whereas outsiders may view terrorists as thugs and hoodlums, they are seen by their supporters as heroes and, in death, martyrs. It is not unreasonable to suggest that one group's "terrorist" is often another's "freedom fighter."

Individual or group terrorism is particularly likely when an unacceptable situation seems permanent and the potential terrorists are frozen out of the political process. At the very least, a terrorist act will get worldwide media attention for the terrorists' cause; at most, it can destabilize the unacceptable situation and provide hope that some future solution will be more acceptable, as illustrated by recent acts in Israel and Great Britain. It is an inexpensive strategy that the weak can use effectively against the strong.

Several Palestinian factions have been open about and adept at using terror against Israel, Israelis, and their allies. Lacking a state, an army, and access to the Israeli political system, they view terrorism as their only hope of ever gaining recognition of their plight and grievances. The Israelis, in turn, have been accused by some of using state terrorism against Palestinians in and outside of Israel, as well as other Arabs. The 1992 election of a new Israeli government under Prime Minister Rabin significantly changed the situation, but it remains unclear whether the subsequent Palestinian agreement will lead to a resolution of the dispute in the aftermath of Rabin's assassination. Hamas, for example, increased its bombing attacks in a desperate attempt to subvert continuing negotiations between Israel and the PLO.

Measures taken by governments against terrorism are most often harsh. Though they may meet with short-term success, the major effect is to increase the terrorists' determination to prevail, even at the risk of losing their lives. If grievances espoused by terrorists can be seriously addressed within the political process, perpetrators will find themselves without a cause. The problem is that there is a countergrievance for every terrorist grievance, and the groups associated with each are not very likely to sit down together to negotiate a mutually acceptable political solution. Until that can be made to happen, terrorist acts will continue, if not increase.

Consequences of Unresolved Domestic Conflict

Two basic choices for approaching domestic conflict have been discussed. One involves the use of politics to bargain and compromise within the framework of political institutions and processes; the other depends on the escalation of conflict to violent levels, using terror, civil strife, and even revolution to achieve one's goals (see figure 4.1). How do governments respond when domestic conflict is unresolved? When politics has failed and violence becomes the norm?

Governments in trouble usually resort to dictatorial measures, using their military or police to enforce what they could not or did not want to achieve by political means—for example, the Chinese government response to demands for democracy in Tiananmen Square in 1989. Incidents like that are why militarism, military governments, and military dictators have been so common in the Other World. When politics and public order collapse for whatever reason, including government abuse or mismanagement, officials will defend authoritarian measures such as martial law as the only alternative to anarchy and chaos. Even those favorably inclined toward political resolution of conflict and who oppose their government will often support force to reestablish order, as seen now in the former Soviet Union. Unfortunately, such response does nothing to resolve the conflict and restore legitimacy. It only postpones dealing with the problems that caused the violence in the first place.

This condition favored military dictatorships in much of the Other World, particularly in the cold war era. Since the problems caused by development are not quickly or easily remedied, the likelihood was that such dictatorships would last for some time. Further, this condition was not conducive to experiments with democratic reforms by military leaders, who generally develop a strong preference for enforced order accompanied by contempt for politicians, politics, and compromise. Since, and partially because of, the end of the cold war, military dictatorships are becoming less common.

These situations were also vulnerable to superpower exploitation. Neither the United States nor the former Soviet Union was anxious to commit aid to states experiencing disorder and instability. Therefore, they in fact favored military regimes and often proffered military rather than economic and other kinds of aid, with the effect of perpetuating them. In the case of the United States, this policy led to the paradox of seeming to support governments that did not come close to adhering to professed U.S. goals and ideals. Needless to say, that appearance became a source of frustration and consternation to peoples in the Other World who felt that both the United States and the Soviet Union were helping to suppress them.

Things began to change in the 1980s and may change still more with the end of the cold war. The United States returned to its "traditional" or Wilsonian foreign policy by withdrawing support from the corrupt regime of Ferdinand Marcos of the Philippines in the 1980s, though the change has yet to produce much stability there. It also withdrew support from President "Baby Doc" Duvalier in Haiti, a second-generation dictator widely despised by his people. Meanwhile, the Soviets learned the same lesson and withdrew their forces, though not all of their support, from Afghanistan in 1989.

While many applauded this trend in superpower disengagement from others' domestic affairs, there was one grave byproduct whose effects are yet to be fully appreciated. States that have had decades of domestic turmoil, followed by long periods of military dictatorship, are not very fertile grounds for democratic political institutions, processes, and culture. On the contrary, as has been demonstrated repeatedly, they are literally barren politically and are therefore ripe for renewed unrest and even new military dictatorships. Two neighboring states that amply demonstrate this problem are Argentina and Brazil. Though their military dictatorships collapsed in the 1980s, they have only a limited pool of experienced politicians and willing citizens to rise to the demands of establishing new partic-ipatory political systems. Most experienced officials and outspoken citizens were imprisoned, exiled, or killed by the old regimes. As a result, both political sys-tems are still ineffectual. Though some dramatic improvements are apparent in both states, their situations have been complicated by massive debt and quadruple-digit inflation. It is difficult, if not impossible, to establish any semblance of nor-malcy under this combination of political, economic, and social conditions.

The former Soviet republics and East Europe find themselves in a similar sit-uation. After decades of enforcing policy from the top down, there are no viable political institutions to facilitate public policy from the people upward. At this point, it remains to be seen whether leaders in the former Soviet Union and East Europe can facilitate the creation of a new order before their armies, nationalists, or those loyal to the old regimes intervene. The precariousness of the situation in the former Soviet Union was amply demonstrated by the August 1991 attempt to overthrow Soviet President Gorbachev and the continuing challenge to the au-thority of President Yeltsin, whose political durability is uncertain at best.

Outlook

The solution to domestic conflict resolution in all cases may be called "institution building," which must be accompanied by the evolution of appropriate political processes and political cultures. As indicated, there is little prospect that trans-planted institutions will work. Considering present opposition to democratiza-tion by many Other World power structures, the biggest hurdle will be convinc-ing these elites to surrender their dominance and control.

INTERNATIONAL CONFLICT

Background

It has been shown how conflict operates within political systems. Now it is time to examine how conflict operates between states in the international system. Although there are important similarities, there are also major differences, the most prominent centering on the mechanisms for maintaining international or-der.[4] International conflict is customarily a euphemism for war. However, it is just as incorrect to think that all international conflict involves war as it is to think that all domestic conflict involves violence. In each case, the vast majority of con-flicts is nonviolent. The world is now and always will be fraught with conflict. It cannot be eliminated. The only question, domestically and internationally, is how to maintain order and control violence in the context of constant conflict at vari-ous levels of intensity.

States have laws, government institutions, political processes, and ultimately police and armies to maintain order within their boundaries. The international system does not. Given the certainty of international conflict and the absence of international government, the question becomes how international order is established and maintained. The answer is that international order has been whatever the stronger members of the international community decided it would be. Specifically, it was whatever the superpowers would accept. In other words, it was and is decentralized rather than centrally guided and controlled like a sovereign state. Before the mechanisms of international conflict resolution are examined, it is useful to see how international order has been managed since the end of World War II and how it may be managed after the precipitous changes brought about by the collapse of the Soviet Union as a sovereign state and superpower.

The Post–World War II International System

Between 1945 and 1989–1990, the world was dominated by the superpowers engaged in the cold war. They and their alliances, the North Atlantic Treaty Organization (NATO) and the Warsaw Pact, dominated the world system by maintaining a balance of power through such mechanisms as containment and massive retaliation. The tension between the alliances, heated at times, imposed a world order that was more acceptable than unacceptable to each. From the perspective of the Other World, it was distinctly neocolonial. When a balance was achieved, the chances were good that it would be maintained because each bloc wanted it that way. The result was a world stalemated in a bipolar, East-West, or communist-noncommunist configuration. Other World countries bargained their resources and strategic locations for domestic and international assistance from one or both of the two blocs. Both NATO and the Warsaw Pact were more important as international organizations than the UN for maintaining international order. Yet, whereas that order was basically acceptable to the superpowers, it was fundamentally unacceptable to most Other World peoples and states because it meant their relegation to underclass status.

One problem bridging the gap between the cold war and the post–cold war international system is the large volume of arms sales by the more developed countries, including the United States, European states, and the former Soviet Union, to the Other World, even though Other World countries are increasingly able to manufacture their own. The arms trade remains big business. In addition, there are significant weapons stockpiles in countries like Somalia and the former Yugoslavia that were accumulated during the cold war and are therefore immune from arms embargoes.

The Post–Cold War System

The international system is changing with the collapse of communism, the fall of the Berlin Wall, and the end of the cold war. Old, unresolved conflicts are resurfacing in places like Bosnia, Rwanda, and Chechnya. One of the Other World's worst fears became a reality when the former Soviet Union opted to move toward cooperation with the West. Since the collapse of the Soviet Union, the new world order will be whatever the United States, the European Community (EC), Japan, and situationally Russia and the Commonwealth of Independent States (CIS) agree on. In this new configuration, countries like Angola, Cuba, Libya, and Nicaragua have lost their Soviet support and will have to rely more heavily than ever on their own limited resources. Other World leaders can no longer rely on sponsors like the Americans, Soviets, or even the Chinese. Meanwhile, some countries, no longer held in check by the superpower stalemate, will seek to set things right from their perspective before the opportunity passes to rearrange the status quo more to their liking. Thus conflict in the Other World and elsewhere has both domestic and international components, which will be discussed later.

The post–cold war era will continue to be characterized by global interdependence, a reality known as the "global village." Industrialized states will continue to seek markets, resources, and cheap labor everywhere they can find them, regardless of ideology. They all need these resources to fuel their economies, and relatively few have enough. The North American Fair Trade Agreement (NAFTA), MERCOSUR and the Andean Free Trade Association in Latin America, the Pacific Rim, and the Asia Pacific Economic Cooperation Conference (APEC) are four regional, international manifestations of the need for economic cooperation to compensate for economic vulnerability.

The UN may become the central component of international conflict resolution in the post–cold war era. If it does, it will be the first time ever that global conflict is managed centrally by a universal institution rather than by its decentralized members. This newly possible approach was severely tested in August 1990, when Iraq invaded Kuwait. For the first time since the Korean War, collective security, backed by U.S. willingness to act unilaterally, was used to check aggression in one of the most explosive regions of the world. The principle of collective security means that an attack on any member of a group is considered to be an attack on the group as a whole. There were two basic ways to respond to the invasion. One was the old, cold war approach: unilaterally dispatching troops and attacking. The other was to capitalize on the newfound collegiality between the United States and the former Soviet Union and to try to use the UN as an arena of diplomatic combat to work out a political solution. As the conflict developed, a combination of the two approaches was attempted. The United States alone, with Soviet consent and Chinese abstention in the UN, dispatched over 500,000 troops to Saudi Arabia and fashioned a UN consensus on embargoes against Iraq. Later, a multinational force, with contingents of British, French, Egyptian, and other troops, launched Operation Desert Storm. A unified UN command was *not* formed, and the United States *did* assume a dominant role. This role may have reflected a lack of confidence in the ability of the fledgling post–cold war system to work, and it supported the suspicion that the United States simply bought UN support with promises of aid.

In the meantime, the relative success of the UN against Iraq has *not* been duplicated in Bosnia, Somalia, or Rwanda. Where consensus among key UN members about its policy toward Iraq was fairly easily achieved, the same was not true of a policy toward Bosnia. Here key members of the UN could not agree on what should be done, in no small part because of the enormous expense and complexity of this and other post–cold war tasks. Eventually NATO intervened. It must be recognized that the UN's role is ineffective when there is no consensus among the major powers.

The Other World and International Conflict

The single dominant feature of Other World states' involvement in international conflict is their relative military, economic, and political disadvantage. Although some countries, such as China, have large standing armies and some sophisticated weapons, they lack the delivery systems to pose any serious military threat to the major powers; although many have an abundance of resources, they usually lack the means to extract and market them; consequently, the political power they can muster is quite limited. The exceptions to this weakness during the cold war were those countries having international strategic importance, making them attractive to the superpowers. For these reasons, Other World countries rarely have much control over their own destiny. This situation has prompted several states like North Korea, Iraq, and Pakistan to try to develop nuclear, chemical, or biological weapons of their own, adding to the problems of arms proliferation, control, and disarmament.

As discussed in the chapter on neocolonialism (chapter 2), most Other World governments depend on major powers for sophisticated weapons and other military hardware. That dependency had two important effects during the cold war era. First, major powers had an interest in the outcome of disputes and did not want any changes that could upset the global balance of power or the status quo. There was always a danger that small wars started by client states could escalate into superpower confrontations. There was U.S. concern during the Vietnam war that the Soviets or the Chinese would dispatch troops to fight there. Likewise, the Soviets had to be concerned that the United States might retaliate against their occupation of Afghanistan (1979–1989). Second, dependency often prevented Other World states from militarily pursuing goals that were not compatible with major-power interests. Major powers have withheld funds, military equipment, replacement parts, or political support from client states to force them back into line. Oddly, this became a kind of safety valve as long as the superpowers did not have an interest in militarily confronting each other. Since the end of the cold war, however, that safety valve is no longer operative in the international system, resulting in increased instability and uncertainty. Some countries appear to feel freer to strike out on their own. Though this does not seem to have been a factor in Iraq's decision to invade Kuwait, it certainly was in both the Bosnian and Chechen declarations of independence in 1991–1992 and 1994, respectively.

Sources of International Conflict

What causes international conflict between Other World countries? Nationalism and territorial disputes are major sources of conflict because of the legacy of artificial colonial boundaries and neocolonialism. After World War II, as colonial empires disappeared, local leaders had the task of making these artificial bound-aries work as viable states. It was not uncommon for state boundaries to divide tribes and ethnic, national, and religious groups, or to combine diverse groups having no bond other than geographic contiguity. Not surprisingly, conflict was intensified and often led to internal or even international disputes. The interna-tional conflict in the Indian subcontinent, variously involving India, Pakistan, Kashmir, Bangladesh, and Sri Lanka, has not subsided since the British colonial presence ended with Indian independence in 1948. Other examples of territorial conflict include Vietnam, Cambodia, and Laos since the end of the French colo-nial presence there.

Political, economic, and social problems are an increasingly frequent source of conflict. Sometimes it is difficult to tell which of the problems is dominant. The Iran-Iraq war was politically motivated but also had territorial, social, and reli-gious implications. Iraq's invasion and annexation of Kuwait was ostensibly mo-tivated by an economic concern—the control of Kuwait's oil—but it turned out to be a vastly more complicated matter. Among other things, nearly landlocked Iraq wanted better access to the Persian Gulf to enhance its access to and influ-ence in the region.

Mechanisms for Resolving International Conflict

Escalation of conflict to a world war between the major powers in the post–cold war era seems a most unlikely prospect at this juncture. However, the removal of the restraints of the bipolar superpower balance may tempt some major pow-ers to resort to war at the regional level, which they can now fight to win for the first time since 1945. Lesser powers may succumb to the same temptation as in the past. The Arab-Israeli wars of 1967 and 1973 and the Iran-Iraq war of the 1980s involved medium-level powers trying to use war to achieve their goals. These wars were possible because the relative weakness of the protagonists "contained" the conflict. In the post–cold war era, major-power conflicts with Other World states will not be restrained and may not necessarily be confined to the area of the original conflict.

The new international system could invite what might be called the "new im-perialism" of post–cold war neocolonialism—the continuation of an era in which Europe, the United States, and elements of the former Soviet Union impose their will by threatening or using force on Other World countries. Instead of relying on ineffectual international conflict-resolving institutions or being checked by the old East-West balance, the "new imperialists" may simply continue to do what they want. Seeing this and being unable to counter it politically or militarily, Other World states may decide they have no choice but to rely on terror or chemical or even nuclear weapons to offset their disadvantage in relation to the major pow-ers. Chemical weapons are sometimes referred to as the "poor countries' atom bomb." The current world order, even if it is "new," is totally unacceptable to most Other World peoples and states. Peace, if it means freezing in place exist-ing boundaries and an unequal distribution of power and wealth, is unacceptable to them. Therefore, other mechanisms for dealing with conflict seem to be even more urgent if war is assumed to be incapable of actually resolving conflicts.

INTERNATIONAL INSTITUTIONS

There are numerous international organizations and institutions.[5] Some, like the UN, are universal, multipurpose organizations involved in conflict resolution and other international problems such as food, health, labor, or education. Others, such as the regional Economic Community of West African States (ECOWAS) or the former Latin American Free Trade Association (LAFTA), now virtually replaced by MERCOSUR (southern market) and the Andean Free Trade Association, and NAFTA (see chapter 5), are functionally narrower in scope, being limited to coordinating the economic policies of their members. They and the UN are known as international government organizations, or IGOs: organizations of countries, not individuals or corporations. Another type, known as the multinational corporation (MNC or MNE—multinational enterprise) or transnational organization (TNO), consists of centrally controlled, nongovernment, international businesses.

Regional International Organizations

Regional international organizations are like their global counterparts except that their membership is confined to one region of the world, usually a continent or part of a continent. In contrast, functional organizations have a common purpose, such as defense, that can encompass countries in different regions. Since the present focus is on conflict resolution, general attributes will be discussed, three examples will be presented, and some regional organizations will be identified. More detailed information about the organizations themselves is found in other chapters.

Three characteristics of regional organizations stand out. First and most obvious, they are defined by geography; that is, they consist of states within a common geographic region—like the Organization of American States (OAS)—and they sometimes espouse a common philosophy—like the Organization of Islamic Conference (OIC). Among other things, they are able to pool political and other resources to deal with common problems. Second, regional organizations are multipurpose, addressing several categories of needs. These generally involve some combination of military, economic, and political cooperation. As might be expected, regional organizations always seem to address most urgent needs first, and these are usually perceived to be military. Some think that military and security cooperation will eventually lead to regional cooperation in other areas like economics and politics. Although this progression may work in Europe, there is little of the same progress in the Other World so far. Finally, some remain hopeful that regional cooperation among states will lay the foundation for the actual integration of states into some larger entity like the European Union (EU), formerly the European Community (EC). Attempts have been made with only limited success to form similar associations in Africa, Asia, Latin America, and the

Middle East. To date, each has been hindered by nationalist and other conflicts among member states. That is not to say, however, that attempts at supranational regional integration cannot succeed at some time in the future.

Functional International Organizations

Some organizations that are neither regional nor universal, but rather functional, merit attention here because of their association with international conflict and with Other World countries. One is the Organization of Nonaligned States (also known as the Nonaligned Movement) and another is the Organization of Petroleum Exporting Countries (OPEC). The Nonaligned Movement is an attempt at the worldwide organization of Other World countries to coordinate their foreign policies, thereby increasing their collective impact on the UN and major powers. Its titular leader is Fidel Castro, and it is significantly less formalized than the organizations noted earlier. Its periodic meetings do not amount to much more than a forum in which to debate Other World issues. Two organizations with similar functions, the United Nations Conference on Trade and Development (UNCTAD) and the Group of 77, created in 1964, have been far more specific—if not much more effective—in representing the cause of their members. Their best-known demand was for the establishment of a New International Economic Order (NIEO) in 1974, which would rectify what they see as the structural, global, economic inequality that operates to the Other World's distinct disadvantage.

In contrast, OPEC is an organization that emerged in 1960 in response to the decline in world oil prices and the sharp elevation of prices for imported manufactured goods from industrialized countries. Its original function was purely economic, but it has experienced periods of substantial political influence and has usually had a moderating influence on conflicts involving its members. What makes it different from all other organizations is a common resource, oil, and the geographical reach of its 13 members, from Indonesia through the Middle East and Africa to Latin America. It is also different because its power and influence are so closely tied to that resource, yet not all oil-producing countries are members, including Mexico, the United States, and the former Soviet republics. OPEC had to struggle for salience during the oil glut of the 1980s, and its viability has wavered ever since. That situation illustrates the vulnerability of Other World countries whose economies depend on one or a small number of resources, so-called "single-crop" economies.

Three regional confederations are highlighted here to provide some insight into what they are and how they operate: the Arab League, the Organization of American States, and the Organization of African Unity.[6]

The Arab League.   The Arab League (or League of Arab States) began in 1945 with 7 members and had expanded to 21 by 1994. It was intended to coordinate the foreign and domestic policies of its membership to benefit the "Arab cause." The central element of that cause has been opposition to the existence of the Israeli state in the Middle East. Although the league benefits from the unifying effects of common culture, religion (Islam), and language, it suffers badly from factionalism. In 1979, Egypt broke ranks by signing a separate peace treaty with Israel following the Camp David agreement. This action resulted in the expulsion of Egypt and the relocation of league headquarters from Cairo to Tunis, Tunisia. Egypt's membership was reinstated in 1989 and the headquarters returned to Cairo. The Iraqi invasion of Kuwait was another serious threat to the league, which continued to be split into shifting factions, consisting of Saudi Arabia, Egypt, and Morocco versus Libya, Jordan, and Iraq. Nationalism has also been a threat to the league and to Arab unity. Despite shared attributes, each attempt to form a single Arab republic has foundered on nationalism at the expense of pan-Arabism.

The post–cold war era has been characterized by at least four major forces that threaten the league's organizational integrity. The first are the religious clerics who want to organize along fundamentalist principles. The second are the traditional royal families in Saudi Arabia, Jordan, Kuwait, and the Gulf states, which espouse a more traditional view of society. The third are the authoritarians like Hafez Assad (Syria) and Saddam Hussein (Iraq), who favor militant, secular nationalism. Finally, there are leaders like President Hosni Mubarak of Egypt who support moderate, secular nationalism and nurture close ties to the West. Ironically, what endears westerners to political leaders like Mubarak is the very attribute that alienates them from the Islamic fundamentalists: secularism and the willingness to engage Western and other states in the politics of bargaining and compromise to resolve international conflicts.

The Organization of American States.   The Organization of American States (OAS), founded in 1948, has 34 Latin American member states plus the United States. Its origins date back to the Pan-American Union, which was an outgrowth of the First International Conference of American States (1890). At one time, it was regarded as one of the most effective regional conflict-resolving organizations in the world. In fact, among its explicit purposes are "preventing difficulties and ensuring the pacific settlement of disputes among its members" and "seeking the solution of political, juridical, and economic problems among members." In the past, it has played a central role in the resolution of many disputes among its members, especially in Central America, but its effectiveness has waned in recent decades.[7] As a result, a faction of OAS members, which came to be known as the Contadora group, was formed during the Panama crisis in the late 1970s in response to the OAS's and others' ineffectiveness in resolving the Central American conflict. It actively attempted to mediate between the United States and the countries in conflict—mainly Nicaragua (see chapter 5).

The Organization of African Unity.   The Organization of African Unity (OAU), founded in 1963, is the African analogue to the OAS, and it had 53 members as of 1995. Its purpose, organization, and effectiveness are similar, but its longevity is not—in large part because most of its members have only recently (since the 1960s) gained independence from colonial powers. Like the OAS of late, the OAU's record in resolving conflicts is spotty at best.[8]

One of its main targets and bases for unity was opposition to the white, minority governments on the African continent, mainly Rhodesia (now Zimbabwe) and South Africa but also Angola and others. Although the organization cannot be credited with freeing Nelson Mandela in South Africa or ending white domination in Rhodesia, it played a major role through the "frontline states"—the independent, black African countries bordering on and surrounding South Africa. Its purpose in ending the reign of the white South African government was similar, though its effectiveness depended largely on its success in mobilizing major world powers behind its cause.

Universal Conflict-resolving Organization: The United Nations

Most states, about 185, belong to the UN, making it the world's only secular, universal, international governmental organization (see figure 4.2). Though designed by the Allied powers toward the close of World War II and chartered in San Francisco in 1945, its membership is now dominated by Other World states because they far outnumber the major powers. Of the many aspects of this successor to the League of Nations, only those that bear directly on its conflict-resolving potential will be addressed here.

The UN is a confederation, which means its only power is what its members grant it. Unlike a sovereign state, the organization is unable to enforce any decisions it makes or policies that it enacts unless it can manufacture a consensus of the membership. Instead, it must rely on goodwill for compliance with most of its directives. As would be expected, voluntary compliance is difficult to obtain from a member state whose national interest is threatened. It has never been easy for countries to place some international, collective, or human interest above their own national interest. Now it is especially difficult because post–cold war tasks like state building, national reconciliation, and social and economic reconstruction are instrinsically harder to accomplish and less amenable to internationally or UN-imposed solutions.

The Security Council is one of the UN's two quasi-legislative bodies, patterned after the Western parliamentary model, and the only one that can take direct action on issues of war and peace. It has ten permanent members—Britain, China, France, Russia, and the United States (Russia assumed the Soviet Union's permanent seat)—each of which has veto power, and ten temporary, rotating members, none of which has veto power. Any one of the permanent ten can veto without cause any agreement of the body as a whole. The World War II Allied victors were not about to create an organization empowered to make decisions inconsistent with their respective national interests, especially considering the frictions that were emerging among the Allies even before the war ended. Not surprisingly, the United States and the Soviet Union were the two permanent members of the Security Council that most frequently exercised their veto. Preliminary post–cold war indications are that the use of the veto may decrease as a new consensus matures among the United States, Russia, and even China.

The Security Council can take direct action if political resolution of conflict has failed by invoking the principle of collective security. If they can agree among themselves, the five major powers can enforce their will, including peace, on the

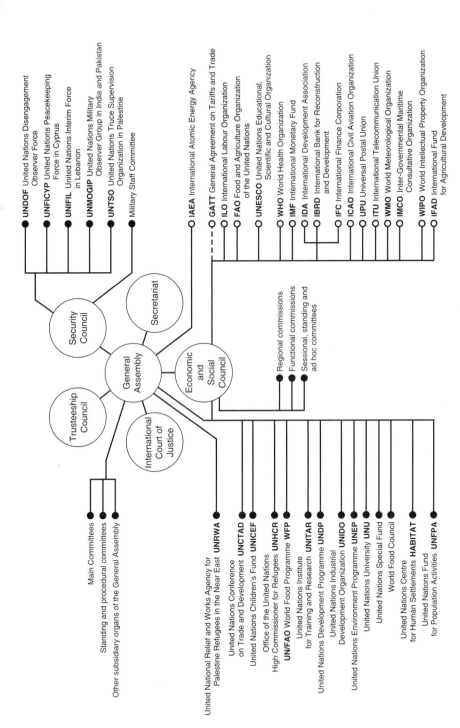

FIGURE 4.2 The Structure and Agencies of the United Nations

SOURCE: United Nations, Office of Public Affairs, October 1983.

UNDOF United Nations Disengagement Observer Force
UNFICYP United Nations Peacekeeping Force in Cyprus
UNIFIL United Nations Interim Force in Lebanon
UNMOGIP United Nations Military Observer Group in India and Pakistan
UNTSO United Nations Truce Supervision Organization in Palestine
Military Staff Committee

IAEA International Atomic Energy Agency
GATT General Agreement on Tariffs and Trade
ILO International Labour Organization
FAO Food and Agriculture Organization of the United Nations
UNESCO United Nations Educational, Scientific and Cultural Organization
WHO World Health Organization
IMF International Monetary Fund
IDA International Development Association
IBRD International Bank for Reconstruction and Development
IFC International Finance Corporation
ICAO International Civil Aviation Organization
UPU Universal Postal Union
ITU International Telecommunication Union
WMO World Meteorological Organization
IMCO Inter-Governmental Maritime Consultative Organization
WIPO World Intellectual Property Organization
IFAD International Fund for Agricultural Development

Security Council
Secretariat
Trusteeship Council
General Assembly
Economic and Social Council
International Court of Justice

Regional commissions
Functional commissions
Sessional, standing and ad hoc committees

Main Committees
Standing and procedural committees
Other subsidiary organs of the General Assembly

United National Relief and Works Agency for Palestine Refugees in the Near East **UNRWA**
United Nations Conference on Trade and Development **UNCTAD**
United Nations Children's Fund **UNICEF**
Office of the United Nations High Commissioner for Refugees **UNHCR**
UN/FAO World Food Programme **WFP**
United Nations Institute for Training and Research **UNITAR**
United Nations Development Programme **UNDP**
United Nations Industrial Development Organization **UNIDO**
United Nations Environment Programme **UNEP**
United Nations University **UNU**
United Nations Special Fund
World Food Council
United Nations Centre for Human Settlements **HABITAT**
United Nations Fund for Population Activities **UNFPA**

rest of the world. Until August 1990, it was virtually unheard of for the five permanent members to agree among themselves, so decisive action was rarely taken. However, in an important, first test of post–cold war United States, Soviet, and Chinese cooperation, the Security Council passed a resolution supporting UN sanctions against Iraq. That action temporarily revitalized the UN and renewed hope that it could be an effective conflict-resolving institution, signaling the potential for a new and intimidating alliance against some, if not all, Other World countries. In the meantime, it has repeatedly demonstrated a remarkable lack of effectiveness in places like Bosnia, Somalia, and Rwanda.

The UN has been involved in as many peacekeeping operations of various kinds since 1988 as in all the previous years of its existence. Some recent examples include Iran-Iraq (1988), Angola (1989), Afghanistan (1989), El Salvador (1989), Cambodia (1990), the former Yugoslavia and Somalia (1992), Rwanda (1994), and Bosnia (1992 to 1995). The Cambodian operation involved about 20,000 "blue-helmet" UN troops contributed by UN member countries and cost around $1 billion. More than 800 UN troops have been killed in the line of duty since 1948.

The General Assembly, the UN's second quasi-legislative body, is open to all members and numerically dominated by the Other World. The General Assembly can act only indirectly on issues of war and peace. Decisions are by majority vote, but there is no authority to enforce these decisions either. Consequently, the organization is basically only a forum for the expression of world opinion. By evolution more than design, the power of the General Assembly has expanded because of deadlocks and inaction in the Security Council. The means used for expressing the position of the assembly is the assembly resolution. Though also not enforceable, the UN assembly resolution is an important political device for Other World countries and has often enhanced cooperation among them.

The third specifically conflict-related component of the UN is the International Court of Justice (ICJ), located in The Hague, Netherlands (Holland). The purpose of the international court, as of domestic courts, is to adjudicate disputes or conflicts in a fair and impartial manner, in this case according to international law. However, it is also unable to compel compliance or enforce punishments. In addition, it suffers from the effect of many different national legal systems. Thus, although there is a body of international law contained in treaties and contracts, there is little agreement on universal, legal principles like justice, human rights, and so on. In consequence, one might think that the court has little influence or much to do. On the contrary, its docket is generally full because the vast majority of its cases involves commercial disputes that conflicting parties want resolved so they can proceed with their various enterprises. The court's main failing is not being able to resolve political disputes among major powers, including the United States, because they usually will not submit themselves to its jurisdiction.

Other International Organizations

As noted earlier, a global village of international interdependence has evolved, which includes international governmental organizations as well as multinational corporations (MNCs). These have an important, if indirect, bearing on domestic and international conflict.

International business in this century earned a bad reputation for contributing to, not lessening, international conflict. Substantial blame for hastening World War I can be placed on firms like Krupp Steel of Germany. It is also widely held that many U.S. problems in Central and South America are the result of exploitative private business ventures like the United Fruit Company (now United Brands). More recently, American, German, Swiss, and other firms have been accused of selling arms and chemical technology to Arab and other states, whether or not consistent with their own country's foreign policies.

Trade, as one important aspect of international business, deserves mention here. It can act as a passive but negative force on mechanisms of conflict resolution, primarily through international associations that control the pricing and marketing of commodities like coffee, sugar, oil, and bananas. Other World countries with single-crop economies are especially hard hit. For example, Cuba's reliance on sugar as a mainstay crop has made it vulnerable to international price manipulation by the United States. Only the former Soviets' aid and willingness to buy up Cuban stockpiles enabled the economy to function at all. Now that aid is gone.

At the same time, international economic involvements have begun to moderate some significant political differences. It is indisputable that economics helped break down the Iron Curtain and the Berlin Wall and generally open up both the former Soviet Union and China. It is also a fact that cooperation in the private sector has increased political cooperation, if only because private interests seek to protect their holdings so they can make their profits. More than once, companies have sought to subdue their parent country's pursuit of national interests to protect their business activities in host countries. The Arabian American Oil Company (ARAMCO) is a case in point. In 1973, that then American-dominated company refused to refuel American warships during the Arab-Israeli war for fear of jeopardizing its relationship with its Arab hosts. In another case, the American-owned Gulf Oil Company paid royalties to the Soviet-backed Angolan government, which the United States was officially trying to subvert. Those revenues accounted for about 70 percent of Angola's foreign exchange earnings.

These situations raise some interesting questions about sources and outcomes of conflict. Would the world be closer to peace and justice if governments left MNCs to pursue their profit-making goals? Are governments, relentlessly pursuing their national interests, the sole or even the major source of international conflict? The jury is still deliberating on these and related questions, but they make food for provocative thought. The ultimate problem is accountability. Public officeholders, on the one hand, must conduct the business of policy-making in the public view and are, therefore, always at least somewhat accountable to their constituencies and world opinion. Business executives, on the other hand, make their policies in the privacy of corporate boardrooms, isolated from public scrutiny and control. Neither source of policy is guaranteed to be in the public interest, but government processes are far more likely to be open and responsive than are corporate boardrooms.

Outlook

In some ways the problem of conflict resolution in the international arena parallels that of the less developed countries in the Other World, but there are differences. The parallel is that there is no international political culture that could focus conflict resolution efforts on international rather than national political institutions and processes. Such a development would represent a quantum leap in the thinking of the world's peoples and politicians, which is not likely in the foreseeable future.

The difference between international and Other World conflict resolution is that mature international political institutions and processes exist. In the Other World, the best conflict-resolving institutions and processes cannot work without sovereign authority and being part of peoples' political thinking and behavior. At the very least, that would require commitment to international interest at the expense of national interests. That is not about to happen either.

SUMMARY AND CONCLUSION

Conflict resolution is the political process of engaging disputants in bargaining and compromise to produce agreements in which all sides have a stake. Conflict is everywhere and is usually nonviolent. Left unattended, it can escalate into violence within and between states. Its resolution requires government and nongovernment institutions plus a political process that people believe in and must have reason to believe will treat them fairly. Such institutions, processes, and political cultures have existed in the Western world for some time, but they are often underdeveloped or nonexistent in the Other World as a whole. In their absence, alternatives to politics, usually violence or force, are likely to be employed to achieve policy goals. Domestic conflict originates in factions within governments, in the population at large, or between the two. Alternative strategies of conflict within states are protests, strikes, civil strife, coups d'état, revolution, and terrorism.

International and domestic conflicts have many of the same characteristics. However, strategies of managing international conflict differ because of the absence of sovereign, centralized, international governmental institutions. First the "balance of power," then the "balance of terror," regulated international conflict during the post–World War II period. The post–cold war era may see the enhancement of the UN as a centralized conflict-resolving institution that will strengthen regional and functional organizations. However, there is a chance that the major powers, including but not limited to the United States and Russia, will engage in a new imperialism against the Other World. Whatever happens, the new era of international interdependence will continue to evolve.

The outlook for the future of conflict and conflict resolution is not as grim as it might first appear. There is little prospect that institutionalized conflict resolution will become an overnight success in the Other World or internationally. However, resolution rather than confrontation and violence has become a necessity, not a luxury. In light of recent events, it appears probable that more Other World states will set about the task of developing institutions and processes for domestic conflict resolution. Meanwhile, it is likely that the current decentralized international system will persist in some form. Traditional mechanisms like treaties and alliances will continue to be used in the effort to maintain some stability, which could buy the time needed to allow international institutions to mature and overcome their historical paralysis. This need is especially urgent now that the bipolar stalemate between the United States and the former Soviet Union has been broken and the world advances into the post–cold war era of multipolarity. Ironically, it may lead to a new stalemate, which has been feared and predicted in the Other World: the United States, some of the former Soviet republics, and Europe (the North, rich, and white) uniting against the Other World (the South, poor, and nonwhite). It does seem likely that the North will continue to project its influence into the South, and it is certain that conflict will be the rule rather than the exception. It is less certain whether the political processes and institutions that have served democracy reasonably well until now will be allowed to evolve and respond to Other World or international needs. Whatever the outcome, much of our collective fate depends on it. From the perspective of people in the Other World, the question as the year 2000 approaches is whether there will be a just "new world order" or simply another version of the same old thing.

ISSUES FOR DISCUSSION

1. Should the UN, NATO, or individual states intervene to stop civil and other conflict in and between Other World states?

One of the ironies of the post–cold war era is that long-simmering conflicts within and between Other World states have escalated in the last several years from their dormancy during the cold war. One need only look at Somalia, Rwanda, Bosnia-Herzegovina, and Chechnya for examples. The reasons for these violent eruptions vary, but the eruptions themselves can be traced to the absence of the "order" that was imposed on much of the world by the superpower stalemate during the cold war period. Ethnicity, nationalism, and the desire for political independence from larger, multinational states are common motivations.

Conflicts like these were usually suppressed or otherwise prevented because they threatened the national interests of the major powers or the cold war order itself. Now that the U.S.S.R. is gone, the world order has changed. The United States as the lone superpower has national interests that are less often threatened. In such a case, morality or human rights issues are increasingly invoked as the justification for outside intervention in Other World conflicts.

Citizens of the major powers have always been dubious about sacrificing their sons and daughters in conflicts that "don't affect them," but the unspeakable atrocities being committed by "neighbors upon neighbors" make it more and more difficult to sit idly by. What some call the "third holocaust" is taking place in the form of ethnic cleansing in Bosnia. Staggering numbers of people were mutilated, tortured, and hacked to death, first by the Hutu, then by the Tutsi tribes in Rwanda.

Is it the duty of the "civilized" states, either singly, in combination, or under the aegis of the United Nations to intervene and try to stop this carnage, or are these kinds of conflicts inevitable, impossibly complex, and immune to intervention and permanent resolution?

2. Is the UN up to the tasks of peacekeeping and peacemaking?

Now that the cold war is over and the post–cold war order is still being defined, it is very clear that traditional mechanisms for reestablishing peace that involve the unilateral action of a single state have been supplanted by collective action. It is no longer possible to have one country police the world. NATO and the UN have the potential to maintain world peace, but each is flawed and in the same way. The UN has no sovereign power and must depend on member states to contribute money and troops. Furthermore, it has an even more serious defect: Any action depends on consensus among Security Council members, each with different and sometimes competing interests. Therefore, the UN's seeming haplessness is no mystery. NATO has the same flaw and acts only when its members are in agreement.

Flaws and defects aside, there are fundamental differences between peace*keeping* and peace*making*. Peacekeeping was the original intent of UN involvement in Somalia. It basically involves interposing a "neutral" force between disputing parties, stopping violence, and policing the imposed order. It does <u>not</u> involve trying to work out a political resolution. This task was accomplished with relative dispatch in Somalia, and television viewers around the world could see positive effects for themselves, in particular the large numbers of starving children and adults who were fed and spared certain death. However, eventually the UN mission in Somalia was changed from peacekeeping to peacemaking. The concept seemed sound but the results were disastrous. The concept is to take advantage of imposed if artificial order by facilitating a politically resolved conflict among the disputing parties. Once that began, the UN itself became the target of the warring parties, particularly General Adid. In consequence, the UN was forced into an inglorious retreat from Somalia in 1994.

Is it desirable or even possible for foreign states, either singly or in combination, to intervene to either make or keep the peace in countries like Bosnia, Somalia, and Rwanda?

3. Does membership in and cooperation with international organizations threaten the sovereignty of the United States and other states or do the advantages outweigh the disadvantages?

There have always been significant numbers of U.S. citizens who fear that the United States is subordinating its sovereignty to international organizations like the League of Nations and its successor, the United Nations. Some feel that the

United States should never have joined either international organization. They charge that the United States needs to get out of the UN to protect its national interests. These people are inclined to think that organizations like the Council on Foreign Relations, which focuses on recommending solutions to international questions, is leading a "conspiracy" against the United States. Calls have become more strident with the passage of GATT, the Organization for Economic Cooperation and Development (1961), NAFTA (1993), and the new World Trade Organization (1993–1995).

Joining any group, whether of individuals or of states, diminishes the amount of unilateral control that can be exercised. By definition, it involves compromise, meaning that no one component or member gets everything it wants. It is indisputable, therefore, that a state's sovereign power over itself is compromised when it joins with others to address global problems cooperatively, be they economic, political, or social.

Not affiliating with any political, economic, or military organization effectively gives states the complete autonomy they have historically enjoyed. It means they decide for themselves what to do and what not to do as determined by their own perceptions of their interests. This is the ultimate expression of the so-called "decentralized international system," which is controlled not by any centralized policymaking body but rather by the sum of what states at the system's periphery do and don't do for and by themselves. In a word, it is total and complete freedom for the state, creating a situation in which survival of the fittest is the operative principle.

In the post–cold war nuclear age, has the time come when international cooperation is more important than ever? Is the need to reassert state sovereignty obsolete or paramount?

4. Is the UN organization adequate to the challenges of the next millenium or is it time for it to be restructured?

The UN Charter was ratified in 1945 by 50 states in San Francisco, California. Though plagued by many of the same problems as its predecessor, the League of Nations, the UN was designed to eliminate as many of the League's weaknesses as possible. It was also designed to be acceptable to all its signatories, but most especially to the Allied powers, which had just emerged victorious from World War II. That in no small part explains how those powers ended up with a veto and five permanent seats on the 15-member UN "action organization," the Security Council. In short, the victors were not about to surrender to lesser powers the supremacy they fought so hard to win on the battlefields.

Since 1945, nearly 150 states have joined the UN. Most of them are Other World states, which achieved statehood after the end of colonial rule. Gradually, the new states came to outnumber the founding powers. That situation was most often reflected in General Assembly resolutions with no binding effect on members. However, major-power control of the Security Council, substantially enhanced by their exclusive veto power, effectively prevented anything from happening that the major powers did not at least passively permit.

As the end of the cold war approached, West Germany and Japan were expressing strong desire to have permanent seats on the Security Council. After the end of the cold war, India joined the call for a permanent seat. However, Germany's situation became complicated with the ratification of the Maastricht Treaty (1991), which included now-unified Germany as one of the 12 original members of the European Union (EU). Should Germany, along with Britain and France, have a permanent seat, or should Britain, France, and Germany join together with the other members of the EU to select one state to represent all of them? That would require Britain and France to surrender their individual seats.

The case for reorganization is strong. Majority Other World members have long held that the current liberal international economic order is structured to their disadvantage. Some deridingly refer to the UN as the "united stations" because of U.S. and Western dominance of the organization. To admit India as a permanent member of the Security Council would be a first step toward dispelling this notion.

The case against reorganization is also strong. Major powers, especially the victorious Allies of World War II, were not willing to subordinate themselves to an organization that might not have worked in their interests in 1945 and probably would not now. The price of their participation was dominance, as witnessed by their exclusive occupancy of permanent seats and possession of the veto. To reorganize the UN so that the great powers are just "one among equals," regardless of size and power, would do much to discourage their participation and thereby render the organization useless. Nevertheless, almost everyone recognizes that the world public has been better served with the UN presence than it would have been without.

Is it time to reorganize?

5. What is the appropriate response to domestic and international terrorism?

One of the most vexing and frightening phenomena since the end of World War II is domestic and international terrorism. Terror is unpredictable and almost always violent. There is no way to exclude the use of chemical or biological agents by terrorists at some time in the future, and they are easy to make, simple to use, terrifying, and deadly.

Whether violent and involving explosives or chemical or biological agents, terrorism is a reality that will most likely become more rather than less serious. Some terrorists are lowly thugs with nothing more than a personal agenda. Those are the people who deserve no mercy and as little attention as possible. Police and military antiterror squads are the appropriate way to deal with them. Others, however, have political agendas that must be reckoned with whether "the establishment" agrees with them or not. They are desperate to have a say about the configuration of a status quo that they believe is structured against them. They are willing to die rather than continue to live under prevailing circumstances. It is increasingly obvious that pretending these people don't exist and don't have legitimate demands only increases their dedication and the frequency of terrorist incidents, although established systems usually have good if not always legitimate reasons for refusing to deal with them. It is a no-win situation for an established society.

Recent years have demonstrated some of the risks and also the advantages of eventually responding to demands of people who have been labeled terrorists. South Africa so far is finding its way peacefully through what has been called an "institutionalized revolution." Incredibly, Nelson Mandela is now president of that country, and the African National Congress (ANC) is now a part of the South African political process. While these changes benefit the overwhelming majority of the South African population, it is also true that life will never be the same for the former white South African political establishment.

That situation is paralleled in many ways by what is happening in Israel. After treating Yasser Arafat and the Palestine Liberation Organization (PLO) as terrorists for decades, the Palestinian agreement was signed by both parties. Now, Chairman Arafat and the Israeli prime minister are working together to implement Palestinian self-rule. While some, even most, Palestinians are at least politically better off, there is no doubt that members of the former Israeli political establishment are without much of the influence and control they once enjoyed.

Oddly, there is an important paradox in each of the above examples, which makes it especially difficult to decide which path to take. It is that radicals among the former "terrorist movements," the ANC and PLO, respectively, are especially angry with their former comrades in arms, Mandela and Arafat, respectively. For the radicals, the compromises that produced new status quos are totally unacceptable. For them, those former comrades are worse than members of the old political establishment. This view has bred a renewed commitment to the use of terror by the perceived losers of the struggle, as illustrated by the assassination of Prime Minister Rabin by a fellow Israeli in 1995.

Should states negotiate with terrorists? Is there any such thing as a "legitimate" terrorist? Is today's terrorist tomorrow's statesman?

NOTES

1. See, for example, the "Civil Disorder Index" in Thomas Kurian, *The New Book of World Rankings* (New York: Facts on File, 1984). See also the "Political Rights Index" and the "Civil Rights Index" in the 3rd ed. (1991).
2. For a discussion of the dynamics of revolutions, see Crane Brinton, *The Anatomy of Revolution* (New York: Norton, 1938).
3. T. P. Thornton, "Terror as a Weapon of Political Agitation," in *Internal War*, ed. H. Eckstein (New York: Free Press, 1964), p. 73. See also J. R. White, *Terrorism: An Introduction* (Belmont, Cal.: Wadsworth, 1991), p. 5.
4. For additional perspectives on international conflict, see I. William Zartman, special ed., "Resolving Regional Conflict: International Perspectives," *The Annals of the American Academy of Political and Social Science*, 518 (November 1991).
5. International organizations, including international governmental organizations (IGOs), are defined in this section. At the risk of adding to the confusion, IGOs are also sometimes called intergovernmental organizations, and both are to be distinguished from

INGOs—international nongovernmental organizations, such as labor unions and churches. The last are not included in this discussion.
6. This discussion of the Arab League, OAS, and OAU draws on A. Leroy Bennett, *International Organizations*, 6th ed. (Englewood Cliffs, N.J.: Prentice Hall, 1995).
7. See J. S. Nye, *Peace in Parts: Integration and Conflict in Regional Organization* (Boston: Little, Brown, 1971).
8. As Nye indicates (*ibid.*), the OAS and the OAU each had successful records by the late 1960s, but this success did not include conflicts that involved one or more of the major powers.

FOR FURTHER READING

Arendt, Hannah. *On Revolution*. New York: Viking Press, 1963.
Bejar, Hector. *Peru 1965: Notes of a Guerrilla Experience*. New York: Monthly Review Press, 1970.
Brecher, Michael, and Wilkenfeld, J. *Crisis, Conflict, and Instability*. New York: Pergamon Press, 1989.
Coser, Lewis. *The Function of Social Conflict*. New York: Free Press, 1954.
Danziger, James N. *Understanding the Political World*. 3rd ed. White Plains, N.Y.: Longman, 1996.
Davies, James C. "Toward a Theory of Revolution." *American Sociological Review*, 27 (1962): 5–18.
Debray, Regis. *Revolution in the Revolution?* New York: Grove Press, 1967.
Fanon, Frantz. *The Wretched of the Earth*. New York: Grove Press, 1963.
Friedland, William. *Revolutionary Theory*. Totowa, N.J.: Allenheld, Osmun, 1982.
Gottlieb, Gidon. *Nation Against State*. New York: Council on Foreign Relations Press, 1993.
Hauchler, I., and Kennedy, P.M., eds. *Global Trends: The Almanac of Development and Peace*. New York: Continuum, 1994.
Huntington, Samuel P. *The Third Wave: Democratization in the Late Twentieth Century*. Norman: University of Oklahoma Press, 1991.
Kennedy, Paul. *Preparing for the Twenty-first Century*. New York: Random House, 1993.
———. *The Rise and Fall of the Great Powers*. New York: Random House, 1987.
Mazrui, Ali A. *The Culture of World Politics: North-South Relations in a Global Perspective*. London: James Currey, 1989.
———. *Cultural Forces in World Politics*. London: James Currey, 1990.
Mills, C. Wright. *Listen, Yankee: The Revolution in Cuba*. New York: Ballentine Books, 1960.
Nkrumah, Kwame. *Revolutionary Path*. New York: International Publishers, 1973.
Palmer, Monte. *Dilemmas of Political Development*. 4th ed. Itasca, Ill.: Peacock, 1989.

PART II
Other World Regions

CHAPTER 5

Latin America

Reginald Gooden

> *[Latin] America is ungovernable, the man who serves a revolution plows the sea; this nation will fall inevitably into the hands of the unruly mob and then will pass into the hands of almost indistinguishable petty tyrants of every color and race.*
> Attributed to Simón Bolívar by Gabriel García Márquez in his novel
> *The General in His Labyrinth*

Latin America, a large portion of the world, is located generally south to southeast of the United States. Traditionally, *Latin America* refers to those countries settled primarily by the Spanish and Portuguese. Portions of this area were also influenced by the British, the French, and to a lesser degree, the Dutch.

Latin America was the first of the Other World regions to experience European colonialism, and it has been struggling with the consequences of political liberation from Europe for at least a century longer. The countries of the Other World have had similar experiences in their courses toward independence and in their struggles for political and economic development. One of the differences between Latin America and the others is that it shares the hemisphere with a nation that underwent European colonialism but then grew to be the dominant world power.

A major theme of this chapter is the external domination that affects the development of public institutions. At just about the time that most of Latin America had succeeded in winning independence from Spain and Portugal, the United States proclaimed the Monroe Doctrine, and the evolution of its various interpretations and applications was keenly felt.

After an initial overview of the geography of the region, specific emphasis will be given to the legacy of colonization and the subsequent movements for political and economic independence. Along with much of the Other World, Latin America is still pursuing the path to development and economic independence. Colonialism gave way to neocolonialism; what these terms mean make up much of the subject matter of this chapter.

Some of Latin America's demographics and social characteristics are contrasted in table 5.1. In addition to the political and physical maps of Latin America,

TABLE 5.1 Characteristics of Latin American Countries

Country	Population (millions)	Population Growth Rate (%) (1992–2000)	Infant Mortality Rate (per 1,000 live births)	Population Under 15 Years of Age (%)	Life Expectancy (years)	Urban Population (%)	UNDP Literacy Rate (%) (1992)	Arable Land (%)	UNDP Per Capita GNP($U.S.)
Caribbean (partial listing)									
Bahamas	.273	1.4	—	30	71.9	—	99	0.8	11,790
Cuba	11.1	0.8	14	23	75.6	75	95	24	—
Dominican Republic	7.8	1.8	57	38	67	62	84	21	940
Grenada	.094	0.4	30	—	70	—	98	15	2,300
Haiti	6.5	2.1	87	40	56	30	55	20	380
Jamaica	2.6	1.0	14	33	73	54	99	19	1,490
Middle America									
Belize	.2	1.9	23	44	68	51	96	2	2,180
Costa Rica	3.3	2.2	14	36	76	48	93	6	1,870
El Salvador	5.6	2.2	46	44	65	45	75	27	1,090
Guatemala	10.7	2.8	49	45	64	40	56	13	940
Honduras	5.3	2.8	61	47	65	45	75	14	590
Mexico	92.2	1.9	36	38	70	74	89	12	3,080

Nicaragua	4.1	3.3	53	46	65	61	78	9	400
Panama	2.6	1.8	21	35	73	54	90	6	2,130
South America									
Argentina	33.9	1.1	29	30	71	87	96	10	3,790
Bolivia	7.7	2.3	86	42	61	52	79	3	650
Brazil	158.7	1.5	57	35	66	77	82	8	2,920
Chile	14.0	1.5	17	31	72	85	94	6	2,360
Colombia	35.6	1.6	30	34	69	71	87	4	1,250
Ecuador	10.7	2.1	58	39	66	58	87	6	1,010
Guyana	.7	1.1	49	33	65	34	97	2	300
Paraguay	5.2	2.6	47	40	67	49	91	5	1,270
Peru	23.7	2.0	77	38	64	71	86	3	1,070
Suriname	.4	1.7	26	—	70	43	96	0.4	3,650
Uruguay	3.2	0.6	20	26	72	89	97	7	2,880
Venezuela	20.6	2.0	33	38	70	91	89	4	2,720
Comparison States									
Austria	8.0	0.3	7	18	76	59	99	18	20,200
Hungary	10.3	0.0	13	19	71	66	99	57	2,750
Ireland	3.5	0.2	7	27	75	58	99	14	11,150
USA	260.7	1.0	10	22	76	76	99	21	22,340

Adapted from *United Nations Demographic Yearbook, United Nations Human Development Report*, and *The World Almanac and Book of Facts*, 1995.

this table will be useful as various countries are discussed. Three case studies illustrate the different paths to independence taken by Cuba, Mexico, and Brazil. The chapter concludes with the Flashpoints on current troublesome areas and issues.

As we move into the late 1990s and the climate of the cold war recedes, the continent faces a promising future at the five-hundredth anniversary of its European discovery by Cristóbal Colón.

GEOGRAPHY

The geography of Latin America is diverse (see figure 5.1) and has presented the region with difficult communication problems, some of which were not overcome until the development of commercial air travel. Even in those places where the mountains did not hinder travel, impenetrable vegetation or treacherous soils did. For example, in the middle of the nineteenth century, when a railroad was being built across the isthmus of Panama, the laborers awoke in the morning to find no trace of the railroad bed they had constructed the previous day; it had submerged into the unstable sand as they slept.

Geologically, an abrupt break with the north-south flow of mountain ranges that characterizes western North America occurs about midway through Mexico. Here a chain of volcanic mountains heads in a west-east direction through southern Mexico, Guatemala, and Honduras and across the Caribbean floor to form Jamaica, southeastern Cuba, Hispaniola, Puerto Rico, and the Virgin Islands. Connecting this region to South America are two chains of volcanic ridges that make up the Lesser Antilles and the highlands of El Salvador, southwestern Nicaragua, Costa Rica, Panama, and western Colombia.

To the west of South America lie the Andes, which contain some of the highest peaks in the Americas. Located at altitudes of more than 10,000 feet, mountain passes tower 3,000 to 4,000 feet over similar passes in the North American Sierra Nevada and Rockies. Mt. Aconcagua (22,835 ft.) is the tallest mountain in the Western Hemisphere. The older highlands of Brazil and Guiana are located on the eastern part of the continent. Between these highlands, heading north, east, and southeast, respectively, lie the plains of the Orinoco and Amazon rivers as well as the rivers flowing south into the La Plata estuary.

The mountains of Central and South America contributed to the rise and development of the high pre-Colombian civilizations of the Aztecs, Maya, and Inca in several ways. They offered a variety of altitudes and climates, which allowed for a broadly based pattern of food production. These mountainous soils were not subject to the debilitating leaching action suffered by land in the tropical rainforests. This generous combination of factors was further enhanced by the availability of a reliable source of water. In South America there was the added benefit of a substantial source of fertilizer to be mined from the Guano Islands off the Peruvian coast. All these factors combined to create an environment conducive to the production of food needed to support a large population. These large concentrations of people would later be exploited by the *conquistadores* to mine the gold and silver of the mountains. In fact, the administrative center of the Spanish

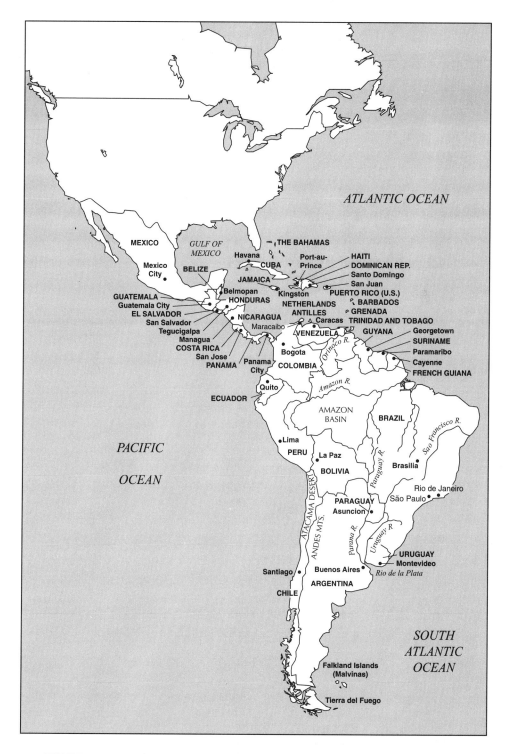

FIGURE 5.1 Political and Physical Characteristics of Latin America

viceroyalty of New Spain was established at the capital of the Aztec empire, Tenochtitlán, which in time became Mexico City.

PEOPLE

In dealing with an area of hemispheric proportion, we should not be amazed by the cultural and physiological variation among the Amerindians present when the first Europeans arrived. These native peoples ranged in sophistication from very primitive to the highly civilized cultures of the Aztecs in northwest and central Mexico, the Maya in Guatemala and Yucatán, the Chibchas of the Colombian highlands, and the Incas in the highlands of Peru, Ecuador, Bolivia, and northern Chile. Their control of the environment was sufficient to account for three-fourths of the population of the area at the time of discovery. The remainder of the native peoples were relegated to isolated and often inhospitable regions, where they sought refuge from the more successful and aggressive cultures.

The arrivals from Spain and Portugal were themselves a rich mixture of cultures and races that had swept across the Iberian peninsula since the time of the Roman conquest. The Christian reconquest of Spain over the Muslims and the later persecution of the Jewish population promoted an overwhelming degree of fervent proselytizing when the Spanish and Portuguese encountered the pagan populations in the New World.

It is estimated that the native populations suffered a mortality rate of from 45 to 90 percent during the first century of contact with the Europeans.[1] This population decline contributed to the forced importation of African slaves. The coastal regions, which grew one of the primary cash crops of the hemisphere, sugar cane, did not have a "reliable" source of native labor. The Indians either died or were able to escape to the interior, which forced the Europeans to bring in Africans as slaves.

Although the dominant religion in Latin America is Roman Catholicism (see box 5.1), the influence of the African religions of the slaves had an important impact on the region's religious culture. Blending African gods with Christian saints, the African religions produced such exotic rites as *Condomble* in Brazil and *Voodoo* in Haiti and Cuba.

Diversity and combination are two important characteristics of Latin American people; the third is the high population growth. Africa may have a higher birthrate, but the population growth in Latin America is among the highest in the world because the relative improvement in health standards has reduced the death rate. Today, more children are surviving, and this is producing volatile social and political results. Population pressure is increasing, requiring more producers to develop a more productive agriculture. Some countries, like Brazil, have vast unsettled regions and are able to relieve the pressure by promoting colonization of the interior. Unfortunately, when this settlement is done carelessly, an ecological disaster can occur as tracts of primeval forest are slashed and burned. In areas where there is no room for expansion, the population pressure may cause migration from thousands of depleted, unproductive minifarms into the cities. Other refugees cross international frontiers and bloody clashes result, as occurred between El Salvador and Honduras in 1969, known as the "Soccer War."

BOX 5.1   Liberation Theology

Along with the military and the landed oligarchy, the Roman Catholic church has been a major influence in Latin America. This triumvirate of power dates to the original conquest of the continent, when the church was given the responsibility of Christianizing the "savages." As in Europe, powerful families would be linked to the ecclesiastical hierarchy, providing sons to serve as bishops, archbishops, and cardinals. Its traditional link with the establishment has generated antagonism between the church and reform movements in the past—often carried to bloody extremes, as with the *cristero* rebellion in Mexico during the 1920s and 1930s. For a long time the church had helped to postpone social unrest by preaching a doctrine of passivity and resignation with one's earthly condition. The Catholic church is itself now undergoing a dialogue concerning its function. Confronted by the blatant social injustice that typifies the life of most of its membership in Latin America, increasing numbers of priests have accepted different strains of church doctrine, which sympathize with the downtrodden, and have combined them into a coherent philosophy that has come to be known as liberation theology. This new perspective has rekindled hope and enthusiasm as well as stimulated practical consequences in the form of community organization. Expectations and demands usually follow when people come together to discuss scriptural passages. These ecclesiastic communities have in turn provoked vicious counterattacks by groups that feel threatened by the prospects of social and economic reform.

Priests and laypersons have been assassinated or marked for extermination. The murderers are often linked with reactionary members of the establishment, who have seldom been brought to trial and are yet to be convicted and punished by a court of law.

Different interpretations of what it means to work toward God's "kingdom on earth as in heaven" have generated conflict within the formal structure of the church itself. Recently the archdiocese of São Paulo (the largest in the Catholic communion) was subdivided to remove poverty-stricken areas from the jurisdiction of Cardinal Paulo Evaristo Arns, thought by the Vatican to be too strident a proponent of liberation theology.

HISTORY

The Colonial Experience

During the fifteenth century, the monarchs of Castile and Aragon were, like their colleagues in other parts of Europe, consolidating power. The system of government used by Queen Isabella to unify her strife-torn realm was later transferred to the New World. To achieve the unification of Spain, the Spanish had to deal with the Moors, Muslim inhabitants originally from North Africa. To the Catholic

Spanish, the Moors were infidels. Ferdinand, king of Aragon, and Isabella, queen of Castile, joined forces in a military effort driven by religious beliefs to expel the Muslims from the region.

In both war and diplomacy, Aragon and Castile presented a united front, although in their internal political operations, Ferdinand and Isabella governed independently. Because the first expedition of Columbus was authorized and financed by the queen, the profits of the enterprise accrued to her and her heirs exclusively. As a result, Mexico and Peru were administered as separate territories, combined with the kingdom of Castile, and Isabella had sole possession of the sovereign rights as well as the property rights. Every privilege and all status, economic, political, and religious, came from her; it was on the basis of this arrangement that the conquest and occupation of the New World proceeded.[2]

So exclusive was Isabella's proprietary sense that during her lifetime only Castilian subjects were allowed to emigrate to the new dominions. A subject of her husband's kingdom required a special dispensation, and these were rare until her death, when Ferdinand assumed the regency. Along with the belief that only her subjects should enjoy the advantages of the new discoveries, there was also the fear that non-Castilians would introduce liberties alien to the much stricter and more centralized institutions controlling Castile. The traces of these Castilian institutions are still apparent in Latin America today (see figure 5.2).

After the initial period, the Spanish monarchs asserted their supremacy more directly. Most of the privileges extended to the original discoverers were withdrawn, and the total political incorporation of the colonies under the sovereignty of Castile was established. This move was to sow the seeds of later defiance. The highest offices of Spanish colonial government were now exclusively filled by *peninsulares*, or those sent to America from Spain. The *criollos*, descendants of the original settlers, who considered themselves to be just as authentically Spanish as the others, were barred from all forms of colonial administration except the *cabildo*, or town council. It was in the town council that the first cries for independence from Spain were uttered in the nineteenth century.

The independence movement in Latin America developed around the *cabildo*, which was the local unit of government. It was the only institution in which the *criollos* were allowed to serve, and as such it became a great source of prestige for American-born Spaniards. A *criollo*, or creole, meant a person of "pure" Spanish heritage who differed only in one respect from a *peninsular*, who could be a relative: The former was born in America and not in Spain.

The Wars for National Independence

The system of centralized government did not produce a smooth operation in the colonies. There were sporadic rebellions and uprisings, but these were not directed so much against the Spanish sovereign as against an oppressive local official. There were also rebellions by the Indian population motivated by reactions against their deplorable situation. In fact, it was the distant, but relatively humane, policies promulgated by Spain that tended to mitigate the abuses heaped on the indigenous people by the colonists. The isolation of the formal seat of power

FIGURE 5.2 European Colonialization of Latin America in 1790

from the daily practical problems of governing engendered the local response of "I obey but do not comply" to the administrative directives arriving from Spain. In effect, the colonists were practicing self-government but in the tradition of authority flowing from the top down. This system tended to stifle development at the grass roots. These "roots" have yet to take hold in a friendly political environment.

With the early exceptions of the United States in 1776 and Haiti in 1804, the wars of national liberation were not initially guided by the liberal ideas produced by the Enlightenment. In Spanish America, the wars of national independence had their origin in the continuing loyalty to the crown. The anticlerical theme of the French Revolution was opposed by the loyal subjects of the Spanish Crown. The attempt by Napoleon Bonaparte to install his brother, Joseph, on the Spanish throne in 1808 stimulated organized opposition in the form of local juntas both in Spain and America. The word *guerrilla* was coined during this time. In Spanish *guerrilla* means "small war" and refers to the resistance directed against the occupying French troops by Spanish nationalists.

As part of its colonial relations, Spain had insisted on the doctrine of mercantilism. This theory prohibited trade between the colonies and non-Spanish ports, effectively excluding creole businesspersons from the profits made by the enfranchised merchants sponsored by the Crown. In the nineteenth century, as English and North American traders gained access to Latin American ports, local merchants, who now enjoyed the profits earlier reserved for privileged *peninsulares*, began to uphold the free-trade doctrines of Adam Smith.

The Napoleonic interlude allowed the colonists to enjoy the results of Enlightenment thought and policies such as equal participation in the empire and proportional representation in the Spanish parliament. Others suggested experimenting with constitutional monarchy. Although the *peninsulares* and *criollos* could unite in their nationalistic opposition to France, they soon fell apart over their visions of life in America after Napoleon.

The clash of ideas soon broke out in armed conflict between the royalists and revolutionary leaders such as Simón Bolívar. As a student in Caracas and Europe, Bolívar had been impressed by the liberal ideas of Rousseau and the French *philosophes*. Returning to Latin America he soon joined those in Venezuela who were plotting independence.

The possibility of returning to an earlier time after savoring some of the fruits of freedom eventually tilted the controversy in Latin America toward independence. By the summer of 1825 the last stronghold of royalist opposition was defeated in Upper Peru. This territory was subsequently renamed Bolivia in honor of the liberator.

The revolutionary wars in Spanish South America were initiated and fought by the middle class in an effort to determine which among them, *peninsular* or *criollo*, would govern. In Mexico the movement took on a different hue. There, from the beginning, the independence movement had the look of class war as the Indians, the mestizos, and the have-nots rose up against the haves. The rebellion began in the provinces, led by a priest named Miguel Hidalgo y Costilla. On

September 15, 1810, the ringing of the church bell in Dolores announced the start of the Mexican war of independence. The rebels, armed with farm implements, were soon defeated, and the liberation of Mexico was quelled for the time being.

In Spain a revolt forced the king to establish a liberal constitution, the anticlerical tenor of which so appalled conservative Mexicans that they organized a new revolt against Spain. The leader of this movement was Agustín Iturbide, who had joined earlier with Spanish loyalists to defeat the revolt launched by Father Hidalgo. Iturbide proclaimed three notions that had popular appeal: the exclusiveness of Roman Catholicism, to be the only faith tolerated in the country; the equality of Spaniards and Mexicans; and an offer to the king to reign over an independent Mexico as a constitutional monarch. When the council in Mexico City took its oath to support the liberal Spanish constitution, Iturbide and his followers declared the independence of Mexico. In May 1822, the junta proclaimed him Emperor Agustín I. Glory was short-lived for the 39-year-old emperor. He was executed by General Antonio López de Santa Anna and the liberals in 1824. Mexican conservatives would have to bide their time as the liberals assumed control of the country.

The independence of Brazil took a different course. On November 29, 1807, as the invading French army came in sight of Lisbon, the Portuguese court sailed down the Tagus River on British ships en route to Brazil. After reaching Bahia, the original colonial capital, the royal court moved on to Rio de Janeiro, which was established as the new seat of the empire. This was the only time that a king ruling from America was the head of a European state. The arrival of the Portuguese court stifled the development of the juntas, which had emerged everywhere else in Latin America, where the great distance between the colonies and Spain had promoted local government.

When the French were finally repulsed, the Portuguese demanded the return of their king, Dom João, who reluctantly departed for Lisbon, leaving his son as regent in Brazil. The independence fever persisted in Brazil. Brazilian representatives to the parliament in Lisbon were slighted by not being allowed to participate fully in debates. They remembered the recent days when they were allowed to play a more important role in the creation of policy. In the presence of this mounting resentment against the metropolis, Brazilian independence came rather quietly. The regent became increasingly sympathetic to the Brazilian cause and refused the summons to return to Portugal. On September 7, 1822, the regent heard the news that his liberalizing decrees had been invalidated and that he himself had been judged a Portuguese traitor. He stripped the Portuguese colors from his uniform and declared, "Independence or Death. We are separated from Portugal."

His declaration was popularly received and he was installed as the constitutional Emperor Dom Pedro I by the council in Rio de Janeiro. The fact that Brazil had gained its independence without straining the government institutions already in place allowed it to avoid much of the internal strife that was to plague the postindependence political, social, and economic development in the rest of Latin America.

Postcolonial History and the Beginnings of U.S. Involvement

One abiding concern of the Latin American governments for much of the remainder of the nineteenth century was the designs that Europe and the United States had on their newly won independence. The United States has played a greater role in the affairs of Latin America than it has in any of the other areas under discussion in this book.[3] Much of the domestic and foreign policies of the nations of the hemisphere are carried out under *Yanqui* influence.

On December 2, 1823, in a message to Congress, President Monroe declared what has come to be known as the Monroe Doctrine. Written by Secretary of State John Quincy Adams, it contains three themes: the noncolonization principle, U.S. abstention from European involvements, and the exclusion of Europe from the Western Hemisphere.[4]

In 1845, war broke out between Mexico and the United States over the annexation of Texas. During the war the Polk administration indicated to the Californians that nothing would interfere with their entry into the Union if they were to gain independence from Mexico. President Polk invoked the Monroe Doctrine in an attempt to forestall French and British opportunism in California.

During the remainder of the nineteenth century the United States limited the extent of the Monroe Doctrine to North America. Not until the advent of the Spanish-American War at the turn of the century, and the beginning of a boundless sense of "manifest destiny," did Latin America have further real cause to worry over Yanqui intentions.

The policy of the United States assumed a more aggressive posture during the twentieth century. The "Roosevelt Corollary" to the Monroe Doctrine represents the policy in its most expansive phase. President Theodore Roosevelt's interpretation held that the United States should prohibit incursions by foreign creditor nations into the hemisphere by undertaking preemptive invasions and occupations of those Latin American countries that failed to honor their debts. Using this inflated view of its self-appointed role, the United States justified military intervention in many of the states of the Caribbean and Central America. This arrogance stimulated vociferous opposition throughout Latin America and created such deep suspicion on their part that they would not agree to a collective defense treaty until 1947.

With the development of the cold war in the late 1940s and the accompanying goal to contain communism, there was a tendency to suspect leftist and reform governments in Latin America. The Johnson doctrine, pronounced in 1964, went so far as to promote the destabilization and overthrow of Marxist governments even if they had been popularly elected.

ECONOMICS

Several social and political phenomena occurred as the economy developed during the twentieth century. One was expansion of the middle class (professionals, shopkeepers, and small businesspersons) who serviced and profited from the export of raw materials and the import of finished goods. These people, not members of the landholding stratum, tended to be concentrated in the cities. The other major change was the development of a more astute urban working class, resulting from the waves of immigrants, mostly from southern Europe, who were encouraged to come to Latin America to work in the new industries.

The presence of a large urban labor force coinciding with severe economic conditions made for a very unstable social milieu. The establishment and the traditional economic doctrine were discredited as a result of the Depression, and the people were willing to accept the stability proffered by a new military leadership. The result was the reemergence of the *caudillo*, the traditional "man on horseback," who had been such a common political landmark in earlier times. Unlike the early postindependence days, however, the new *caudillo* voiced a populist doctrine. Populism supplemented his military connection and mobilized mass support among the members of the working class, who were now tamed and incorporated into the political system. The influence of these leaders, Juan Perón in Argentina, Getúlio Vargas in Brazil, and Lázaro Cárdenas in Mexico, is still important today.

After World War II, Latin American countries ran up against a new reality: To remain competitive with a reindustrialized postwar Europe, they would have to be able to match its new and sophisticated production methods. The most modern developments were occurring in Europe and the United States, and to obtain them Latin America had to produce the necessary foreign exchange. It could do so only by reverting to the sale abroad of its traditional export commodities, and a new cycle of "colonial" economy reemerged. Extreme examples are the so-called banana republics of Central America, who were so dependent on the North American market and shippers for their well-being that they had to place themselves at the disposal of large corporations like the United Fruit Company. Added to these problems was the fact that the latest technology tended to be capital intensive. That is, it reduced the need for human labor, which is what Latin America had (and continues to have) in surplus. Reducing the size of the local labor force by using capital-intensive production methods compounded the problem because it reduced the demand for the products as it decreased employment.

Three Views on Development

Why is Latin America as a whole still considered underdeveloped? Several explanations have been offered to describe this phenomenon.[5] The most traditional explanation holds that there is no qualitative difference between Latin America and the other, "advanced" nations of northern Europe and Japan. Development is just a matter of degree, and Latin America has not as yet launched itself. Advocates of this theory split into conservative and liberal camps. The conservative position often heard in the United States is that Latin America needs to create the proper climate for foreign investment. What foreign investment conservatives have in mind, in this case, is generated by private funding. Such an approach works to the advantage of wealthy investors in the United States.

The liberal view argues for public investment. This view speaks of the need to develop an infrastructure, including transportation, communications, and power-generating systems, before the economy can be self-sustaining. Because the development of the infrastructure is so expensive and because everybody benefits, not just the industry that will be using the particular resource, it is felt that such projects should be public undertakings and the type of venture to which foreign governments could contribute. This was the kind of rationale that was heard during the mid-1960s in support of the Alliance for Progress. Of course, another reason given to support the alliance was the urgency to provide an alternative to the rising popularity of the Cuban revolution and the temptation for many reformers to turn to radical and violent solutions to the problems facing their countries.

The second, and more recent, view goes under the name of dependency theory. Unlike the older perspective, dependency theory is pessimistic about the prospects for the evolution of healthy socio-politico-economic development in Latin America because its economies depend on external systems. The economics of the various Latin American countries have evolved as the result of a system that is driven by exports. To the degree that an infrastructure has been developed, its primary function is to transport the resources of the nation beyond its boundaries to foreign lands, thereby neglecting local needs. According to this theory, Latin America will never develop under these conditions. This view sees no improvement until the area, and all of the Other World for that matter, breaks out of the dependency mold. Because the problem is structural in nature, breaking out is equivalent to overthrowing the system. The United States has not been receptive to such "solutions" since Castro's experiment in Cuba. These two theories underlie much of the controversy about what needs to be done in Latin America today to achieve the life-style of the so-called developed nations.

The third answer to the lack of development is not economic in nature but, rather, explains the situation in historical terms. This theory claims that Castile, unlike many of the other countries in Western Europe, was particularly centrist in its political administration. In contrast with England, Castile lacked a "true" feudal system, did not have a Protestant and nonconformist religious tradition, and also lacked the entrepreneurial establishment that caused England to be considered "a nation of shopkeepers." Even in those countries, like Mexico and Cuba, that had a true revolution (as opposed to the interminable round of palace coups endemic to the area), the end result was a centrist, authoritarian government. The three factors contributing to the rise of liberalism in North America were lacking in the Castilian political and economic tradition.

GOVERNMENT

In the 1970s one could count the "free" governments of Latin America on four fingers: Mexico, Costa Rica, Colombia, and Venezuela. The major countries of South America—Argentina, Brazil, and Chile—had military-installed bureaucratic, authoritarian regimes. Authoritarian government also occurred in Uruguay, which had formerly been referred to as the Switzerland of South America because of its democratic tradition. The exception was Peru, which initiated a peculiar variation in that it was not controlled by the traditional power groups. Its government was able to institute some minor revolutionary reforms, including extensive land redistribution. Peru's experience resembled to a lesser degree the revolutionary governments of Mexico and Cuba of the 1920s and 1960s, respectively.

The bureaucratic, authoritarian state seems to be a recent phenomenon and is distinguished from the tradition of authoritarian governments in Latin America by several characteristics. Military officers are not in charge of the different bureaus that run the government because these offices are filled by career bureaucrats. The working class is eliminated from directly influencing policy because political parties and labor organizations are curtailed or prohibited altogether. The government favors the establishment and, to some degree, the middle class because groups from this sector are in the best position to define policy and protect their interests as the influential bureaucrats come from their ranks. This condition results in an acute case of bureaucratic or military myopia, which interprets all problems as technical in nature and reducible to an administrative solution rather than negotiation. This kind of government provides the appearance of stability so satisfying to foreign investors and has often succeeded in attracting business from abroad. In time, however, it aggravates the members of the local middle class, who might have originally welcomed the military "solution" to the rising social chaos because the entry of foreign investment threatens their economic status.

As the tenuous base of support for the military from the middle sectors erodes under the economic strain of reentry into the neocolonial economic mode, the ruling groups have exercised several options. One is to call for a constitutional convention and return power to the people, as the Brazilian military did in 1985 after 21 years in power. Another is to increase repression and attempt to suppress dissent, as happened in Chile under General Augusto Pinochet until the military returned to the barracks in March 1990 after 16 years of military dictatorship. In Argentina, the military attempted to divert rising discontent and defiance through a nationalistic diversion that led to the invasion of the Falkland islands. Argentina was defeated in this 1983 war with England, and the country was so humiliated that the military lost all ability and will to continue the repression. It is inconceivable that regardless of their level of incompetence, the military rulers intended the outcome they obtained.

Conflict Resolution through Regional Organization: The Organization of American States

The notions of nonintervention and the sovereign equality of all states, along with the principles of mutual security, peaceful settlement of disputes, and a commitment to democracy and human rights, combined in three separate treaties to establish the Organization of American States (OAS). These treaties are the Inter-American Treaty of Reciprocal Assistance (Rio Treaty), 1947; the Charter of the Organization of American States (Charter of Bogotá), 1948; and the American Treaty on Pacific Settlement (Pact of Bogotá), 1948.

The Rio Treaty, which provides for collective defense under the provisions of Article 51 of the UN Charter, is seen as a regional arrangement, although the treaty makes no mention of this fact. This omission led to much controversy because all of the disputes in the area have a regional origin. According to Chapter VII of the UN Charter, every effort at achieving a peaceful settlement of regional disputes shall be exhausted before they are referred to the Security Council.

Problems arose between the United States and the other members of the OAS because North American administrations tended to interpret communist "intrusion" into the area as "external" aggression to be responded to by the full force of "collective measures" (usually initiated and led by the United States). The Latin American states are usually more modest in their interpretation of the "threat," seeing it as local in origin and protected against interference by the fact that all members have officially upheld the principle of nonintervention.

Because of the superior political, military, and economic power of the United States in comparison with all of the other members of the hemisphere together, another problem arises. Is the OAS a collective security arrangement in any authentic sense? Or is it merely a convenient aggregation of states through which the United States can give a collective cast to its own unilateral decisions? It is often the case that in major controversies, such as the Dominican intervention in 1965, there is a struggle between the "Colossus of the North" and the other members of the OAS about which international organization should deal with the crisis. The United States likes to keep a crisis within the confines of the OAS and, hence, under its control; many of the other hemispheric nations would like to take it to the UN, where the United States can be balanced by Russia and the other major powers in the Security Council.

Given the differences in power between the United States and Latin America, why did not the latter reject the OAS as nothing more than a convenient apparatus for the United States to reimpose the Monroe Doctrine in a multinational disguise? The answer seems to be that the OAS is better than nothing or, worse, a return to the bad old days before its inception. Its existence at least confirms the legal equality of all states, a tenuous acknowledgement perhaps but a straw that small states can grasp in disputes with larger states. Furthermore, because substantive policies must gain a two-thirds majority before adoption by the organization, it acts as a brake on actions contemplated by the United States. Thus, the OAS persists because it is of mutual benefit to the member states. The end of the cold war and Canada's recent membership in the organization should improve its effectiveness during the 1990s.

During the summer of 1991, at its meeting in Santiago, Chile, the OAS resolved to take a more active role in promoting democracy in the hemisphere (see box 5.2). This resolve was partly the result of Latin American displeasure with the recent invasion of Panama by the United States, but it also followed from the fact that all the members at least nominally represented democratically elected regimes for the first time since the OAS was founded. They have an interest in telling the military not to interfere and were quick to adopt economic sanctions against Haiti in October 1991, when that country's military deposed the popularly elected Jean-Bertrand Aristide. In April 1992, the OAS met to denounce the termination of the democratic process in Peru by President Alberto Fujimori and the military. The organization sent a delegation headed by Secretary General João Baena Soares to convince the president to reverse the course that his "frustration" with the legislature had precipitated. As with Haiti, the OAS is in a difficult position; it is now on record as opposing undemocratic turns, but it knows that the imposition of economic sanctions will hurt the innocent more than the guilty.

BOX 5.2   Contadora Peace Initiative and the Arias Peace Plan

Contadora is an island off the coast of Panama where the presidents of that country, Colombia, Venezuela, and later Mexico convened to devise plans to alleviate the tensions mounting in Central America. The primary intent of the Contadora peace initiative in the mid-1980s was to prevent an escalation of the conflict between the Sandinista government of Nicaragua and its neighbors (Honduras and Costa Rica) who had been harboring contras. These counterrevolutionaries, many of whom were members of the despised Somoza military, were being assisted by the United States in their attempts to overthrow the Sandinistas. The Contadora peace initiative also sought to address the turmoil in El Salvador and initiate a dialogue between the Reagan administration and Fidel Castro. The Contadora nations saw the causes of political and social unrest in the area as the results of underdevelopment and a long tradition of social injustice. Intent on devising a political solution, they felt that, being Latin American, they had a sounder grasp of the issues engendering the conflict than did the United States, which tended to blame the problem on the Soviet Union and its Cuban ally.

The plan recognized the existing governments, set limits on foreign troops, and restricted the use of military maneuvers and bases in the area. It also abolished economic sanctions. Although claiming to support the plan's pacific intentions, the Reagan administration succeeded in thwarting any concrete development by prevailing on its allies to reject the provisions.

President Oscar Arias of Costa Rica was able to achieve greater success with his plan by changing the focus to emphasize dialogue, amnesty, and elections while skirting the military components that made the other proposal too unpalatable for the United States. For this work he was awarded the Nobel Prize for Peace. Opinion in the United States after the eruption of the Iran-contra scandal made it easier for Congress to oppose the administration on military support for the contras, and the transformation of the Soviet Union modified the nature of its support for the Sandinista government; thus, by March 1988, the two contending parties to civil strife in Nicaragua signed an accord. The conditions for the process of reconciliation allowed for an election in February 1990, which resulted in the surprising defeat of the Sandinistas at the hands of a factitious coalition of opposition groups and the election of Violeta Barrios de Chamorro as president.

> **BOX 5.2   (continued)**
>
> The decade of violence in El Salvador, resulting in over 75,000 deaths, may have reached an end with a cease-fire on February 1, 1992, between the Farabundo Martí Liberation Front (FMLN) and the right-wing ARENA party. The arrangement was worked out by the former UN Secretary-General Javier Pérez de Cuellar and depends on the international organization to guarantee the peace. The U.S. support of the military in El Salvador had frustrated a termination of hostilities in the past.
>
> These examples of peace initiatives in Central America provide a miniature portrait of the ongoing tension between the United States and the Latin American nations, who believe they have a more intimate understanding of their problems than does their occasionally paternalistic North American neighbor.

The subsequent development of Haiti will be pursued in a later section. The impasse between the dedication to democratic governments echoed in the OAS resolutions and the "self coup" (*auto golpe*) staged by President Alberto Keinya Fujimori in Peru illustrates the ironies hidden in what would appear to be obvious forces in collision: democracy and dictatorship.

When Fujimori took office the Peruvian economy was in shambles. Inflation was soaring out of control, and the previous socialist administration of President Alán García Pérez had defaulted on the country's external debt. Adding to the turmoil were the depredations of two guerrilla factions—the more notorious of the two being the Shining Path (*Sendero Luminoso*), led by a former philosophy professor, Abimael Guzmán Reynos, who espoused a Maoist ideology.

Terrorists compound the economic problems of the countries in which they operate. Assassinations and destruction of property increase the price of doing business. Workers who fear extermination migrate. This is especially so for those who are in the middle class because they are most often targeted by guerrillas and also have the skills and means to seek employment elsewhere. Also, more resources go into buying protection, such as walls, insurance, police, and military, that could more productively be spent on trucks and tractors. Linked to these terrorists is the narcotics trade, which is used to finance their operations. This introduces another avenue for corruption into the institutions and relations of a society.

Four different attempts at stabilization of the economy had failed before Fujimori's inauguration. There are social and economic costs associated with stabilization plans, and each failure makes it more difficult to convince those that suffer that they should try again.

Frustrated by the legislature and what he perceived to be a corrupt judiciary, Fujimori instigated his coup d'état. The grip on the police and military was relaxed, and Peru rose in the ranks of those countries who are the worst offenders of human rights. He instituted a severe economic reform (fujishock) along the lines prescribed by Washington and the IMF. Fujishock brought down the rate of inflation. Guzmán was captured and given a life sentence in September 1992, which dimmed the exploits of the Shining Path. Fujimori had assuaged the ire of the democracies abroad by inviting them to supervise the election for a constitutional convention later that year. The new constitution enhanced the powers of the president and allowed Fujimori to succeed himself in office. The relative stability associated with his administration led to reelection in 1995 in a race against former UN Secretary General Javier Pérez de Cuellar (1982–1992).

The causes of the violence persist in Peru. There is still devastating poverty and a chasm separating the poor from the economic and political elites. Authentic democracy will be postponed until these structural problems can be mitigated, but progress in that direction is more likely through greater opportunity for popular participation. In the meanwhile, foreign banks are satisfied because Peru is back on the amortization schedule.

CASE STUDIES

MEXICO

> Poor Mexico, so far from God and so near the United States.
> José de Ia Cruz Porfirio Díaz

Under the leadership of Benito Juárez, Mexico experimented momentarily with republican institutions and a new constitution in the mid-nineteenth century. The period is known as the Reform. Out of this brief republican interlude there emerged Porfirio Díaz, a man cast in the mold of the traditional Latin American dictator. Under his influence (1877–1911) the country underwent its first round of economic development, but the costs of progress were excruciating for the majority of the population.

Díaz and his administration came under the spell of the doctrines of the French philosopher Auguste Comte, who argued that social integration and development would occur if social scientists were in charge of state planning. A group of self-proclaimed social technicians surrounded the Mexican dictator and opened up the country to thorough exploitation by foreigners. Railroad track increased fivefold in four years when Díaz granted the concession to external interests in 1880. Foreign trade increased by a factor of nine, and the United States became Mexico's chief trading partner.

In spite of such progress, the Mexican middle class was excluded from decision making and became increasingly resentful of the foreigners, who flaunted a rich European life-style. The forces that would soon erupt into one of the few revolutions in Latin America gathered momentum with the exile of Díaz in 1911. These forces are personified by some of the famous leaders emerging from the period: Emiliano Zapata, the head of the peasant movement demanding land and the restoration of traditional communal holdings; Venustiano Carranza, repre-

A Mexican Election Poster: Power to the People with
Rafael García Vazquez

SOURCE: Joe Weatherby

senting the landed oligarchy and favored by the administration of President
Woodrow Wilson; and Francisco ("Pancho") Villa, in command of what amounted
to an agrarian proletariat comprising cowboys, small ranchers, and agricultural
workers from the northern state of Chihuahua. Mexico remained in turmoil until the presidency of Alvaro Obregón (1920–1924), who began a tradition of the
peaceful devolution of power of Mexican presidents in the twentieth century. He
also appreciated the need to reign in the turbulence unleashed by the revolution.
There were hundreds of associations, armed bands, and ideological groupings
that had to be organized if Mexico was to acquire the status of a civil society. The
effort to legitimize the revolution found its expression in the formation of an official political party by President Plutarco Calles. This creation was initiated by
the revolutionary elite and was imposed from the top down. Like many other po-

litical organizations in Latin America, it provided a structure through which the major social, political, and economic forces in the state could seek expression. It also provided a means by which they could be controlled by the establishment.

Elected in 1934, Lázaro Cárdenas is the most admired president in the hearts of the Mexican people and is seen as the embodiment of the revolution. He distributed 44 million acres of land to the dispossessed, almost twice as much as had all of his predecessors. Not all this land was turned over to individuals, for much of it went into communal holdings that contained hundreds of families. One of his most popular acts, and one that fueled a sense of national pride, was the nationalization of Mexico's petroleum resources.

The National Revolutionary party, as it was originally named, underwent several transformations and today is known as the Institutional Revolutionary party (PRI). As presently organized, it comprises three major sectors: labor, peasants, and a segment of the middle class and bureaucracy. It is the dominant force in Mexican politics and until recently the presumed winner in any partisan contest.

The president of Mexico has extraordinary power. Not only does he exercise all the traditional powers of a Latin American chief executive, but also he is the chief arbitrator of conflict arising among the groups constituting the sectors of the dominant party, as well as the chief determiner of who is to succeed himself in the presidency.

Since the 1970s, the sectors in Mexico's ruling party have experienced increasing tension because of the growing pressures brought on by the need for development and the repayment of the nation's debt. The strain has tempted the party leadership to opt for a solution reminiscent of the Porfirio Díaz days, represented outwardly in a succession of presidents from the technocratic and financial areas of the government bureaucracy. In the 1987 presidential election, Carlos Salinas de Gortari received 50.7 percent of the votes. In earlier times, that would have been an impossibly slim margin. The ballots have still not been made available to public scrutiny. His closest rival, and the person who claims to have been denied the victory through fraud, was not the candidate from the traditional opposition party of National Action (PAN), located on the right of the political spectrum. Cuauhtémoc Cárdenas, son of the revered Lázaro Cárdenas, who bolted in opposition from the party his father helped to establish, led a leftist attack on the PRI under the banner of the recently formed Democratic Revolutionary party (PRD).

President Salinas de Gortari had made a commitment to honest elections, which has contributed to PAN victories in Baja California, Guanajuato, and Chihuahua. He has also begun the process of moving the country's industry out of public control and into the private sector. The reforms he instituted have arrested the rate of inflation and increased economic growth. In 1993, Canada, the United States, and Mexico established a free-trade area for North America. Proponents of this extended market see it as a boon to the development of the larger region. If, in addition, the price of petroleum were to climb again, Mexico would be in a better position to address the narcotics trade, which continues to irritate relations between it and the United States. (See the sections on NAFTA, the Chiapas uprising, and narcotics traffic for a more specific treatment of these issues.)

Another source of friction between the two countries is the flood of undocumented aliens from Mexico and Central America. Many of these people are fleeing stagnant economies or political repression at home. Their desperation makes them easy victims of abuses by predators along their journey to the United States. While residing in the United States, the fear of exportation often perpetuates their exploitation.

On New Year's Day 1994, the day that was to initiate implementation of the North American Free Trade Association, Mexicans awoke to the sound of gunfire as members of the Zapatista Army of National Liberation (*Ejército Zapatista de Liberación Nacional*, EZLN) invaded the towns of San Cristóbal de las Casas, Las Margaritas, Altamirano, and Ocosingo in the state of Chiapas. This violence was different from that which had killed Cardinal Juán Jesús Posadas Ocampo in a Guadalajara airport crossfire between drug thugs. Although the roots of both may ultimately have emerged from poverty, the former resonated support throughout rural Mexico, recalling demons of the country's recent history. Later that year the top executives of the Banamex bank and Giant (*Gigante*) supermarket chain were kidnapped and held for ransom.

In March, Luís Donaldo Colosio Murrieta, the presidential candidate for the PRI, was assassinated while campaigning in Tijuana. Five months later, the newly appointed candidate Ernesto Zedillo Ponce de Leon won with 51 percent of the vote, and the PRD candidate, Cárdenas, placed third behind PAN with a mere 16 percent. How could a candidate who many claim would have won in 1988 but for election fraud fare so poorly against a "substitute" in the face of so much social and political discontent? Much of the PRI success results from its political savvy, which is discussed in the segment on NAFTA; the rest probably results from a shaken public's hesitancy to switch regimes during tumultuous times.

The situation would not improve for the people of Mexico. On December 20, 1994, 19 days after Zedillo's inauguration, the *técnicos* (bureaucrats with Ph.D.s in economics and finance from Harvard, Yale, Stanford, Chicago, and MIT) devalued the peso.

BRAZIL

> *God is a Brazilian.*
> Anonymous

Brazil's transition to national independence was relatively peaceful. Brazil had no military tradition and, therefore, avoided the phenomenon of dictatorial rule until much later. The army did not become a factor until it emerged as the result of a prolonged war initiated by the dictator of Paraguay in 1865. In 1889 the military declared the end of constitutional monarchy and the beginning of republican government. Since then, the military has been a dominant player in Brazilian politics.

As with the rest of Latin America, Brazil had a single-crop economy for most of its history. Originally the crop was sugar, which was the force behind the establishment of slavery. Sugar plantations were concentrated in the northeast and had generated as much as one-third of Brazil's foreign exchange. Later, the dominant crop became coffee, grown in the southern highlands, which produced half the country's trade. The shift in crops from sugar to coffee also represented a geographical change in the economic fortunes of the respective areas. In modern times, the northeast became one of the most depressed regions. Tremendous demographic pressure is exerted on the other areas as emigrants from the northeast populate the shantytowns overlooking large urban centers such as Rio de Janeiro. These economic refugees also trek into the formerly impassible jungles of the interior, following recent inroads by teams of bulldozers. Consequently, an important ecosystem in the midst of a tropical rainforest had now been breached and laid open to wanton exploitation of resources and the indigenous tribes.

The economic depression of the 1920s and 1930s compounded the political and social problems of a single-crop economy. Exercising a traditional role, the military stepped into the turmoil and installed a man who would influence Brazilian politics into the twenty-first century: Getúlio Vargas, a politician from the southern state of Rio Grande do Sul.

Vargas was quick to override the traditional autonomy of the states, which were organized around political machines led by local bosses. He replaced the governors with intervenors and succeeded in augmenting the power of the federal government, which reached its apex on November 10, 1937, when Vargas proclaimed the New State, designed a new flag, and declared the new motto to be "Order and Progress." Order and progress was the battle cry of positivism, a doctrine imported from France that emphasized science and technology as the means of solving social problems. Earlier the doctrine justified revamping the curriculum of the military academy to emphasize science and engineering. Faith in the technological solutions promised by positivism continues to tempt military officers despondent over the apparent insurmountable problems facing their country.

During Vargas's tenure in the 1940s, the labor unions were brought under government control. Brazil achieved more stability, while remaining an authoritarian state. However, in the euphoria from the defeat of the Axis powers in World War II, it became harder to justify the dictatorship. Vargas attempted to widen his popular support by espousing a populist rhetoric and promoting antimonopolistic policies with the intent of reducing foreign involvement in the domestic economy. This course alienated him from influential policymakers in the United States, and the army asked him to resign in 1945. He retired to Rio Grande do Sul and was elected a federal senator later in the year. Five years later, in 1950, he again won the presidential election. Although his program was moderate, the inflation rate would not abate, the balance of trade grew increasingly unfavorable, and the administration in the United States was having a difficult time convincing itself that it should assist Brazilian development with public funds.

Vargas was attacked from the left and right. The left denounced him for becoming a lackey of foreign exploiters, and the right claimed that his policies alienated Brazil from its allies. An assassination attempt on one of his vocal detractors was traced to a member of his own security guard. Although Vargas was innocent, the corruption that had begun to swirl around him must have depressed him to the point that he committed suicide. This act resulted in his martyrdom, and those who had exploited the issue of corruption against him now found themselves on the defensive.

The legacy of Vargas continues to influence Brazilian politics. After a series of caretaker governments, President-elect Juscelino Kubitschek was allowed to assume office in January 1956. The vice president, João "Jango" Goulart, who was elected independently, won by a larger margin. Neither of them was able to win by more than a plurality. There was an attempt to deny them office by the anti-Vargas interests, but the major force in the military prevailed to support the constitution.

During the remainder of the 1950s, Kubitschek pursued a policy of economic development. The construction of a new national capital in Brasília was his lasting contribution in focusing development inward. But the great effort for economic advancement also brought rising inflation, which had to be addressed with unpopular programs. Adding to the problem was the fact that economic development resulted in a growing urban workforce, which grew in political sophistication as well as in numbers. Agricultural workers had become more active politically by organizing in "peasant leagues" to deal with their problems. These factors became a point of concern to the urban middle class, the landlords, and the military, which saw the leagues as threats to their social position.

Into this heated political atmosphere entered Jânio da Silva Quadros, who had risen quickly in the politics of the pivotal state of São Paulo. He offered a more positive program than the conservatives and at the same time avoided the rampant populism that alienated the middle class. The vice president was, again, "Jango" Goulart. The eccentric Quadros abruptly resigned from the presidency in an attempt to force the legislature's hand. This act precipitated a coup d'état by the military, who were troubled over the fact that the vice president was visiting the People's Republic of China.[6]

The military relented after 16 months, but the Brazilian situation continued to deteriorate by the time João Goulart was allowed to assume the presidency. Attempting to deal with the economic impasse, President Goulart promoted a plan that sought to reduce inflation while simultaneously boosting growth. This plan devastated the economically vulnerable, further aggravating their discontent. Increasing acts of insubordination in the military worried the generals, and the agricultural establishment was resentful over an agrarian reform program that did not compensate them adequately for expropriated land. In the United States, the Johnson administration was prepared to assist the Brazilian military with the intervention of naval and airborne forces if necessary.[7]

The recent Cuban revolution was too vivid in the minds of the Brazilian middle class, and when the military took control on March 31, 1964, they sighed with relief. Suspending democratic practice provided the stability needed to force the reforms that the technocrats felt would develop the country. After several years there was talk of the "Brazilian miracle" as economic growth attained the heights of the Kubitschek era, although the shantytown dwellers were ground down into further poverty.

After 21 years of dubious accomplishments the "legalists" in the military were able to convince the hardliners to allow the people to choose between slates of candidates approved by the military to start the return to democratic government. In 1985 Tancredo Neves was elected president. He was denied the victory but not because of the military. On the eve of his inauguration he underwent abdominal surgery from which he never recovered. The vice president, José Sarney, struggled in vain to correct the nation's economy.

Brazil currently confronts economic and development problems similar to those facing many of the countries in the Other World. The United States and the IMF have continually stressed the need to "privatize" the economy by reducing government ownership of industries and services, to encourage foreign investment and competition and diminish inflation. A country of tremendous natural resources, Brazil suffers the consequences of their poor distribution. One percent of the population owns over 50 percent of the wealth. It is a country with 12 million landless and impoverished peasants and an estimated 1.24 billion acres of arable land, two-thirds of which is owned by 5 percent of the population, which in turn farms only 15 percent of the total. Nevertheless, these powerful individuals are capable of defeating any attempt at effective land reform. Years of drought and rural hardship have driven millions to seek refuge in the urban areas, where they add to the inflationary pressure by causing the government to spend more on social services.

Carnival Participants in the Brazilian Colonial Capital of Bahia. A float depicts the IMF as "Uncle Sam" with the slogans hunger, misery, exploitation, violence, and oppression emblazoned on his jacket.

SOURCE: Domingo/Lenderts

This was the political context in 1989 when Brazilians directly elected their president for the first time since 1960. Fernando Collor de Mello, the candidate of the center-right National Reconstruction party, beat Luís Inácio "Lula" da Silva of the Worker's party by a vote of 53 to 47 percent. Faced with the highest foreign debt in the Third World ($115 billion) and an inflation rate that was projected to be 1,900 percent for 1990, Collor instituted reforms that collided with da Silva and the military. Collor offered to privatize state-owned industries and, simultaneously, to address the external debt by exchanging ownership of the former for reduction in the latter. This move created some consternation with the more nationalistic members of the armed forces. His attempt to impose a presidential decree that would have suspended a 166 percent wage increase authorized by the Regional Labor Courts was rejected by the federal courts. His reorganization of the economy resulted in the layoff of 350,000 government workers. Fear of unemployment stimulated protests and strikes by workers, which further destabilized the economy and promoted greater recession.

With his popularity waning, Collor suffered the additional indignity of having his brother denounce him for misappropriating campaign funds. Collor resigned from his office on December 28, 1992, to avoid certain impeachment by the legislature. A sad day for President Collor is a memorable one for Latin American democracy as a chief of state, forced to resign, is followed in office by his constitutional successor.

Though honest, the new president, Itamar Franco, did not have an economic recovery plan. He eventually appointed Fernando Henrique Cardoso to fill the vacant post of finance minister. In an earlier time Cardoso was driven from his post as a professor at the University of São Paulo by the military dictatorship. During his exile the sociologist collaborated with Enzo Falleto to write one of the basic texts on "dependency theory," called *Dependency and Development in Latin America*.

In the last eight years, Brazil has gone through five different currencies, and the 1980s were regarded as the "lost decade." Per capita GDP in 1990 was what it was in 1980, the last year of the "economic miracle." The new finance minister installed the *Real Plan*, and inflation declined from 50 percent per month to around 3 percent. The plan was launched early enough in the approaching presidential campaign so that candidate Cardoso could reap the benefits of its apparent success. Most important, the leading opposition candidate, "Lula" da Silva, thoroughly frightened the political and economic establishment to such an extent that they backed Cardoso with every means at their disposal. Cardoso won the election with 53 percent of the votes cast, a margin of more than 2:1 over da Silva.

As President Cardoso was inaugurated in January 1995, and Brazil's social problems persisted, Amnesty International reported the slaughter of thousands of "street children" at the hands of death squads. In the countryside peasant leaders and environmental organizers were murdered with impunity. A recent Hollywood film (*The Burning Season*), starring the late actor Raul Julia, portrayed the exploits and assassination of unionist-environmentalist Chico Mendes. Earlier this year, the governor of the state of Rio de Janeiro requested the army to intervene in the famous city with the same name because the local police could no longer control the gang violence. Governor Marcello Alencar did not seem concerned over the fact that General Nilton Cerqueira, who commands the 10,000 army troops and 5,000 police, headed one of the country's notorious secret police operations during the "dirty war" of the 1960s and 1970s. City Councilman Chico Alencar is concerned. Referring to the general as a 65-year-old "Rambo," he commented, "That's what we have now, Rambo, just more violence on top of violence."[8] As in other countries in Latin America, true reform will require structural transformation; but it will take a lot to convince the powerful interests arrayed against change of the need for a more equitable distribution of resources.

CUBA

> It is my duty . . . to prevent, through the independence of Cuba, the U.S.A. from spreading over the West Indies and falling with added weight upon other lands of Our America. All I have done up to now and shall do hereafter is to that end. . . . I know the Monster, because I have lived in its lair—and my weapon is only the slingshot of David.
>
> José Martí

Cuba, the largest of the Caribbean islands, looms larger yet in the eyes of current North American policymakers. The island was late in severing colonial ties with Spain. Although the Cubans had initiated several independence movements throughout the nineteenth century, the final attempt came on the eve of the twentieth. A mysterious explosion, which sent the American battleship *Maine* to the bottom of the Havana harbor in 1898, provoked an uninvited North American intrusion into Cuba's war of independence. As a result of the North American intervention and the Spanish defeat, Cuba became a U.S. protectorate for the next 35 years.

Cuban pride was trampled when Cubans were forced to accept the provisions of the Platt Amendment in exchange for nominal independence. The amendment stipulated, among other things, that Cuba could not enter into substantial foreign agreements without approval by the United States. It ceded to the United States the right to intervene to maintain a "stable government" and the right to "acquire and hold the title to land for naval stations." Cuba was forced to incorporate the amendment into its constitution before the United States would agree to remove occupying troops. This passage provided the justification for intervention in Cuban affairs by the United States from 1906 to 1920. In 1934, the treaty was abandoned as part of President Franklin D. Roosevelt's "good neighbor policy." However, the naval base at Guantánamo is still under U.S. control. Until the revolution of 1959, Cuba was seen as an extension of the United States. Its economy was so integrated with that of its northern neighbor that it was treated as another of the 50 states.

The development of the sugar cane industry in Cuba is a good illustration of how the cultivation of an exclusive crop can affect a nation's economic status. By the middle of the 1800s, Cuba was producing close to a third of the world's supply of sugar, in part because of the labor of over half a million blacks transported against their will from Africa. Sugar soon came to dominate the island economy during the time of the American protectorate. The mills dwindled in number as the smaller agriculturists were bought out and an increasing amount of land was given over to sugar production. These larger operations came under American control, and the development of the island's infrastructure was planned to exploit the transportation of the main cash crop. By 1928, Americans owned over two-thirds of the island's sugar production,[9] a situation that contributed greatly to the anti-American tenor of Cuban nationalism during the overthrow of the dictator Gerardo Machado in 1933.

Sugar cane requires infrequent replanting, so that the demand for labor comes only for three months during the harvest. The remainder of the year is referred to by Cubans as *tiempo muerto*, or dead time. Since there was nothing much to do around the sugar mills most of the year and the small farms had been bought up and given over to producing cane, a growing rural proletariat emerged, which would drift into the urban areas in search of employment.

In 1903 Cuba and the United States worked out a reciprocal trade agreement that gave sugar a 20 percent reduction from existing U.S. tariffs in exchange for a 20 to 40 percent tariff reduction for Cuban imports from the United States. Because sugar was to become the source of 80 percent of Cuba's foreign exchange, this relationship increased dependence on the United States. This and other arrangements contributed to Cuban prosperity in the good years. However, its own economy and politics became susceptible to the plotting of the American sugar lobby, which had its own interests to protect. When the Great Depression racked the United States, the social and political devastation was felt in Cuba as well.

The leftward potential of the groups that overthrew the dictator Gerardo Machado in 1933 was thwarted by Washington's refusal to accept the provisional presidency of Ramón Grau San Martín. Instead, the United States sided with Sergeant Fulgencio Batista, who had led the rebellion in the army that contributed to Machado's downfall. The politics that dominated the next 26 years was a struggle between an ineffective reforming element and the forces backing Batista. It was an era of rampant corruption and abuse of power.

On the eve of the 1952 presidential elections, Batista staged a coup and captured the executive office. This act stimulated a romantic and vain attack on the Moncada Barracks by Fidel Castro and a group of 165 youths on July 26, 1953. The attack was a disaster. Fidel and his brother Raul were lucky to avoid the fate of half of the party, which ended in casualties, capture, and death. In an effort to terminate military reprisals against any comrades associated with the attack, the Castro brothers surrendered and were sentenced to 15 years in prison.

Good luck always followed Fidel Castro. In an attempt to appease the opposition, Batista declared an amnesty and the Castro brothers were released in 1956. They were exiled to Mexico, where they were joined by others in training for the overthrow of Batista. Later that year a band of 82 revolutionaries sailed for the island. The landing was another disaster. The popular uprising that was to erupt on their arrival never materialized. After several days of mishaps, all that survived from the invasionary expedition were 12 *guerrilleros* (guerrilla fighters) who managed to slip into the Sierra Maestra mountains, where they would remain pretty much unnoticed until their interview by Herbert Matthews of the *New York Times* the following year.

The interview gave "the bearded ones" the exposure they needed to mobilize the latent anti-Batista sentiment throughout the island. Every revolutionary act would elicit a repressive countermove by Batista, which in turn only stimulated further disobedience and subversion until his support dissolved and he fled from Cuba on New Year's Eve, 1959.

What accounts for Fidel's subsequent rise? Unlike other revolutions in Mexico or China, the Cuban revolution emerged after a relatively brief period of conflict. The corrupt politics of the previous half century had thoroughly discredited the establishment. There was no one to compare in stature with the popular and charismatic revolutionary hero. The *Partido Socialista Popular* (PSP), which was the name under which the Cuban communist party operated, had been slow to back the *guerrilleros* in the Sierra Maestra, joining in the revolutionary movement only at the last minute. The PSP was also suspect because of its long alliance with Batista and its contribution to the organization and maintainence of workers' support during his regimes. So why did Fidel become a communist?

Any authentic reform of the Cuban political and economic structure would have to break the U.S. control of the sugar economy. That act would also entail a thoroughgoing agrarian reform because sugar production was the foundation of the system. The alternative would have to be a socialist or some other economic system with strong central direction from the state. The question was, would it be Cuban or Soviet socialism?

Washington's imperialist reaction to Castro's revolution darkened the atmosphere. Boycott and sabotage during the Eisenhower administration were followed by the unsuccessful Bay of Pigs invasion in 1961 and assassination plots against Fidel sanctioned by the Kennedy administration. Castro had to consolidate the revolution, and to do so he availed himself of the only antibourgeoisie apparatus in existence at the time, the PSP. He remained the revolutionary dictator and was quick to move against any regular party leader who wanted the institution to take the lead and govern. He drew on the communist party and Soviet advisers to replace the fleeing technicians dissatisfied with the increasing socialist direction of the revolution.

The growing indigenous opposition to socialism rejected assistance from those who had exiled themselves and were plotting a counterrevolution, with the aid of the Central Intelligence Agency (CIA), from afar. The abortive Bay of Pigs invasion had the effect of terminating the internal opposition because it had now become equated with the external counterrevolutionaries in the eyes of the people who had joined in defending the nation. This event gave Castro the support he needed to discredit and eliminate the opposition.

For a time in the 1960s Fidel sounded independent of the Soviet Union. He denounced the traditional communist parties throughout the hemisphere as reactionary. He squandered Soviet support on pet economic projects and played host to revolutionary leaders from the Other World at a Tricontinental Congress in an attempt to gain the leadership of the "nonaligned" nations. But his support of the Soviet invasions of Czechoslovakia in 1968 and Afghanistan in 1979 and the Russian suppression of the free labor movement in Poland in more recent years indicates how dependent on the Soviet Union Cuba had become for its survival. Many believe that Cuba was more dependent on the Soviet Union than it was on the United States in the pre-Castro years. Fidel's luck may be changing.

At a time when the former Soviet bloc is dissolving, the two Germanies are reunited, and the Commonwealth of Independent States (CIS) is experimenting with a free market, it is tempting to speculate that perhaps Cuba will go in the same direction. This is unlikely as long as Fidel Castro remains in control. Socialism did not enter Cuba in the wake of an occupation by the Soviet army. Communism was introduced by an extremely popular leader as a way of freeing his country from half a century of Yanqui domination, as well as a means by which he could solidify his control of the revolution.

The Soviet Union supported Cuba with about $5 billion in assistance in 1989, but as of the COMECON meeting in January 1990, Russian trade would be based on market price and hard currency. In the span of a year sugar exports to the island's primary buyers fell by 50 percent. In spite of all the efforts at agrarian reform, Cuba was as dependent on sugar then as before the revolution, and to make matters worse, the dietary trendsetters in the developed world were using less sugar, relying on sugar beets or other chemical sweeteners. Russia could no longer afford to subsidize the island's petroleum needs, and Cuba could not afford the 80 percent cash payment demanded by Mexico and Venezuela as partial payment on a special rate to sister nations bordering the Caribbean.

Cement plants came to a halt. Power would be rationed at night. Farm machinery and other essential vehicles were sidelined for lack of gasoline, and there was talk of bringing back the use of oxen. A deal with China resulted in the importation of two bicycle factories. The hope was that they could persist until the Juragua nuclear power plant could be finished. Costing $1.1 billion so far, the island's biggest industrial project also came to a halt. The Russians were demanding $200 million in cash to continue; there was a $300,000 monthly payroll and $200 million more was needed for financing. The prospect of an industrial resurgence by 1995 dimmed. Rationing increased, and visitors to Cuba reported being mugged when they strayed from the vicinity of their hotels.

From one of the bright spots in the Other World in quality of life for the worker, Cuba had taken a plunge. Given this drop in the standard of living, how secure is Castro now? The execution of General Arnaldo Ochoa—a "Hero of the Republic," the popular commander of the Cuban expeditionary forces in Angola and Ethiopia—on the charges of corruption and drug trafficking sent the powerful message that no one is safe. A move to depose Fidel would not come from above, as such persons have too much to lose without him. Fidel personifies the revolution. Those below would have an extremely difficult time in trying to plot against him. Intelligence channels permeate the society in large part because of the need to maintain readiness against the omnipresent threat of an external invasion. The more the United States threatens Cuba, the easier it is for Fidel to rally mass support for the defense of the revolution. The very security precautions that must be instituted against the eventuality of a U.S. invasion are the same ones that prevent the success of any domestic uprising. When Jorge Mas

Canosa and the Cuban-American National Foundation set up a real estate registry in Miami, Florida, for the purpose of recovering the properties of returning exiles when they overthrow the Castro brothers, they play into Fidel's hand—such actions serve only to rally the faithful in support of the regime.

Why did the U.S. government pass the Cuban Democracy Act (1992) sponsored by Representative Robert Torricelli (D–N.J.)? Among other things, the act denies docking facilities in the United States for a period of 180 days to ships trading with Cuba, as well as prohibiting subsidiaries of American firms from doing business with the island. Such actions, opposed by American businesses, only reinforce Castro's claim that Cuba is a U.S. target. The cold war is over. Cuba cannot in any way continue to be perceived as a security risk for the hemisphere, much less for the United States. Is it a revanchist reflex from the past or a policy tailored to satisfy the needs of an exiled community concentrated in Miami? As long as the cold war lasted, U.S. administrations found it convenient to curry favor with the Miamians; policies against Castro at the time served a mutual interest. But as we have seen in Haiti and Panama, embargoes do not hurt the elite of the targeted country, who are buffered from its effect. Fidel, even more so than Manuel Noriega, is able to turn the embargo to his purpose.

A change in U.S. policy toward Cuba may have arrived with the first wave of Cuban refugees fleeing the island in unseaworthy rafts (*balseros*). Clinton's support of the Torricelli bill in an attempt to gain the support of the Republican Cuban community of South Florida during the 1992 presidential campaign had failed when only 20 percent voted for him. Perhaps their bitter defeat at the Bay of Pigs soured them on the Democratic party forever.

As the boat people arrived on the Florida coast along with the fleeing Haitians, both groups 146were shipped to the Guantánamo Naval Base. This treatment of the Cubans was an affront to the 1966 Cuban Adjustment Act, which had given the Cuban exiles a special status. Now they were being lumped together with other unlawful immigrants. On May 6, 1995, a few days after they had been picked up at sea, a U.S. Coast Guard cutter returned 13 boat people to the Cuban naval base at Bahía de Cabanas.[10] The Miami Cubans saw this as an act of betrayal: Their special status had been revoked. Does this signal a break from past policies? It remains to be seen whether the Clinton administration will seek a foreign policy with Cuba independent from that of the Cuban exiles, who persist in wanting to punish Fidel Castro. That policy might better be guided by what means we should pursue to integrate Cuba into the hemisphere and advance democracy and economic development.

LOOKING AHEAD

Contemporary Latin America continues to reflect its long colonial experience. The political institutions developed in that part of the hemisphere were extracted from a strong central administration, mitigated only by the great distance between the colonies and the seats of empire. On top of that experience has been layered the ideologies of liberalism, positivism, socialism, and Marxism. Regardless of the fact that these influences tug at cross-purposes, the prevailing result has been some sort of highly centralized government. Whether the chief executives are garbed in civilian or military dress, their authority and power eclipse all other political institutions associated with liberal government.

Nevertheless, change is in the air. The prospects for economic development in the region do not appear as bleak in the 1990s as they did a decade ago. Latin Americans are willing to experiment again with regional integration. Earlier efforts toward establishing free-trade areas and common markets in the 1960s floundered. At that time countries were not willing to transcend national interests for the sake of the greater good. The mutual trust required for such an experiment to succeed deteriorated as military regimes pursued their separate agendas.

Staggered by an enormous foreign debt and fearful of the consequences of European economic integration, Latin Americans are now more receptive to economic cooperation. The nations of the southern cone (Brazil, Argentina, Paraguay, and Uruguay) signed the Treaty of Asunción, which established MERCOSUR (southern common market), modeled on the 1959 Treaty of Rome, which erected the framework for the European Common Market. Tariffs are scheduled to decline over time, along with other restrictions on trade. At the other end of the hemisphere, Canada, Mexico, and the United States launched the North American Free Trade Agreement (NAFTA) on January 1, 1994. The countries of the isthmus are attempting to revive a free-trade area, as are the 13 English-speaking countries that make up the Caribbean Commonwealth (CARICOM).

After an epoch of import substitution, industrialization and its associated macroeconomic devices for protecting domestic industries, government subsidies, public ownership, and intrusive economic programs, what had caused the receptive mood in the hemisphere to free trade, international competition, privatization, and serious attempts at installing those policies that would rein in galloping inflation? To a great degree it was a response to the economic debacle of the 1980s, coupled with the demise of the Soviet model and the need to change its ways if it was to obtain a sympathetic ear with the international lending organizations.

Flying to Mexico to celebrate the ratification of NAFTA by the U.S. Congress, Vice President Al Gore announced that his country would host a summit meeting of the Western Hemisphere leaders in 1994. The summit, held in Miami in December 1994, was attended by 34 heads of state. In the discussions leading up to the event, the Latin American and Caribbean nations stressed their interest in a free-trade area encompassing the two continents. Having just finished a difficult fight over NAFTA ratification, the Clinton administration suggested the topics of narcotics trafficking, government corruption, and women and the environment in development. All these topics found their way into the list of principles that emerged on December 11.

Nine days after the summit, Mexico devalued the peso and the rosy days of the "tequila sunrise" were followed by the "tequila hangover." What was expected to be a 15 percent devaluation of the overvalued Mexican currency soon had the peso in free fall. Contributing to the skittishness of the foreign investors were a string of unsolved assassinations of high officials in the Mexican society and the peasant uprising in Chiapas. Mexico, one of the few governments in Latin America that had maintained a semblance of civilian-led stability during the period of the "dirty wars," which racked so many of its neighbors, appeared to be just as fragile as they and no place to risk an investment. Soon all investments in Latin America were suspect, and the other countries suffered collateral economic damage. What happened?

The 1990s were an economic improvement over the 1980s. Average growth in the area between 1985 and 1989 was 1.5 percent, not the 3 percent since 1990. To this was added the announcement that the countries were liberalizing their economies, controlling inflation, privatizing state industries and resources, and opening their economies to foreign investment, coupled with diminished controls on repatriation. Liberalization of trade along with foreign investments stimulated an increase in imports. Lacking the sophistication and capacity to compete internationally, Latin American exports fell behind imports. The difference could be masked momentarily by the influx of capital investment, as well as portfolio investments held in Latin American stocks and bonds—which looked more inviting at a time when the United States was paying low interest rates. In contrast with Asia, where the foreign money was used mainly for investment, in Latin America it was going toward consumption. This is understandable given the economic doldrums of the 1980s. The influx of foreign money increased the value of the local currency, and this had the happy effect of cheapening imports; however, it also made exports more expensive, thus distorting the balance of trade even further.

The expectation that the U.S. Federal Reserve would be raising interest rates caused portfolio investors to pause. Even more significant, however, were the domestic problems emerging in Mexico. When the *técnicos* decided to correct the value of the peso while all the other alarms were going off, the system crashed. Money managers in New York, London, and Tokyo, watching the peso sink on their computer screens, withdrew their volatile portfolio accounts. Nobody wants to hold pesos now, and the Mexican currency will probably sink below its true value. The more stationary investments—foreign money that bought up the public industries and resources that were being privatized—are still good. The oil is still there, but it is going to take a while before foreigners will want to take another chance.

Throughout Latin America it will take longer to address the structural problems we have been discussing. Latin America has one of the worst distributions of wealth in the world. The macroeconomic reforms imposed by the lending institutions are having an excruciating effect on the majority of the population. Investment in education, health, and food is essential but can come about only through fundamental restructuring of the societies. The more the effort to address the social imbalance is ignored, the more Chiapas we will see.

The author V. S. Naipaul has written, "So many words have acquired lesser meaning in Argentina: *general, artist, journalist, historian, professor, university, director, executive, industrialist, aristocrat, library, museum, zoo*; so many words need inverted commas." Moises Naim, who quotes Naipaul, then states that throughout Latin America things would be better if other words such as "Ministry of Education," "Child Nutrition Board," and "Technological Research Institute" could recover their authentic meaning.[11]

It will take a while longer before the principles espoused at the 1994 Miami summit (free trade, democracy, sustainable development, honest government, termination of drug trafficking, and liberation of women) will lie together comfortably.

FLASHPOINTS

NARCOTICS TRAFFIC

> *The answer to the problem of drugs lies more in solving the demand side of the equation than it does the interdiction.*
>
> George Bush

As long as the demand for drugs exists, it will be difficult, if not impossible, to stifle the sources of supply in Latin America. The supply of cocaine has economic as well as cultural and political bases in Bolivia, Colombia, and Peru. Culturally, the native populations of Bolivia and Peru have traditionally relied on chewing coca leaves to relieve the fatigue, thirst, hunger, and cold that are endemic to life in the bleak environment of the Andean altiplano. Lake Titicaca, located at one end of this intermountain plateau, has an elevation of 12,508 feet above sea level. The medicinal and religious uses of the coca leaf date back to the Inca civilization, and the cultivation of the plant is allowed by contemporary Peruvian administrations at controlled levels.

The economic value of coca production is significant. It was estimated that in the 1980s Bolivia supplied over one-third of the U.S. market for cocaine. This amount results in a gross income of about $3 billion, which represents a figure six times that country's legal exports. Family farmers growing coca on plots of less than 3 acres have an average income of $1,000, as opposed to the $160 their neighbors would earn for other crops. The primary exports of Colombia (coffee and petroleum), Peru (copper and petroleum), and Bolivia (tin and natural gas) have been declining; and when one adds the falling standard of living associated with the austerity programs imposed by the international lending agencies, it is difficult to see how an impoverished people would choose the traditional way of doing business over the more lucrative one of producing and transporting cocaine.

The United States argues that all countries should share the burden of eradicating drugs. Critics counter that if the foreign demand did not exist, the problem would take care of itself. This dialogue points up conflicting approaches. On the one hand, the problem is one of economic development, that is, improving a country's balance of trade by increasing its exports. Such an approach is expensive because it involves the transformation of an entrenched socioeconomic structure at a time when these countries are faced with a large foreign debt. On the other hand, it is tempting to see the problem of narcotics as merely a matter of eradicating a troublesome crop and delivery system. This approach looks easier but engenders indigenous opposition because politicians can play on latent anti-

American feeling by defining it as another example of U.S. intervention. Mexican officials were incensed that the United States violated the sovereignty of their country by paying bounty hunters for the delivery of Humberto Alvarez Macháin, a physician alleged to have been in charge of overseeing the torture death of DEA agent Enrique Camarena in 1985.

The tragic results of the drug trade in Colombia are well known. There the Medellín cartel pursued a deadly game of intimidating the government by assassinating officials, political candidates, and journalists. The "extraditables," those at risk of extradition to the United States, tried for some time to reach a compromise with the government. They offered to curb their local violence in exchange for criminal trials at home, where "justice" might be more lenient than in the United States. In 1991, the alleged kingpin of the Medellín cartel, Pablo Escobar, arranged a plea bargain with President César Gaviri Trujillo whereby he surrendered himself in exchange for asylum in Colombia—to the chagrin of the Bush administration. After staging a successful jail break during the summer of 1992, he was cornered and killed by a special drug enforcement unit on December 2, 1993.

Closer to home, the link between narcotics traffickers, politicians, and officials of the Mexican government have combined to produce what some term a "narco democracy." Narco tyranny would be a better description of a vicious association of people who have produced an awesome collection of well-connected cadavers. The victims include the Roman Catholic cardinal of Guadalajara, a federal police commander, the Tijuana police chief, the former state attorney general of Jalisco, the general secretary of the ruling party, and that party's presidential candidate. The crimes remain unsolved.

The rise of narcotics violence in Mexico is attributed by some to the relative success of our interdiction of the conduit between Colombia and Florida. The squeeze caused the barons of the Cali and Medellín cartels to employ the smuggling channels already in place from California to Texas. The transfer of contraband along the U.S.-Mexican border goes back before Prohibition and has been passed down among families engaged in the trade. American agents have devised a rule of thumb that claims that the payoff is $1,000 per kilo of cocaine. The loads flying into central Mexico no longer rely on single-engine, propeller-driven Piper Cubs and Cessnas. The vehicle of choice today is the 727 and other jets capable of carrying 10 tons. There was a scandal in Zacatecas involving a shootout between the federal transportation police and the federal judicial police over possession of a plane that was so overloaded it had blown out its tires upon landing. The judicial police won, and the cargo disappeared. Because of its distinct packaging, it was discovered a few days later, making its way through the American drug market. The vast sums of money generated by drug traffic require laundering as well as protection. In no time at all the guardians of law and order are compromised and the corruption rises to the top, where assignments are made to the lucrative exchange points for a fee.

Mario Ruiz Massieu, brother of the slain Fransisco Ruiz (general secretary of the PRI), who had been married to the sister of President Carlos Salinas, was the former deputy attorney general and antinarcotics chief. He is currently being held in New Jersey while Mexico sues to extradite him. A search of his assets showed ownership of homes in Texas and Acapulco and deposits of $9.4 million—$1 million for each month he had served as chief narcotics investigator.

The corruption does not remain below the border. Members of San Diego street gangs were transported into Guadalajara for the gun fight that took Cardinal Juan Jesús Posadas Ocampo's life. A senior banker at American Express Bank International of Beverly Hills was convicted of laundering $30 million. The concern now is that access and transport to the United States will be made easier with the implementation of NAFTA.

PANAMA

Ever since the discovery of gold in California, the United States has been interested in Central America. Americans were looking for a way to expedite transportation across the continent. With the publication of *The Influence of Sea Power* by Admiral Alfred Thayer Mahan in 1890, the idea that the Caribbean was analogous to the Mediterranean Sea encouraged the U.S. Navy to build a canal in "our Mediterranean." The necessity of a canal became apparent when the battleship *Oregon* had to steam 12,000 miles around Cape Horn on a trip from San Francisco to Havana in response to the sinking of the battleship *Maine*. Panama was selected as the site. Political differences with Colombia required the United States to assist a group of rebels who wanted to disassociate Panama from its former status as a province of Colombia. Curious circumstances were associated with the treaty drafted between Secretary of State John Hay and Philippe Bunau-Varilla of France, who was acting as envoy extraordinary and minister plenipotentiary until the Panamanian delegates arrived in Washington, D.C.

Bunau-Varilla had an interest in securing the canal for Panama, which was in competition with Nicaragua. To ensure the passage of the treaty in the U.S. Senate, he agreed on November 18, 1903, to terms more generous than even John Hay had proposed. This event created discontent between Panamanian nationalists and the United States. These feelings of resentment, which on occasion erupted violently, underlay the tensions in U.S.-Panamanian relations. In 1977 President Jimmy Carter and General Omar Torrijos abrogated the Hay–Bunau-Varilla Treaty and returned the canal to Panama.

The story of the two nations might have had a happy ending, but Torrijos, who died in a mysterious helicopter accident in 1981, was replaced by his subordinate, General Manuel Antonio Noriega. Relations between the Reagan and Noriega administrations soured in 1988 when the latter was indicted on drug-trafficking charges by two Florida grand juries. The Reagan administration put pressure on the dictator to remove himself. Noriega refused and began denouncing the United States for reverting to its imperialist tradition; he claimed that President Reagan, who had led the opposition to the revision of the treaty, was seeking a way to revoke the document. The United States began to apply a tourniquet to the Panamanian economy. Finally, President George Bush intervened with a force of 27,000 troops on December 20, 1989, citing as justification the protection of U.S. citizens in the Canal Zone, the promotion of democracy, and the apprehension of an accused felon. The action was condemned by both the UN and the OAS.

In January 1990, the month following his confirmation as president of the republic by the U.S. military on a Canal Zone army base, support for the coalition government of President Guillermo Endara stood at 70 percent. By October 1990, it had fallen to 40 percent and was down to 10 percent by May 1992. The bond that held the coalition of parties together when they opposed the dictator disintegrated with his departure.

By May 8, 1994, the time of Panama's general elections, 16 parties had come up with six presidential candidates. The victor, with 33 percent of the vote, was Dr. Ernesto Pérez Balladares, leader of the *Partido Revolucionario Democratico* (PRD)—the party of captured General Manuel Noriega. Was the U.S. invasion for naught?

Perez Balladares was able to refurbish the image of the PRD by disassociating it from the National Defense Forces and the memory of the deposed dictator. Instead, he recalled its populist past and those policies that had linked it and the popular Omar Torrijos with reforms favoring rural Panama at the expense of the urban areas favored by the oligarchy. Torrijos had struck a responsive nationalistic chord in the hearts of his countrymen with the return of the Canal. The United States, more concerned with the process of democratization, broke with its past by refusing to interfere in the election. The exercise was exemplary. Citizens complimented themselves on achieving the standards set for Central America by Costa Rica. On September 1, 1994, President Perez Balladares was inaugurated.

ZAPATISTA UPRISING IN CHIAPAS, MEXICO

The contentious period in mid-nineteenth century Mexico, *La Reforma*, was a struggle between forces calling themselves liberal or conservative. Much of the dispute had to do with the role of the Roman Catholic church. The liberals, led by Benito Juárez, wanted to reduce the influence of the church and passed a law, *Ley Lerdo*, that required all corporations to sell their lands. The state could now go after one of the largest landowners in the country. This law was later incorporated into the liberal constitution of 1857. During the dictatorship of Porfirio Díaz, the original intent of *Ley Lerdo* was subverted and the constitutional provision was used instead to divest the indigenous agriculturists of their communal lands. This resulted in a system of peonage, as the now-landless peasants were forced to work for the large landowners whose properties had just multiplied.

It was from this sector that Emiliano Zapata, the revolutionary leader from the state of Morelos, emerged. Proclaiming the *Plan de Ayala* in November 1911, he denounced Francisco Madero, the man responsible for the overthrow of the dictator Díaz. Madero was himself a large landowner and indicated no interest in addressing the problems of the landless peasants. The new Querétaro Constitution, adopted in 1917, empowered the state in ways that preceded the radical ideas of the Russian Bolsheviks. Article 27 detailed the basis for land reform: It restricted the purchase of land by foreigners and reaffirmed the tradition of *ejidos*. Although subsequent administrations paid lip service to land reform and engaged in minimal attempts at redistribution, the agrarian problem was not seriously addressed until the Lázaro Cárdenas administration (1934–1940). Reinforcing the agrarian basis of the revolution, he distributed 44 million acres, which was twice the amount provided by the preceding administrations. Rather than breaking the land into minuscule subsistence plots, he relied on the tradition of communal landholding. He also provided the necessary support services to sustain his program. These holdings, which could include hundreds of families, were also provided with schools, hospitals, and agriculture credit.

This being the case, why did the peasants embarrass the Salinas administration on New Year's Day, 1994, by staging an uprising, capturing towns in the southern Mexican state of Chiapas and demanding agrarian reform and political democracy? Was not this the administration that had pledged itself to honest elections? How could it be that the Ninth Congressional District, which included the town of Ocosingo, now occupied by members of the Zapatista Army of National Liberation (EZLN), cast a 100 percent vote for the PRI in the 1991 federal elections? It was clear that no party could capture 100 percent of the votes in an honest election.

Perhaps better endowed than other rural areas, Chiapas in many ways represents rural Mexico. It is an area rich in resources. The region contains fertile farmlands, pastures, and forests, as well as petroleum. The mountains along its eastern border drain the clouds ladened with moisture that float in from the Gulf. That water irrigates the dense Lacandón rainforest, which controls its flow downhill to where it spins the turbines that produce three-fifths of the electricity empowering all of Mexico. The oil and the power plants belong to Mexico, but most of the population of Chiapas does not share in the common wealth. Article 27 of the 1917 constitution mentions "equitable distribution of the public wealth," but in the town of Ocosingo, only one-third of the homes have electricity and that proportion decreases as one travels into the countryside.

By various means, the rich few have acquired most of the landholdings over the years. These few wealthy families have been allied with the politicians and army and employ forceful tactics in dealing with that portion of the indigenous population that objects to their demands. They have always controlled the judges and frustrated legal attempts to stop them.

Now they can change the law to their liking, as the Salinas administration did in modifying Article 27 of the constitution to allow the subdivision and sale of common lands. The move to do so results from the current liberalization of the Mexican economy, which has cut back on agricultural subsidies while increasing the privatization of state industries and foreign agricultural competition in the wake of NAFTA. One hears the argument that liberalizing the economy will improve everyone's standard of living. It may be more profitable to develop mechanized, export-oriented agricultural products for U.S. markets and import the cheaper beans and grain grown in the fields of Canada and the United States. But if the peasants do not have access to credit and the means to compete in exporting crops, they will sell off their lands. As population pressure on diminishing agricultural land increases, peasants will invade the lands of the ranchers and provoke retaliatory strikes by the owners and their private armies or with the cooperation of the state's armed forces. The National Solidarity Program (PRONA-SOL), launched by President Salinas to ameliorate some of these problems, distributed generous amounts, but these usually filled the pockets of the local bosses.

The regional elites resort to extreme measures in dealing with the native populations and others who have the audacity to organize peasants, workers, or even meetings. These violent measures have provoked the bishop of San Cristobal de las Casas into forming a human rights center to document the abuses. Governor Patrocino González Garrido, a Salinas relation, has responded by jailing two priests. This treatment of the native population is not something new: The Zapatistas did not emerge overnight. In 1980, after numbing delays while waiting for the legal system to resolve titles to lands that they had claimed, the Indians began to occupy these holdings. The landowners were furious and demanded that the authorities take positive action to remove the intruders. A priest mediated a dialogue between the squatters and the governor. But at the appointed time, instead of the appearance of the governor, General Absalón Castellanos and his troops massacred the Indians.[12] The general, whose holdings amounted to 77 square miles and 10,000 head of cattle, had a personal message to give to the squatters. Ironically, portions of the general's ranch intrude into lands granted by President Cárdenas to the community of Las Margaritas. Instead of the target of an investigation, the general became governor of Chiapas from 1982 to 1988.

When the Zapatistas demanded the replacement of the PRI by a more democratic government, they were rejecting the combination of forces in the PRI intent on perpetuating their exploitation. The same governor of Chiapas, Patrocino González Garrido, was then appointed Salinas's secretary of government in 1993. The year before the 1994 presidential election, his responsibility would be to prepare for and supervise, among other things, the election. Maybe this explains how the polls showed total support for an administration the people of the district rejected.

The movement launched by Francisco Madero, which erupted into the Mexican Revolution, pursued the ends of effective representation coupled with the associated notion of no reelection. To that was added the Zapatista demand of agrarian reform. The PRI, the party whose name institutionalizes the Mexican Revolution, could be expected to provide Mexicans with its goals. The neo-Zapatistas remain unconvinced.

NORTH AMERICAN FREE-TRADE AREA

Not as formal as the European Economic Community (EEC), which contemplates a common currency and the creation of more centralized controls, and not as loose as the Association of South-East Asian Nations (ASEAN), NAFTA is a regional free-trade area with implications for the entire hemisphere. Already the inclusion of Chile has arisen, and as the membership grows, more Latin American and Caribbean nations will fret about being excluded.

Hemispheric regionalization makes sense for environmental, economic, and trade reasons. For instance, pollution on the Great Lakes or the Colorado River affects residents on both sides of the border. Clearly, it is in the mutual interest of countries that share a frontier to cooperate. The largest proportion of U.S. foreign investment resides in Mexico and Canada. Most of the exports of Canada and Mexico are to the United States. For the United States, Canada is the largest market, with Mexico a close second.

The treaty includes the following objectives: First, a gradual reduction in tariffs on some protected items, such as textiles, over the next 15 years. Second, no distinctions made between foreign and domestic investors in most industries. Third, by the year 2000 the protection of Mexican banks will be lifted. Fourth, trucking across borders will be open to all. Fifth, intellectual property is protected. Sixth, the United States will spend up to $90 million to train its displaced workers. Seventh, there will be a cooperative venture by Mexico and the United States both to clean up pollution along the border and to assist communities affected by the termination of tariff barriers. Commissions to investigate environmental and labor abuses will be established.

But more important for our understanding of contemporary Mexican politics and similar regimes throughout the hemisphere is an appreciation of how the ruling party went about achieving the inclusion of Mexico in the North American free-trade area. Since its establishment over 65 years ago, the PRI, Mexico's ruling party, has offered the example of an authoritarian corporatist regime. The party is the state and controls the politics of the country from the top down. The different social factors of the society are incorporated into the institution, and at the top is the president and his enablers.

In an attempt to bring stability to the country, the party has intruded into all aspects of society. The state is involved in the energy, banking, and transportation industries and in the organization of most of the nation's composite groups (labor, bureaucrats, teachers, military, etc.). Nevertheless, most of the population is excluded from sharing in the distribution of resources. When one is the dominant institution in a country, it is hard to avoid the blame for what goes wrong. The party's control was severely challenged in the 1988 presidential election. Cuauhtémoc Cárdenas led the "democratic current" out of the party and challenged its candidate, Carlos Salinas de Gortari. Educated at Harvard, Salinas returned to Mexico imbued with the virtues of liberal economic doctrine. This perspective was easier to convey in Latin America in the wake of the Soviet demise and the economic troubles exhibited in Cuba nearby. But to adopt the tenets of NAFTA was to depart from the tradition of the PRI, which had promoted nationalism, protectionist barriers to foreign competition and investment, and government ownership of important industries. To privatize the Mexican economy by selling off enterprises and liberating trade and investment would alarm the traditionalists in the party. Some speculate that the assassinations of Salinas's hand-picked successor, Luís Donaldo Colosio, and the secretary general of the party, José Francisco Ruiz Massieu, were the result of retaliation from the old guard against the *salinistas*. This whole area remains murky because it was complicated by the intrigues of the drug cartels.

In Mexico, the politics of NAFTA can be seen as the employment of authoritarian means to achieve liberal economic ends. Representing a boon to well-connected members of the Mexican elite, NAFTA would provide access to one of the richest markets in the world; those who could afford to invest in the selling off of state-owned operations would reap a handsome return. (The July 1994 issue of *Forbes* showed 24 Mexican billionaires.) New foreign investment in Mexico would raise the economic status of all, and the PRI could recover the luster it had lost in recent times. The new regional arrangement would protect it from exclusions implicit in other regional arrangements, such as those of the EEC. The incentives to the private sector were fairly apparent. To bring around those who would find themselves in the most vulnerable condition, Salinas instituted the Program of National Solidarity (*Programa Nacional de Solidaridad*, PRONASOL) to inject $1.7 billion by 1991 into local communities, infrastructure, schools, and services. By moving in this direction, the PRI stole the thunder of the PAN, which had traditionally located itself on the right and had pushed the interests of business. On the left, the PRD was left to warn of foreign intrusion and, together with the PAN, grouse that there should be more democratic participation in pursuing NAFTA.

Large Mexican industries, such as cement, did not have to be convinced of the benefits that would flow from integration. Small agricultural operations would suffer the brunt of competing with the north in grain, but business groups integrated into the PRI organization went along. The same was the case with labor organizations associated with the party. Most were convinced that increased foreign investment could only help them.

The PRI succeeded in projecting a new image, at least in the area of liberal economic ideology, away from its earlier links with populism. It triumphed in the 1994 presidential campaign but still has the problem of overcoming its link with corruption. If the PRI is to remain in power, it must make real improvements in the lives of average Mexicans. The PRI will progress in its attempt to recapture the confidence of the people if the actual benefits match the rhetoric used in marketing NAFTA.

ENVIRONMENT

The concern for sustainable development, which is another term for protection of the environment, was one of the principles incorporated in the declaration of the summit of the Americas, which took place in Miami, Florida, in December 1994. Is economic and political development compatible with protection of the environment? It has become a contentious issue, separating the northern industrial nations from the developing countries generally located to the south of them. The developing world sees it as the height of hypocrisy on the part of the industrialized world to change the rules of the game as the former are attempting to come into their own.

Although the evidence is controversial at times, which allows some to postpone corrective measures, on the whole people can agree that we are affecting the environment in significant ways and that it will take cooperation by all of us to address the issue because the consequences of local indifference are global. Humans are now the principal driving force behind global environmental change (barring the occasional eruption of a Mount St. Helens). We are becoming aware that these forces transcend local concerns; that the time required to deal with these conditions may take decades; and that the policies required will take skill, flexibility, and the reconciliation of diverse and antagonistic interests.

Many of the demands of the free traders are opposed by the environmentalists, who criticize them for moving too fast and being dependent on environmentally destructive fuels. Although there are leaders in the United States sympathetic to sustainable development, such as Vice President Al Gore, it is difficult to reach a unified policy on environmental issues because of partisan opportunism, concern over the loss of sovereignty, and at times sincere disputes over the proper interpretation of scientific evidence.

Demand for tropical products in the United States is going to influence the land use in Central America as tropical forests are converted into furniture or the biodiversity of the natural forest is transformed into the biomonotony of a banana plantation. It is claimed that the conversion rate of going up the food chain is 10:1; that is, each pound of beef requires 10 pounds of grain. This is another way of saying that as the ranchers in Chiapas increase their cattle herds, they are pushing the indigenous population off the land because 10 pounds of beans could just as well have become 1 pound of Juan Doe. The natives can either migrate to the cities, where they become an urban problem and later perhaps one for the Immigration and Naturalization Service (INS, or *migra*), or to the Lacandón forest. There they will slash and burn and in time destroy or remove the nutrients, which in a rainforest are locked up in the biomass. The depleted forest will no longer be able to arrest the falling rain, and erosion will silt up the streams, affecting the wildlife and in time interfering with the reservoirs and the generation of power.

In Haiti 63 percent of those employed are rural workers laboring on land that is denuded, exhausted, and no longer able to support the population. Their earnings account for 28 percent of the GDP. Coffee is the leading export crop. Haiti cannot afford to degrade its agricultural base any further, and it has no other option but to engage in sustainable development.

Development will take cooperation, but one cannot escape the environment. Now that the cold war is over, we may be able to focus on a more subtle but no less consequential form of international security.

HAITI

On February 7, 1991, Jean-Bertrand Aristide, Haiti's first democratically elected president, was inaugurated. He was overthrown seven months later by a military coup led by General Raul Cedras and others associated with the former discredited regimes of François "Papa Doc" Duvalier and his son, Jean-Claude "Baby Doc," who had been waiting for the opportunity. This overthrow was a blatant disregard for the democratic progress that had been achieved by a people tyrannized since their declaration of independence from France in 1804. It was also an affront to the recent resolutions to uphold constitutional regimes passed by the Organization of American States. The OAS responded by calling on October 8 for a hemispheric trade embargo on Haiti. The message was subverted when the Bush administration exempted the assembly plants associated with U.S. corporations.

Increasing repression resulted in an exodus of Haitians, who left the island on just about anything that would float. Many refugees were lost at sea but enough reached American shores to prompt an order from President Bush on May 24, 1992, calling for their repatriation to Haiti. Reports of the mistreatment awaiting the returnees created a sympathetic response in America. This attitude prompted Bill Clinton to claim that, if elected, he would change our Haitian policy. He was elected but continued with the repatriation policies of the previous administration. However, an attempt was launched to put more pressure on the Haitian military by imposing an oil embargo, sponsored by the United Nations, on June 23, 1993.

On July 3, 1993, President Aristide and General Cedras met at Governor's Island in New York. At that meeting they reached an accord that allowed Aristide to return in exchange for amnesty for Cedras and his supporters. After the embargo was lifted, Cedras reneged on the deal. Things then turned uglier for supporters of Aristide. Armed civilians supported by the military, known as *attachés*, engaged in the most outlandish depredations against the general population. In September Antoine Izmery, an ally and financial backer of Aristide, was dragged from church and murdered in front of a horrified congregation. Then, as a supreme act of defiance to the international community, a mob prevented the docking of the *U.S. Harlan County*, which was bringing 200 noncombat troops to prepare for Aristide's return.

The Security Council unanimously approved a blockade by the U.S. Navy, and a worldwide oil embargo took effect at midnight October 18, 1993, all to no avail. Many of the elite in Haiti profited from the embargo because they controlled smuggling on their part of the island and gained from the increased cost of gasoline on the black market. More pressure was needed to resolve the standoff. The U.S. administration froze the American-held assets of the military's supporters and suspended flights out of Haiti. The UN approved a resolution authorizing the use of force. President Clinton was able to overcome partisan politics in the United States by approving a last-minute attempt to reach an accord through the mediation efforts of a peace delegation comprising former President Jimmy Carter, Senator Sam Nunn, and retired General Colin Powell. They convinced Cedras to accept a peaceful solution and withdraw from power. At the same time President Clinton had dispatched an invasion force to Haiti. Those troops were already underway as the discussions were concluding on September 19, 1994. To the relief of everyone, the force was able to land on the island without opposition.

The record of U.S. intervention in Haiti is not good. The American military previously occupied the island from 1915 to 1934. There is still controversy about the motivation for this earlier occupation. Was it concern for the violence in Haiti or was it to secure the investments of Chase Manhattan Bank? Some say the occupation was the result of a threat to the Caribbean by the Germans. The U.S. presence was resented during that period, and American troops had to fight against Haitian guerrillas. Although the occupation brought about some improvements in health, for example, others, such as roads, resulted from forced labor by Haitians who were supervised by an army of occupation. American involvement resulted in the concentration of power in Port-au-Prince and consolidation of the army, which had the unintended effect of supporting Papa Doc's eventual rise to power.

To succeed, democracy is going to have to transform almost 200 years of misrule and oppression. Will the popular Jean-Bertrand Aristide, who promised to leave office when his term as president concludes in 1996, have sufficient time to begin a process of reform that, in effect, would be revolutionary? Will he receive the economic support required to transform an infrastructure devastated by years of neglect and pillage? His supporters won a majority of seats in the legislature during the summer 1995 election. If the military and police can be reformed and the elites controlled, the people of Haiti might be able to restart the journey to independence they began in 1804.

NOTES

1. Nicolas Sanchez-Albornoz, *The Population of Latin America*, trans. W. Richardson (Berkeley: University of California Press, 1974), p. 86; in Jack W. Hopkins, ed., *Latin America: Perspectives on a Region* (New York: Holmes and Mier, 1987), p. 11.
2. C. W. Harring, *The Spanish Empire in America* (New York: Harbinger, 1963), p. 5.
3. Abraham F. Lowenthal, ed., *Exporting Democracy: The United States and Latin America, Themes and Issues* (London: Johns Hopkins University Press, 1991).
4. Samuel Flagg Bemis, *The Latin American Policy of the United States* (New York: Norton, 1967), pp. 63–66.
5. For a straightforward contrast of many of the contending theories about economic and political development, see Ronald H. Chilcote, *Theories of Comparative Politics: The Search for a Paradigm* (Boulder, Col.: Westview Press, 1981), chap. 7, "Theories of Development and Underdevelopment." See also Hernando de Soto, in collaboration with the Instituto Libertad y Democracia, *The Other Path: The Invisible Revolution in the Third World*, trans. June Abbott (New York: Harper & Row, 1985), for a critical study of the causes for economic stagnation in his country by a Peruvian businessperson. De Soto describes the internal roadblocks to development, such as the interminable formal requirements imposed on newcomers by the economic establishment. For example, an effort to establish a typical one-owner garment factory required 10 months and a loss of net profits equivalent to 32 times the minimum living wage, as well as 11 permits. The owners were asked for bribes 10 times to "expedite" approval, but they paid only the two without which the project would have been killed. Enormous resources are being squandered daily in much of Latin America because of the control associated with the old economic order. See also Jan Knippers Black, *Development in Theory and Practice: Bridging the Gap* (Boulder, Col.: Westview Press, 1991).
6. Thomas E. Skidmore, *Politics in Brazil, 1930–1969: An Experiment in Democracy* (New York: Oxford University Press, 1967), p. 206.
7. Jan Knippers Black, *United States Penetration of Brazil* (Philadelphia: University of Pennsylvania Press, 1977).
8. *Los Angeles Times*, May 19, 1995, p. A-13.
9. Hugh Thomas, *Cuba: The Pursuit of Freedom* (New York: Harper & Row, 1971), p. 557.
10. *Los Angeles Times*, May 7, 1995, p. A-19.

11. Moises Naim, "Latin America the Morning After," *Foreign Affairs*, 74, 4 (July/August, 1995): 60–61.
12. Andrew Reding, "Chiapas Is Mexico: The Imperative of Political Reform," *World Policy Journal*, 11, 1 (Spring 1994): 14.

FOR FURTHER READING

Atkins, G. Pope. *Latin America in the International Political System*. 3rd ed. rev. Boulder, Col.: Westview Press, 1995.

Cardoso, Fernando H., and Faletto, Enzo. *Dependency and Development in Latin America*. Berkeley: University of California Press, 1979.

Cockcroft, James D. *Neighbors in Turmoil: Latin America*. New York: Harper & Row, 1989.

———. *Latin America: History, Politics, and U.S. Policy*. Chicago: Nelson-Hall, 1996.

Domínguez, Jorge I., and Hernández, Rafael, eds. *U.S.-Cuban Relations in the 1990s*. Boulder, Col.: Westview Press, 1989.

Lowenthal, Abraham F., and Treventon, Gregory F., eds. *Latin America in a New World*. Boulder, Col.: Westview Press, 1994.

Molineu, Harold. *U.S. Policy toward Latin America: From Regionalism to Globalism*. 2nd ed. Boulder, Col.: Westview Press, 1990.

O'Donnell, Guillermo. *Modernization and Bureaucratic-Authoritarianism: Studies in South American Politics*. Berkeley: Institute of International Studies, University of California, 1973.

Pastor, Robert A. *Whirlpool: U.S. Foreign Policy toward Latin America and the Caribbean*. Princeton, N.J.: Princeton University Press, 1993.

Petras, James, and Morley, Morris. *Latin America in the Time of Cholera: Electoral Politics, Market Economics, and Permanent Crisis*. New York: Routledge, 1992.

Silva-Michelena, José A., ed. *Latin America: Peace, Democratization & Economic Crisis*. United Nations University. Studies on Peace and Regional Security. London: Zed Books, 1988.

Skidmore, Thomas E., and Smith, Peter H. *Modern Latin America*. 2nd ed. New York: Oxford University Press, 1989.

Stein, Stanley, and Stein, Barbara. *The Colonial Heritage of Latin America*. New York: Oxford University Press, 1970.

Trouillot, Michel-Rolph. *Haiti: State against the Nation: Origins and Legacy of Duvalierism*. New York: Monthly Review Press, 1990.

Veliz, Claudio. *The Centralist Tradition of Latin America*. Princeton, N.J.: Princeton University Press, 1980.

Wiarda, Howard J. *American Foreign Policy toward Latin America in the 80s and 90s: Issues and Controversies from Reagan to Bush*. New York and London: New York University Press, 1992.

CHAPTER **6**

Sub-Saharan Africa

Richard Kranzdorf

Seek ye first the political kingdom and all other things will be added unto you.
Kwame Nkrumah

Viewed from the standpoint of the last half of the 1990s, these words from one of Africa's leaders in the post–World War II generation seem quaint or naive. Independence from colonial rule did not bring "all other things." As this chapter emphasizes, Africa's internal problems have multiplied and worsened in the past decade. In addition, foreign interests now appear to be focusing their attention elsewhere in the world. The political instability, economic decline, social unrest, and environmental degradation that became commonplace in most of the states of the region will not quickly improve.

From 1957 to 1980, more than three dozen African colonies achieved independence, some peacefully and others violently. Despite the different roads taken, a common theme ran through these new states in their early years: hope, excitement, deliverance.

This early enthusiasm struck a responsive chord in the West. Some leaders were genuinely supportive of the new order. British Prime Minister Harold Macmillan declared that "the winds of change" were blowing through Africa and would have to be accommodated. Youthful President John F. Kennedy embraced the notion of a Peace Corps, with Africa to be a major recipient of hundreds and then thousands of practical idealists. Further, it was believed that the East-West conflict would be fought in the Other World, and the battle for the hearts and minds of the people of Africa was seen as an important objective.

If this earlier period was one of optimism and gains in Africa, then the 1980s was one of pessimism and losses. In fact, the period has been described as "the lost decade." Although there are success stories and some recent encouraging signs, the overall situation is disheartening. It is true that the 1990s have witnessed a modest increase in participatory political systems. Further, as will be seen in the

Case Studies and Flashpoint sections of this chapter, several of the wars in Africa have abated or ended. However, many countries continue to be under either military rule or strict civilian governments in which democracy, at least as we understand it in the West (e.g., freedom of speech and press, competitive elections, and an independent judiciary), is significantly restricted or nonexistent. In a number of states significant human rights abuses still occur.

By virtually any index, the economic situation has worsened. Per capita income, already the lowest in the Other World, actually declined during the 1980s. The international monetary debt of most African states soared. Unemployment or underemployment continued its upward climb. Most agricultural products and minerals are fetching lower world prices than 10 or 15 years ago, and many millions simply do not get enough to eat.

Nor is the picture any brighter in other areas. The population explosion continues unabated, again far higher than in the rest of the Other World. Food production has not kept pace with population growth, and despite rising food imports, the average African has less to eat now than in 1980. Environmental degradation increases yearly, and the underlying support systems sag under the onslaught. More and more species are endangered as impoverished humans encroach on their habitat, sometimes killing the animals for profit. Similarly, the quality of education is in serious straits, and new health problems such as AIDS dwarf older ones, which have been curbed or eliminated.

The history and geography provide some clues to the causes of this unhappy situation. A discussion of the political, social, and economic realities within and beyond Africa today provides additional explanations (see table 6.1). The case studies illustrate the dilemmas the peoples of Africa are facing. The chapter concludes with Flashpoints on current trouble spots. (Discussion of the five North African states bordering the Mediterranean is included in chapter 8.)

GEOGRAPHY

Africa, second in size only to Asia, has some of the world's mightiest rivers and abundant mineral resources. Nevertheless, the region has more than its share of natural impediments to development, including its relative isolation from other areas of the world. The Atlantic Ocean is located to the west of the continent and the Indian Ocean to the east. Prevailing wind patterns on the west coast minimized maritime contacts between Africans and Europeans until the fifteenth or sixteenth century. With the Sahara desert in the north, it is easy to understand why overland transportation from Europe and North Africa was and is spotty. The Kalahari desert in the southern part of the continent is an additional obstacle.

Africa's great rivers—Nile, Zaire (Congo), Niger, Zambezi, and Orange—all have cataracts, sand bars, or other obstructions, which also undermine rather than enhance communications. The continent's smooth coastline, and thus its lack of natural harbors, has been another problem, although today coastal cities such as Dakar, Lagos, Luanda, and Dar es Salaam are highly important.

TABLE 6.1 Africa

Country	Population (millions)	Population Growth Rate (%) (1992–2000)	Infant Mortality Rate (per 1,000 live births)	Population Under 15 Years of Age (%)	Life Expectancy (years)	Urban Population (%)	UNDP Literacy Rate (%) (1992)	Arable Land (%)	UNDP Per Capita GNP ($U.S.)
Northern									
Algeria	27.9	2.7	52	44	66	50	61	3	1,990
Egypt	59.3	2.1	76	40	61	45	50	3	610
Libya	5.1	3.4	63	47	62	76	66	2	—
Morocco	28.6	2.3	50	40	63	40	52	18	1,030
Tunisia	8.7	1.9	34	37	67	—	68	20	1,500
Western									
Benin	5.3	3.0	110	47	46	38	25	12	380
Burkina Faso	10.1	2.7	118	—	48	21	20	10	290
Cape Verde	0.4	2.8	58	44	67	44	67	9	750
Côte d'Ivoire	14.3	3.5	95	47	52	39	56	9	680
Gambia	1.0	2.5	124	45	46	26	30	16	360
Ghana	17.2	2.9	83	45	56	34	63	5	420
Guinea	6.4	3.0	139	—	44	26	27	6	500
Guinea-Bissau	1.1	2.1	120	—	43	—	39	11	180
Liberia	3.0	3.2	113	45	55	43	42	1	—
Mali	9.1	3.1	106	46	45	22	36	2	270
Mauritania	2.2	2.8	85	44	47	39	35	—	510
Niger	8.6	3.2	111	49	46	15	31	3	310
Nigeria	98.1	5.1	75	—	52	16	52	31	350
Senegal	8.7	2.7	76	47	49	39	40	27	730
Sierra Leone	4.6	2.6	142	45	42	32	24	25	200
Togo	4.3	3.1	89	49	54	29	45	25	410

Region / Country								
Eastern								
Burundi	6.1	2.7	114	46	48	6	52	43	220
Djibouti	0.4	2.9	111	—	49	77	—	—	—
Ethiopia	58.7	3.0	106	49	46	—	71	12	120
Kenya	28.2	3.3	74	49	59	25	81	3	340
Madagascar	13.4	3.2	89	—	55	22	—	4	210
Malawi	9.7	2.6	141	48	45	17	80	25	230
Mauritius	1.1	0.9	18	30	70	39	34	54	2,380
Mozambique	17.3	3.2	129	44	47	—	52	4	80
Rwanda	8.4	3.3	119	48	47	55	—	29	290
Seychelles	.72	0.8	12	35	71	50	—	—	5,070
Somalia	6.7	3.1	126	—	46	24	27	2	—
Sudan	29.4	2.7	80	—	51	23	28	5	—
Tanzania	28	3.2	110	47	54	21	—	5	120
Uganda	19.9	2.8	112	47	43	11	51	23	170
Zambia	9.2	2.7	85	48	46	49	75	7	420
Zimbabwe	11	2.8	74	48	56	27	69	7	670
Middle								
Angola	9.8	3.5	145	—	46	28	43	2	—
Cameroon	13.1	2.8	77	45	55	41	57	13	860
Central African Republic	3.1	2.5	137	41	47	47	40	3	410
Chad	5.5	2.8	132	41	47	32	33	2	210
Congo	2.4	2.9	111	—	52	41	59	2	1040
Equatorial Guinea	0.4	2.5	103	43	47	—	52	8	290
Gabon	1.1	3.2	95	—	53	46	62	1	3,980
São Tomé and Príncipe	0.1	2.0	64	—	67	—	—	1	400
Zaire	42.7	3.1	111	45	52	40	74	3	—
Southern								
Botswana	1.4	2.9	39	48	60	26	75	2	2,580
Lesotho	1.9	2.5	70	41	60	—	—	10	570
Namibia	1.6	3.1	62	—	58	33	—	—	1,520
South Africa	43.9	2.3	47	39	62	57	—	10	2,540
Swaziland	.9	2.7	93	47	57	23	—	8	1,130

SOURCE: Adapted from the *United Nations Demographic Yearbook*, *United Nations Human Development Report*, and *The World Almanac and Book of Facts*, 1995.

Most of the region's interior is flat or gently undulating. The major exception is the great Rift Valley system in eastern Africa, which runs north to south for hundreds of miles and digs deep trenches, 20 to 50 miles wide, into the earth. Inactive volcanoes, frequent earth tremors, and occasional earthquakes occur in the area. Lake Victoria is the largest lake in Africa and Mount Kilimanjaro is the continent's highest mountain, 19,340 feet above sea level.

Whatever the focus, African geography runs the gamut from scarcity to abundance. Although temperatures are generally high, rainfall, when abundant, gives rise to lush vegetation; more often, the absence of rainfall contributes to a parched landscape. Varying soil quality also helps produce rainforests, savanna, or deserts. Mineral resources follow the same oscillating pattern. Some areas in central and southern Africa are uniquely blessed, whereas other locales are virtually void of substances valued in the modern world (see figure 6.1).

The complex interaction of temperature, rainfall, population growth and distribution, and soils is of crucial significance in Africa today. The human habitat was once more hospitable. Thirty-five hundred years ago what is now the Sahara was green. Just 40 years ago the Sahel, which includes the area lying just south of the Sahara, was able to sustain a population of perhaps 20 million. Today, famine is an ever-present danger. Millions of nomadic herders, traders, and small farmers have been turned into refugees trying to eke out a living in an increasingly unforgiving environment.

As a result, both the farmer, whose land becomes more difficult to till, and the herder are forced to move to overcrowded cities. Nouakchott, for instance, the capital of Mauritania and on the edge of the Sahel, has grown from 20,000 people in 1960 to more than 350,000 today. Many of its people barely survive; some starve. The same might be said of Khartoum, the capital of Sudan, some 3,000 miles away. In the last few years, eastern and southern Africa have been affected in a similar way. In fact, the encroaching desert, aided by drought, has affected some two dozen African states.

In the past, Africa's strategic importance rested on its mineral wealth in the central and southern parts of the continent and its geographic "chokepoints" on the perimeter of the region. High-tech industries of the West relied on platinum, chrome, and vanadium, which are found almost exclusively in Africa. Gibraltar, the Suez Canal, Bab el Mandeb, and the Cape of Good Hope at the southern tip of the continent were strategic areas of interest to both East and West. With the end of the cold war, both the economic and geopolitical standing of the region declined.

PEOPLE

Africa's people have been divided by many factors including race, ethnicity, religion, country, and class. The importance of race was established as early as the fifteenth century. Later, it was tied to class when positions in society became dominated by Europeans. Because of the colonial legacy, the belief that one race is superior or inferior to another still has considerable significance in Africa. The em-

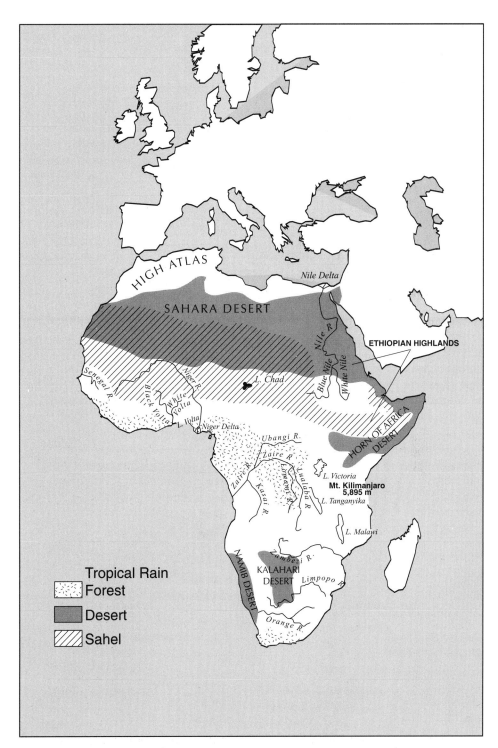

Tropical Rain
Forest

Desert

Sahel

FIGURE 6.1 The Physical Geography of Africa

155

phasis on race was clearest in South Africa, where apartheid, a form of separate development based on race, was officially proclaimed by whites in 1948 and rescinded only in 1990.

Race still remains important in many other African countries. In several former French colonies, there are almost as many Europeans now as there were at independence more than three decades ago. There, as elsewhere, Europeans have many of the most prestigious and best-paying jobs. Often being white gets one a better seat in a van or truck or allows one to be waved through a checkpoint while others with a darker skin must wait. For the present then, Europeans, a name often given to all whites, still enjoy a high social status and life-style far above that of most of the indigenous residents.

Between the Europeans and the Africans on the ladder of success are the Indians of East and South Africa and the Lebanese of West Africa. Both groups are major forces in retail and wholesale merchandising and in the economy generally. Because of their positions, both are also targets of protest from those below them on the ladder.

When discussing language, ethnic groups, cultures (and subcultures), and religions, the key concepts are diversity and complexity. There are, conservatively, many hundreds of different ethnic groups. (Because of the negative connotations of the words *tribe* and *tribalism*, the terms *ethnic group* and *ethnicity* have replaced them.) Thus, there are many hundreds of distinct languages and cultures. While some groups number in the millions of members, others have only hundreds. The sheer number of such groups throughout Africa makes this dimension unique to the continent. Ethnic divisions are a powerful force today. Ongoing struggles in such diverse states as Angola, Burundi, Ethiopia, Kenya, Liberia, Mauritania, Nigeria, and Rwanda may be explained, in part, by deep-seated ethnic divisions.

African religions, again diverse and complex, have generally accommodated external religions, accepting some aspects and modifying others. Christian missionaries, who preceded colonial officials, remained after their government's departure. Although numbers are hard to come by, there is a consensus that the number of people embracing either the monotheism of Christianity or Islam in some form is growing rapidly. The Roman Catholic population, for instance, has grown considerably in the last decade to more than 120 million, and Pope John Paul II has visited the continent no fewer than 11 times. Local customs and beliefs, however, have challenged Rome's pronouncements; indigenous churches therefore abound. Islam has been an important political factor in many countries in the Sahel and the Horn of Africa.

Most people in the West give their primary support to the nation-state, but such a commitment is rare in Africa. Race, ethnicity, and religion have historical and deep-seated appeals that compete with the nation-state. With a large majority of Africans still continuing to live in the rural areas, developing support for the nation-state is a challenge. Only rarely do state and ethnic boundaries coincide. Nationalism is further hampered by the small size and population of many of the countries, as well as their lack of resources.

A belief in a shared past or shared future, in myths or traditions, in joint economic or social institutions, or in a common culture is in short supply on the national level. Rarely is there a common indigenous language. In fact, in most African states, the official language is a European tongue. In conflicts between personal, family, or ethnic ties on the one hand, and a national perspective on the other, the larger focus usually loses. National leaders and others in the intelligentsia have the media at their disposal in their call for increased support for the state, and expanding education for children and adults helps. Nevertheless, developing a broadly-based nationalism is proceeding only slowly.

As in the Commonwealth of Independent States and Eastern Europe, class formation is expanding and perhaps sharpening. With few exceptions, the emergence of a small elite class, often tied to one ethnic group, has become the norm. For the time being, a comfortable life-style is beyond even the aspirations of the great majority. With the move to privatization described in the section on economics, some will dramatically improve their lot, but many others will become more embittered as life passes them by.

At the beginning of the twentieth century, the continent of Africa had fewer than 100 million people. Its population now is about 700 million. During the 1970s and 1980s, the population growth rate increased to more than 3 percent a year. Different sources say that the region's annual population increase is now anywhere from 2.8 to 3.4 percent. At most, that means a doubling in 25 years.

The birthrate in sub-Saharan Africa has declined slightly in the past generation but the death rate has declined more. More specifically, the infant mortality rate declined by about 30 percent between 1970 and 1992. With fewer babies dying, there will be one less reason for parents to want more children. Nevertheless, births per married woman in the region declined only from 6.7 in 1960–1965 to 6.6 in 1985–1990. Botswana, Ghana, Kenya, and Zimbabwe have achieved varying degrees of success at population control. Kenya, which a decade ago was averaging close to 4 percent growth per year, the world's highest, is now nearing 3 percent. Widespread government programs enacted there since the late 1970s have reduced childbirth rates in Kenya by a third.

However, only 14 percent of married women between 15 and 49 use contraceptives in many African countries. Information and distribution systems for population control are stunted. Some governments still believe family planning will curb the economic potential of their states. In most countries, the status of women is low and their sex education lags behind that of men. The religious admonition calling for large families is another factor driving population growth.[1] It is feared that unless fertility rates soon decline, the continent's life-support systems will be overwhelmed and the mortality rate will increase. Over the past 30 years, economic growth has barely kept pace with population growth.

HISTORY

Africa's history before the arrival of the Europeans was rich, varied, and complex. It involved many types of political systems, social structures, and economic patterns. It also involved considerable interaction with the peoples of North Africa, the Arabian Peninsula, and even China. Africa has been called "the cradle of human history," "the cradle of mankind," and "the first habitat of man." These phrases apply, as the oldest human remains, dating back at least 3 million years, were found in eastern Africa. Nevertheless, many people did not think Africa had a history because, to them, history was based on written language. This bias has now been corrected. In certain areas south of the Sahara, written Arabic was in use a thousand years ago. More important, we now realize that oral traditions, archaeological exploration, comparative linguistics, art styles, ethnography, radio carbon dating, and a host of other tools can provide a rich history, predating the written word.

The domestication of cattle is 6,000 to 7,000 years old in Africa. Working with metal and iron, planting crops, and engaging in long-distance trade are occupations that go back millennia as well. In fact, there is much discussion today over how much impact on Egypt, often referred to as the cradle of civilization, came from areas further south. The Khoi-Khoi (Hottentots), San (Bushmen), and Twa (Pygmies) had long inhabited much of central and southern Africa until incursions from West Africa around the eleventh century began to reduce their spheres.

African kingdoms of great size and wealth predate the European colonial presence by many hundreds of years. Some of the best-known empires—Ghana, Mali, and Songhai—which together lasted over a thousand years, were in the western Sudan, south of the Sahara. Here Islam made its presence felt, especially among the rulers of Mali and Songhai. Great Zimbabwe in southern Africa, with its imposing stone structures, reached its apex in the fifteenth century.

By the eighth century, Arab traders had brought Islam to the Horn of Africa, from which it gradually spread south and west. The Arab presence, however, went back much further, especially along the east coast. In succeeding centuries, traders pushed into the interior, although African culture remained dominant throughout. The Arab influence was great, however, from the formation of towns along the Indian Ocean to the rise of Swahili as the most important language in the region. The arrival of the Portuguese, with their superior military power, at the end of the fifteenth century signaled the rapid decline of Arab culture in the area.

Until the latter half of the nineteenth century, there were few Europeans in sub-Saharan Africa, especially in the vast interior. Despite their small numbers, however, they had a profound and lasting impact on African life. The institution of Western-style slavery cost the continent anywhere from 12 to 50 million men, women, and children. In the seventeenth and eighteenth centuries, slavery was the major export from the west coast of Africa.

By 1850, the European presence in Africa had existed along narrow coastal strips for over 350 years. The Portuguese in the fifteenth and sixteenth centuries, the Dutch in the seventeenth century, and the British in the eighteenth and first part of the nineteenth centuries had been dominant because of sea power. By about 1850, newfound European attention to the "Dark Continent" coincided with turbulence in several parts of Africa and resulted in greater penetration of the interior than ever before. The European objectives in Africa included raw materials to feed the industrial revolution, new markets, promising investments, naval bases, the renewed drive to "save souls," and a multifaceted quest for new knowledge.

THE COLONIAL EXPERIENCE

Despite the increasing presence of the Europeans, 90 percent of the continent was ruled by Africans until the last two decades of the nineteenth century. The European powers had not thought the benefits of occupation were worth the costs. As the foreigners jockeyed for power and prestige on the continent and around the globe, the situation quickly changed. The European states moved to establish a whole series of colonies in the region, and the possibility that the new competition would result in war was seen as a real danger. From October 1884 to February 1885, a conference to discuss the future boundaries of Africa was held in Berlin, at which almost all of the important European powers were represented. The decisions reached there—and elsewhere in Europe in the remaining 15 years of the nineteenth century—established the basic political map of the continent to this day.

Africa was artificially divided to suit the objectives of the colonial governments. Preexisting ethnic, linguistic, and cultural units were ignored. The maps in figures 6.2 and 6.3 are only 11 years apart, but the contrast is striking. Throughout Africa, closely-knit people speaking the same language were suddenly separated. It was from these diversions that future generations' secessionist movements and border claims, known as *irredentism*, would spring.

The heyday of European colonial rule in Africa lasted for only 50 or 60 years. However, those few decades changed the face of the continent forever. The impact of colonialism depended on the type of rule instituted, the presence or absence of white settlers, and the particulars of the African elite. Most important, each African ethnic group had its own political and social system. Each responded to colonial rule in a different way, ranging from willing acceptance to bloody resistance of the outside powers. The Baganda people of East Africa welcomed the European presence. But the Ndebele-Shona Rebellion (1896–1897) against English-speaking settlers in what is now Zimbabwe, the Ashanti and Fulani resistance against the British in West Africa (1900–1901), and the Maji Maji rebellion contesting harsh German rule in East Africa (1905–1907) all resulted in a strong European show of force followed by occupation.

The British generally practiced indirect rule, a system in which they were removed from day-to-day activities; instead they used the traditional authorities, who were now responsible to them. The other colonial systems employed direct rule, in which the European administrators played a much more extensive role in everyday African life. The British, concerned about costs, emphasized the economic dimension and were more aloof; the French, the leading practitioners of direct rule, were more intimately involved, held out the slight possibility that their subjects might become French citizens, and had a more lasting effect on their colonies.

Whatever the differences, the similarities were more important. The colonial powers' dominance occurred everywhere. Different peoples were divided or united by fiat, and long-time trading patterns were subject to fundamental change as the societies themselves were transformed in a hundred different ways. The indigenous populations suffered altered political arrangements, alien tax struc-

FIGURE 6.2 European Colonization in Africa, 1884

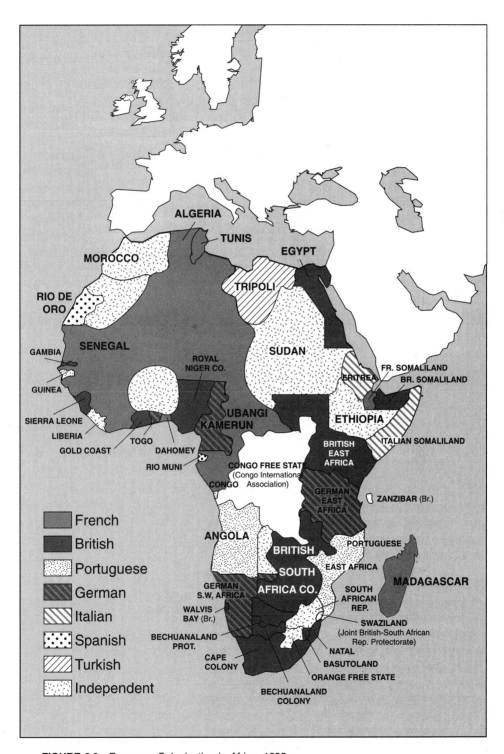

FIGURE 6.3 European Colonization in Africa, 1895

tures, forced labor, and directed changes in individual wants and societal norms. By shifting the roles and selection processes for traditional political leaders, the colonial authorities unintentionally sowed the seeds for far greater political changes in years to come. Much of the economy fell under the influence, if not control, of the Europeans, who wished to substitute one or two cash crops or minerals for subsistence farming. Foreign goods and the widespread use of colonial currencies were also introduced. In addition, the missionary and soldier added their particular persuasions to that of the administrator and merchant. By 1920, only Ethiopia, Liberia, and the Union of South Africa were free from formal European control, and the last was run by a white minority.

The new order scarcely touched the lives of the masses in many of the colonies. The people had little contact with Europeans, except when it was necessary to pay some new tax, live under some new law, or adopt a new plan for local land use. For the majority living in the rural areas, change or adaptation was to be a very gradual thing.

In the Portuguese, German, and Belgian colonies, the rule was far more harsh and the impact was often far more devastating. Villagers were routinely taken, with or without their leaders' approval, to work on roads or other projects. But impressment was the least of it. The Congo Free State, for instance, was the private preserve of the Belgian king, whose control was so inhumane that after about 20 years he was forced to cede his 900,000-square-mile playground to the government of Belgium, which then established an only slightly more benevolent rule over this mammoth colony in the middle of Africa.

The movement to independence can be described in two ways: structurally or chronologically. Among the most important structures in the movement, especially to the generation coming of age at the turn of the century, was the church. This institution was part of the white establishment, with its distinction between superior and inferior values, but it was also a source for Western-style education and a breeding ground for future nationalists. Although Christianity first undermined local cultures and traditions, later, independent, indigenous Christian churches came to question colonial government policies. Other institutions of change were located in the fast-growing cities. These included the tribal unions and associations; trade unions or workers' solidarity organizations; the rudimentary mass media; the soldiers and ex-servicemen, who had traveled beyond the colony; and finally, overt political movements. All contributed to the requests for greater responsibility by the local, African elite; to calls for autonomy or power sharing by the growing nationalist movement; and ultimately, to demands for independence, now backed by the masses.

Chronologically, the trickle of restrained nationalism before 1885 became a torrent of calls for independence in the years after World War II. West Africa moved ahead more quickly than East Africa, which in turn led the southern part of the continent. Overall, the British colonies were in advance of the French, who led the Portuguese. But even the British were cautious, expecting at most a slow devolution of power. The British anticipated that black parliamentary governments would be established by local leaders, who would be "properly" educated and trained. For the French, those few Africans who gained political power would do so not in African political structures but as overseas representatives in the French National Assembly in Paris. The other European powers believed that any growth of political consciousness would change the status quo and thus was unthinkable.

When World War II began in 1939, no one would have guessed that independence for most of the African colonies was only a generation away. Despite the depression of the 1930s, colonial rule appeared immutable. Certainly, there were the firebrands who agitated for greater rights for Africans, but they were few in number and cautious in method, despite an occasional protest or even riot at a particular location.

The war, however, had a tremendous effect on all parties. Tens of thousands of soldiers saw action beyond the continent. They returned home with newly honed skills and ideas and settled in the cities rather than returning to their homes in the rural areas. They became a part of the mass independence movements that were destined to sweep the continent. The new militancy was fueled by large numbers of students returning to Africa from overseas, the demands of an increasingly urbanized population, and a new generation of political leaders. The battered European powers, meanwhile, were simply hoping to hang on at home and had little interest and few resources for the colonies, thousands of miles away.

Africans under French rule were ready for a new day. Early in the war, General Charles de Gaulle had promised greater local autonomy (but not self-government) and increased rights for the peoples of French West Africa (FWA) and French Equatorial Africa (FEA) if they supported him in his battle against Vichy France and Nazi Germany. Similarly, in 1941, U.S. President Franklin Roosevelt and British Prime Minister Winston Churchill promised in the Atlantic Charter "to respect the right of all peoples to choose the form of government under which they will live." At the end of the war, the newly founded United Nations called for self-determination, and the two emerging superpowers—the United States and the Soviet Union—both supported changes in the existing colonial order.

The beginning of the end for colonial rule began with a railway workers' strike in FWA in 1946, followed by disturbances over economic issues in the Gold Coast, a presumed model British colony in West Africa, in early 1948. This latter protest, in which ex-servicemen played a major role, spread to the other British colonies in the area. In those postwar years, a new law and a new constitution in Paris also accelerated change throughout FWA and FEA. In the years that followed, Africans living thousands of miles apart, speaking hundreds of different languages, and subjects of several colonial powers took up the unifying cry of self-government.

Independence came first to the Gold Coast (renamed Ghana) in 1957. The next year, President de Gaulle angrily accepted Guinea's vote to follow suit.[2] At the same time, the other colonies that had been carved out of FWA and FEA chose federation with France, allowing Paris continuing control of foreign affairs, internal security, and defense. In 1960, the logjam broke as the remaining 11 French-speaking colonies became independent. The same year Nigeria ended its colonial relationship with Britain to become a regional magnet. For the next 20 years the march to independence continued, and by the end of 1980 only Namibia, on the southwest coast of Africa, remained in a dependent status (see figure 6.4); South Africa, despite UN resolutions, refused to give up its controlling interest over the former German colony it had inherited as a mandate after World War I. Finally, in 1990, even this dependency ended, as a general agreement on regional relations in southern Africa was reached (see the Angola-Namibia case study).

Independence throughout the region had been achieved. But if this was a time for celebration, it was also a time of great concern since there was never a consensus on future directions within each state, let alone within regions or the continent as a whole. Older animosities that sometimes had been kept under wraps by the colonial power burst forth. Opposing local, national, and supranational forces threatened the stability of the fragile new states. Furthermore, the economic dimension was no more secure than the political, as local economies remained vulnerable to both domestic and international interests. The former colonial states were independent, but their governments lacked the sustained support of the people or, in some cases, the international community. Without such support, unity and economic well-being were unlikely.

GOVERNMENT

To understand African government in the 1990s, one must realize that there has been an incredible compression of major political events. People who are now middle-aged grew up in the heyday of colonial rule, lived through World War II and the nationalist rush to independence, and finally have experienced the instabilities of the postindependence years. The scholar Ali Mazrui quoted former Tanzanian President Julius Nyerere as saying that whereas some countries are trying to reach the moon and beyond, many Africans are still trying to get to town.[3] Today, such traditional institutions and values as the extended family and communal ownership of property are under attack while a new set of institutions and beliefs are not yet in place.

Instead of rule by the people, African independence has usually resulted in the continued rule of the few, though now the new elites are indigenous, not foreign. The urban community, not the majority in the countryside, gets the bulk of state-run programs. In the cities, it is the small middle and upper classes who benefit from government. Despite a long history of group participation in decision making in many societies, pronouncements today are usually still made by and for the few. Women are rarely a political or economic force, except in retail or wholesale trade. The result is too often an elite driven by self-interest and even greed, while the many are disregarded.

Political solutions tried elsewhere in the Other World have faced opposition and inertia from societies in Africa. A major problem for the social elites is that the people have little faith in them. Although a few traditional authorities such as Chief Gatsha Buthelezi of the Zulu people in South Africa exercise considerable political influence, such examples are rare. For one thing, almost all African states comprise many ethnic groups, and traditional authorities may be unsuccessful in reaching out to those who owe them no special allegiance. Moreover,

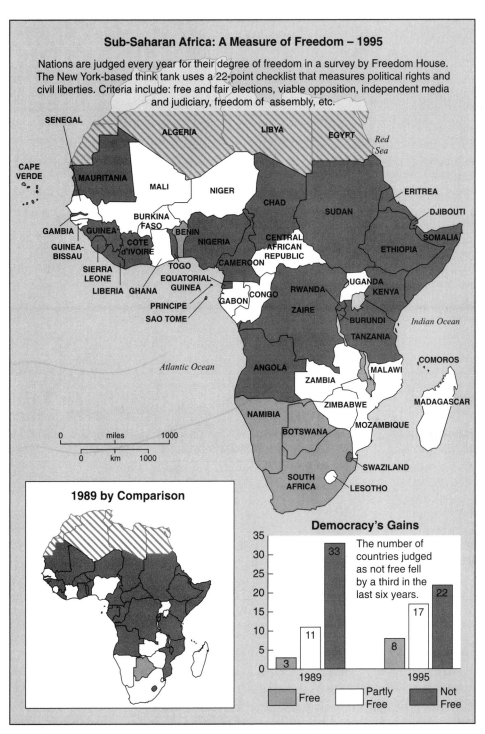

Sub-Saharan Africa: A Measure of Freedom – 1995

Nations are judged every year for their degree of freedom in a survey by Freedom House. The New York-based think tank uses a 22-point checklist that measures political rights and civil liberties. Criteria include: free and fair elections, viable opposition, independent media and judiciary, freedom of assembly, etc.

1989 by Comparison

Democracy's Gains

The number of countries judged as not free fell by a third in the last six years.

1989: Free 3, Partly Free 11, Not Free 33
1995: Free 8, Partly Free 17, Not Free 22

Free | Partly Free | Not Free

FIGURE 6.4 Sub-Saharan Africa: A Measure of Freedom—1995

165

few of these authorities have real political power. They may also carry the baggage of colonial days, when their functions were usually altered by their European overlords, thus leading to the loss of respect from their subjects.

By the early 1980s, competitive political party systems in Africa were a rarity. This fact would have surprised earlier generations since, in many cases, the political party was in the forefront of the march to independence and in doing so gained mass support. Some parties managed to gain the grudging blessing of the colonial rulers, who looked fondly to their own political parties as models.

In the last years of the twentieth century, two trends are observable: First, democracy is on the rise in Africa. Second, the situation remains very fluid. Each year, Freedom House, an organization based in New York City, issues a global assessment of the level of "freedom" in each country in the world. Free speech, independent media and judiciary, freedom of assembly, free and fair elections, and viable opposition are among 22 criteria used. As figure 6.4 makes clear, in 1995, 8 countries in Africa were listed as free, 17 as partly free, and 22 as not free. From the standpoint of democracy, this is a significant improvement over a few years earlier.[4]

What are the reasons for this change? The end of the cold war meant that the United States and the Soviet Union would no longer back rival groups or countries; the cessation of the resulting political turmoil is thus one explanation. The rise of democratic governments that serve as models in other parts of the world is a second. Greater willingness of human rights activists, journalists, and other courageous individuals to step forward to criticize the status quo is apparent. Rising levels of education, health, and economic well-being in some countries have also helped. That African states spend less money on the military frees funds for more productive uses.[5] Finally, more people simply demand a say in the way their government is run. Such devices as cellular phones and the Internet allow more instantaneous communications, enabling Africans to become aware of conditions elsewhere.

The fluid nature of most political systems in the region tempers the comments of the previous paragraph. Given the many other contemporary elements mentioned in the chapter, it cannot be otherwise. Cote d'Ivoire, for instance, had an election in late 1995. While opposition parties were permitted, their leaders were banned from running and critical newspapers were muzzled. Few democratic governments have established themselves in this part of Africa.

Pan-Africanism and Regional Cooperation

In the 1990s, a number of countries were involved in civil wars. The governments themselves seemed incapable of dealing with the many problems they faced, yet relying on grass-roots movements invited challenges to the regimes' authority and stability. The remaining alternative was to look beyond individual borders to common efforts in the region. The notion of a common heritage, common values, and a common future again resonated deeply among a growing minority. After all, pan-African congresses had been held during early decades of this century.

In the early 1960s, it was clear that there was a struggle between more militant governments who wanted to work for continental fusion and Mother Africa and those who, having just gained independence, did not wish to be swallowed up by some larger entity. Antagonistic blocs of countries formed. Trying to stem the hostilities, 30 African states met in the Ethiopian capital of Addis Ababa in May 1963. The result was the creation of the Organization of African Unity (OAU), whose principles included

1. National independence over continental unity
2. Nonintervention in the affairs of another state
3. The sanctity of national boundaries
4. The responsibility of Africans for peacefully solving their own problems
5. The adoption of a nonaligned or neutralist stance
6. Equality of all sovereign states

Support for liberation movements was agreed to in a resolution, but it was not a principle on which the organization was founded.

In the ensuing years, OAU membership swelled as more than three dozen colonies became independent. Annual meetings of heads of state and foreign ministers were held to promote political, economic, and cultural cooperation. But, as in the UN, hard decisions involving action were in short supply. The acrimony of the early years was papered over, only to reignite over a number of issues in the late 1970s. By the mid-1980s, the OAU was so deeply in debt that its day-to-day operations were in jeopardy.

In the past decade, financial problems and the traditional unwillingness to intervene "in the affairs of another state" loomed very large. In any case, as we know from Bosnia, regional intervention is difficult and perilous. The OAU has attempted to play a calming role in the long-festering conflict in Liberia but with only limited results. The OAU was all but invisible in the civil wars in Somalia and Rwanda in the 1990s.

Regional organizations have been somewhat more active, though there have certainly been more disappointments than successes. Although there are more than 200 organizations for regional cooperation, most in Africa have been simply façades and not cost effective. Large bureaucracies, an unwillingness to decentralize control, politicized appointments, and marginal interest among African states limited the importance of regional institutions. Further drawbacks have included the uneven distribution of benefits and costs, inadequate budgets, duplication of efforts among different organizations, and problems of coordination.

By all odds the most important and successful of the regional entities is the Southern African Development Community (SADC), which includes the states of Angola, Mozambique, Botswana, Lesotho, Swaziland, Zimbabwe, Zambia, Malawi, Tanzania, Namibia, and beginning in 1994, South Africa. This organization, which had worked to counter white-ruled South Africa, became vastly more important with the addition of its 11th member. In short order, the emerging bloc entered into a trade concession agreement with the European Union. There was also a treaty forwarding political and economic cooperation between member states. With trade between the members only 25 percent of total trade, and trade between the original 10 states only 4 percent of the total, there is plenty of room for growth. The large turnout from governments and business leaders at the 1995 Southern Africa Economic Summit seemed to underscore the optimism. And with the possible exception of Angola, the countries in the area also appeared to be on a more stable political footing.

African Relations with Outside Powers

Over the past century, Africa's relations with outside powers have gone through several stages and may now be entering a new one. As the earlier discussion in this chapter suggested, the colonial powers consolidated their control over most of the continent in the 1890s. At least through World War II, the United States, the Soviet Union, and China did not challenge the domination of the existing order. Even the advent and pursuit of the cold war did not at first change this order. The Other World, and especially Africa, was not seen as a major theater of competition. Conflicts might flare around the perimeter of the Soviet Union and even to a limited degree in Latin America, but Africa was a backwater.

As African states began to achieve independence in the late 1950s, however, this situation began to change. The U.S.-Soviet rivalry became global, and soon the Chinese entered the maneuvering. In addition, the French continued their strong economic and military presence in the region. For 20 years the jousting continued unabated.

By the 1980s, this foreign competition began to ebb. The superpowers and China became more selective as all African states were no longer contested for by East and West. The ideological orientation of any one state was not viewed as very important. The Soviet Union was the largest supplier of military aid to the region, but then, under Mikhail Gorbachev, it reduced military material bound for Mozambique, helped broker the Cuban pullout from Angola, played a supportive role in achieving Namibia's independence, and withdrew its commitment to what had been its closest ally in the region, Ethiopia.

The United States abandoned anticommunism as the linchpin of its African policies. Long-time ally Sese Seko Mobutu, president of Zaire, was rebuked for activities that made him one of the richest men on the continent, if not the world, while silencing any potential opposition. On a more positive note, Washington played a major role in mediating the end to long-festering civil wars in Angola and Ethiopia. Nevertheless, the Pentagon remained involved in training local armed forces in a number of countries.

The Western influence has been much in evidence economically. France was the country that had long had close relations with its former colonies. By the mid-1990s, this was changing. For one thing, almost all of the first generation of African postindependence leaders who embraced France have passed from the scene. More important, in late 1993 France greatly reduced its support for the common currency used in almost all of French-speaking Africa. These former colonies became more vulnerable to the shifts in world markets as their ties with France loosened.

The United States, after encountering serious problems while intervening in

Somalia in 1993, also curbed its interest in Africa. Getting bogged down in quagmires that involved revamping police and security forces, reestablishing basic services, rebuilding infrastructure, and creating jobs did not have support in Washington. The Republican Congress was intent on slashing foreign aid, especially in most African states, where no vital American interests were seen at stake.

In the 1980s, the largest recipients of U.S. aid in sub-Saharan Africa were Somalia, Zaire, Liberia, and Sudan. All were corrupt but willing to do our bidding in the last years of the cold war. Now, in the 1990s, Africa is at the bottom of America's priorities. Foreign aid for the fiscal year that ended September 30, 1995, for the entire region was $1.2 billion. With the exception of South Africa, there has been a tendency for the United States to withdraw from the area without distinguishing between more and less worthy governments. Even claims of genocide in Rwanda in 1994 did not stir the American public or government to any major action.

ECONOMICS AND NATURAL RESOURCES

It has already been suggested that African physical geography, including temperature, rainfall, coastlines, rivers, soils, and the like, created difficult conditions for its peoples. Moreover, foreigners abused the natural habitat in many parts of the region. For instance, the colonial powers instituted cash crops and the export of livestock, which in turn meant widespread clearing of the land and sometimes depletion of the soil. Similarly, Europeans carving up the continent created or heightened local rivalries, which resulted in conflicts that also affected the landscape. The decline of large areas of present-day Africa has been caused more by human than natural factors. Exploding populations, the movement from countrysides to cities, and the shift from a nomadic to a sedentary way of life have major ramifications.

Economic patterns established in Africa a century ago continue to have great relevance today. The search for legitimate trade in the decades after the abolition of slavery resulted in the introduction of such cash crops as cocoa, coffee, tea, cotton, ground nuts, and palm oil, as well as renewed exploration for minerals. Gradually a shift from subsistence farming to exports took place. In almost all cases, the colonies depended on no more than a total of three crops or minerals for almost all of their earnings. Thus was Africa gradually drawn into the global capitalist system, albeit as a minor player. This pattern remains true today.

After independence, the future at first looked promising. Some countries followed the Western model of letting free enterprise dominate the economy; others chose to have the state play the major role. in either case, the 1960s and early 1970s was a period of growth throughout the continent. Unlike Asia, most of the countries were feeding themselves; unlike Latin America, most of the land was either communally owned or run by small farmers. Foreign investment was forthcoming and commodity prices were high.[6]

With the first oil price shock in 1973, this rosy picture began to change. Only a few African states had appreciable amounts of oil; others were forced to spend more of their precious capital and then to borrow money at high rates of interest to secure oil for industry. By the late 1970s, prices had peaked and were beginning to fall, for both agricultural products and minerals. Deindustrialization resulted from declining domestic demand brought on by reduced income and shortages of foreign exchange. Poor maintenance and lack of spare parts, the protection of inefficient basic industries, and political considerations accelerated the economic decline. Drought became more pronounced in the Sahel region south of the Sahara. Sub-Saharan Africa's total debt, which had been $6 billion in 1970, rose to $125 billion by 1987.

By the early or mid-1980s, stagnation had been replaced by economic decline. Governments were living way beyond their means. African per capita income began to decline. Millions who had only barely been eking out a living now fell deeply into poverty and, in some cases, faced starvation.

These problems give a sense of the enormity of the economic disaster Africa is weathering (see box 6.1). By 1990, 325 million people, or 62 percent of the region's population, minus South Africa, were living in absolute poverty.[7] Per capita income hovered in the $300-a-year range.

How can this situation be changed? For more than a decade, the answer most often given by foreign governments and international lending agencies is privatization. That is, outside help, including additional loans and the restructuring of outstanding loans, will only be made available to African countries if they agree to major policy reforms that substitute market forces for state-directed economies.

Reforms focusing on currency devaluations, reductions in government expenditures, and limits in domestic credit were begun by the IMF in the early 1980s. The World Bank, noting that little had been accomplished, added other "structural adjustments." It sought to increase producer prices, reduce or eliminate sub-

---

BOX 6.1   Facts and Statistics on Sub-Saharan Africa

1. Forty-five percent of the region's population is under the age of 15.
2. The African economy expanded by 1.6 percent in 1993, up from 0.4 percent the preceding year but still barely half the rate of population growth for the same year.
3. At the end of 1992, Africa had 5.4 million refugees, second only to Asia, which had 7 million. Africa's population, however, is less than one-sixth that of Asia.
4. More than half of sub-Saharan Africans lack safe drinking water.
5. Grain production more than doubled in Africa from 1950 to 1994. Nevertheless, because of population growth, grain production per capita has declined, and only imports have curbed widespread malnutrition.
6. The region's debt in 1994 was $180 billion, three times that of 1980 and 10 percent higher than its entire output of goods and services.

7. The lifetime risk of dying from pregnancy-related causes in Africa is 1 in 21. It is 1 in 51 in Asia and 1 in 6,366 in the United States.

8. The gross national product per capita declined by 0.8 percent per year between 1980 and 1992 in the region. In many countries, people's incomes fell by 20 percent or more. In Niger it was down more than 45 percent; in Côte d'Ivoire it fell more than 50 percent.

9. Life expectancy in Africa is 51.1 years, the lowest for any region in the world.

10. In the industrial countries, on the average there is 1 doctor for every 400 people; in sub-Saharan Africa the figure is 1 doctor per 36,000 people.

11. In the past 50 years, 65 million hectares of productive land have turned to desert in the region.

12. The proportion of regional gross domestic product devoted to military spending in sub-Saharan Africa increased from 0.7 percent in 1960 to 3.0 percent in 1991.

13. Between 1985 and 1990, 60,000 middle and high-level managers left the area for other parts of the world.

14. Of the 173 countries listed in the 1994 edition of the *Human Development Report*, 22 of the bottom 25 countries are from sub-Saharan Africa, as measured by the *Human Development Index*.

15. According to 1992 figures, 101 of every thousand infants die in the first year of life.

In contrast, some conditions have markedly improved in Africa when compared to years past.

1. Life expectancy in the region was just 40 years in 1960, compared to 51.1 years in 1992.

2. Infant mortality in Africa declined from 165 per thousand in 1960 to 101 in 1992.

3. Twenty-five percent of the area's population had access to safe drinking water as recently as 1975–1980, compared to 45 percent from 1988–1991.

4. Children of primary school age attending school in the region increased from 50 percent in 1970 to 66 percent in 1991; the comparable figures for those of secondary school age were 7 percent and 18 percent.

5. Adult literacy in Africa increased from 28 percent in 1970 to 51 percent in 1991.

SOURCE: Most of the facts and statistics above are taken either from *Vital Signs 1994* or the *Human Development Report 1994.*

sidies and trade restrictions, improve education and health systems, pay far more attention to the environment, encourage foreign investment, and champion small producers. A domestic bicycle industry or low-cost local roads for nonmotorized vehicles were looked on favorably. Above all, it emphasized private enterprise.

By the mid-1990s, more than two dozen countries in Africa adopted major economic policy reforms. These states embraced the reforms or capitulated to Western prescriptions. World Bank personnel worked closely with local officials; in Washington, a private enterprise bureau was set up with the U.S. Agency for International Development to back further American investments in Africa. Even former socialist countries such as Angola and Mozambique accepted the structural adjustment reform package. Outside criticisms of these programs included the reduction in the quality and quantity of government services; the introduction of user fees, which disproportionately hurt the poor; and the increased cost of basic foodstuffs and transportation.

Structural adjustment at the national level may be inadequate unless the Western countries open their markets, pay decent prices for African goods, and curtail or suspend debt repayments. Any benefits for African states are likely to take years, if not decades, whereas adverse effects of reform are instantaneous. If discontent rises, government instability and repression will be the likely results.

The IMF and World Bank argue that several countries, including Burkina Faso, Ghana, and Zimbabwe, that have practiced the adjustments have slowly improving economies. The banks also submit that states taking the plunge have done better than those that have not. That is small consolation to millions of individuals who have experienced worsened conditions.

On balance, sub-Saharan African economies in the mid-1990s are a bit improved over the beginning of the decade, if not over 10 or 20 years earlier than that. What could quicken the pace? As mentioned elsewhere, a thriving South Africa could make a big difference. More small-scale loans would undoubtedly help. Reorienting social spending toward the rural poor and away from large prestigious projects is overdue.

CASE STUDIES

SOUTH AFRICA

The key point about South Africa is that although blacks outnumbered whites by five to one, political and economic power remained with the minority until 1994. Over the generations, white domination wore many faces. At the turn of the twentieth century, the British defeated the Afrikaners in a bloody civil war. The Afrikaners were a people whose ancestors came mainly from the Netherlands beginning in the seventeenth century. For the next few years there were four separate states, with Great Britain in charge of them all; then in 1910, the four fused into one Union of South Africa, and London became all but invisible. Fearing for the future of blacks in the country, a forerunner to the African National Congress (ANC) arose two years later. However, it could do nothing to prevent the Land

Divided Highway Ends: The Main Road between
Malindi and Lamu, Kenya
SOURCE: Emmit B. Evans, Jr.

Act of 1913, which prevented blacks from owning land in most areas and from owning quality land in all parts of the country. Another important date is 1948, the year that the Afrikaner-backed National party won the whites-only national elections. The newly elected party formally instituted a policy of apartheid, or separate racial development. From then on, blacks; to a lesser extent Indians; and those of mixed race, called coloreds, were treated as inferior beings. Brute force, including the arrest of the leaders; legislation; and custom enshrined the new order. For the next 36 years, despite nonviolent protests and occasional acts of sabotage, the status quo of white domination and black subordination prevailed.

Beginning in late 1984, disturbances became more widespread, and violence by both the state and opponents of apartheid intensified. Arrests numbered in the thousands. A year later, the government declared a state of emergency in much of the country. Authorities tried to keep order by imposing controls on dissidents, including the media. The economy began a downward spiral, helped along by damaging strikes. Limited sanctions imposed by several governments, including the United States, and the loss of many foreign companies also hurt. Nevertheless, the white ruling class held firm.

In the late 1980s the South African government tried both the carrot and the stick to impose its will. The authorities offered minor reforms, and relations improved with some surrounding black-run states. However, several thousand people died because of political unrest, and a second emergency decree resulted in tens of thousands of additional arrests. A change of direction seemed impossible.

Change did come, however, and it came rapidly. There are several explanations for the shift. First, Frederik W. de Klerk succeeded P. W. Botha as prime minister and head of the National party in 1989. There was nothing in de Klerk's past to suggest that he was any different from his predecessors. Nevertheless, he quickly called for a national conference to prepare a new constitution, approved peaceful political protests, ousted several hard-liners from the cabinet, and announced his willingness to talk about some method of sharing power.

At the same time, the situation fundamentally improved in neighboring Namibia and Angola. South African leaders perceived that the abating U.S.-Soviet confrontation would lessen the threat of communism within their own borders. Many in the country also noticed democratization in other parts of the world. Both the South African government and the ANC saw a military solution to the internal unrest as unlikely. In addition, the economy continued to sag, and Western powers warned that tougher sanctions were a possibility. Demands for change came from all directions.

The winds struck with gale force. Nelson Mandela, jailed in the early 1960s for promoting the violent overthrow of the government, was released by Prime Minister de Klerk in early 1990 along with other dissidents. The government also lifted the 30-year ban against the ANC, the Pan-African Congress, the South African Communist party, and many other organizations. Over the next few months the government rescinded the state of emergency throughout the country, curbed the secretive state security system, reduced the military budget, and ended political censorship. It also repealed the Separate Amenities Act, thus opening public hospitals, restaurants, libraries, buses, and parks to all.

The first half of 1991 shook apartheid to its roots. Its pillars—the Lands Acts, Group Areas Act, and Population Registration Act—were repealed, and the Internal Security Act was severely amended. Before the year was out, discussions were held on the shape of the political system to come. In early 1992, more than two-thirds of whites endorsed de Klerk's reform program in a referendum.

It took two more years of maneuvering by many parties before the ultimate goal of one person, one vote was achieved. The rival ANC and the Zulu-based Inkatha movement, led by Chief Gatsha Buthelezi, clashed, resulting in thousands of deaths. There were divisions among the whites as well, with a small minority refusing to consider any changes. But in late April 1994, the people of South Africa, including the millions of black citizens, went to the polls for the first time in the country's history.

As expected, the ANC was the big winner, receiving 63 percent of the vote as Nelson Mandela became president. By not getting two-thirds of the vote, the victorious party had to work with non-ANC members in Parliament in the writing of a new constitution. The National party finished second and became the official opposition. In addition, de Klerk became one of two vice presidents. The Inkatha Freedom party finished third. In a bid to form a government of unity and reconciliation, Mandela offered a number of cabinet positions to members of the other two parties. Buthelezi became the home affairs minister.

Many people predicted that given the struggle that preceded the election, the following months would be ones of upheaval. It did not work out that way. There were growing pains, yes, but both in political circles and throughout the country there was relative tranquility based on a foundation of gradual change. From international outcast to liberal democracy in one year was phenomenal. While some complained that Mandela was moving too slowly to institute reforms, most were supportive of the pace and direction of change. Racial strife gradually eased. Economic growth caught up with population growth for the first time in a decade. There were a number of strikes, but they did not divide the country or undermine the ANC. Finally, in late 1995, tranquil local elections took place throughout the country.

All of which is not to say there are not serious problems ahead. Gaining political power is a lot different than gaining economic power. Economic disparities between blacks and whites are still four times as great in South Africa as they are in the United States, and that ratio will not change quickly. The reconstruction and development program, which is to bring about economic improvements for the impoverished black majority, is slow in getting started. While other countries and international lending institutions have helped, such assistance pales in comparison with that given to countries in the former Soviet orbit or in the Middle East. And while there has been a steady stream of foreign companies coming or returning to South Africa, again it is less than expected.

Probably the biggest issue is land. The Restitution of Land Rights Act, passed in late 1994, allows thousands of blacks stripped of their land in past decades to return to their homes. But money for the buy-back program is limited. In any case, there are millions who will not fit under provisions of the act but who were moved from land they still see as theirs. Regardless of circumstances, the government, with private-sector backing, has committed itself to aiding the poor by building 1 million homes before 1999 and, in addition, offering loans and subsidies for first-time homeowners.

Other sticking points are the meshing of old-time military and police personnel and the guerrilla fighters who opposed them. In the fall of 1995, a former defense minister from the old regime and 10 high-ranking military compatriots were indicted for allegedly approving a 1987 massacre in a Zulu township. There have been charges of continuing police abuses, unresolved claims of torture and murder against white security personnel, and an upsurge in violent crime. There are still very high rates of black unemployment. A need to rebuild the educational system and demands by Chief Buthelezi for autonomy for KwaZulu-Natal Province must be addressed. Finally, there is Nelson Mandela himself, in good health in his late 70s but still mortal. The president has said he will not run for reelection in 1999.[8]

RWANDA

In 1993, few people in the United States had ever heard of Rwanda, let alone knew anything about the Maryland-sized country in the middle of Africa. In 1994, Rwanda gained its "15 minutes of fame" in the world media as 1 million people, mostly Tutsi, died in terrible massacres. They were the victims of the worst genocide that the world had seen since World War II.

At one level, the killings were a continuation of the ethnic rivalry between the Hutu and the Tutsi people that had gone on since the fifteenth century. It also involved differences between the more militant Hutu in the north of Rwanda and their more moderate counterparts to the south. The Tutsi, although only 15 percent of the population, were wealthier and had for many generations been in charge.

Mass killings occurred periodically from the 1950s until the early 1970s. Ethnic conflict was one way of describing the situation; class conflict was another. A struggle for land in this densely populated country and children made orphans by the fighting and AIDS, who were thus cannon fodder for the recruitment, were indirect explanations of the building tensions.[9]

In late 1993, there were warnings at the United Nations that a simmering three-year-old civil war might erupt into something much worse. A fragile peace accord was foundering on the makeup of a transitional government. There was a small peacekeeping force already in Rwanda, but after the failure of the UN experience in Somalia, its mandate was very narrow. It was in this atmosphere that the presidents of Rwanda and Burundi were killed when their plane mysteriously crashed in April 1994 on a flight from Tanzania, where they had been discussing how to resolve the conflicts in the two neighboring countries.

What ensued was a terrible massacre in which both Tutsis and moderate Hutu were slaughtered. Astoundingly, at this critical time, the UN Security Council delayed and then refused to allow those peacekeepers who remained in the country to try to stop the killings.

After weeks of only token opposition, the Rwandan Patriotic Front (RPF), a Tutsi-dominated organization, some of whose members had been living in neighboring Uganda for more than a generation, engaged government forces and gradually pushed them back. With international action at a standstill, France, which had backed the Hutu-led government four years before, now sent 2,500 troops to act as a buffer. Ultimately, more than 2 million Rwandans who feared Tutsi retribution for earlier massacres fled the country.

From one grisly chapter to another, the mass exodus created appalling conditions at refugee camps in neighboring countries. Despite belated UN humanitarian assistance, cholera epidemics and dysentery took tens of thousands of additional lives. Ultimately, the camps were shut down and some destitute souls returned to an uncertain future in Rwanda. Others, fearful of returning to Rwanda, continued to live as refugees in Zaire, Burundi, Tanzania, Uganda, and Kenya.

A Rwandan interim parliament was sworn in in late 1994. The RPF, however, continues to be the power in the country, although elements of the Front's army have abused that position. Many thousands of Hutu languish in overcrowded, inhumane Rwandan jails, with charges yet to be brought against them. The government barely functions, the infrastructure is in tatters, many of the farms are unattended, the country is basically broke, and international aid is sparse. Meanwhile, the exiled Hutu army of the former regime rearms and elements infiltrate into their former homeland.

Are there other "Rwandas" lurking? Neighboring Burundi has many of the same elements that engendered the Rwandan horror. There, more than 100,000 people have been killed since the first Hutu president was assassinated in October 1993. Several of the Case Studies and Flashpoints in this chapter also point to danger, and there are other countries that could go the route of Rwanda.

ZIMBABWE

Zimbabwe became independent in 1980 after a lengthy struggle to end white-minority rule. In the ensuing years, the country has moved forward. On the positive side, economic growth has more than kept pace with population growth. There are many family-planning programs involving both sexes, and fertility rates are declining. Tribal disputes between the majority Shona and minority Ndebele have faded. The 80 percent literacy rate is one of the highest on the continent. Racism has been contained, if not eliminated. There is a good health-care system, a thriving tourism industry, a police force that no longer generates fear, and a functioning infrastructure. Because officials give local residents an economic stake in the survival of wildlife, species that are in decline elsewhere are growing. Most of the country has clean air and clean water. In general, there is a reasonable level of political stability.

But there is another side. There was a very serious drought in 1992 and another one in 1995. Better stockpiling of food the second time cushioned the blow, but hundreds of commercial farmers faced bankruptcy and major crop production fell by more than 50 percent. The much-commended economic prosperity of the 1980s was in jeopardy as living conditions for most of the population fell. The cost of living soared, interest rates of over 30 percent a year caused a decline in the business climate, government red tape discouraged investment, the official unemployment rate was above 50 percent, and popular discontent rose. Zimbabwe developed one of the highest HIV-positive rates in Africa, and AIDS became the leading cause of death for children under five; it was also a major mortality factor for middle-level managers in their 30s and 40s.

As in South Africa, probably the most volatile issue is land ownership. Until recently, 4,500 white farmers owned more than 70 percent of the country's most fertile land, leaving the 7 million black farmers to engage in mainly subsistence farming. Government laws aim to change the situation by giving the poor a chance to acquire better land. White farmers and the World Bank have objected, claiming the economy of the state will suffer under these reforms. Government officials have responded with charges of racism. In 1994, a High Court decision upheld the state's land seizure powers, which could result in almost half of the country's 4,000 white-owned farms being turned over to landless blacks. President Robert Mugabe threatened to deport whites who claim that the compensation for their farms is inadequate.

In the past, President Mugabe attempted to make Zimbabwe into a single-party state. He failed, but such is the political dominance of his Zimbabwe African National Union–Patriotic Front (ZANU-PF) that it maintains control of the nation. In 1995 parliamentary elections, ZANU-PF captured 118 of 120 seats. The following year the president was overwhelmingly reelected. The Mugabe government also controls all radio and television stations and major newspapers. It provides millions of dollars a year in funding to the one major party but none to the tiny opposition. There are opposition charges of voter intimidation and inaccurate voting lists. Even with all these blemishes, Zimbabweans still have much to be proud of in the 15 years since independence. By the standards of much of Africa, Zimbabwe is a success story.

ANGOLA-NAMIBIA

As you have read, there have been a few recent changes for the better in sub-Saharan Africa. One area where there appeared to be improvement was the neighboring countries of Angola and Namibia. Until a late 1988 agreement, the Angolan government, long locked in a civil war, had the support of some 50,000 Cuban soldiers. Simultaneously, while South Africa continued to control Namibia, it was forced to battle both guerrillas fighting for independence there and neighboring Cuban and Angolan government troops.

Presently, Namibia is doing very well, while Angola teeters. With the twin goals of easing tensions in southern Africa and achieving Namibian independence, the United States pressured South Africa to bring its forces home. Working with Washington, the Soviet Union persuaded Cuba to remove its troops from Angola. The UN Transition Assistance Group, a 6,000-person peacekeeping force, provided the mortar for the complicated transition. On March 21, 1990, the century-long period of colonization in Africa ended as Namibians took control of their destiny. Over 20,000 people had died during the 23-year war for independence. The fighting was over, and a democratic constitution and elected government were in place.

On balance, the first half of the 1990s was a time of advancement. As in neighboring South Africa, the leadership has followed a policy of reconciliation with the economically important white minority, and overt racial friction was rare. As in South Africa also, the major political party, the South West Africa People's Organization (SWAPO), propounded Marxist rhetoric until it came to power and then became far more pragmatic. Problems faced by the government included corruption and mismanagement in tourism and fishing concessions, as well as a continuing problem of poaching. There was criticism of some government leaders living in an extravagant manner. Little effort was made to reduce widespread poverty, with its immense gap between rich and poor. Slow progress in educational and environmental matters are other weak areas. The elections in December 1994 proved that reelected President Sam Nujoma and SWAPO were more popular than ever. The dominant party won more than two-thirds of the seats in Parliament in what international observers deemed fair elections. Indeed, Namibia's slip from the world's attention was an indication of national tranquility.

On May 30, 1991, a peace treaty was signed in Angola, officially ending a 16-year-old civil war between the Soviet-backed government and the opposition, which was supported by the United States. Both outside forces had continued to pour large-scale military aid into a country that had known perpetual misery for 30 years. The brutal struggle for independence from Portugal had been achieved only in 1975. Then came the internal fighting, which took some 300,000 lives. In addition, starvation afflicted more than a half million people; one-half of the country's export earnings went for the war; refugees numbered in the hundreds of thousands; a cholera epidemic raged; and the economy, even with oil revenue and considerable outside assistance, remained in tatters. Life expectancy was among the lowest on the continent. Under the U.S.-Soviet brokered agreement, the former enemies were to build a unified armed force, promote a multiparty political system and market economy, and plan for elections monitored by a UN observer force. After the votes were counted in the elections of 1992, the losing side claimed fraud and ballot stuffing.

In the succeeding months, thousands more were killed in renewed fighting. In November 1994, the government and the rebels signed a peace treaty, which called for the United Nations to monitor the cease-fire and for the opposition to have a share of the power. Early in 1995 thousands of UN peacekeepers began to arrive. While rich soil, diamonds, and oil provide great economic potential for Angola, political instability clouds the future.

FLASHPOINTS

AFRICA AND AIDS

"The best estimates place [Africa's] actual share [of AIDS cases] at about 67 percent [of the global total]."[10] In other words, about two-thirds of all people suffering from AIDS are African. "An estimated 1.5 million people died of AIDS in 1994 and four-fifths of them had lived in sub-Saharan Africa."[11]

More than 10 million people in the region are believed to have the HIV virus, a figure that is expected to grow to 15 million by the end of the decade. Some 2 million Africans have acquired the disease itself. In some urban areas HIV rates are as high as 30 percent of the adult population. Uganda, one of the most infected countries, has between 1 and 1.5 million HIV cases in a population of 17 million. One projection states that the country, which had a life expectancy of just 43 years in 1992, would see that figure drop to 32 by 2010. In Malawi, a country of just over 9 million, more than 4,000 people die of the disease every month.

In 1993, more than a million HIV-positive infants were born in Africa. Just as wrenching, more than 2 million HIV-*negative* children from the region have lost their mothers to AIDS, thus setting up growing numbers of orphans without adequate health and human care. Many of the AIDS orphans are avoided for fear of contagion. Sixty percent of new cases in Africa in 1993 occurred among people between the ages of 15 and 24.

Not so long ago the AIDS virus was mainly in East and Central African cities. No longer. Nigeria, on the continent's west coast, now has a major problem. In most states, the number of HIV cases in the countryside has risen dramatically. Finally, in Africa, unlike the United States, women make up a large percentage of those contracting the virus. In fact, four out of five women with AIDS live on the continent.

Health care is completely inadequate to the challenge. Although AIDS education and improved mass communications are helping in some countries, the enormity of the challenge dwarfs any effective response. Some hard-hit countries could face bankruptcy in the next decade. International assistance pales next to the enormity of help needed.

HORN OF AFRICA

Sudan, Ethiopia, Eritrea, Somalia—four different countries, all poor, and four different histories that affect one another. All have known war recently, and in at least two the fighting continues. Drought, soaring populations, and depleted natural resources are endemic to the Horn of Africa. Ethiopia is one of the oldest countries in the world and Eritrea among the newest; both are carving out new directions. Sudan and Somalia, however, seem involved in upheaval without end.

From the 1890s until independence in 1956, Sudan was formally under joint Anglo-French control. In 1958, a coup brought a change of regime and ushered in an era of unrest and military uprisings, the most recent of which occurred in 1989. Alleged plots, such as one resulting in the arrest of military officers and civilians alike in the summer of 1991, are even more common. Still, the sudden changes at the top have had little effect on the on-again, off-again civil war, which has raged for more than 30 years. The opposing forces comprise 16 million people in the mainly Muslim north and 7 million in the non-Muslim south. The northern-based government, dominated by Islamic fundamentalists, has imposed itself on an ever more hostile south. Both sides have used food as a weapon. To make things more complicated and more terrible, those opposing the government have now split into two groups and spend as much time fighting each other as the common enemy. The warring factions have varying ethnic support. One side wants nothing less than independence, while the other supports autonomy within Sudan. Whatever the source, up to 2 million people in the south have died from fighting, famine, and disease since 1983, and maybe twice that number have been internally displaced. The United States added Sudan in 1993 to its list of countries that aided terrorism, claiming that the government is helping individuals and groups bent on destabilizing other states in Africa and beyond. The tragedy in Sudan rivals that in Rwanda but has received much less attention by the media or the nation-states of the world.

Because of inhospitable terrain and no obvious exportable economic resources, Ethiopia was able to keep its independence and its monarchy until conquered by Italy in 1935. Six years later the British drove the Italians out and restored Emperor Haile Selassie to power. In seeking to enlarge his diverse state and alter the country's land-locked status, the emperor, with British approval, in 1952 claimed the former Italian colony of Eritrea. He did not, however, receive the Eritreans' approval. A military coup in 1974 swept away the old Ethiopian order. A self-proclaimed Marxist government asked the Soviet Union to replace the United States as the primary outside power. In trying to consolidate its control, the government of President Mengistu Haile Mariam became ever more dictatorial. Eritrean nationalism then burst forth. Over the years, two guerrilla fighting units succeeded in pushing the central government out of most of the province. Other ethnic groups' increasing discontent further weakened President Mengistu's hold in other parts of the country. The Soviet Union and its allies ended their economic and military aid.

The end came in the spring of 1991 with the collapse of the central government and the flight of Mengistu. Two million people had died under his reign. In the following months, representatives of 27 ethnic and political groups, including the Ethiopian People's Revolutionary Democratic Front (EPDRF) and the Eritrean People's Liberation Front (EPLF), met to work out the future of the country. Meles Zenawi of the EPDRF headed a transition government. More attention began to be paid to the rural poor as Zenawi balanced state and private ownership. Despite new programs, food shortages continued as population growth outstripped grain production by ever-widening amounts. At the end of 1994 a new democratic constitution was adopted that promised ethnic groups the right to secede if they wished. The leadership was Tigrean-dominated, much to the displeasure of the more populous Oromo and Amhara peoples. In 1995 elections, the ruling coalition was victorious. Several major parties boycotted the proceedings, claiming their members had been harrassed and even jailed when they tried to campaign.

With Ethiopia's consent, Eritrea had invoked its right to self-determination in 1993. Following almost 30 years of war in which 250,000 people were killed, it became the first territory in Africa to secede successfully from another African country. In a referendum, 99.8 percent of the approximately 1.1 million Eritreans voted for independence. Transitional institutions were established, and EPLF leader Issaias Afewerki was elected president by the new National Assembly. The country is nearly equally divided between Muslims and Christians. The government has received very high marks for its political sensitivity and economic programs, which focus on small-scale peasant agriculture. It is referred to as an "oasis of stability" in the Horn, though it broke diplomatic relations with Sudan after charging its neighbor with supporting border clashes in the hope of toppling the broadly-based government. Relatively fertile soil on the high plateau; promising resources of gold, oil, and fish; land reform; upgrading of the rights of women; a lack of crime and corruption; and optimism about the future all create a counter to the discouraging events of surrounding countries. The government has promised a new constitution and multiparty elections before the end of the decade.

Somalia may in years to come be looked on as an example in which an Other World country was briefly noticed by the world at large and then returnd to global anonymity. Southern Italian Somaliland and northern British Somaliland were fused at independence in 1960. Nine years later, Mohammed Siad Barre seized power and became a ruthless president for the next 22 years. Even though the overwhelming majority of the people are from the same ethnic group, competing clans and subclans formed the basis for challenges to Barre and each other.

The 1970s and 1980s were also a time of U.S.-Soviet rivalries around the world. In the Horn of Africa, the United States first backed Ethiopia while the U.S.S.R. supported Barre's version of socialism. In the late 1970s, a new Marxist government in Ethiopia led to the superpowers switching sides, both stuffing their beneficiaries with weapons. Despite Barre's deplorable human rights record, the United States continued to funnel military and economic aid to Somalia until the late 1980s.

In 1991, Barre was finally ousted and a struggle for power between different individuals and subclans or lineages began. Life in much of the interior, which was never easy, became harder as famine took its toll. In the months that followed, the United Nations hesitated. As pictures of starving children filled television screens, however, the world body began to supply food to hundreds of thousands of people. With provisions being hijacked or blocked at the capital of Mogadishu, UN observers, and then U.S. troops, arrived to assist. Gradually the mission's objective changed from ending starvation to establishing a measure of peace and security to the country by ending the tribal struggle for power. Later it was hoped that the UN could rebuild the infrastructure, the economy, and finally the government itself. This changed objective involved the UN as a participant in the conflict.

By 1993, there were 25,000 American military personnel, thousands of other UN peacekeepers, and countless private parties, all attempting to provide assistance. In October of that year, 18 U.S. Army Rangers lost their lives in a futile attempt to capture a Somali leader who was accused of fomenting strife. Although President Clinton announced an immediate increase in U.S. troops to be sent to the country, the future direction of American and then UN personnel was to hunker down and then to get out. All military personnel were gone by early 1995, though a few relief agencies braved the dangers and stayed. Some see the operation as saving great numbers of lives and offering hope during a time of misery; others believe that UN members came too late and got too enmeshed in local politics and in "nation building."

Elsewhere, there has been a slow improvement of the economy, with farming on the increase, schools reopening, and local-level authority being restored. But there is still no functioning national government, and local militias still fire on one another.

AFRICA ON THE MOVE

Africa is on the move. It may be movement from the countryside to the cities as the region becomes increasingly urbanized. The population shift may be from one part of a country to another because of famine, or it may be from one country to another because of war or lack of jobs. In any case, untold millions move and few go in style. Most have little more than the clothes on their backs and maybe a bag or two as they trudge from one destination to another.

In the past few years, armed conflicts in Rwanda, Mozambique, Somalia, Ethiopia, Liberia, Angola, and Sudan resulted in the migration of millions of people. Sometimes, as in Mozambique, the fighting ebbs and the refugees return. But in other cases, such as Liberia, the strife shows no sign of abating and the misery continues, seemingly without end. Africa has almost a third of the planet's 23 million refugees.

In Ethiopia, there is simply not enough locally grown food, largely the result of the population doubling in the past four decades. In Somalia, clan warfare, population growth, heavily eroded and overgrazed soil, and deforestation have all taken their toll on living conditions. In densely populated Rwanda, the horrors of 1994 caused over 2 million Hutu to heed their leaders' call to flee to neighboring countries. And then there are the large numbers of people from Angola, Mozambique, Namibia, and Zambia who have flooded into the postapartheid South Africa to look for a better life.

Rising crime rates, health problems including the lack of safe drinking water, and declining foreign assistance also contribute to migrations. Like most other issues, there is no one single reason why people move and no one magic wand to improve their situation.

NIGERIA

Next to South Africa, Nigeria is viewed as the country in sub-Saharan Africa to have the greatest potential. But recurring political instability and economic mismanagement for the past quarter century have taken their toll, and for many of its citizens the hope for a positive future is dim.

Nigeria's population of almost 100 million people is by far the largest on the African continent. Twenty years ago the country was an economic powerhouse as well. In 1977, per capita GDP was $1,000. Ten years later the figure had dropped to $370; in 1992 it was $320. For the period 1980 to 1992, Nigeria's economic growth rate was minus 0.4 percent. In that period, the country slipped from the Other World's middle-income to low-income group.

A major factor in the decline was the precipitous drop in oil prices. The government and many upwardly mobile people lived way beyond their means during this period. Yet the masses saw little of the new wealth. As the decade drew to a close, the international debt soared to $35 billion, and the government agreed to begin a very stiff structural adjustment program (see the section on economics). In this environment, social unrest further undermined foreign investment.

The military government that came to power in a 1985 coup (there have been seven coups since independence in 1960) promised elections and the return to civil rule at the beginning of 1993. Indeed, elections were held, but when the military rulers did not like the results, they simply annulled them. Since then, there has been turmoil, with strikes and even riots, the people demanding that the victor, billionaire K. O. Abiola, be allowed to serve as president. But the military, now under the control of General Sani Abacha, put Abiola in jail instead and cracked down very hard on any dissent. Rule by decree was the watchword. The military has ruled in Nigeria for 23 of the past 27 years. In March 1995, an attempt to overthrow the government failed. Its leaders, including a former head of state, were to be put to death, but after national protests the sentences were commuted to life imprisonment. General Abacha also attempted to head off further criticism by belatedly promising a return to civilian rule by late 1998.

Before the year was out, nine other dissidents including Ken Saro-Wiwa, a prominent author and playwright, were executed. The government charged that they had fomented strife that led to the murder of several rivals in a major oil-producing area. Saro-Wiwa had protested that the production had resulted in serious pollution in the area. He also railed against the refusal of the corrupt government to give even a fraction of the riches to his poor Ogoni people living in the oil-rich coastal sector. Worldwide condemnation followed the hangings, with none other than South African President Nelson Mandela calling for a worldwide oil embargo. Under the best circumstances, however, it is difficult to get approval for such a global action and even more difficult to enforce it. Nigeria, for instance, is the fifth-largest foreign supplier of oil to the United States and owes over $30 billion to Europe and Japan. Thus, while Nigeria has become an international pariah, the government remains defiant.

Shell Oil, which had been the main multinational corporation extracting the oil until driven from the region in 1993 by the turmoil, announced within days of the executions that it would go ahead with a $3.8 billion liquefied natural gas project. If completed, it would be the most expensive foreign enterprise on the entire continent.

How long can the downward spiral continue? Oil prices hover around $20 a barrel. External debt exceeds 100 percent of gross domestic product per year. Annual inflation ranges from 65 to 100 percent. Up to 90 percent of the people live in poverty amid massive corruption, starting at the very top. To give one example, before a general stepped down as president in 1993, he bestowed on each of 3,000 loyal officers a $21,000 automobile even though the country was virtually bankrupt. The very future of Nigeria as a unified state is now in doubt.

MOZAMBIQUE

Two statistics on Mozambique, a former Portuguese colony, stand out: First, *The 1994 World Development Report: Infrastructure for Development* listed Mozambique's $60 per capita annual GDP as the lowest in the world.[12] Second and more encouragingly, since the end of a civil war in the early 1990s, about 95 percent of the 1.7 million refugees who fled the country because of the fighting have returned.[13]

The Front for the Liberation of Mozambique, or Frelimo, led the fight for independence from Portuguese rule, gaining its objective in 1975 and forming the new government. Two years later, the Mozambican National Resistance, or Renamo, was created as an opposition force by the white minority in preindependence Rhodesia. Over the years, 600,000 to 1 million people, half under the age of five, were killed by former Portuguese soldiers, disaffected members of Mozambique's ruling party, and white South African–backed authorities. Countless thousands of others were maimed by some 2 million mines strewn around the country. Even with improved conditions, the infrastructure will take years to rebuild.

While all of the privations that the people have been through are acknowledged, Mozambique is another country in southern Africa where conditions appear to be improving. The government renounced its former Marxist orientation in 1990, opting for a new constitution and a multiparty democracy instead. The international financial community has embraced the country, and the United States made Mozambique its biggest aid recipient in sub-Saharan Africa.[14] South African investments and tourism continue to rise.

In October 1992, after two years of negotiations, Frelimo and Renamo finally signed a peace pact. In addition to a cease-fire, both armies were to be demobilized, reconstruction of the country was to begin, and elections were to be held. It took two more years of delays and posturing plus the positioning of 7,500 UN peacekeepers, but in the end elections did take place and the results were accepted by all sides. While Frelimo won a close victory, South African President Nelson Mandela lobbied for power sharing between the two main parties. President Joaquim Chissano said he was amenable to the idea. The economy is still in the doldrums and the repatriation of refugees will be a lengthy process, but conditions in Mozambique may finally be looking up.

LAND MINES

One of the more distressing consequences of recent wars is that a greater and greater percentage of those injured, maimed, or killed are civilians. In Africa, millions of mines are strewn across many countries, ready to exact a fearful toll on innocents even years after a conflict has ended.

Angola is a case in point. The UN has estimated that in this country of between 10 and 11 million people, some 25 million mines are deployed. Other countries with significant numbers of these devices are Mozambique, Somalia, Sudan, Uganda, Ethiopia, and Eritrea. A program has been started in Mozambique to rid the country of the mines, but the work is slow. Meanwhile, mines continue to be laid in other countries, resulting in thousands of casualties each year.

A few countries, including South Africa, have halted export of mines in conjunction with the 1980 Land Mines Protocol of the United Nations Weapons Convention. However, many have not, and a recent UN conference to restrict or ban land mines failed to make any progress. China, Romania, and Russia are still among the leading suppliers of land mines in Africa.

ZAIRE

Zaire has lush forests, fertile croplands, and prodigious mineral deposits. But its colonial experience as the Belgian Congo made it totally unprepared for independence in 1960. Not surprisingly, chaos resulted, in which racial, ethnic, and ideological conflicts brought the country close to disintegration. Outside states threatened to intervene, but a UN peacekeeping operation, despite many problems, provided the glue that kept the country together. After the UN departure in 1964, however, instability grew again. A year later, General Joseph Mobutu staged a coup and began to put his mark on the country, a mark that has become all-pervasive.

Thirty years later, Zaire is going back in time. It is a country where political and economic conditions have gotten about as bad as they can get. The general has become President Sese Seko Mobutu and runs a "kleptocracy," government by theft. While Mobutu is a billionaire who maintains several residences in Europe, the World Bank has declared Zaire bankrupt since 1994. The economy declined by 12 percent in 1992 and 17 percent in 1993. Massive corruption including diamond smuggling, hyperinflation, and hunger are only three of the people's problems. Because of the disintegration of the government infrastructure, civil servants and soldiers are not paid and stage mutinies.

Because of the cold war, Zaire for many years was the largest recipient of U.S. aid in sub-Saharan Africa. Indeed, Mobutu came to power with the help of the CIA, which used the country as a staging area for activities throughout the continent. Dissolution, decay, and undevelopment are all terms now used to describe this country, one-quarter the size of the United States.

There have been attempts at democratic reform during the 1990s. President Mobutu originally agreed to step down in mid-1991 but has used political guile and muscle to keep from doing so. A rival government is in place, new elections are promised, and Washington now condemns Mobutu. The longtime president still remains the dominant figure in Zaire. How much longer he will have a country to rule is another question.

ENVIRONMENT

In recent years, a whole cottage industry has been formed of experts bemoaning the environmental present and future in Africa.[15] All essentially have said the same thing: that the region's environment is being overwhelmed. This chapter has offered several reasons why more and more countries cannot feed themselves. Civil wars are making whole areas unfit for human habitation. Only minor advances have been made in limiting population growth. Poverty cuts like a scourge through the area, forcing Africans to mutilate their remaining forests, grasslands, and croplands. The continent is becoming increasingly urbanized as millions each year migrate to the cities, placing additional stress on these areas.

African food dependency is growing. Drought, pests, and insects destroy agriculture. New seed varieties, greater use of chemical fertilizers, and better management are offered as remedies, but the first two again increase dependency on fickle sources beyond the continent.

Rising population and growing consumption are raising levels of air and water pollution. The burning of wood for heat and cooking has long choked local skies, and coal-burning power plants in South Africa affect the health of crops and humans. Industrialization throughout the continent is growing and with it the attendant ecological problems. As in Eastern Europe and Russia, industrialization and providing jobs threaten to take precedence over air quality.

Industrialization is also affecting water quality, especially on Lake Victoria, the world's second-largest freshwater lake, and other inland waters in East Africa. An invasion of giant water hyacinths, nourished by pollutants, are choking the inland sea, impeding navigation, and modifying aquatic ecology. Some of the ports on the lake have sustained 50 percent declines in trade, and commercially significant fishing has disappeared in certain areas. In fact, the whole regional ecosystem is at risk. To the north, Lake Chad is shrinking, perhaps because of global warming.

Population growth and poverty are also endangering other species on land. While poaching of some species has been contained in several countries, more

Under Sail: Traditional Fishermen Headed
Home Off the East Coast of Africa
SOURCE: Emmit B. Evans, Jr.

land-poor people and rising populations generally are making it ever more difficult for threatened animals and plants to survive.[16] International treaties and private preserves are helping, but the long-term prognosis is not good.

The life-support systems throughout Africa are now at risk. Land degradation from overgrazing, deforestation, and agricultural mismanagement is severe.
Fishing off the southwest coast of Africa is declining. Coral reefs adjacent to East
Africa are being affected by nearby land clearing and development. Tropical rainforest devastation is continuing.

SUMMARY

Natural geography and history impede positive change in Africa. Population,
health, education, food, energy, and environmental concerns are troubling problems. Politically, the continuing quest for legitimacy, the social diversity and conflict, the lack of regional and pan-African cooperation, and the lessening international interest in Africa do not bode well for the years ahead. Finally, by many
indicators, the economic well-being of the peoples of the region actually declined
in the 1980s and early 1990s, while dependency on external agencies that prescribe privatization increased.

As Africa moves toward the twenty-first century, there has been no dramatic
turnaround for the region. However, politically and economically there are glim-
mers of hope. Developments in South Africa are exciting, and so are those in several other countries in southern Africa. More people are participating in political
matters without fear than at the beginning of the decade. In 1994, economic growth
exceeded population growth for the first time in years. In places, there are in-

creased incidents of grass-roots political empowerment. Africa has great potential, but there is much to do and there may be little time left to do it.

NOTES

1. Figures in the last four paragraphs came from the United Nations Development Programme, *Human Development Report 1994,* and publications of the World Watch Institute.
2. "Angrily" is an understatement. With independence, France cut all ties with Guinea and withdrew, taking with them everything from government vehicles to telephones.
3. Mazrui related the anecdote in the 1986 television series "The Africans."
4. Karen Norris Schneider, "Sub-Saharan Africa: A Measure of Freedom—1995," *Christian Science Monitor,* March 13, 1995, pp. 10–11.
5. Despite the fact that most of the region's people live in absolute poverty, more than $8 billion was spent on weapons in 1993.
6. Jennifer Seymour Whitaker, *How Can Africa Survive?* (New York: Council on Foreign Relations, 1988), pp. 30–31.
7. Alan B. Durning, "Ending Poverty," in Lester R. Brown et al., *State of the World, 1990* (New York: Norton, 1990), p. 139.
8. For an excellent summary of contemporary South Africa, see "Coming of Age," a special supplement in *The Economist,* May 20, 1995.
9. Hal Kane, "Leaving Home," in Lester R. Brown et al., *State of the World, 1995* (New York: Norton, 1995), p. 142.
10. Worldwatch Institute, *Vital Signs, 1994* (New York: Norton, 1994), p. 102.
11. Worldwatch Institute, *Vital Signs, 1995* (New York: Norton, 1995), p. 18.
12. World Bank, *The 1990 World Development Report: Poverty* (Washington, D.C.: World Bank, 1990), p. 178.
13. The number of refugees dwarfed those from any other country on the continent until the 1994 Rwandan civil war.
14. As of December 1994, 71 percent of Mozambique's budget came from outside donors.
15. Impressive books, devoted in major part or entirely to African environmental stresses, include Paul Harrison, *The Greening of Africa* (New York: Penguin Books, 1987), and *The Third Revolution* (New York: Penguin Books, 1992); and Lloyd Timberlake, *Africa in Crisis: The Causes, the Cures of Environmental Bankruptcy,* new ed. (London and Toronto: Earthscan, 1988).
16. Since 1989, for instance, Kenya's elephant population has grown by some 60 percent to an estimated 25,000. In the same period, Kenya's human population has grown by 6 million, an increase of about 27 percent.

FOR FURTHER READING

Bayart, Jean-François. *The State in Africa: The Politics of the Belly.* London and New York: Longman, 1993.

Boahen, A. Adu. *African Perspectives on Colonialism.* Baltimore: Johns Hopkins University Press, 1987.

Chazan, Naomi; Mortimer, Robert; Ravenhill, John; and Rothchild, David. *Politics and Society in Contemporary Africa.* 2nd ed. Boulder, Col.: Rienner, 1992.

Clough, Michael. *Free at Last? U.S. Policy toward Africa and the End of the Cold War*. New York: Council on Foreign Relations, 1992.

Davidson, Basil. *The Black Man's Burden: Africa and the Curse of the Nation State*. New York: Times Books, 1992.

Gordon, April A., and Gordon, Donald L., eds. *Understanding Contemporary Africa*. Boulder, Col.: Rienner, 1992.

Harbeson, John W., and Rothchild, Donald, eds. *Africa in World Politics: Post–Cold War Challenges*. Boulder, Col.: Westview Press, 1995.

Harrison, Paul. *The Third Revolution: Population, Environment, and a Sustainable World*. London and New York: Penguin Books, 1992, 1993.

Hiltzik, Michael. *A Death in Kenya*. New York: Delacorte Press, 1992.

Hochschild, Adam. *The Mirror at Midnight: A South African Journey*. New York: Viking Press, 1990.

Houser, George M. *No One Can Stop the Rain: Glimpses of Africa's Liberation Struggle*. New York: Pilgrim Press, 1989.

Khapoya, Vincent B. *The African Experience: An Introduction*. Englewood Cliffs, N.J.: Prentice Hall, 1994.

Klitgaard, Robert. *Tropical Gangsters*. New York: Basic Books, 1990.

Malan, Rian. *My Traitor's Heart*. New York: Vintage Books, 1990.

Mazrui, Ali. *The African Condition*. New York: Cambridge University Press, 1980.

Mazrui, Ali, and Tiday, Michael. *Nationalism and New States in Africa*. London: Heinemann, 1984.

Ramsay, F. J., ed. *Global Studies: Africa*. 6th ed. Guilford, Conn.: Brown and Benchmark, 1995.

CHAPTER 7

Asia

Earl D. Huff

> *There have been in Asia, generally, from immemorial times, but three departments of government: that of finance, or the plunder of the interior; that of war, or the plunder of the exterior; and, finally, the department of public works.*
>
> Karl Marx

It cannot be overemphasized that the segment of the vast Eurasian land mass that we call Asia is by far the largest and most diverse of the continents. Indeed, as we focus our attention on that vast area spanning one-third of the Earth and containing two-thirds of its people, we are immediately confronted with the necessity of limiting the areas to be touched on in this brief chapter.

Our discussion will be limited to those nations that do not fall either within the Western industrialized bloc or the rapidly changing former Soviet one. Therefore, Japan and the former Soviet states of Asia will be excluded entirely from the Asia of our Other World. Also excluded are the states of Southwest Asia, which along with the states of North Africa are discussed in chapter 8 under the more commonly used heading the Middle East. Consequently, this consideration of Asia is confined to the territory on the continent south of the states of the former Soviet Union, extending from Pakistan in the west to the Korean peninsula in the east, as well as the various island states southward to Indonesia. Although we have placed vast areas of Asia beyond the scope of this chapter, this limitation does little to reduce the difficulty we will encounter in dealing with the great geographic, cultural, and ethnic diversity that remains. The countries and the physical characteristics of this vast region are depicted in figure 7.1.

Two decades ago, the noted author and journalist Robert S. Elegant told of a conversation that illustrates some of the difficulties that may be encountered when those reared in the cultures of the West come into contact with Asia. Elegant's secretary asked a Hong Kong parking lot attendant if he had seen a

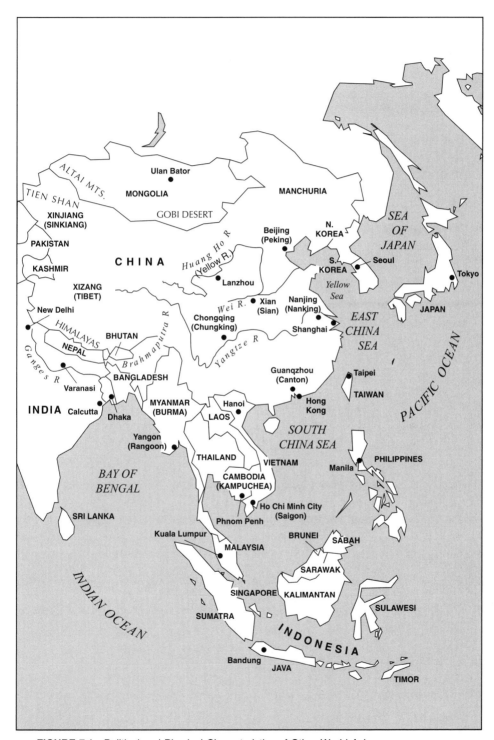

FIGURE 7.1 Political and Physical Characteristics of Other World Asia

191

Hong Kong $100 note that had been lost shortly after Elegant and a Chinese friend had parked their car.

> "Yes," the attendant recalled. "I remember that a devil-person and a human being came by talking Mandarin Chinese. The devil-person tried to pay with a $100 bill but the human being paid with a smaller bill. Then the devil-person put the $100 in his pocket."

Elegant noted, "The attendant was neither making a personal remark nor being deliberately rude." He was simply using the term *gwai lau* ("devil-person") as normally used by Chinese who speak the Cantonese dialect to refer to non-Chinese. Had the attendant spoken Mandarin, the official language, he might have referred to Elegant as *yang kuei-dze*, literally, "overseas devil."[1] Elegant went on to say, "Even Chinese from different areas are accorded distinctive insults. Northerners often refer to other Chinese as *nan-man* (Southern savages). Southerners return the compliment with *pei-yee* (Northern barbarians)."

Elegant's experiences illustrate several points to be remembered as we examine contemporary Asian political issues. First, we must recognize that there is perhaps no other segment of the Earth in which the influence of history is stronger. The quoted comments by Elegant reflect an attitude of superiority born of a 4,000-year period when China came into direct contact with no country that was by any measure its equal. Even the Chinese name for the country, *Chung-Kuo*, means "the middle (of the world) country." It is only in the last two centuries that such a view has been challenged by the "overseas devils" from Europe. We would do well to overcome any tendencies toward ethnocentricity as we deal with nations that are often the products of civilizations predating our own. Indeed, in times past, many of these civilizations could, with justification, have viewed Europe as an "underdeveloped" land. Second, we must resist the tendency to overestimate the impact of even the most sweeping contemporary political changes. The attitudes quoted above are strikingly similar to those encountered in China in centuries past, regardless of the regime in power.

Perhaps even more relevant to this chapter is the degree to which the quotations reveal divisions within one of the most politically and culturally unified Asian states. These divisions must be kept in mind as we consider the extent to which the words of various Asian politicians reflect the sentiments of national populations that are often highly fragmented. Certainly, if such divisions exist within a single state, we must greet with even greater skepticism generalizations that purport to explain "Asian" attitudes on issues of the day.

A brief review of the information contained in table 7.1 will do much to illustrate the great variety of conditions in Other World Asia. Such diversity makes it unwise, or perhaps impossible, to attempt an analysis of the region as a whole. It seems equally inappropriate to attempt a state-by-state analysis. Rather, after briefly sketching the geographical features, the ethnic composition, and the historical setting, we will divide the region into three geographic areas: East Asia, South Asia (the Indian subcontinent), and Southeast Asia. We will discuss the recent history and current outlook of major states in each of those areas and note any forces that seem likely to affect significantly their international behavior.

TABLE 7.1 Characteristics of Asian Countries

Country	Population (millions)	Population Growth Rate (%)	Infant Mortality Rate (per 1,000 live births)	Population Under 15 Years of Age (%)	Life Expectancy (years)	Urban Population (%)	Literacy Rate (%)	Arable Land (%)	Per Capita GNP ($U.S.)
Middle South									
Afghanistan	16.9	4.2	156	—	43	18	32	12	—
Bangladesh	125.1	2.4	107	44	52	14	37	67	220
Butan	1.7	2.3	121	39	48	—	41	2	190
India	919.9	1.8	78	36	60	26	50	55	330
Maldives	.3	2.9	54	47	63	26	—	10	470
Nepal	21	2.4	84	44	53	8	27	17	180
Pakistan	121.9	2.7	102	44	58	28	36	26	400
Sri Lanka	18	1.2	22	35	71	22	89	16	500
South East									
Brunei	.29	2.1	25	—	74	—	—	—	—
Myanmar (Burma)	44.3	2.1	64	36	57	25	82	15	—
Cambodia	10.3	2.4	111	—	50	13	38	16	200
Indonesia	200.4	1.7	67	37	62	31	84	8	610
Laos	4.7	2.8	102	—	50	19	—	4	220
Malaysia	19.3	2.1	26	36	70	51	80	3	2,520
Philippines	69.8	2.0	51	39	65	44	90	26	740
Singapore	2.9	0.9	6	23	74	—	—	4	14,140
Thailand	59.5	1.1	37	29	69	19	94	34	1,650
Vietnam	73.1	2.0	96	39	63	21	89	22	—
East Asia									
China	1190.4	1.2	52	28	71	28	80	10	370
Korea, North	23.1	1.7	28	29	71	60	95	18	—
Korea, South	45.1	0.8	22	24	70	71	96.8	21	6,350
Mongolia	2.4	2.6	43	—	63	57	—	1	—
Comparison States									
Japan	125.1	0.4	4	17	79	77	99	13	26,840
Belgium	10.1	0.1	7	18	76	97	99	24	19,010
Italy	58.1	0.1	8	16	77	68	97.4	32	17,040

SOURCE: Adapted from the *United Nations Demographic Yearbook, United Nations Human Development Report,* and *The World Almanac and Book of Facts, 1995.*

GEOGRAPHY

Throughout Other World Asia, geography greatly affects population distribution and standard of living. Perhaps the first image that comes to mind when westerners think of Asia is of a densely populated land of grinding poverty. Although such an image is not totally incorrect, it is incomplete. Some areas of Bangladesh, eastern India, and elsewhere do fit that image. However, other areas such as Singapore or northwest China do not, the former because of a relatively high per capita income, largely attributable to its highly industrialized modern economy, and the latter because of the generally very sparse population of that remote region. With approximately four out of five Asians living in a rural environment, the densest populations tend to occur in the alluvial valleys and flood plains of the major rivers and in other regions where agricultural activity is relatively easy to sustain. Not surprisingly, the vast desert regions of northern China, Pakistan, and India tend to be very sparsely settled. Similarly, the population is quite sparse in the high Himalayan "backbone" of Asia. With altitudes averaging 20,000 feet and much of its land surface perpetually under snow, that vast region does not encourage economic activities.

From the Indian subcontinent to the Yellow Sea, the dominant climatic influence to which virtually all activities must adapt is the rhythm of the monsoon. The term *monsoon* is derived from Arabic and means "seasonal trade wind." Such seasonal shifts in prevailing winds result in distinct wet and dry seasons. Although each region of Asia has its own seasonal pattern, the situation in the Indian subcontinent is illustrative. India's monsoon climate divides the year into three distinct seasons. The arrival of the monsoon in June begins a wet, humid season that lasts through September or October. A cool, dry season extends from October to March. The hot season fills the remainder of the yearly cycle. With over two-thirds of India's population living directly off the land, any change in this cycle can have dramatic social and/or political consequences.

With almost all of India's rainfall occurring between June and September, it early became apparent that irrigation was vital if large populations were to be sustained during the remaining eight months of the year. Although Karl Marx's knowledge of Asian history was not his strongest quality, he was correct in his assessment that Asia's "climate and territorial conditions . . . constituted artificial irrigation by canals and waterworks, the basis of Oriental agriculture."[2]

China, on the eastern rim of monsoon Asia, has a climate rather similar to that of the eastern United States, with four distinct seasons. However, as a result of the great size of the Eurasian land mass, China tends to be somewhat colder and drier than similar latitudes in the United States. Rainfall is nearly adequate for agriculture in the south of China but inadequate in the north. Consequently, for thousands of years, China's rivers, along with highly developed canals and irrigation systems, have been of vital importance as providers of a life-sustaining substance, as means of transportation, and as shapers of social attitudes. An age-old dependence on irrigation has taught the Chinese the need for cooperation and for a higher authority to maintain public works and settle disputes.

PEOPLE

India's numerous ethnic groups converse in about 600 languages and dialects, 15 of which are officially recognized as being of national importance and none of which is universally understood across that vast state. Conflicts in recent years among Hindu, Muslim, and Sikh religious groups in India, Sinhalese and Tamil ethnic groups in Sri Lanka, and nationalist uprisings in the Indian segment of Kashmir are indicative of internal tensions that threaten the unity and stability of South Asian states. Indeed, the assassination of former Prime Minister Rajiv Gandhi was believed to be the work of discontented Tamils. His mother, Prime Minister Indira Gandhi, was assassinated by Sikh separatists.

Today's China remains a land in which the vast Han majority (approximately 94 percent) shares territory with numerous non-Chinese nationalities, many of whom reside in the sometimes tense regions along China's periphery. There may be found sizable Manchu, Mongol, Tibetan, and Turkic minorities along with many other, less numerous ethnic groups. In many such regions, these ethnic groups have, in fact, constituted the majority. Current Chinese policy encourages the Han majority to respect the efforts of minorities to maintain their separate identities while simultaneously promoting the immigration of Han Chinese into the sparsely settled regions where such minorities have traditionally dwelt. It seems only a matter of time until the Han constitute a majority in every region of China.

Throughout Southeast Asia, ethnic Chinese are a small but important minority, making up 1 to 3 percent of the population of Cambodia, Indonesia, Vietnam, the Philippines, and Myanmar, formerly known as Burma. In Thailand, they number approximately 14 percent of the population. In Malaysia, around one-third of the population is ethnic Chinese. In Singapore, one of the most prosperous states in the region, they are, in fact, the majority, numbering around 77 percent of the population. Throughout Southeast Asia, the Chinese are a relatively small, clannish, and affluent element of the population who constitute both a significant influence beyond their numbers and a convenient target for possible ethnic conflict.

Southeast Asia is also diverse in religion, with some representation of each of the world's great religions in virtually every state. To generalize, Buddhism is the predominant religion in Myanmar (Burma), Cambodia, Thailand, and to a lesser extent Singapore, Laos, and Vietnam. In Indonesia, Brunei, and Malaysia, Islam is the dominant religion, although there are significant pockets of other religions; for example, in the Indonesian island of Bali, Hinduism is the primary religion. In Malaysia, the huge Chinese minority constitutes a significant island of Confucianism and Taoism. In the Philippines, Christianity is by far the dominant religion, yet there is also a small and sometimes militant Muslim minority. As might be suspected, the interplay of the many faiths and the many animistic religions as well provides a rich cultural mosaic in Southeast Asia. Likewise, it contributes additional breeding grounds for conflict both within and among the states of the region.

HISTORY AND GOVERNMENT

Two of the great early civilizations of the world originated in Other World Asia. In the west, the Indus civilization began in the Indus River valley about 2300 B.C. In the east a few hundred years later, the Chinese civilization arose in the valley of the Hwang Ho, or Yellow River. It is perhaps not too great an oversimplification to view these two great cultures as the foundations for subsequent Asian civilization.

South Asia

Throughout history, Indian civilization and its dominant religion, Hinduism, have dominated South Asia. Both began in the Indus civilization but were modified by cultural influences of the Aryan invader of 1500–1200 B.C. and by native Dravidian people from other regions of India. Later invasions brought Islam to South Asia, an influence that led to 400 years of Muslim domination of India and may be found today in the predominantly Muslim states of Pakistan and Bangladesh, as well as in the approximately 11 percent Muslim population that remains in India.

The last great foreign invasion of India began with Portugal's capture of Goa in 1510 from the Muslim state of Bijapur. From that date until the Portuguese were driven from Goa in 1961 by Indian forces, there was a European presence in India. However, the European state that most profoundly influenced South Asia was not Portugal but Great Britain.

The British East India Company came to India solely for trade when it established its first settlement in Surat in 1612. However, the first century of British presence in India coincided with a period of considerable disorder, which to British thinking necessitated a military response and eventually led to the conversion of the East India Company from a mere trading organization into the de facto ruler of India. Finally, in 1858, the British government replaced the East India Company when Queen Victoria appointed the first British viceroy of India. As the nineteenth century drew to a close, India under British rule was achieving a measure of economic development. In the cities, the emergence of an Indian industrial class was well under way. In rural areas, new lands were being brought under cultivation as huge irrigation works were developed.

Also developing in late nineteenth-century India was a politically aware middle class educated along Western lines and demanding a greater role in the affairs of India. Many such individuals were present in December 1885, when the self-appointed Indian National Congress first met to discuss social and political issues. In a manner not unlike certain moderate American colonists, who over a century before had petitioned Britain to grant them the rights of Englishmen, these middle-class and mostly Hindu intellectuals sought reform, not revolution. However, by 1906, a more militant Indian National Congress demanded nothing less than self-rule, altbough that position was not then generally held among educated Indians. But by 1920, even relatively pro-British Indians such as Mohandas Gandhi were openly and actively opposing continued British rule. Gandhi's non-violent resistance movement provided an effective base of mass support that complemented the efforts of the Indian National Congress. However, the congress continued in many ways to cooperate with the British by participating in numerous elections held during the two decades preceding World War II.

In the same year that the Indian National Congress first demanded self-rule for India, another organization of nearly equal significance was formed. In 1906, the Moslem League was organized to speak on behalf of that minority as mutual suspicion increased between Hindu and Muslim nationalists and communal violence raged between the two religious groups. In spite of the efforts of Gandhi and others, relations continued to degenerate as independence approached. By 1940, the Moslem League was actively demanding the creation of a separate Muslim state, Pakistan.

As World War II ended, Britain reluctantly recognized its inability to continue governing the Indian subcontinent. It turned instead to the task of withdrawing from that region in an honorable and orderly manner that, insofar as possible, might satisfy the demands of both nationalist elements. In February 1947, amid growing communal violence, the new British Labour government announced its decision to withdraw from India and set about developing a plan to partition the area into a predominantly Hindu India and a new Muslim state of Pakistan. On August 15, 1947, that plan was rather arbitrarily put into effect.

Unfortunately, that relatively simple political act did not dampen ethnic hostilities, whose roots extended centuries into the past. The Muslim population was not neatly clustered in only a few regions. Hundreds of years of political and economic integration under the British and before them had resulted in numerous clusters throughout the whole of British India. Massive dislocations and tremendous bloodshed occurred as around 15 million individuals, both Muslim and Hindu, participated in one of the largest and most violent mass migrations in human history. Even after the conclusion of that migration, it soon became apparent that the conflicts that had divided Muslim and Hindu within British India would be played out on a larger stage between the newly created states of India and Pakistan.

It should also be noted that the creation of two distinct states did not end communal strife in either. Experience seems to indicate that whenever numerous distinct ethnic or religious groups live in close proximity to one another, the potential for such conflict exists. Just as conflicts between Muslims and Hindus were instrumental in the division of British India into two states, later tensions between Punjabi-dominated West Pakistan and the Bengalis of East Pakistan resulted in the creation of a separate Bengali state, Bangladesh, in the east.

East Asia

From its origins in the lower Yellow River valley, Chinese civilization spread first to contiguous regions of northern China between the great Yellow and Yangtze river systems. Then, with the Han dynasty (206 B.C.–A.D. 222), South China came under centralized control. It is the people of these regions who were the progenitors of the largest ethnic group or nationality in China, the Han Chinese.

By around 500 B.C., when in the West ancient Greece was reaching its greatest height, China came under the influence of the secular ideology of Confucianism, which was to dominate the social order of China up to the present century. Like his contemporary Plato, Confucius (*kung-fu-tzu*, or "master Kung") speculated on the ideal form of the state. Confucianism teaches that all elements of society, including the government, should be bound by firm codes of behavior and ethical principles. Each person, from peasant to emperor, could contribute to the collective well-being by observing proper conduct. In short, good government and all other human endeavors are a matter of ethics rather than divine revelation. Confucianism was the glue that bound the Han Chinese leadership together for millennia and provided a cultural and material superiority that was recognized both by the Chinese and by all other people with whom they came into contact until very modern times. Even invading non-Chinese peoples such as the Mongols and Manchus chose to emulate the Chinese culture and utilize Han officials and methods.

We find in China a unique situation in which the current government maintains centralized control over essentially the same territory as that of Chinese regimes over the past 2,000 years. However, neither that centralized control of the Chinese nor the extent of the territory itself has been totally consistent over time. Often during its long history, China has degenerated into numerous warring states or de facto decentralized control by local officials. Historically, as a dynasty's power grew, the extent of the territory it controlled became enlarged to include peripheral regions such as Tibet, Indochina, and Manchuria. As a dynasty's power waned, such regions might simply recognize Chinese suzerainty through the payment of tribute or perhaps openly defy Chinese authority. Figure 7.2 illustrates the extent of China's rather indefinite boundaries during the late eighteenth century and demonstrates the extent to which history provides a basis for possible future territorial claims by the Chinese.

The last Chinese dynasty, the Ch'ing, or Manchu, was at the peak of its power during the reign of Emperor Ch'ien-lung (1736–1795). Its authority extended throughout the territory currently governed by China and on to Indochina, Burma, Nepal, Outer Mongolia, and beyond. But only a half century later, that proud nation was well on its way to a status later described by Sun Yatsen, the founder of the Chinese republic, as a "subcolony"—an area whose international status was inferior to that of a colony, like India, dominated by a single master. The Opium War (1839–1842), the first war between China and a European state, demonstrated the inability of China to defend itself against superior Western military technology. The Treaty of Nanking, which ended that conflict, and other such unequal treaties forced on a declining dynasty by imperialist powers gave China numerous masters, each demanding most-favored-nation status as they carved out spheres of influence within the territory of the nominally sovereign nation.

With the final collapse of the Ch'ing dynasty in 1912, China once again fell victim to internal divisions and continued foreign pressures. In varying degrees, both problems continued to plague that nation to the midpoint of the twentieth century. Indeed, if there is any common bond between Kuomintang (Nationalist) and communist China during the last half century, it is the desire to bring an end to the humiliations suffered by China at the hands of foreigners and to return a united country to its rightful place as a major actor in the world community.

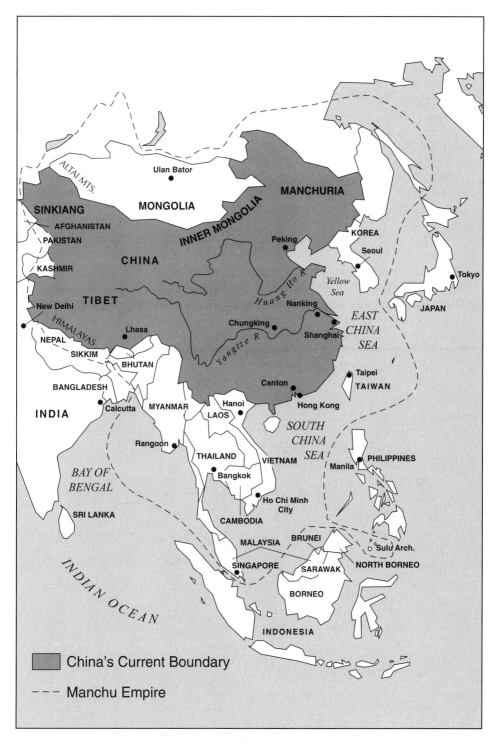

FIGURE 7.2 The Boundaries of China (as Perceived by the Chinese in the 1960s) and at the Height of the Ch'ing Dynasty in the Late Eighteenth Century

SOURCE: Modified version of map in Harold Hinton, *Communist China in World Politics* (Boston: Houghton Mifflin, 1966). Reprinted by permission.

Southeast Asia

Southeast Asia has historically been subjected to the gravitational pull of the two dominant civilizations just discussed. Like South and East Asia, it is populated by numerous and diverse peoples. Unlike those regions, it has not developed an indigenous independent civilization comparable to those of the Indus or Yellow River valleys.

From around the third or fourth century B.C., the various native peoples of Southeast Asia were greatly affected by massive migrations of those from India, who brought Hinduism, Buddhism, Islam, and other cultural influences. Likewise, regions near China such as northern Indochina came under both cultural and military pressures from their great neighbor to the north. For centuries, many areas of Indochina were either under direct Chinese control or served as tributary states.

Mixed with the cultural influences of China were the native cultures of the Malay, Thai, Vietnamese, Miao, Khmer, Filipino, and numerous other ethnic divisions within Southeast Asia. To that mix was added the influence of the Western colonial powers and a renewed Chinese influence brought by waves of Chinese immigrants during the colonial period. During that time, these "overseas Chinese" rose to dominant positions in many areas of business, first as retail merchants and later as bankers and industrialists.

CASE STUDIES

EAST ASIA: CHINA

As generally defined, East Asia comprises China, the Koreas, and Japan. With Japan outside the scope of this chapter, China is unquestionably the East Asian state with the greatest impact on world affairs and thus invites our closer attention. For our purposes, the word *China* will be used to refer to the People's Republic of China (PRC). The Republic of China (RC) on Taiwan will be referred to as Taiwan.

One further source of confusion involves the transliteration of Chinese names into the Roman alphabet. Unfortunately, several systems are currently in use. The most common is the Wade-Giles system, which is used by most Western scholars and in Taiwan. A second system that is finding increasing use worldwide is the Chinese phonetic alphabet, or "pinyin" system, developed and used by the PRC. This chapter will generally utilize the Wade-Giles system when referring to places in China and to all but the most current personalities. Pinyin will be used to refer to individuals who more recently achieved prominence in China. Several major personalities whose careers have spanned long periods will be referred to in the Wade-Giles transliteration and will also be followed by the pinyin transliteration in parentheses. Finally, it should be noted that the names of Chinese and many other Asians begin with the surname rather than the given name. Thus, the first U.S. president would have been referred to as Washington George had he been Chinese. Likewise, a respected former Chinese premier, Chou En-lai (Zhou Enlai), should be referred to as Premier Chou (Zhou).

Listed below in both systems of transliteration are several common names of major Chinese places and persons.

Wade-Giles	*Pinyin*
Teng Hsiao-ping	Deng Xiaoping
Mao Tse-tung	Mao Zedong
Chou En-lai	Zhou Enlai
Yang Shang-kun	Yang Shangkun
Peking	Beijing
Tientsin	Tianjin
Kwangchow	Guangzhou
Sian	Xian
Sinkiang	Xinjiang

In area, China is the third largest country on earth, behind Russia and Canada. It is only slightly larger than the United States, although its population of around 1.2 billion, easily the world's largest, is more than four times greater. However, this statement is an oversimplification because it fails to take account of the vast differences in population density within China. Although it contains several of the world's largest cities, most Chinese do not reside in the urban regions. Rather, approximately 80 percent of Chinese live in a rural setting, and the vast majority earn their livelihood by toiling on the land. Unfortunately, approximately two-thirds of China's territory is mountainous or desert and has limited capacity to support a large rural population. Indeed, China's atomic test area in the Lop Nor region of Sinkiang province is among the world's most sparsely populated areas. At the other extreme are the fertile Yangtze and Yellow River regions, which along with South China contain some of the world's most densely populated agricultural lands. As one travels through these regions, the pressure of vast numbers of people farming every available piece of arable land becomes immediately apparent to even the most casual observer.

It was the late Mao Tse-tung (Mao Zedong) who first recognized the central role that the vast peasantry would play when he tried to adapt Marxist-Leninist principles to conditions in China. In 1927, in regard to a peasant revolt in his native province of Hunan, Mao wrote that it was "necessary to establish the absolute authority of the peasants" as revolutionaries sought to "bring about a brief reign of terror in every rural area." To his more traditionally Marxist comrades, who saw the urban areas as the central focus of revolutionary activity, Mao argued that in "semi-colonial and semi-feudal" China, "the broad peasant masses" had simply "risen to fulfill their historic mission to overthrow the rural feudal power. Every revolutionary comrade should know that the national revolution requires a profound change in the countryside."[3]

Over a decade later, after Mao had assumed the leadership of the Communist party of China (CPC), he pointed out that the "reactionary forces have long occupied China's key cities." However, he continued to stress his view that "the Chinese revolution can be victorious first in the rural districts. . . . It is evident that the protracted revolutionary struggle conducted in such revolutionary base areas is mainly a peasant guerrilla war led by the Chinese Communist Party." From those secure rural areas, Mao urged his comrades to engage in protracted guerrilla warfare to defeat eventually a more powerful enemy. Although the peasantry would be the prime force, Mao also recognized that the chance of success could be enhanced by working within a revolutionary "united front of all revolutionary classes under the leadership of the proletariat"—in other words, directed by the CPC, the vanguard of the proletariat.[4]

With the proclamation of October 1, 1949, which established the PRC, Mao and his associates turned their attention to governing the world's most populous nation. However, their experiences in the long rise to power lived on for decades in the form of a militancy unmatched in any other communist state and enunciated in the "thoughts of Mao Tse-tung." By the mid-1960s, Mao led an assault on all intellectual dissent that pitted him and his supporters against relatively more moderate party officials, such as Liu Shao-chi (Liu Shaoqi) and eventually Teng Hsiao-ping (Deng Xiaoping), in a struggle culminating in the so-called Great Proletariat Cultural Revolution (GPCR). The GPCR resulted in a period of chaos, terror, and suffering that was only partially remedied by Mao's use of the army to suppress his militant student allies, the Red Guards, in late 1968. Indeed, the GPCR did not officially end until the critical transition year, 1976. As late as March 1978, a new constitution of the PRC referred to the "triumphant conclusion of the Great Proletariat Cultural Revolution" that had "ushered in a new period of development in China's socialist revolution and socialist construction."

Beyond China's borders, Mao's "thoughts" provided an ideological framework for a variant of Marxism that used the Chinese experience as a guide for other Third World states. By the mid-1960s, Mao's late "close comrade-in-arms" and heir apparent, Vice Chairman Lin Piao, utilized Mao's "thoughts" to urge "peoples' wars" (i.e., protracted guerrilla warfare) modeled on China's experience as a way to bring about the fall of the West. In an article published on September 3, 1965, in Peking's *Renmin Ribao (People's Daily)* and later in the booklet *Long Live the Victory of People's War*, Lin argued that the encirclement of the cities and control of the countryside during the CPC's long struggle for power were "of outstanding and universal practical importance" for all the nations and peoples in Asia, Africa, and Latin America who were struggling against U.S. "imperialism and its lackeys." In the following paragraph, Lin clearly articulated the Maoist view of the Third World's role in world revolution:

> Taking the entire globe, if North America and Western Europe can be called "the cities of the world," then Asia, Africa and Latin America constitute "the rural areas of the world." . . . In a sense, the contemporary world revolution also presents a picture of the encirclement of cities by the rural areas. . . . The socialist countries should regard it as their internationalist duty to support the people's revolutionary struggles in Asia, Africa and Latin America.[5]

In the eyes of Lin and of Mao, once this process was complete, the "cities of the world" would eventually fall like ripe fruit.

Nearly three decades have passed since these statements by Lin were made. In many ways, the China of today is quite a different society than that of the mid-1960s. Following the death of Mao in October 1976, and the subsequent reemergence of Teng Hsiao-ping as the most powerful individual in the Chinese hierarchy, a more pragmatic leadership succeeded in its power struggle against more radical elements and set China on a somewhat different course.

Today's Chinese leaders acknowledge that grave errors were made by Mao and the party during the two decades preceding Mao's death. They clearly state that Mao "overestimated the role of Man's subjective will" and that he must be held chiefly responsible for the mistakes made during this period.[6] But it is perhaps neither prudent nor possible to discredit totally a leader who has so indelibly influenced a nation as did Mao. Rather, the current regime seeks to institutionalize Mao's "thoughts" and bend them to the service of a more pragmatic and inwardly oriented form of communism than anything he envisioned.

> Mao Zedong Thought, coming into being and developing in the course of the Chinese revolution, is the crystallization of the collective wisdom of our Party and a summing-up of the victories in the gigantic struggles of the Chinese people. . . . Its theories have all added new and original ideas to the treasure house of Marxism. . . . Mao Zedong Thought has been and will remain the guiding ideology of our Party.[7]

Under the guidance of such "thought," China has turned away from Mao's insistence on rigid self-sufficiency and is actively encouraging the transfer to China of foreign investment and technology as it pursues the "Four Modernizations": industry, agriculture, national defense, and science and technology. To that end, "special economic zones" have been established to cooperate with foreign and overseas Chinese investors in a form of "state capitalism." On a vast scale, China is putting its economic house in order, with the assistance of foreign capital. Rural reforms were initiated in the late 1970s, revamping China's collectivized agriculture to reward individual initiative. By the mid-1980s, such reforms had spread to the larger economy as, in the name of Marxism-Leninism, the CPC set about the reduction of centralized state planning and moved toward a pricing structure based more on market forces. By the mid-1990s, China's gross domestic product was increasing at a rate of well over 10 percent a year.

Although somewhat preoccupied with its internal affairs, China has also turned a more moderate face outward. In 1990 it cooperated with the UN effort to reinvigorate the concept of collective security by forcing an Iraqi withdrawal from Kuwait. Similarly, it participated in international efforts to end the conflicts in Cambodia and Afghanistan. On the unfinished business of national reunification, the new leadership stressed that the Taiwan and Hong Kong issues must be settled peacefully under a policy of "one country, two systems." This policy would allow the areas to remain capitalist for a period of 50 years after reunification. In the case of Hong Kong, an agreement to that effect was signed in December 1984. Hong Kong officially reverts to Chinese sovereignty in 1997. Although no such

Advertising in China. This advertisement on a Beijing street illustrates the extent to which present-day China is turning away from Maoist self-sufficiency in favor of increased trade with the West.

SOURCE: Earl Huff

agreement has been reached regarding Taiwan, by the mid-1990s contacts between the RC and the PRC were increasing in various ways, ranging from trade to rapidly expanding travel between Taiwan and the mainland and numerous semiofficial contacts between representatives of the two governments. It seems unlikely that this process will be reversed unless Taiwan precipitates a crisis by more vigorously asserting its claim to sovereignty.

Today, although China increasingly seeks a major role among the world's great powers, it also continues to view itself as a developing country and as a major spokesperson for the interests of such nations. Unlike the 1960s, its leadership now seems primarily influenced by a need to promote mutual economic progress and technological cooperation. Although China continues to see itself as an opponent of the hegemonism of great powers and as an ally of various elements that it feels have been under attack by such states or their proxies, it has been far less vocal since the end of the cold war. However, in recent years it has supported opposition groups in Cambodia, Afghanistan, Palestine, southern Africa, and Central America. Furthermore, as events along its border with Vietnam a decade ago demonstrated, China remains prepared to act militarily to defend its interests if need be.

In short, the past two decades have witnessed dramatic changes in China both internally and in its international behavior. Although the apparent success of internal changes may well limit the ability of future Chinese leaders to return to the extremely militant policies of the past, given the events of June 1989 there is room for skepticism. Faced with a growing demand for political as well as economic reforms, the Chinese government chose to resort to military force against demonstrators in Beijing's Tiananmen Square and throughout China. That brutal response was followed by a massive propaganda campaign against "bourgeois liberalism" that seemed very much in keeping with the mass campaigns and other forms of thought reform that characterized an earlier period of the PRC. Each anniversary of the Tiananmen massacre has been preceded by renewed efforts to suppress Chinese dissidents.

Although communist regimes in Europe and elsewhere have undergone thorough and perhaps irreversible political reform, the aging Chinese leadership seems unwilling to commit to such a course. Today, the rigidly hierarchical CPC remains the dominant force in China, with the ability to reach into and direct virtually every aspect of life in that state. China is still a considerable distance away from a democracy in the Western sense. The newly burnished and institutionalized "thoughts" of Mao Tse-tung, together with highly centralized CPC control, provide rather flexible and potent devices for leading China in whatever direction its leaders deem appropriate. For the time being, they seem to have concluded that China's interests will be best served by a rather moderate foreign policy and domestic economic reforms alongside a rigidly authoritarian political system. It remains to be seen how long such a combination can be sustained by an aging leadership. By the mid-1990s, possible lines of division within the CPC were already forming as the aging Teng Hsiao-ping's health worsened and party leaders began to position themselves for a succession struggle.

Perhaps the most significant conclusion to be drawn from current Chinese behavior is that China has been communist for less than five decades, whereas it has been Chinese for more than 4,000 years. During those four millennia, pragmatism has been rather constantly a major element of the Chinese national character. In that light, it may be asserted that the current pragmatic leadership is more "Chinese" than were Mao and the radicals who once dominated China. However, as the events of 1989 demonstrated, should elements within that pragmatic leadership conclude that more militant policies better serve either China's interests or their own, potent means remain for them to reverse current policies abruptly. Indeed, given the dramatic policy reversals over the past decades, such a turn of events should not surprise any knowledgeable observer.

SOUTH ASIA

As noted, Indian civilization and Hinduism are traditionally the dominant forces shaping South Asia. However, today that region is made up of six independent states, four of which have populations that, although certainly influenced by Indian civilization, are not predominantly Hindu. As already indicated, Pakistan and Bangladesh are predominantly Muslim. Two other South Asian states, Bhutan and Sri Lanka, have populations that are approximately 60 percent Buddhist. The sixth state, Nepal, like India, is predominantly Hindu.

Although each of these states plays a role in the political behavior of South Asia, our attention will focus on the two largest states on the Indian subcontinent, India and Pakistan. The former will receive somewhat greater attention both because of its greater size and because it was one of the founders and most influential members of the nonaligned movement.

India. With the assassination of Mohandas Gandhi on January 30, 1948, Jawaharlal Nehru soon became the most influential political leader in the Congress

Once Elegant Buildings from India's Imperial Past, a Backdrop for Trade in Today's Calcutta

SOURCE: Earl Huff

party and in India. As such, he became India's first prime minister, a post he held until his death in 1964.

Under Nehru, India advocated a policy of nonalignment with either of the two major-power blocs. It should be noted that this policy was quite different from simple neutrality and implied an active role in solving the great issues that divided the world. India sought to further world peace by offering an alternative to the bipolarity that characterized world relations in the years following World War II. It wanted to gain the acceptance by other nations of the nonalignment principle and to serve as the primary voice of that part of the Other World that saw the East-West confrontation as only one of many major international problems. By the early 1950s, India had largely achieved those goals and had assumed a degree of influence in world affairs that was quite out of proportion to its material resources.

A second basic element of Indian foreign policy during this period was anti-imperialism. Under Nehru's direction, India actively sought an end to colonialism wherever it existed in Asia and beyond. Indeed, it is perhaps this aspect of India's foreign policy that cemented its leadership position within the Other World. Such a policy was eagerly received by Other World nationalists still striving for independence and, perhaps more significantly, by those who had recently achieved that status.

In 1949, Nehru described his nonalignment philosophy as

a positive, constructive policy deliberately trying to avoid hostility to other countries. It follows, therefore, that we should not align ourselves with what are called power blocs. We can be of far more service without doing so and I think there is just a possibility that at a moment of crisis our peaceful and friendly efforts might make a difference and avert that crisis.[8]

On April 29, 1954, the validity of this policy seemed confirmed as India concluded an agreement with China on Tibet, a region that had nearly brought the two Asian states to armed conflict during the previous four years. The preamble to the treaty for the first time listed the *Panchsheel,* or "Five Principles," that Nehru saw as an alternative to the military alliances then occupying many nations, both East and West. In 1954, China, then a Soviet ally and a state that had until recently branded leaders of most emerging Asian nations as "running dogs of Western imperialism," suddenly turned a more moderate face to the world and agreed to the following principles:

1. Mutual respect for each other's territorial integrity and sovereignty
2. Mutual nonaggression
3. Mutual noninterference in each other's internal affairs
4. Equality and mutual benefit
5. Peaceful coexistence

It is beyond the scope of this chapter to analyze the reasons for China's sudden acceptance of the *Panchsheel.* However, it should be noted that these principles have had something of a lasting effect on the foreign policies of both countries. Although they did not prevent the two states from going to war in 1962, in a border dispute, both have continued to espouse the five principles. Indeed, the Shanghai Communiqué signed by Chou En-lai and Richard Nixon in 1972 contains a more recent enunciation of the principles as China again sought to present a more moderate face to the world community.

With India's defeat in the 1962 border conflict with China and the death two years later of Jawaharlal Nehru, India's position of preeminence among the nonaligned nations drew to a close. Although India has remained a major regional power and significant international actor, subsequent Indian leaders have been less concerned with global issues and more concerned with Indian economic development and security.

By the time Prime Minister Lal Bahadur Shastri governed India (1964–1966), events had demonstrated that the country was faced with possible threats to its security from two neighboring states, China and Pakistan. A 1963 agreement between these two states concerning the borders of the segment of Kashmir held by Pakistan did nothing to lessen Indian concern. A second Indo-Pakistani war was fought in 1965, with Pakistan using armaments it had received as an ally of the United States.

When Nehru's daughter, Indira Gandhi, began her first term as prime minister in 1966, India was increasingly concerned about its relations with both China and Pakistan. Although nonalignment remained the focus of India's foreign policy, it was adjusted somewhat by the new prime minister. As the 1970s began, India sought a dependable means to protect itself from the two states, which in-

The Ganges. This river is of great religious significance. Here at Varanasi, Hindus bathe in its sacred waters.

SOURCE: Earl Huff

creasingly were cooperating with each other. With the United States utilizing the "good offices" of Pakistan to begin a process of normalization of relations with China, support from the West against the two states seemed, at best, unlikely. Eventually, on August 9, 1971, India concluded a 25-year treaty of peace, friendship, and cooperation with the Soviet Union that required consultation between the two states in the event of an attack or threat on either. Although the agreement recognized India's desire to remain nonaligned, it was no doubt intended to act as a deterrent to both Pakistan and China and to increase trade and other forms of cooperation with the Eastern bloc.

In December 1971, India again became involved in armed conflict with Pakistan over the events then occurring in East Pakistan. By supporting the independence movement of the moderate Bengali leader, Sheikh Mujibur Rahman, India sought both to create order along its eastern borders and to install a friendly regime in the newly created state of Bangladesh. Simultaneously, the weakening of a diminished Pakistan gave India unchallenged supremacy on the subcontinent.

On May 18, 1974, India reconfirmed this position of supremacy and perhaps gained a large measure of independence by lessening its need for Soviet support. On that date, India exploded a nuclear device and became the world's sixth nuclear power. In the years since, it tried with limited success to achieve political and economic self-reliance and, for the most part, has followed an independent foreign policy. In accordance with that policy, India long promoted the concept that the Indian Ocean should remain a "zone of peace" free from East-West competition. However, both the Soviet Union and the United States increased their naval presence in that region. Now, although East-West competition has ended, given the proximity of the vital and volatile Persian Gulf region, it seems likely that a large foreign naval presence will continue in the area.

Although India's anticolonialist foreign policy has remained an article of faith, in this decade it has begun to turn away from economic policies of rigid self-reliance and state micromanagement. By the mid-1990s, as Prime Minister P. V. Narasimba Rao's freer market policies both welcomed and received considerable business participation and direct investment from abroad, the World Bank forecasted that India would have the world's fourth-largest economy by the year 2020.[9]

Today perhaps the greatest threat to India lies within its own borders. It remains a state with often deep divisions among many of its numerous ethnic, linguistic, and religious groups. Active independence movements such as those by Sikhs in the Punjab and Muslims in Kashmir are constant reminders that India's nation-building efforts, although substantial, are as yet incomplete. The Indian constitution's promise of a "secular, democratic republic" was greatly diminished in the early 1990s when it experienced its worst religious violence since independence. Nearly 2,000 Indians died following mass riots, which occurred after politicians from the Bharatiya Jamata party (BJP) spoke at a Hindu religious ceremony near an unused Muslim mosque at Ayodhya. Most of the dead were Muslims who had been killed by Hindu police or by Hindu mobs as the police looked on. One Muslim member of Parliament asserted, "In India today you have 120 million Muslims . . . under threat from a fascist party." Although that may be an overstatement, the BJP is indeed a right-wing Hindu movement. With 119 of 545 seats in India's parliament, it is also the official opposition party.[10]

In short, the India of the 1990s is a major regional power whose anticolonialist and nonalignment credentials remain intact, albeit on a diminished scale. Its energies are increasingly directed inward toward its own development as it has become relatively more secure against conflict with either Pakistan or China, both of whom have undergone considerable internal changes since the previous conflicts occurred. In recent decades, increased U.S. military aid for Pakistan caused some concern and was countered by the availability of increasingly sophisticated Soviet military weaponry to India. Russian weapons continued to flow to India even after the dissolution of the Soviet Union. Finally, in early 1995, the United States sought to improve its security relations with both India and Pakistan and to reduce the likelihood of a fourth war on the subcontinent. In January 1995, after assuring Pakistan that he was "not envisioning that the United States would be proposing arms supplies" for India, U.S. Secretary of State William J. Perry concluded "a modest but groundbreaking security agreement" with India. The agreement provided for stronger bilateral military ties and expanded defense research and production.[11] India's willingness to conclude such an agreement and its earlier efforts to avail itself of Soviet weaponry underscore the fact that now, as in the past, its policy of nonalignment is the work of political realists. Its leadership remains eager to defend India's national interests through any means it deems to be productive.

Pakistan.   As noted, Pakistan's view to the east has been marked by mutual suspicion and conflict with its immediate neighbor, India. It is perhaps understandable that Pakistan has generally looked westward for support. As an Islamic state, its first efforts after achieving statehood were aimed at taking its place in the affairs of that segment of the international community. By 1954, without abandoning its previous commitment, Pakistan looked even further westward, becoming an active member of the Western military defense system. In May of that year, a Mutual Defense Assistance Agreement was signed by Pakistan and the United States. The following September, Pakistan joined the United States, Britain, France, Australia, New Zealand, Thailand, and the Philippines in signing the South-East Asia Collective Defense Treaty. In early 1955, Pakistan moved even further into the Western camp by joining Britain, Iraq, and Turkey in the Baghdad Pact of Mutual Cooperation. Following the addition of Iran and the later withdrawal of Iraq, that group changed its name to the Central Treaty Organization (CENTO).

In making these moves, Pakistan was motivated in large part by a sincere belief that the tenets of communism were incompatible with the strongly held religious convictions of a Muslim state. Beyond that, membership in the Western military defense system provided a significant measure of protection against further conflict with India. As noted, Western armaments were indeed utilized when such conflicts later occurred.

It should be noted that Pakistan's anticommunist stance was always somewhat tempered in respect to China. From the time of the Bandung Conference in April 1955, Pakistan's leadership seemed to look beyond China's Marxist government to view that state as a fellow Asian state with similar problems and often compatible aims. Perhaps the most compatible policy of the two states was that each, for its own reasons, viewed India as a rival. The Sino-Indian border war in late 1962 clearly demonstrated China's military superiority and bolstered its ambition to be the dominant power among Afro-Asian states. It also strengthened the ties of mutual interest between Pakistan and China. From that time until the present, the two states have increased their contacts in many areas and have enjoyed quite cordial relations. Indeed, it was Pakistan's ability to bridge two worlds that permitted the initial U.S. contact with China during Henry Kissinger's secret trip in 1971.

In recent years there have been massive internal conflicts within Pakistan's neighboring states of Iran and Afghanistan. On a lesser scale, numerous political conflicts have also occurred within Pakistan. In a military coup in 1977, Pakistan came under the authoritarian military regime of President Mohammed Zia ul-Haq. However, political parties cautiously began to operate again after martial law was lifted in late 1985. The Zia regime ended following his death in a mysterious 1988 plane crash and the election that same year of Prime Minister Benazir Bhutto, the Harvard- and Oxford-educated daughter of the former populist Prime Minister Zulfikar Ali Bhutto, whom Zia ul-Haq had overthrown and hanged.

In 1990 Prime Minister Bhutto's government was charged with corruption, nepotism, and incompetence and was dismissed by Pakistan's conservative President Gulam Ishaq Khan with the support of the military. Elections followed in October 1990, and Bhutto was defeated. However, exactly three years later, she was returned to office in an upset election that was described as the freest election in Pakistan's history. With a close ally, Farooq Leghari, serving as president, Bhutto soon instituted policies aimed at securing foreign investment and privatizing key segments of the economy such as energy and telecommunications. In an apparent break with Pakistan's past, its 577,000-person military force remained neutral during the political struggles that accompanied those dramatic reforms. Although Pakistan remains a state in which the frequently corrupt institutions of democracy must compete for power with a well-organized and influential military establishment, a degree of cooperation between the two seems to have emerged.

Unfortunately, Pakistan's leadership must also deal with a bewildering variety of often violent conflicts within its borders. Violent attacks regularly occur between Sunni and Shiite Muslims, between locals and Muslim immigrants from India, and by Muslim fundamentalists on various minority religious groups. In addition, tribal wars have erupted in the deserts of Baluchistan. Such strife is, at best, a complication for Bhutto and her Pakistan Peoples party as they seek to achieve their avowed aim of "progress and prosperity" for Pakistan's nearly 122 million people.

Today, Pakistan continues to view itself first and foremost as a member of the Muslim world as it moves toward its own form of Islamic state; for example, in 1991 it introduced *Sharia*, or Islamic law, into Pakistan. In reaction to upheavals in neighboring Iran and Afghanistan, it increased its ties to moderate Arab states and sought accommodation with the Iranian and Afghan regimes. For years, relations with the latter have been complicated by the presence of millions of Afghan refugees in Pakistan. With the fall of the Soviet-imposed government in 1992, the refugee problem began to diminish, but continuing civil war within Afghanistan keeps the refugee problem alive. Some observers believe that Pakistan covertly supported one Afghan rebel force, the Taliban, when it gained control of nearly 40 percent of Afghanistan in early 1995.

After 1981, relations with the United States improved as Pakistan again received considerable American economic and military aid. By 1990, it was the third-largest recipient of such aid, behind only Israel and Egypt. The aid totalled more than $700 million annually and included a $3.2 billion five-year arms agreement. Although the Soviet withdrawal from Afghanistan and the subsequent dissolution of the Soviet Union would seem to reduce the usefulness of Pakistan as a U.S. ally, Muslim Pakistan's support of U.S. allies and interests in the Persian Gulf region is still a valuable asset.

Relations with China remain cordial. Relations with India, although less hostile than in the past, continue to be tense and are made more so by continued friction over the Kashmir issue and by indications that Pakistan now has a nuclear capability to match that of India. Indeed, concern on this issue is not limited to the Indian subcontinent. American aid was suspended in late 1990 when Pakistan refused to permit international inspection of its nuclear facilities. However, as part of a U.S. effort to improve its security relations with both Pakistan and India, in early 1995 the U.S. and Pakistan resumed joint military exercises, officer training, and yearly exchanges on security issues.[12] This occurred in spite of the fact that Pakistan's former prime minister, Nawaz Shariff, had, on August 23, 1994, clearly proclaimed that his country possessed nuclear bombs.[13]

SOUTHEAST ASIA

With one exception, Thailand, the nations of Southeast Asia share a common past—colonization by various Western powers. Until the years following World War II, Burma, Malaysia, Singapore, and Brunei were British; Indonesia was Dutch; Indochina (Vietnam, Cambodia, and Laos) was French; the Philippines were first a colony of Spain and then of the United States. Typically, boundaries drawn by the colonial powers paid little attention to the ethnic makeup of the region they administered, and people with well-established cultural identities were often divided. Just as often, numerous diverse ethnic groups were combined into a larger political unit and were joined by other peoples, such as Indians or Chinese, who had been either transported or encouraged to settle there by the colonial power. Consequently, when the colonies within the region were granted independence in the decades following World War II, the newly formed states had populations that were exceedingly diverse and often lacked the sense of nationhood implicit in the term *nation-state*. Cohesion, when it existed, was often nothing more than the common impulse to rid the region of the colonial power. The resulting demand for "self-determination" was quite unlike that which motivated nineteenth-century European nationalists such as Mazzini. Southeast Asian nationalists such as Sukarno in Indonesia or Ho Chi Minh in Vietnam accepted the colonial boundaries drawn by the European powers. Their objective was simply to achieve sovereignty over the territory and provide their own, indigenous leadership.

Today's Southeast Asia comprises 10 sovereign states: Brunei, Cambodia, Indonesia, Laos, Malaysia, Myanmar, the Philippines, Singapore, Thailand, and Vietnam. Given such a diverse group, generalizations become rather risky, although some areas of continuity may be discerned. Common problems relating to ethnic diversity and arbitrary boundaries have already been noted. In addition, it should be recognized that this region, like other regions of the Other World, is faced with those problems typically related to the modernization process as discussed in chapters 1–3. Beyond that, post–World War II Southeast Asia has generally been a hotbed of revolutionary activity. At various times, extensive guerrilla warfare has occurred in Burma, Indonesia, Malaysia, the Philippines, and of course the three states of Indochina. It continues today, in diminished form, in the Philippines, Cambodia, and Myanmar.

In 1978, Vietnam, with Soviet support, sought to complete its hegemony over Indochina by invading Cambodia and ousting the Chinese-supported Khmer Rouge regime of Pol Pot. During its three-year reign, that regime had brutally reorganized Cambodian society at a cost of over a million lives. The Cambodian conflict continued as a guerrilla war, with the Khmer Rouge and two noncom-

Local Market. Relatively abundant local produce is displayed in this market on the Hindu island of Bali in predominantly Muslim Indonesia.

SOURCE: Earl Huff

munist guerrilla forces opposing the Vietnamese-supported government of Hun Sen from bases near the Thai border. The rebel coalition, under the nominal leadership of Prince Norodom Sihanouk, was recognized by the UN, the United States, China, and most other states as the legitimate government of Cambodia. Conditions also remained tense along Vietnam's own border with China, where several limited military engagements between the two states occurred.

By the early 1990s, the Soviet Union, China, and the United States seem to have determined that a changing international environment made continued conflict in Cambodia no longer in anyone's interest. Faced with diminished support from an overextended Russia, Vietnam withdrew most of its forces from Cambodia and sought to better its relations with China. With Sino-Soviet relations improving, China reduced its support of the brutal Khmer Rouge. Perhaps finally emerging from the trauma of Vietnam, the United States withdrew recognition of the rebel coalition and began formal contacts with both Vietnam and the Vietnamese-supported Hun Sen regime in Cambodia. On October 23, 1991, the four warring Cambodian factions signed a peace agreement, which provided for a cease-fire and a new coalition government to be headed on an interim basis by Prince Norodom Sihanouk. In 1993 UN-sponsored elections were held to select a permanent government. However, during the two years between the signing of the agreement and the elections, the cease-fire was violated by both the Khmer Rouge and the interim government. The Khmer Rouge eventually refused to participate in the elections, in which the royalist FUNCINPEC party achieved a narrow victory over the Vietnamese-supported former Communist party led by Hun Sen. Eventually, a power-sharing arrangement was devised and a coalition government was formed between the two parties. By the middle of the decade, the forces of the Khmer Rouge and the new government were again engaged in extensive armed conflict in the Cambodian countryside, and the former Communist party, now known as the Cambodian Peoples party, seemed to be extending its influence within the governing coalition.

Politically, the states of Southeast Asia have generally evolved toward authoritarian regimes of both the left and the right. The former is centered in Indochina, Vietnam serving as the dominant power. Authoritarian regimes of the right are typical throughout the remainder of Southeast Asia. However, there is at least some reason to believe that this situation may be weakening somewhat. In 1992 Thailand's former supreme military commander, Prime Minister Suchinda Kraprayoon, was forced to resign in disgrace, and legislation was passed by the Thai parliament reducing the power of the long-dominant military leadership. Suchinda was replaced as prime minister by Chuan Leekpai, who held office for two years and eight months, the longest term ever served by a civilian prime minister in Thailand. His replacement, Barnharn Silpa-archa was elected in 1995 amid numerous charges of voting fraud in the still fragile Thai democracy. In 1992, in neighboring Myanmar, the leader of the ruling military junta retired, and some very limited political reforms were instituted. Some movement toward greater democracy may have occurred in Myanmar in July 1995, when Nobel Peace Prize-winner Aung San Suu Kyi, the leader of the popularly elected opposition party, the National League for Democracy, was "unconditionally" released after six years under house arrest.[14] However, the military regime remains in power. In Indonesia, although the military remains in control under the leadership of President Suharto, a former general, somewhat greater freedom of the press and of speech is tolerated. Nevertheless, such limited reforms, as yet, only slightly modify regimes that remain essentially authoritarian.

The primary vehicle for regional cooperation in Southeast Asia has been the Association of Southeast Asian Nations (ASEAN), comprising Indonesia, Malaysia, the Philippines, Singapore, Thailand (the original members), Brunei, and since 1995 Vietnam. The organization's origins date back to 1967, when the five original member states sought to avoid involvement in the Indochina conflict and to oppose any form of renewed great-power rivalry in Southeast Asia. Although the ASEAN states were then noncommunist and generally conservative in outlook, regional order and the avoidance of rivalry seem to have been of relatively greater importance than their opposition to communism. With the conclusion of the Vietnam war, the leaders of that state were generally viewed by the ASEAN leadership as successful nationalists who had undergone a struggle for independence similar to their own. With limited territorial ambitions and a strong nationalistic regime that might serve as a check on Chinese influence in the region, Vietnam was seen as a state that should be included in ASEAN's efforts to promote regional cooperation.

This view changed dramatically when, in November 1978, Vietnam concluded a treaty of friendship and cooperation with the Soviet Union and almost immediately took steps to invade Chinese-supported Cambodia. Such actions made Vietnam a vehicle for the very sort of great-power rivalry that the ASEAN states sought to avoid in Southeast Asia. As a result, they opposed the Vietnamese effort by working within the UN and elsewhere to deny recognition to the Vietnamese-installed Cambodian government. Thailand, the ASEAN state most immediately threatened by the Vietnamese action, went even further, informally working with China to permit resupply of the Cambodian insurgents and providing a sanctuary for those forces in the Thai regions bordering Cambodia.

In recent years the ASEAN states have somewhat reduced their reliance on ties with the West. Economically, Japan's investment now exceeds America's throughout the region. Politically, from Fiji to Australia to New Zealand, the ASEAN states have begun to play a larger role among states of the Western and South Pacific regions. Relations with the former U.S.S.R. and China improved as the ASEAN states came to see them as the key to peace in Indochina and to the reduction of Vietnamese influence in the region. With the signing of a peace agreement in Cambodia in late 1991 and the formation of an ASEAN free-trade zone in early 1992, the ASEAN states again expressed their desire to build a relationship of friendship and cooperation with Vietnam, Laos, and Cambodia. Finally, in July 1995, Vietnam was officially admitted to ASEAN. Today, in spite of occasional disagreements and the failure as yet to include the other states of Indochina in its order-building efforts, ASEAN has become a vital political force in the region and seems likely to play an even greater role in the future.

Southeast Asia's diversity may also be seen in the economic realm. The three poorest states, Cambodia, Vietnam, and Laos, have per capita yearly incomes of $280, $230, and $200, respectively. Vietnam excluded, the 350 million citizens of the six remaining ASEAN states have a combined GDP of well over $200 billion and an annual economic growth rate of over 7 percent over the past two decades. The wealthiest members, Singapore and Brunei, have per capita incomes of around $16,500 and $8,800, respectively. In general, agriculture is the dominant economic activity in the region. However, Indonesia and Brunei are major oil-exporting states. Singapore contains a vast array of industries within its tiny territory of just under 225 square miles and serves as the region's largest port and trading center. At the other extreme is Myanmar, which since the l960s sought to isolate itself from foreign trade and influence. In recent years, that policy has been reversed, and Myanmar is slowly beginning to emerge from its self-imposed cocoon. However, by the mid-1990s, both its economic and its political future were uncertain as its military remained unwilling to yield power to a democratically elected civilian government.

In short, there are great disparities in wealth among the states of Southeast Asia. Today, some of the most sophisticated industrial techniques are being utilized alongside traditional agricultural and manufacturing techniques that remain essentially unchanged from those of centuries past. At the current time, Southeast Asia is an exceedingly diverse and sometimes violent region. However, the possibility of interstate conflict seems increasingly to be mitigated by habits of cooperation, relatively stable governments, and the generally growing economies of the ASEAN states. Should major conflicts occur, they seem more likely to arise at the intrastate level as a consequence of the still incomplete nation-building process within these very diverse states.

Myanmar (Burma). This picture, taken from northern Thailand in early 1992, conveys some flavor of the inward-looking authoritarian nature of the military regime in Myanmar at that time. The sign at the entry gate warns that tourists are not permitted.

SOURCE: Earl Huff

FLASHPOINTS

AFGHANISTAN

In 1978, a coup d'état brought a Marxist government to power in Afghanistan. However, splits within the Afghan Communist party over both Islam and socialist reforms soon threatened the very survival of the Marxist revolution. It was this volatile situation that caused the Soviets to intervene on the night of December 24, 1979. The Afghan prime minister was killed, and in his place the Soviets installed Babrak Karmal. Soviet forces eventually swelled to around 120,000 before their withdrawal in 1989.

The Soviet intervention provoked open civil war. A number of loosely organized resistance fighters calling themselves the *mujahedeen* ("holy warriors") were able to tie down the Soviet military for a decade. Soviet policy throughout much of the Other World was subjected to harsh criticism until the "new thinking" of Mikhail Gorbachev brought a Soviet withdrawal, coupled with military and economic support for the last Soviet-installed government, led by former Afghan secret police chief Najibullah. Tainted by its association with the Soviets, that government failed to establish legitimacy either at home or abroad. More than 5 million refugees fled Afghanistan, most settling in Pakistan near the Afghanistan border.

A stalemate, which had characterized the final years of Soviet intervention, continued for a time after the Soviet withdrawal. However, the combatants looked for support to outside states such as the former Soviet Union, China, the United States, Pakistan, Saudi Arabia, and Iran. Given the drastic changes that had occurred in the international environment, such support soon diminished as other priorities emerged. In April 1992, the Najibullah government collapsed, and several mujahedeen rebel groups entered Kabul, the capital. Burhanuddin Rabani was elected in December 1992 for a two-year term as president. In the months and years that followed, the nine mujahedeen factions that had waged war against the old Soviet-installed governments increasingly turned their weapons on one another. With Rabani refusing to relinquish the presidency at the end of his term, a tenth faction appeared in early 1995. The new faction, known as the Taliban, or "Seekers," was originally made up of students of Islam from the southeastern city of Kandahar. Its avowed aim was to end Afghanistan's internal conflicts and lawlessness and to institute an Islamic government in that state. Within a few months the new factions had gained control of 8 of Afghanistan's 28 provinces.

Today, Afghanistan remains a state with serious internal divisions. Now that the common enemy is removed, it is difficult to envision Afghanistan as quickly overcoming its vast political, ethnic, linguistic, and even religious divisions in order to function effectively as a single nation-state. Indeed, there is no precedent in its past to indicate that it can do so.

CAMBODIA

In a sense, the recent conflict in Cambodia between Vietnam and the coalition of guerrilla forces headed by Pol Pot, Prince Sihanouk, and Son Sann may be viewed as a proxy war between China and the Soviet Union, with the United States and others playing lesser roles. In addition, it was an effort by successful Vietnamese nationalists to establish their hegemony over all of the former French colony. By the 1980s, the latter objective was essentially achieved by the Vietnamese and their Soviet patrons. However, as sporadic military conflicts along the Sino-Vietnamese border proved, China retained both an interest and an ability to affect events in Indochina. As the 1990s began, relations among China, Russia, and the United States had improved to the point that each sought to influence the combatants to end the conflict. In January 1990, the five permanent members of the UN Security Council drafted a peace plan calling for a UN-supervised transition administration and elections. The plan was formally achieved with the signing of the October 1991 agreement and the 1993 elections noted earlier in this chapter.

Today, the Khmer Rouge remains a well-armed and politically unified force that controls much of Cambodia's countryside. It is still a significant threat to the stability of Cambodia and Southeast Asia in general.[15]

CHINA'S BORDERS

China has consistently argued that it is not bound by the so-called unequal treaties and agreements forced on it by the imperialist powers during the nineteenth and early twentieth centuries, when a weakened China made numerous territorial concessions. Although China later resolved by force of arms the exact location of its border with India, the "proper" location of its northern borders, with the former Soviet republics, remained largely unresolved until late 1994 when Presidents Jiang Zemin and Boris Yeltsin met in Moscow to sign agreements that delineated the final 34-mile segment of their disputed border. Only three small islands in rivers along this border remain in dispute. Perhaps more important, the agreement does not bind all the states of the former U.S.S.R. The border issue may yet be complicated by disorder within those states, by a desire for political unity between some of China's minority nationalities and their ethnic kin north of the border, or by a more militant leadership in either China or Russia.

As noted earlier and illustrated in figure 7.2, the regions over which China has historically exercised sovereignty have enlarged or diminished with the power of its central authority. Consequently, it is able to assert a historic connection to vast regions beyond its current borders. In the final years of this century, perhaps the most volatile such region lies in the South China Sea, a major waterway and a likely site of large deposits of underwater oil and gas. Today, China claims sovereignty over about 80 percent of the South China Sea and has forcefully asserted its claim, first, by seizing control of the Paracel Islands at the conclusion of the Vietnam war and, second, following a brief naval conflict against Vietnam in 1988, by occupying and fortifying several of the Spratly Islands, a chain of hundreds of islands, reefs, and atolls located between Vietnam and the Philippines. Vietnam continues to claim part of the Spratlys, called the Nansha Islands by the Chinese. Taiwan, the Philippines, Malaysia, and Brunei also claim all or part of the chain. Following a 1995 confrontation with a Filipino naval vessel, the Chinese ministry reaffirmed its "action to safeguard its sovereignty over the Nansha Islands" and assured the world community that its actions would "not affect the freedom and safety of foreign vessels or foreign aircraft to navigate through international sea lanes under international laws."[16]

Though located farther from the Spratlys than any of the other claimants, China is better able to assert its claims because of its relative power and the divisions among the ASEAN states on this issue. Significantly, the larger world community, including the United States, seems to have adopted a hands-off policy on the Spratly dispute because of both Chinese assurances regarding freedom of navigation and a desire not to provoke China at a time of delicate political maneuvering associated with the struggle over the successor to Deng Xiaoping.

CHINA'S LEADERSHIP

By 1995 the health of China's "senior leader" Deng Xiaoping was failing and his ability to influence the course of China's politics relied increasingly on indirect means. For decades he had worked to weed out opposition within the party and to place into positions of power individuals in whom he had trust. His chosen successor, Jiang Zemin, seemed well positioned for any succession struggle. He served as general secretary of the CPC, head of state, and perhaps more important, as chairman of the commission that directs China's military. However, things are usually not so simple in Chinese politics. For one thing, formal titles often mean very little. When Deng edged aside Mao's chosen successor, Hua Guofeng, in 1979, Deng was only a vice premier. He continued to dominate Chinese politics when, during his declining years, his only formal title was "Most Honorary Chairman of the All China Bridge Association." Along with Deng, former President Yang Shangkun, Bo Yibo, and other "retired" elder statesmen played major roles behind the scenes. They continue to do so.

To complicate matters further, there is growing evidence that pressures from reform elements within the Communist party may bring about a reassessment of the 1989 Tiananmen incident after the death of Deng Xiaoping. Such a reassessment could have a major impact on a succession struggle. A quiet visit by Jiang in 1995 to the tomb of reform leader Hu Yaobang was perhaps an early effort by Jiang to distance himself from the incident. It was the death of Hu that sparked the first demonstrations in Tiananmen Square.

Given the secrecy that shrouds such important decisions in China, it is risky to predict the outcome of a succession struggle. However, it is quite certain that China's management of its transition to the post-Deng era will have major implications for the Chinese nation and for the world.

DEVELOPMENT VERSUS ENVIRONMENTAL DESTRUCTION

A trip to a local clothing or hardware store leaves little doubt that Asia is at the forefront of development within the Other World. First there was Japan, emerging from the destruction of World War II. Then came the "four little dragons": Hong Kong, Taiwan, Singapore, and South Korea. More recently Thailand, Malaysia, and Indonesia have joined the group of rapidly developing Asian states. Then, emerging from its Maoist policy of rigid self-sufficiency, China opened its doors to the world and began a process of rapid development that in recent years has consistently produced a double-digit rate of economic growth. Now another Asian giant, India, has begun to stir. With all the vast differences that exist among these states, there is one significant similarity: Economic growth came at a price, a massive degradation of the environment.

Today, throughout Other World Asia, one can witness the results of policies and activities that place a far lesser priority on preservation of the environment than on rapid economic growth. China now has one of the most polluted capitals in the world. Bangkok and Taipei, with their enormous traffic jams, are also rivals for that title. Even Kuala Lumpur, the smallest Asian capital, is now beset with air pollution and traffic congestion. Acid rain and chemical pollution of both air and water in China, along with rapid deforestation in Malaysia, Myanmar, Thailand, and elsewhere in Asia, are typical of the assault on the environment that is occurring as Other World Asia seeks to achieve the level of economic development demanded by its growing population.

Is this an irreversible process, or is it simply a necessary stage in development? There is no certain answer to this question. However, it may be argued that numerous other states achieved rapid economic development with little regard for environmental implications, then vigorously and generally successfully attacked environmental problems. Japan is a prime example. Unfortunately, such a process has generally occurred only after the state concerned was both satisfied with its level of development and convinced that its quality of life was threatened.

INDIA-PAKISTAN

The suspicion and distrust that divides these two South Asian states have long and deep roots, extending far beyond their independence in 1947. Indeed, the very creation of two states from British India was an attempt to resolve at least some of the enmity that even then existed. Since 1947, the hostility between India and Pakistan has resulted in three wars, each of which did nothing to lessen tensions. The first two wars ended in stalemates, the cease-fires resulting largely from pressures exerted on the two states by outside forces. The immediate cause of each conflict was territorial in nature and, for the most part, involved a dispute over the divided Kashmir region. The 1971 conflict was more general and more conclusive in its outcome. Unlike the previous conflicts, it was an all-out war with fighting on all fronts. When it ended, a victorious India received the unconditional surrender of Pakistani forces in Bangladesh and then declared a unilateral cease-fire in the West. A dismembered and demoralized Pakistan had little choice but to end the conflict.

It would seem that India would no longer feel threatened by a nation whose population and GDP are less than 20 percent of its own. However, such is not the case. India continues to oppose any U.S. move to provide armaments for Pakistan, believing that such arms will ultimately be used against India itself.

Although Pakistan has repeatedly denied any such intentions, it should be noted that there is some cause for India's concern. During the 1980s both the United States and China increased their support for Pakistan as a counter to Soviet actions in the region. Substantial military support continued even after the Soviet withdrawal from Afghanistan. Pakistan today has a well-equipped and well-trained military of over a half million men, and a former prime minister has admitted that it also has nuclear weapons. Given the enmities of the past and the fact that issues such as Kashmir are still unresolved, it is not surprising that suspicion and distrust continue to cloud relations between India and Pakistan.

Two of the past three wars between the two states were fought over the Kashmir issue. Since 1990, the Indian army has been immersed in a bloody battle with Kashmiri separatists that continues to aggravate relations between Pakistan and India. In 1995, following numerous atrocities and the burning of an Islamic shrine, tensions again grew tense in India's only state with a Muslim majority. Given such conditions, and the fact that Kashmiri separatists now demand total independence from *both* states, it seems unlikely that a negotiated settlement will end the longest significant unresolved territorial dispute since World War II. However, such a settlement may be necessary if the world is to avoid its first true nuclear war.

ISLAMIC FUNDAMENTALISM

Although Islamic fundamentalism is a phenomenon usually associated with the Middle East rather than Asia, it has been a major force in the Afghan conflict. There are now indications that it is spreading even further eastward.

Early in this decade a rebellion in the northern Sumatran region of Indonesia resulted in several thousand deaths. That area contains the most radical Muslim clergy in the country. Just to the north, in Malaysia, the central government's ruling National Front was defeated in 1990 by the Parti Islam in the state of Kalantan. The government in that state soon banned gambling, alcohol consumption by Muslims, singing groups of men and women together, and so on. In 1992 it replaced the existing secular criminal laws with Islamic law. Although the National Front won an electoral landslide in other regions of Malaysia in the 1995 elections, it was unable to unseat the Parti Islam in Kalantan.

Traditionally, both Malaysia and Indonesia have had secular governments and have been regarded as among the most moderate and tolerant of Muslim states. However, with Muslim majorities of 60 percent and 80 percent, respectively, they provide fertile ground for the further spread of Islamic fundamentalism. It should be noted that existing national leaders seem to recognize its potential force. In 1991 even President Suharto of Indonesia, who in the past has discouraged Islamic activism, found it prudent to make his first pilgrimage to Mecca. Similarly, Malaysian Prime Minister Mahathir Mohammed, who once ridiculed Islamic law, decided not to oppose its adoption in the state of Kalantan.

In short, for the moment Islamic fundamentalism is more a potential threat to the secular regimes of Southeast Asia than a current threat. However, given the volatility of its message and its past success in Iran and elsewhere, it is not a force to be ignored.

NORTH KOREA

Although North and South Korea share a common language, history, and culture, they remain bitterly divided politically. In recent years, under the leadership of President Kim Young Sam, the rapidly industrializing South Korea has vigorously moved toward democracy, first at the national level and then, in 1995, at the local level when local government elections were held for the first time since 1961. In contrast, North Korea remains an authoritarian Marxist state whose secretive and unpredictable leadership presides over East Asia's only declining economy. Faced with a loss of aid and trading partners after the fall of world communism, North Korea's 1994 trade plunged to about half its 1990 level.[17] As a consequence, it seems to have concluded that there is no alternative to accepting some modification of its long-standing policy of self-reliance. It has therefore indicated a desire to attract foreign investment and has accepted emergency shipments of rice from South Korea and Japan.

North Korea's leadership also presides over a state that caused international concern when its intention to develop a nuclear weapons capability became known. However, that concern has diminished somewhat since October 1994, when North Korea agreed to halt its nuclear program and accepted an offer by the United States, Japan, and South Korea to replace its graphite-moderated nuclear reactor with light water reactors, which produce less of the plutonium needed for such weapons.

World concern was also raised by the sudden death in July 1994 of Kim Il Sung, who had led North Korea since its inception in 1945. Although his son, Kim Jong Il, was his chosen successor, there was little evidence that he was firmly in control. Indeed, there is considerable speculation that a power struggle continues within the leadership between those who wish to continue past isolationist policies and those who favor increasing economic and political ties with the outside world. Given North Korea's history of belligerency, the outcome of any such struggle is of considerable importance both to its neighbors and to the larger world community.

SRI LANKA

According to the most recent census, taken in 1981, the population of Sri Lanka is 74 percent Sinhalese, most of whom are Buddhist, and 18 percent Tamil, who are primarily Hindu; almost all the remainder are Muslim. Historically, the island has seen numerous clashes between the Tamils, descended from the dark-skinned Dravidians of southern India, and the lighter-skinned Sinhalese, who trace their origin to the Aryan invaders noted earlier in this chapter. However, modern conflict began in the late 1950s when the Sinhalese-dominated government made Sinhalese the sole official language, began resettling Sinhalese in predominantly Tamil areas of the island, and passed other legislation viewed by Tamils as discriminatory. Conflict increased in the 1970s and became more violent when the militant Tamil Tiger guerrillas launched their first armed attack in 1978. Since that time violence has escalated as the Tigers and other Tamil separatists have sought the establishment of an independent Tamil state, Tamil Eelam, to be carved from northern and eastern Sri Lanka. Anti-Tamil riots and massacres by both sides have followed.

By the mid-1980s the Indian government apparently feared that the conflict might threaten the stability of India, where 18 miles away, in the southern Indian state of Tamil Nadu, an additional 50 million Tamils reside. With many Indians urging their government to act to support the Tamils, the Indian and Sri Lankan governments reached an agreement in July 1986 that provided for greater autonomy in the Tamil regions of Sri Lanka and obliged the Indian army to help enforce the accord. When that agreement broke down a few months later, the Indian army became embroiled in the conflict against the Tamil separatists. Finally, a measure of order was restored and Indian forces withdrew, although violence between the Tamils and Sinhalese by no means ended.

In August 1994, the newly elected government of Chandrika Bandaranaika Kumaratunga promised a renewed effort to reach a peace agreement with the Tamil separatists. In January 1995, her government and the Tamil rebels announced that they had agreed to a truce, ending their 12-year conflict. However, war erupted again the following April when the Tamil Tigers blew up two naval patrol boats, killing 12 sailors, and a week later shot down two air force transports, killing 97 more people. Large-scale military operations then resumed.[18] Obviously, the ingredients for conflict are still present within Sri Lanka.

TAIWAN

In a dramatic break with the past, China's current leadership has stressed that the reunification of Taiwan with the mainland must be accomplished peacefully. However, the iron determination to accomplish that reunification is no less now than in the past. Clearly, until recently the Chinese leadership felt time was on its side. It sought to put its own house in order and to isolate the Taiwan regime in the international community as it simultaneously continued to show a moderate face toward its compatriots on that island. In recent years the government of Taiwan has responded by permitting a dramatic increase in individual travel and other personal contact between Taiwan and the mainland. There has been a similar increase in trade between the two states. Such cooperation was further promoted when semiofficial representatives met in Singapore in 1993 to set up a system of regular meetings between the two sides and to sign agreements pledging cooperation on trade, technology exchanges, copyright protection, and other outstanding issues.

There is, however, one issue that may lead to renewed Chinese militancy regarding Taiwan. Until recently both the PRC and the RC agreed that Taiwan was a part of China but argued over which government was its legitimate ruler. Recently, Taiwan has sought recognition as a separate state, representing a distinct segment of the Chinese nation. Taiwan's President Lee Teng-hui seemed to be embracing that concept when in early 1994 he proposed "a state of Taiwanese people" and sought support for "returning [Taiwan] to the United Nations." China's position was again clearly illustrated in several articles in the semiofficial publication *Beijing Review*, which argued that "Taiwan is an inalienable part of China and the people on Taiwan Island are Chinese."[19] Chinese sensitivity on the issue of Taiwan and its sovereignty was again illustrated by China's "strong protest to the U.S." on the occasion of an "unofficial and private" visit by Lee to the United States in June 1995. The Chinese Foreign Ministry warned that the visit,

> under whatever name or in whatever way, will inevitably cause the serious consequence of creating "two Chinas" or "one China, one Taiwan". . . . On this major issue of principle which bears on China's fundamental interests, the position of the Chinese government is firm and unswerving. Any act aimed at undermining China's sovereignty and creating "two Chinas" or "one China, one Taiwan" is absolutely unacceptable to the Chinese government and people. . . . To the Chinese people . . . nothing is more important than state sovereignty and reunification of the motherland.[20]

Further evidence of China's concern came during the weeks preceding the March 1996 reelection of Lee Teng-hui when China carried out military maneuvers near Taiwan. China seems prepared to continue with its relatively moderate policies only insofar as it believes they lead to an eventual reunification. Should that strategy continue to achieve results, armed conflict seems unlikely. However, even the pragmatic and patient leaders of China cannot be expected permanently to rule out other means to complete their unfinished revolution if a moderate course does not succeed.

SUMMARY

As stated at the outset of this chapter, Asia is the largest and most diverse continent and, as such, largely defies generalization. However, it is to be hoped that the foregoing pages conveyed something of the geographic, political, and historical forces that have shaped the current attitudes of Other World Asia. To varying degrees, each part of that region has been shaped and has reacted, sometimes violently, to a major historical force, European imperialism. Today, the Asian heirs to some of the world's earliest and greatest civilizations remain determined to be masters of their own destinies. The means by which they seek to do so are nearly as diverse as the region itself. China rather quickly reasserted its independence from the Soviet Union and continues to forge its own course toward Marxism. India remains a parliamentary democracy and seeks to develop its own substantial resources as it continues to espouse nonalignment as its fundamental foreign policy. Pakistan looks toward the United States and China for support and continues its efforts to find its place among its fellow Islamic states. The ASEAN states actively seek order in their region as they vigorously nurture their expanding economies. Vietnam utilized Soviet support while retaining much of the nationalist revolutionary ardor that permitted its successful drive to establish itself as the dominant force in Indochina. That ardor has cooled somewhat now that Soviet aid has disappeared and contacts with its neighbors are becoming warmer.

The diversity among the states of Other World Asia is matched in most by an equally diverse citizenry. The leaders of each state must continue to build diligently the social ties and the habits of cooperation that are necessary to unite such diverse elements into a single nation. This process is already well under way, and its successful completion may be the most important challenge faced by those who lead this vast segment of the Other World.

NOTES

1. Robert S. Elegant, "To the Chinese, You're a Devil-Person," *Los Angeles Times*, June 24, 1974, II, p. 7. All other references to Elegant's comments are also from this source.
2. Karl Marx, "The British Rule in India," in *Crisis and Continuity in World Politics*, ed. George A. Lanyi and Wilson C. McWilliams, 2nd ed. (New York: Random House, 1966), p. 85. These remarks originally appeared in an article written by Marx for the *New York Tribune*, June 25, 1853.
3. Mao Tse-tung, "Report of an Investigation into the Peasant Movement in Hunan," *Selected Works of Mao Tse-tung* (Beijing: Foreign Languages Press, 1965), vol. I, pp. 23–59.

4. Ibid.
5. Lin Piao, *Long Live the Victory of People's War!* (Beijing: Foreign Languages Press, 1966), pp. 48–49.
6. Communist Party of China, *Resolution on CPC History* (Beijing: Foreign Languages Press, 1981), pp. 28–31. The resolution was adopted by the Sixth Plenary Session of the Eleventh Central Committee of the CPC on June 27, 1981.
7. Hu Yaobang, "Speech at the Meeting in Celebration of the 60th Anniversary of the Founding of the Communist Party of China," *Resolution on CPC History* (Beijing: Foreign Languages Press, 1981), pp. 94–95.
8. Jawaharlal Nehru, *India's Foreign Policy* (New Delhi: Publications Division, Ministry of Information and Broadcasting, Government of India, 1961), p. 46.
9. *Los Angeles Times*, December 6, 1994, p. H4.
10. Tomar Masland et al., "Holy War in India," *Newsweek*, December 21, 1992, pp. 46–47; and *Los Angeles Times*, January 28, 1993, p. A8.
11. *Los Angeles Times*, January 13, 1995, p. A6.
12. Ibid.
13. *New York Times*, August 25, 1994, p. A7.
14. *Los Angeles Times*, July 11, 1995, p. A1.
15. *New York Times*, May 4, 1994, p. A5; and *Los Angeles Times*, January 3, 1995, p. H3.
16. "News Briefing by the Chinese Foreign Ministry," *Beijing Review*, June 5–11, 1995, p. 19.
17. *Los Angeles Times*, July 9, 1995, p. A6.
18. *Los Angeles Times*, July 10, 1995, p. A6.
19. Ren Xin, "Lee Teng-hui's Separative Words Refuted," *Beijing Review*, July 18–24, 1994, p. 20.
20. "China Issues Strong Protest to US," *Beijing Review*, June 12–18, 1995, pp. 18–19.

FOR FURTHER READING

Barnds, William J. *India, Pakistan and the Great Powers*. New York: Praeger, 1972.
Beijing Review, a Chinese weekly of news and views.
Burki, Shahid J. *Pakistan under the Military: Eleven Years of Zia ul-Haq*. Boulder, Col.: Westview Press, 1991.
Cooper, John Franklin. *China Diplomacy: The Washington-Taipei-Beijing Triangle*. Boulder, Col.: Westview Press, 1992.
Fairbank, John K.; Reischauer, Edwin O.; and Craig, Albert M. *East Asia: Tradition and Transformation*. Boston: Houghton Mifflin, 1989.
Falkenheim, Victor C., ed. *Chinese Politics from Mao to Deng*. New York: Paragon House, 1989.
Fang, Percy J. *Zhou Enlai: A Profile*. Beijing: Foreign Languages Press, 1986.
Ganguli, Shivaji. *U.S. Policy toward South Asia*. Boulder, Col.: Westview Press, 1990.
Johal, Sarbit. *Conflict and Integration in Indo-Pakistan Relations*. Berkeley: Centers for South and Southeast Asia Studies, University of California, 1989.
Kleinberg, Robert. *China's "Opening" to the Outside World: The Experiment with Foreign Capitalism*. Boulder, Col.: Westview Press, 1990.
Liang, Heng, and Shapiro, Judith. *Son of the Revolution*. New York: Vintage Books, 1984.
Palmer, Ronald D. *Building ASEAN: Twenty Years of Southeast Asian Cooperation*. New York: Praeger, 1987.

Schlosstein, Steven. *Asia's New Little Dragons: The Dynamic Emergence of Indonesia, Thailand and Malaysia*. Chicago: Contemporary Books, 1991.

Sisson, Richard. *War and Secession: Pakistan, India and the Creation of Bangladesh*. Berkeley: University of California Press, 1990.

Snow, Edgar. *The Long Revolution*. New York: Vintage Books, 1973.

Terrill, Ross. *Mao: A Biography*. New York: Harper & Row, 1980.

Tzou, Byron N. *China and International Law: The Boundary Disputes*. New York: Praeger, 1990.

CHAPTER **8**

The Middle East and North Africa

Joseph N. Weatherby

Both the East and the West want to corrupt us from within, obliterate every distinguishing mark of our personality and snuff out the light which guides us.

Muammar al-Qaddafi

There is a saying in the West that the Middle East is a region too important to the outside world to allow it to be governed by Middle Easterners. The Middle East has played a pivotal role in world affairs since ancient times. Forming the land bridge between Asia, Africa, and Europe, the Middle East has the strategic attention of both the East and the West (see figure 8.1).

The Middle East is also the birthplace of the world's three great monotheistic religions: Judaism, Christianity, and Islam. For almost 1,400 years, Islam has been the religion of 90 percent of the region's inhabitants. The effect of religion on politics is more pronounced in the Middle East than probably in any other region in the world.

The twentieth century has witnessed one of the greatest transfers of wealth in history, as vast supplies of oil have been discovered in both the Arabian Peninsula and North Africa. This development has prompted the bitter Western comment that "where there are Middle Easterners, there is oil." In the 1990s, Saudi Arabia, Kuwait, Iran, and Iraq account for more than 53 percent of the world's petroleum reserves. This oil is a primary fuel for the industries of Europe, the United States, and Japan. As newspaper headlines indicate, more issues critically important to the future of the United States and the Western world converge in the politics of the Middle East than anywhere else in the Other World.

The purpose of this chapter is to offer a brief introduction to the Middle East and North Africa. After a discussion of geography and economics, we will trace the history of the Middle East; the story of Islam; and the subsequent rise of na-

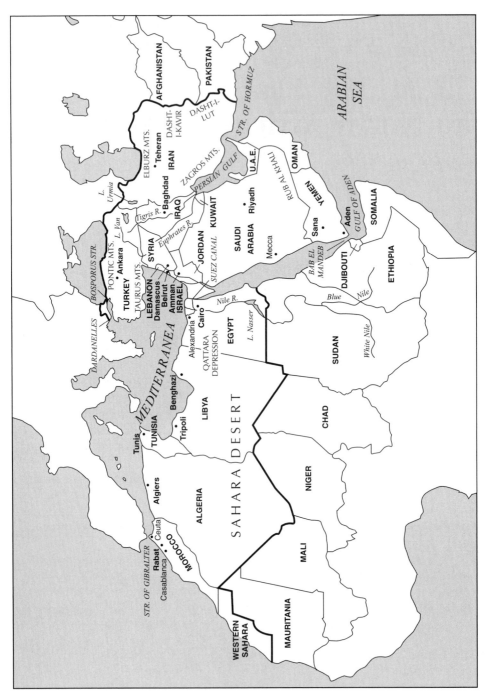

FIGURE 8.1 Political and Physical Characteristics of the Middle East and North Africa

tionalism in Egypt, Turkey, Iran, and Israel. The essential aspects of Arab nationalism will also be discussed. Finally, the central points of the Arab-Israeli dispute will be outlined in the Flashpoints. The data in table 8.1 illustrate the vast differences in population, wealth, and conditions of life in the North African and Middle Eastern countries.

Although most Americans can point to a map and identify some countries located in the Middle East, few have any idea what nations are actually included in the region. Even scholars fail to agree on the subject. The U.S. Department of Defense states categorically that there is no precise, generally accepted definition of the region variously called the Near East or Middle East.

Because, at times, all the area from the Atlantic coast of Morocco to Afghanistan has been included in this region, no one term seems to describe adequately the whole. The words *Middle East* and *Near East* are inadequate, misleading, and culturally biased. They are misleading because they have been used to describe different places at different times in history. Originally, the Near East referred to the lands of the eastern Mediterranean, and the Middle East described the Indian empire controlled by Britain. The terms converged geographically only during World War II, when the British based their Near Eastern and Middle Eastern operations in Cairo. Because the active involvement of the United States in the region began during this period, Americans have tended to use the term *Middle East*, whereas Europeans continue to use the more traditional designation, the *Near East*, to describe the same area. Even in the absence of this confusion, the terms *Middle East* and *Near East* are culturally biased from the standpoint of inhabitants of the region. Both terms describe the Other World in ways that are meaningful only in reference to the former colonial powers in Europe.

In an effort to avoid these pejorative labels, writers sometimes use the phrases *the Arab world* and *the Islamic world* as substitutes. Unfortunately, these words often confuse as much as they inform. *The Arab world* cannot accurately describe the region as a whole because the phrase ignores 65.6 million Iranians, 62.2 million Turks, and 4.5 million Jews living in Israel. Much of the same problem arises with the use of *Islamic world*: Although Muslims account for most of the area's population, large Christian and Jewish minorities play pivotal roles. This term also implies a religious unity in Islam, which simply does not exist except on the most superficial level.

Despite these concerns, the terms *Middle East* and *North Africa* will be used in this chapter because of their common usage in the United States. The Middle East will be understood to include the Arab states of Arabia and the eastern Mediterranean, Turkey, Israel, and Iran. It will also contain the North African states of Egypt, Libya, Tunisia, Algeria, and Morocco. This selection may seem arbitrary because it omits Afghanistan, Somalia, the Sudan, and Mauritania, which form transition areas between the Middle East, North Africa, and other adjacent regions.

In the Middle East, one encounters strange-sounding names with a regional significance. The Holy Land, Maghreb, Levant, Judea, Samaria, and the Fertile Crescent are all examples of special places that require more explanation. The *Holy Land* was traditionally associated with pilgrimages and crusades to the sites

TABLE 8.1 Characteristics of Middle Eastern and North African Countries

Country	Population (millions)	Population Growth Rate (%)	Infant Mortality Rate (per 1,000 live births)	Population Under 15 Years of Age (%)	Life Expectancy (years)	Urban Population (%)	Literacy Rate (%)	Arable Land (%)	Per Capita GNP ($U.S.)
Middle East									
Bahrain	.6	2.6	19	32	71	81	79	2	7,150
Iran	65.6	3.0	60	47	67	57	56	8	2,410
Iraq	19.9	3.1	67	48	66	70	62	12	—
Israel	5.0	2.6	9	31	76	90	95	17	12,110
Jordan	4.0	3.4	32	41	67	70	82	4	1,060
Kuwait	1.8	1.4	13	43	75	95	74	1	—
Lebanon	3.6	1.9	40	33	68	86	81	21	6,140
Oman	1.7	3.5	37	—	69	12	—	—	—
Qatar	.5	2.3	22	—	70	86	—	3	15,040
Saudi Arabia	18.2	3.3	52	43	69	79	64	1	7,900
Syria	14.9	3.5	43	48	66	51	67	28	1,170
Turkey	62.2	1.9	49	35	67	61	82	30	1,790
United Arab Emirates	2.8	2.1	22	—	71	81	—	1	22,180
Yemen	11.1	3.9	113	—	52	31	41	6	520
North Africa									
Algeria	27.9	2.7	52	44	66	50	61	3	1,990
Egypt	59.3	2.1	76	40	61	45	50	3	610
Libya	5.1	3.4	63	47	62	76	66	2	—
Morocco	28.6	2.3	50	40	63	47	52	18	1,030
Tunisia	8.7	1.9	34	37	67	52	68	20	1,500
Comparison States									
Canada	28.1	1.3	7	21	77	77	99	5	20,510
Poland	38.7	0.4	13	25	72	62	99	46	—
Italy	58.1	0.1	8	16	77	68	97.1	32	17,040

SOURCE: Adapted from the *United Nations Demographic Yearbook, United Nations Human Development Report,* and *The World Almanac and Book of Facts, 1995.*

venerated by Christians because of their association with the life of Jesus. Today, the term also includes sites sacred to Jews and Muslims, most of which are in or near the city of Jerusalem.

The Maghreb is a phrase literally meaning "the west," and by tradition it implies "the setting sun in the west." This term is used to describe the North African countries of Morocco, Algeria, and Tunisia, and some writers also include Libya. Like the Maghreb, *the Levant* signifies a direction, the eastern point of the compass. The Levant is generally understood to include the present states of Lebanon and Israel.

Judea and *Samaria* are ancient Hebrew names currently applied by the government of Israel to the former Jordanian-held territories on the West Bank of the Jordan River. The old biblical names are used to remind the world that Israel claims a historic right to bring Jewish settlers into these Arab-populated territories. These terms are used by those Israelis who support the expansion of the borders of Israel to include all of the territories that biblical tradition teaches were promised by God to the ancient children of Israel.

The term *Fertile Crescent* is familiar to many in the West because it is the traditional site of the birthplace of Western civilization. It includes the present countries of Israel and Lebanon as well as Syria and Iraq. Some writers say that the Fertile Crescent arches like a bow from the eastern Nile delta to the mouth of the Shatt al-Arab river in Iraq. Other authorities hold that the western terminus of the bow is Palestine, not the Nile delta. What is important to remember is that this is an area of relatively good agriculture, low population, and a reasonable climate. As in ancient times, this area offers the best hope for the development of a nonpetroleum-based economy.

GEOGRAPHY

Western perceptions of the Middle East are simultaneously accurate and misleading. The greatest expanse of desert in the world does exist here, but although there are still camel-mounted Bedouins in parts of the Middle East, most people now live in villages, towns, and cities. Even those Bedouins who have not settled into permanent residences are now likely to be exchanging their "ships of the desert," the camel, for Toyota trucks. Like many parts of the Other World, the Middle East is an area of both variety and dynamic change.

In its simplest form, the Middle East can be divided into three distinct geographic regions: the plains of North Africa and Arabia, the Fertile Crescent, and the northern tier. These areas are surrounded by five seas and five straits and are bisected by two of the world's great river systems.

The Plains of North Africa and Arabia

The vast deserts of the Sahara and the Rub al Khali cover over 95 percent of this region. Because of their immense size, it should not be surprising to learn that the surfaces of these two deserts vary from gravel to rock to sand.

Camels Gathered Around One of the Government-prepared Watering Holes
in the Sahara Desert
SOURCE: Joe Weatherby

The Qattara Depression, larger than 4,000 square miles, is located near the Mediterranean in Egypt's portion of the eastern Sahara. From time to time, proposals have been made to divert the waters of the Mediterranean over the precipice to the Qattara floor, which is 400 feet below sea level. Engineers estimate that enough falling water could be diverted through generators to create an electric power complex that would rival the Nile's Aswan High Dam. A combination of environmental concerns and a shortage of capital in Egypt has postponed serious consideration of this project for the foreseeable future. There has been another, perhaps more feasible, Qattara proposal to tap an abundant ancient water supply, believed to exist beneath the depression floor, to create a new Nile delta in the desert. Whether the Egyptian government will find the development funds that would be required to attempt either of these ambitious schemes is doubtful at the present time.

The Rub al Khali of Saudi Arabia is famous for sand mountains that are hundreds of feet high. This desert may contain the largest area of sand on Earth. For the first time since the ancient caravan routes flourished, westerners are again penetrating the unknowns of the Rub al Khali, but this time in modern vehicles and engaged in the search for oil.

The remaining 5 percent of the plains of North Africa and Arabia is a transitional territory that includes two distinct areas: desert scrub country and a rich Mediterranean coastal zone. This zone stretches from the Nile delta westward for most of the length of North Africa and to the Atlantic coast of Morocco as far south as Casablanca. The desert scrub country does contain some soil, moisture, and vegetation, and much of it resembles the high plains of the western United States. The conditions that produce desert scrub occur elsewhere in the Middle East, including southern Turkey, western Iraq, western Iran, and parts of Jordan and Syria. The nomads live in the desert scrub with their ever-migrating herds of sheep and goats.

Most of the residents of the plains live in the narrow coastal zone of the Mediterranean rather than in the deserts. The North African coast of the Atlantic and the Mediterranean generally conforms to what is known as the Mediterranean climate, which features hot, dry summers, with brown or dormant vegetation, and cool, wet winters, when the plant life has its growth period. In North Africa, this coastal zone ranges from only a few miles in width in parts of Egypt and Libya to as much as 50 miles in Algeria. In Egypt, the coastal zone and Nile valley and delta combined average 2,700 people per square mile, representing one of the world's densest populations. Remarkably, unlike other high-density areas, such as the Netherlands, the people of Egypt are still largely engaged in traditional Other World occupations including subsistence agriculture (see box 8.1).

Some of the great cities of both Africa and the Middle East are located in or near the Mediterranean coastal zone. Cairo, with a population of over 11 million people, is the largest and most important city on the African continent. Other important North African cities are Alexandria, Egypt (3.3 million); Tripoli, Libya (610,000); Benghazi, Libya (400,000); Tunis, Tunisia (700,000); and Algiers, Algeria (2 million). Both Rabat (982,000) and Casablanca (2,600,000) are located in the coastal zones of Morocco. Saudi Arabia in the Arabian Peninsula contains the historic cities of Mecca (810,000) and Medina (250,000). The commercial centers of Jedda (1 million) and Riyadh (1,976,000) are also located in Saudi Arabia.

These statistics may have more meaning if we compare the size of North African and Arabian cities with those found in the United States. Cairo has 4 million more people than New York City; Alexandria and Casablanca are larger than Houston; Tunis and Mecca are slightly smaller than San Antonio; Jedda, Rabat, and Riyadh are all larger than San Francisco.

The North African and Arabian plains contain a number of mountains, including the Atlas and Rif mountains of Morocco and the Tell Atlas of Algeria and Tunisia. The highest point in Egypt is the 8,600-foot Jabal Musa (Mount Sinai), lo-

---

BOX 8.1   Water

The greatest shortage in the Middle East is water. Since ancient times, Mediterranean people have used ingenious methods to carry water to the fields. Following are several traditional irrigation methods still used in the region.

The *qanat* is a tunnel sometimes over 10 miles long that taps the groundwater in the foothills and transports it to the fields in the valleys. This system is used in Iran and other mountainous countries in the northern tier.

The *shadoof* is an ancient system using a goat-skin bag attached to a pole that is pivoted from the river to the field. This water system is used extensively along the banks of the Nile River in Egypt. The water wheel is a device used to lift and transport water. This system is usually animal-powered.

The *Archimedes* screw is a portable gear used to raise water from a river or pond to the fields.

cated in the southern Sinai. Tradition holds that God gave the Ten Commandments to Moses on Mt. Sinai. The Arabian peninsula is mountainous in Yemen and Oman. In both places, peaks reach heights of 12,000 feet.[1]

The Fertile Crescent

Perhaps nowhere in the world has so much human history been tied to one single geographic area as in the Fertile Crescent. Everywhere the visitor looks, on the hills or in the valleys, important events in the history of humankind have occurred. Here are the ruins of ancient civilizations, the land of prophets, and the birthplace of Judaism and Christianity. Geographically, the Fertile Crescent includes a narrow coastal zone flanked by the sea on one side and a rather low coastal range of mountains, running north to south, on the other. Along the southern border of Turkey, the Fertile Crescent arches eastward through a gap in the mountains to include the desert scrub lands of Syria and Iraq before joining the rich river basins of the Tigris and Euphrates. The region terminates at the northern end of the Persian Gulf.

The coastal zone of the Fertile Crescent is similar in many respects to the coast of California. Although this analogy has limitations apparent to any geographer, it may be useful to consider the following comparisons. If we were to travel the coastal route south from San Francisco to Los Angeles, we would pass

The Souk. Located next to the coral-colored walls of the old kasba, the market, or souk, is the focal point of life in this Moroccan town.

SOURCE: Joe Weatherby

through countryside that is similar in many respects to the coastal zone of the eastern Mediterranean, with Beirut being comparable to the Bay Area, Haifa to Monterey and Carmel, the Lebanon Mountains to the California coastal range, the Bekaa valley in Lebanon to the Salinas valley, and Tel Aviv to the area between Santa Barbara and Los Angeles.

With the exception of Beirut, which has a population of 1.5 million, the cities of the eastern Mediterranean do not rival either those of North Africa or the interior of the Fertile Crescent. Tel Aviv has a population of 368,000 and Jerusalem 544,000. Tripoli, the second-largest city in Lebanon, has a population of 245,000 people.

The two major cities of the Fertile Crescent are Baghdad, Iraq, and Damascus, Syria. Baghdad, with a climate similar to the southwestern United States, has a population of over 3.8 million. The population of Damascus is over 2 million. Syria and Iraq are the most important states of the Fertile Crescent. Both are considered to have a good chance to develop well-rounded economies, maintain low population densities, and establish reasonable standards of living. At the present time, their problems are mainly political, not geographic or economic.

The Northern Tier

The northern tier is an area of mountains and plateaus linked to a mountain system that stretches from the Alps in the west to the Himalayas in the east. Although Afghanistan and Pakistan are often included in this region, this discussion of the northern tier is limited to Turkey and Iran.

Both countries are located on high plateaus surrounded by mountains. Turkey is situated on a peninsula jutting out into the Mediterranean. Turkey is about the size of Texas and Arkansas combined. The Anatolian plateau, a high, dry region about 3,000 feet above sea level, is located in the center of Turkey. Here, the Turks produce most of their wheat and cereals. Two mountain ranges run east to west along the edges of the plateau. The Pontic Mountains are located on the north and the Taurus Mountains on the south of the peninsula. Eastern Turkey is extremely mountainous along the Iranian border. Mount Ararat, the traditional site of the landing of Noah's ark, is near this border. It is worth noting that Turkey has a long, varied coastal region that includes both a Mediterranean climate along the south and west and a wet area near the Black Sea city of Rise. This city receives as much as 98 inches of rain a year. With such climatic variety in the coastal zone, Turkey raises a number of crops including tea, tobacco, and cotton. Although most people live in villages, Turkey has several large cities. Istanbul, with a population of 6.6 million, is the largest. Ankara, the capital, has a population of 2.5 million, and Izmir has 1,700,000 people.

Nature has played a cruel trick on Iran. Larger than Alaska, Iran consists of a high desert surrounded on all sides by rugged mountains that prevent moisture from penetrating into the interior. The Zagros Mountains run along the length of the eastern shore of the Persian Gulf, and the Elbruz Mountains are located along a line parallel to the southern coast of the Caspian Sea. The jewel of the

Elbruz is a partially snowcapped volcano 18,376 feet high. This volcano, Mt. Damavand, is clearly visible from Tehran. Tehran is built in the foothills of the Elbruz and has a setting and climate closely resembling Salt Lake City, Utah.

Most of the interior of Iran consists of two terrible deserts, where some of the world's highest temperatures have been recorded. The Dasht-I-Kavir, or "Salt Desert," and the Dasht-I-Lut, the "Desert of Death," are largely untraveled even today. The hostile environment in Iran's interior has caused over 70 percent of the country to remain uninhabited. The people of Iran live either along the narrow coastal plain of the Caspian Sea or in scattered urban centers in the north and west. Tehran, the capital, totally dominates these urban centers with a population of over 6 million people. The nation's second-largest city, Meshed, has a population of more than 2 million.[2]

Strategic Geography

The Middle East contains two of the world's great river systems: the Nile and the Tigris and Euphrates. The area also has two lesser waterways that are important in the politics of the region: the Suez Canal and the Jordan River.

Flowing 4,037 miles, the Nile is the world's longest river. Rising in Ethiopia and Uganda, it crosses the Sudan, enters Egypt at Lake Nasser, passes through the dam at Aswan, and flows past Cairo to the delta and the Mediterranean. If there is a central feature to Egypt, it is most certainly the Nile, which has been the life-support system for this nation's residents for over 5,000 years. The need to secure the Nile in upper and lower Egypt is as important today as it was when the pharaohs ruled the nation in ancient times. As in the past, today's Egyptian leaders pay particular attention to politics in the Sudan. To the Egyptian, the fate of the Sudan still affects the security of the Nile.

Both the Tigris and the Euphrates begin their journey to the sea in central Turkey. The Euphrates passes through Turkey, Syria, and Iraq, and the Tigris through Turkey and Iraq. The Karun flows from Iran to join with the Tigris and the Euphrates, forming a new river called the Shatt al-Arab just before reaching the northern shore of the Persian Gulf. It is in this meandering delta of the Shatt al-Arab near Basra where much of the war between Iraq and Iran was fought during the 1980s. This same area was a strategic objective of American forces during the 1991 war with Iraq.

The Suez Canal has been strategically important since its opening in 1869. One hundred and one miles long, the canal separates the Red Sea from the Mediterranean, saving ships the costly and time-consuming trip around the tip of southern Africa when traveling from the Persian Gulf and points further east to and from Europe. For further information, see the Flashpoints at the end of this chapter.

The Jordan River and its system of lakes and seas are historically significant as the site of many events sacred to Christians and Jews. The Jordan is also politically important because it is the disputed border between Jordan and Israel. The river flows through a valley for about 80 miles between the Sea of Galilee (Lake Tiberias) and the Dead Sea. The Jordan's economic significance is limited.

Ranging from 50 to a few hundred feet in width, its potential for irrigation cannot possibly meet the exaggerated hopes for agricultural development of either the Arabs or the Israelis.[3]

No area of the globe is as strategically located as the Middle East. For centuries, it has been the invasion route of Egyptians, Persians, Romans, Christians, and Muslims. Today, its important location as a passageway between Africa, Europe, and Asia is without challenge. The Middle East is surrounded by five easily traversed seas: Arabian, Red, Mediterranean, Black, and Caspian. There are three gulfs of importance: the Gulf of Aden, located at the tip of the Arabian peninsula; the Gulf of Oman, situated between Oman and Iran; and the famous Persian Gulf. Entry and egress to all but two of these bodies of water are controlled by narrow straits: the Straits of Gibraltar, controlling the western Mediterranean; the Dardanelles and the Bosporus, dominating entry to the Black Sea; the Bab el-Mandeb, controlling the southern end of the Red Sea and the Suez Canal; and the Straits of Hormuz, which must be passed to enter the Persian Gulf. Only the Arabian Sea, which is part of the Indian Ocean, and the Caspian Sea, which has no outlet, are not dominated by strategic straits.[4]

PEOPLE

A popular misconception is that there is a homogeneous race of people in the Middle East. This notion is fostered by some of the region's religious institutions, whose traditions allude to Arab, Jewish, or even Aryan races. However, these terms have little meaning in the Middle East today unless they are limited to linguistic or cultural associations.

Although there are no recognizable groupings about which everyone would agree, authorities acknowledge that the region contains Semitic, Turkish, and Persian-speaking people. Of the Semitic-speaking population, the Arabs are the most numerous. Although there are many dialects, there is only one written Arabic, and it is understood by educated Arabs everywhere. Arabic is spoken from the Atlantic coast of Morocco to the shores of the Persian Gulf. By this definition, approximately 150 million Arabs live in the region. Although there is a single Arab nation in theory only, the common bond of language has meant that unification is an aspiration of many of the region's inhabitants.

The other large Semitic group lives in Israel. Reviving a formerly ritualistic language as a symbol of their nationalism, the more than 4 million Jews of Israel have again made Hebrew a living language.

The 56 million Turkish-speaking people in modern Turkey came to the Anatolian peninsula in the eleventh and twelfth centuries from central Asia. They have lived in a single identifiable state since the Turkish Republic was created from the breakup of the Ottoman Empire following World War I.[5]

Persian is an Indo-European language written with a modified Arabic alphabet. There are about 34 million Persian-speaking Iranians in Iran. Finally, it should be pointed out that the region also contains people who speak different languages, including the Kurds, Armenians, and Greeks.

RELIGION

Two great forces are shaping the character of the modern Middle East. One is the Islamic religion and the other is nationalism.

Islam is the youngest of the three great monotheistic religions that arose in this region; the other two are Christianity and Judaism. Islam has been the dominant religion in the Middle East for almost 1,400 years. Today less than 10 percent of the population is non-Muslim. Thus, to understand the Middle East, it will be necessary to have some knowledge of Islam.

First, however, a distinction should be made between what is often referred to as the popular or folk religion and the formal religion of mosque and church. It is next to impossible to generalize about Middle Eastern folk religions except to point out that the popular practices of Christians, Jews, and Muslims are similar. All have their local saints, sacred places, and symbols. Many of these traditions spill over from one religion to another. For example, people of all religions in the Mediterranean traditionally paint the windows and shutters of their homes blue to ward off the evil eye. The distance between this popular practice and the formal religion of the scholars is often as great as that of the Pentecostal snake handler in the Appalachian Mountains and the pope in Rome. This inquiry will be limited to the formal religious practices of the majority religion, Islam.[6]

Much of the universal appeal of Islam is found in its straightforward simplicity. Unlike Christianity, there are no priests dispensing sacraments, no catechism, and no complicated theology. Islam demands a belief in only one God, called Allah in Arabic. Muslims believe that Mohammed is the prophet of God. The word *Islam* means "submission"; thus, a Muslim is a believer who has submitted to the will of God. This simple theology may be summarized as belief in the oneness of God, the prophecy of Mohammed, judgment day, and life after death.

Islam is more than a religion as that term is generally understood in the West. It is a way of life, 24 hours a day, 7 days a week, 365 days a year. Muslims do not concern themselves with what is the truth because truth is contained in the profession of faith and the word of God as revealed through Mohammed in the Koran. The great questions of Islam are centered around how a good Muslim should live and relate to others, not what a Muslim should believe in order to enter paradise. Although it is easy to make a profession of faith in Islam, it is difficult to live the life of a good Muslim. As a guide for living, Muslims observe five religious obligations, called the Five Pillars of Islam: professing faith, observing ritual prayer, giving alms, fasting during the month of Ramadan, and making a pilgrimage to Mecca.

The Profession of Faith (Shahadah)

Muslims believe that there is no God but God and that Mohammed is his prophet. The implications of this profession are threefold. First, in contrast to most Christians, who believe that there is one God, expressed as Father, Son, and Holy Spirit, Muslims hold to an uncompromising monotheism: "There is no God but God." Second, Muslims believe that although other prophets, including Jesus, have received revelations, Allah's words as revealed through Mohammed are the

North African Door. Popular culture in North Africa holds that either the "hand" door-knocker represents the hand of Mohammed's daughter, Fatima, or that the fingers represent the Five Pillars of Islam.

SOURCE: Joe Weatherby

final, complete message from God to humankind. Third, Muslims believe that this message is contained, in full, in a book called the Koran.

Prayer (Salat)

Traditionally, Muslims pray at five prescribed periods a day: in the morning before sunrise, noontime, afternoon, sunset, and late evening. The prayer is ritualistic and keeps the believers in constant contact with God. Islam differs from those forms of Christianity in which believers pray through mediators inasmuch as Muslims believe that they have direct access to God.

Alms Giving (Zakat)

Muslims believe that they are obliged to pay a percentage of their income to the poor and needy. They do not believe that poverty is a crime. For Muslims, there is little or no stigma attached to this system of voluntary religious welfare.

Fasting (Sawm)

During Ramadan, the ninth month of the Islamic calendar, all Muslims are called on to observe the fast by abstaining from all food, drink, and other earthly pleasures during daylight hours. This month-long fast, longer than anything practiced in either Christianity or Judaism, teaches Muslims self-denial and moderation.

Pilgrimage to Mecca (Hajj)

If possible, all Muslims are enjoined to visit the Great Mosque in Mecca at least once. Here, facing the Ka'bah and wearing the same ritual white, Muslims from every station in life, from every country in the world, both male and female, pray as equals before God.[7]

Holy War (Jihad)

Many consider the jihad, or holy war, to be almost a "sixth pillar of Islam." This duty, often misunderstood in the West, has two meanings: one inner and one external. The inner meaning calls on Muslims to fight constantly against their own evil inclinations. The external command offers salvation to those Muslims who

Center of the Islamic World. The Sacred Mosque and its black-draped Ka'bah at Mecca teem with life during the pilgrimage season.

SOURCE: Courtesy, Saudi Research and Marketing, Inc., Washington, D.C.

fight to promote a universal Islamic doctrine. The confusion concerning *jihad* arises because the term has been used in a political manner by some Islamic leaders to further their own purposes. When used in this way, there is some doubt whether it is anything more than a symbolic gesture.[8]

The Muslim community is governed by a hierarchy of principles expected to guide the faithful in all matters of life. These principles, or authorities, are collectively called the *Shari'ah*, or "the path to be followed." This path includes, in descending order of importance, the Koran, the tradition (*Hadith*) of how Mohammed lived, consensus (*Ijma*) of the religious scholars on issues, and deduction (*Qiyas*) where there is no precedent. Not all Muslim communities accept this hierarchy in its entirety.

The great split in Islam began because of a dispute over how the successor (caliph) to Mohammed should be selected. The Shiia branch of Islam is based in Iran. Shiites believe that the first caliph should have been Ali, the son-in-law of Mohammed, and that successive caliphs should have come exclusively from the descendants of Ali. Sunnis, who make up approximately 80 percent of the world's Muslim population, believe that the caliphs should have been chosen by election of the faithful from members of Mohammed's tribe. Over the centuries, many other differences have developed between these two branches, and their disputes still color Middle Eastern politics hundreds of years after the original split occurred.[9]

HISTORY

Since the seventh century, the history of the Middle East has been inexorably bound to the history of Islam, which includes at least five distinct periods: the life of Mohammed, the rightly guided caliphs, the Umayyads, the Abbasids, and the Ottomans.

The Life of Mohammed (A.D. 571–632)

Mohammed was born in A.D. 571 in the city of Mecca. Orphaned while young, he was reared by a grandfather who was a leader of the Meccan Quraysh tribe. Mohammed is traditionally believed to have traveled with caravans to other parts of the Middle East as a young man. His visits may have exposed him to other religions. When he was 40 years old, he started receiving revelations commanding him to tell the world that there was one God, that Mohammed was his prophet, and that there would be a judgment day. These revelations were revolutionary ideas that threatened existing society in Mecca. In the summer of 622, opposition from the Meccans forced Mohammed to flee from Mecca 200 miles north to the city of Medina. The date of Mohammed's flight, called the Hijra, marks the beginning of the Islamic calendar. After converting Medina to Islam, Mohammed lived to see not only Mecca but also the entire Arabian peninsula become Muslim before his death in 632. It should be remembered that Muslims do not ascribe divine qualities to Mohammed. He is considered to have been a human being who, while living a perfect life, served as a messenger from God.

Mosque of Mohammed Ali. Located on the Citadel towering above Cairo, this mosque was begun in 1824. Today, it remains the most imposing landmark in the city.

SOURCE: Joe Weatherby

The Rightly Guided Caliphs (632–661)

Mohammed's death left the movement without a clearly designated successor. This vacuum initiated a struggle for power that ultimately led to the Sunni-Shiia split. Although some of the faithful believed that Ali had been designated by Mohammed as his successor, Abu Bakr (the prophet's father-in-law) was chosen to be the caliph. After only two years, Abu Bakr chose Umar to be the caliph, and under Umar's leadership, Islamic armies conquered the Fertile Crescent, Persia, and Egypt. Much of what is familiar to westerners about Islam, including the veiling of women and the ban on alcohol, was institutionalized during Umar's tenure. Uthman succeeded Umar, who was assassinated in 644, but he too was assassinated 12 years later. Ali was finally selected as the fourth caliph, only to be challenged by the powerful Umayyad family from Mecca. The Umayyads backed another leader named Mu'awiyah. There was a civil war between the Umayyads, who had the support of Muslims in Syria, and the Muslims who supported Ali. Eventually, Ali was assassinated in 661. Shiites still maintain that Ali was the only legitimate successor to Mohammed.

Muslims look with fondness at the period of the first four caliphs as a time when the religion had a purity of purpose that ultimately was lost. Modern Muslims tend to stress the exertions of the period, the justice, and the humanity and ignore the disturbing reality that three of the four "rightly guided caliphs" were assassinated. Nevertheless, if there ever was a time that Muslims long to return to, it is this one.

The Umayyad Dynasty (661–750)

Under the first Umayyad caliph, Mu'awiyah, the election of leaders was ended in favor of a dynastic approach, and the political capital of Islam became Damascus. During the almost 100 years that the Umayyads ruled, the Islamic faith spread to three continents. However, it was only a question of time until the non-Arab elements of the empire began to believe that they were being treated as second-class members of the Damascus state. In 750, the non-Arab dissidents of the empire arose and ended the Arab domination by destroying the Umayyads. In place of the Umayyads, a new multicultural system was established, called the Abbasid dynasty.

The Abbasid Dynasty (750–1258)

With the rise of the Abbasids, the so-called Golden Age of Islam began. The empire's new capital in Baghdad saw Muslims lead the world in philosophy, literature, mathematics, and medicine. Many developments that were to bear fruit in the explosion of the arts and sciences during the Renaissance in Europe originated in the streets of Abbasid Baghdad. The rule of the Abbasids came to an end in the year 1258, when Mongol armies from central Asia conquered Baghdad. After the fall of the Abbasids, no single power was able to dominate the Middle East until the Ottoman period.

The Ottoman Empire (1453–1918)

Tradition holds that the Ottomans came to Anatolia from central Asia in the early Middle Ages. By the mid-1300s, they were in the process of establishing an empire that would again extend Muslim control to parts of Europe, Africa, and the Middle East. Although it is difficult to generalize about an empire that lasted for over 600 years, it is safe to state that many of the conditions found in the modern Middle East began in the practices of the Ottomans. For example, the Ottomans were able to rule a diverse multicultural empire stretching over much of the Mediterranean world because they established a system of religious and cultural autonomy called the Millet. Sectarian separation was institutionalized and even encouraged by the Ottomans as long as loyalty and taxes were paid to the caliph. This system of religious toleration resulted in the survival of small Christian and Jewish groups, which otherwise would have disappeared. Middle East groups still divide along sectarian lines after the fashion of the Millet.

During the eighteenth and nineteenth centuries, Ottomans were in retreat in the face of increasing Western power. Many of the negative stereotypes that westerners have about the Middle East come from this period of Ottoman weakness. The Ottomans survived the nineteenth century but collapsed with the defeat of the Central Powers in World War I. The subsequent partition of the non-Turkish elements from the empire resulted in the creation of the modern Turkish Republic.

Islam Today

Much has been written in recent years concerning the resurgence of Islam as a unifying force in the Middle East. Although it can be said that Islam is not a form of nationalism, it is clear that Islamic attitudes and symbols are used and manipulated by nationalists in the Middle East to legitimize their respective political objectives.

It is possible to identify certain important attitudes that Muslims have concerning non-Muslims. Islam victoriously entered the world scene over 1,300 years ago and remained so for almost 1,000 years. This long period of dominance has led to a collective mind set that is reflected in the commonly used Muslim expression "Islam dominates and may not be dominated." Thus, for Muslims, some religions may be tolerated, but none will be allowed parity, much less dominance, if there is power to prevent it.

Although some Muslims view the defeats of the recent past with the rationalization that "Islam gains strength with every testing," there is no denying that it is particularly galling to have unbelievers dominating believers after all these centuries. This attitude is reflected in the responses of many people from the Middle East when they come in contact with the outside world. In the nineteenth century, the early military defeats administered by the West were rationalized on the grounds of technological inferiority. Attitudes eventually evolved into a conspiratorial view of history in which the West was blamed for every problem in the region.

In this century, continuing defeats, both external and internal, have led to a further sense of helplessness that is reflected in an almost irrational rage against anything Western or modern because it is believed to represent colonialism in a new form. This attitude can be seen in a number of ways, including the actions of students studying in the West, Islamic resurgence movements in the region, and the return to conservative Islamic dress by many university-educated women. Although it is difficult to forecast the direction these frustrations will take, it is safe to say that they have a real basis in fact and can only become a major unsettling element in Middle Eastern politics.

In part, the Islamic resurgence occurred because Islam has avoided the stigma of failure that has accompanied the secular philosophies. In the twentieth century, capitalism, socialism, Marxism, and secular nationalism have all been tried, and each has ended in failure. Only Islam offers hope for a renewal of Middle Eastern society without the taint of defeat, corruption, or association with colonialism. In whatever form it takes, Islam is today, as it has always been, the central factor in the lives of millions of people.[10]

THE COLONIAL EXPERIENCE

For the better part of 1,300 years, Christians from Europe have fought Muslims from the East. During the last 200 years, this traditional conflict has been worsened by the impact of Western colonialism. It began with the French invasion of Egypt in 1798. Although this occupation was cut short by the British victory over the French fleet at the battle of Aboukir, it signaled a growing European interest in the area. Soon Britain, France, Italy, and Spain pursued their imperial objectives. Germany and Russia were absent only because their ambitions were frustrated by the British and the French. The British began their imperial adventure on the periphery of the Middle East by developing a series of strategic colonies on the shores of the Persian Gulf. By the opening of the Suez Canal in 1869, Britain controlled colonies stretching from Aden, at the mouth of the Red Sea, across southern Arabia all the way to India. Later the British leased the Ottoman island of Cyprus and used it as a naval base to check the Russian attempts to enter the Mediterranean.

The British military occupied Egypt in 1882 because of a fear that the Egyptian government would not pay debts owed to foreign investors. This occupation was considered to be temporary, but the British did not leave Egypt until 1956. They were also interested in expanding their influence along the Red Sea. After much fighting, the Anglo-Egyptian forces occupied the Sudan in the last decade of the nineteenth century. By this time, Britain was the European country with the most extensive presence in the Middle East.

When the Ottoman Empire was disbanded at the end of World War I, the British gained custody of Iraq, Palestine, and Transjordan. Semi-independent, these territories were administered by the British as mandates until the end of World War II. For the most part, British colonies in the Middle East were established as strategic colonies either to protect the lifeline to India or to create a stable environment for business investment.

After their earlier occupation of Egypt, French imperial activity was limited to the establishment of a colony in Algeria in 1830. Throughout the nineteenth century, this colonial bridgehead was expanded by French settlers until it included a large portion of North Africa. In the twentieth century, these holdings grew to include the southern portion of Morocco. France gained control of Syria and Lebanon as part of the partition of the Ottoman Empire. Regardless of their official status, the French administered these territories as colonies.

Spain and Italy developed imperial ambitions in North Africa during the early part of the twentieth century. Italy began a military occupation of Libya in 1911, when the territory was taken from the Ottomans. Building on several ancient enclaves, the Spanish joined the French in the partition of Morocco by occupying the northern portion in 1912. Although established largely for prestige purposes, these colonies proved difficult to pacify completely and expensive to maintain. It is doubtful whether these colonies ever justified the blood and treasure required to hold them.

Although Germany never actually controlled any territory in the Middle East, it did play an active political role as a participant in the great-power struggle of the nineteenth and twentieth centuries. Before World War I, it sent military advisors and agents to both the Ottoman Empire and to Persia. It also participated in the planning and partial construction of the Berlin-Baghdad railway. Because the Germans were only in the Middle East in a financial or advisory capacity, and because they were opposed to the British and French, they were the most admired Europeans active in the region.

With the exception of the navy in the war against the Barbary pirates, the United States avoided involvement in the Middle East until the end of World War II. Before President Truman played a leading role in the establishment of the state of Israel, the United States escaped the colonial stigma applied to most other developed countries. Since that time, the United States has been blamed for almost every ill that plagues the region.

During the last 200 hundred years, almost every area in the Middle East has suffered under colonial occupation. Many of these areas fell under European control after World War I. As a result of this experience, the worst forms of imperialism are well remembered. At times, the Western powers have denied that they were officially in the Middle East in an imperial capacity. Nowhere in the Other World was Western imperialism implemented in a more hypocritical or cynical fashion.

GOVERNMENT

By the last quarter of the twentieth century, the countries of the Middle East had received formal independence. The end of colonialism resulted in the creation of one of the most politically complex regions in the Other World, containing democracies, authoritarian civilian states, military-dominated regimes, and monarchies. Morocco, Saudi Arabia, Jordan, and the Arab states of the Persian Gulf are monarchies. Iraq, Libya, and Syria are regimes in which the military plays an important role. Egypt, Tunisia, and Turkey are civilian authoritarian states. Iran is an Islamic republic. In the past, both Israel and Lebanon have been considered Western-style democracies, but a civil war, Palestinian intrigues, Syrian military intervention, and the 1982 Israeli invasion have combined to kill the short-term hope for an independent democracy in Lebanon.

It is important to remember that since independence, few Middle Eastern regimes have demonstrated a sustained commitment to constitutional government as it is understood to exist in the West. During periods of crisis, decision making has often reverted to informal systems that exist outside the formal mechanisms of government. Thus the Middle East is dominated by personalities and politics rather than law as it is understood in the West, where following procedure is more important than winning. Middle Eastern government institutions must be considered as only a part of a greater cultural whole that is involved in political decision making. Traditional social, cultural, and religious institutions still play a disproportionate role in the politics of the region.

ECONOMICS AND NATURAL RESOURCES

It is popular to state that with the exception of petroleum there are no significant mineral deposits in the Middle East. Although it is true that the resources of the region are limited, it is also true that much of the Middle East has not been thoroughly surveyed. Nevertheless, important mineral resources have been found in limited areas. Phosphate deposits are mined in Morocco, the former Spanish Sahara, Tunisia, Jordan, and Egypt. Iron ore is found in both North Africa and Turkey. Some gold has been discovered in Egypt and Saudi Arabia.

Clearly, oil is the great natural resource of the region. The Persian Gulf states provide significant amounts of the oil needed by Europe, Japan, and the United States.[11] What is perhaps more important is the realization that the oil states of the Middle East and North Africa control more than 60 percent of the world's proven reserves of oil and 25 percent of the reserves of natural gas. Because of these resources, this region will play an important economic role in world affairs for a very long time.

There is a vast contrast between oil-rich states with low populations and non–oil-producing states with high populations. For example, Qatar's per capita GDP is about $17,000; that of the most populated Arab country, Egypt, is only $700. This discrepancy is a destabilizing element for the entire region. Iraqi President Saddam Hussein cited economic inequity as a justification for his 1990 invasion of Kuwait: "The malicious Westerners intentionally multiplied the number of countries with the result that the Arab nation could not achieve the integration needed to realize its full capability. When fragmenting the Arab homeland, they intentionally distanced the majority of the population and areas of cultural depth from riches and their sources."[12]

The scarcity of water is the most serious impediment to improving agricultural production in the region. In an experiment, the Gulf states and Saudi Arabia have made great strides, at high cost, to start an agricultural industry. There have been calls from some of the poor states to use Arab oil money to make the non–oil-producing states breadbaskets for the region. This pan-Arab agricultural vision for the present is still a dream.

Turkey, with a better supply of water than the Arab states, does have a well-developed agricultural system. The Turks rank among the top 20 nations in the world in the production of wheat, potatoes, barley, olives, tomatoes, sunflower seeds, cotton, tea, and wool. Iran produces wheat and grapes, and Egypt is famous for its high-quality cotton and oranges. Grain products and oranges are also produced in the Levant.

CASE STUDIES ON MIDDLE EASTERN NATIONALISM _____

Despite their diversity, the countries of the Middle East underwent similar experiences that shaped their attitudes toward the outside world. All of them felt the humiliation of Western colonialism in one form or another. As was the case elsewhere in the Other World, reaction to the colonial experience served as a spark that ignited the fires of nationalism. Much of the force of Middle Eastern nationalism has centered around a resistance to Western colonialism.

Over the years, the competing nationalism of the Turks, Iranians, Egyptians, and Israelis has resulted in irredentist claims against one another. When one looks at the territorial aspirations of Turks, Kurds, Iranians, Iraqis, Israelis, Palestinians,

Jordanians, Egyptians, and Libyans, it becomes obvious that if all of their hopes are to be realized, the people of the Middle East will have to stack countries on top of one another. The final solution for these competing nationalistic objectives is one of the great political problems of the late twentieth century.

The traditional goal of Middle Eastern nationalism has been to achieve independence. Certainly, here, as elsewhere in the Other World, there is no agreement about what independence means or how it can be realized. The case studies in this chapter demonstrate that Middle Eastern nationalists have used a variety of approaches to achieve their objectives. Some have totally rejected the political and religious institutions of the past, as in Turkey, whereas others have sought independence by returning to what they believe to be the traditions of early Islam, as in Saudi Arabia and Iran. Finally, some nationalists have sought to chart a middle course similar to that of Egypt.

Although included in this discussion, the experience of Israel cannot readily be identified with other nationalism in the region. Israel is a settler state based on Western traditions. However, the Israeli experiment is interesting because the Zionist form of nationalism is becoming more sectarian and Middle Eastern in its point of view.

In chapter 2, nationalism was described as it has developed in the West. Among the features discussed were exclusivity and suspicion of others. Nationalism also supported the establishment and maintenance of the modern nation-state. We will see from the case studies in this chapter that this process also occurred in the Middle East. However, some Middle Eastern nationalism is moving in new directions, making it difficult to categorize in traditional terms. These nationalistic movements no longer identify with the state boundaries that currently exist. They favor a new unification through supranational units like the Levant or the Maghreb.

Many of the new nationalists view their own governments as illegitimate, and they almost repudiate those goals of their fathers 40 or 50 years ago. At that time, nationalistic efforts were directed at the overthrow of the colonial rule of Britain and France. The changed attitude has been articulated by some Palestinians, who occasionally refer to, along with opposition to Israel, a repressive Arab system. They are voicing opposition to Arab governments of both left and right, and they are hoping to use the Palestinian revolution as a catalyst to spread change to all of the states of the Middle East.

It should also be pointed out that Middle Eastern nationalistic sentiments are primarily products of the urban centers. In much of the countryside, people still have loyalties similar to those found in prenationalistic Europe. To these people the first contact with the authority of the state is often a point of contention and not an expression of loyalty. The villagers' contact with the government is limited to paying taxes and watching the state take their village sons away to the army. In many of the rural areas, the values of the central government have little or no legitimacy.

Traditional nationalism has failed to fulfill regional aspirations, so it is being either modified or discarded. In the past, nationalistic goals included political unity and freedom from both colonial and neocolonial domination. Arab nationalism also hoped to establish a classless society, a democratic political system, and an effective challenge to Israel. However, after years of formal independence, these stated goals remain unfulfilled dreams.

TURKEY

Emerging from the Ottoman defeat of World War I, Turkish nationalism drew on the struggles and writings of the previous 50 years to create a movement based on the unifying aspects of the Turkish language and Turkish identification. This idea succeeded in ways in which the similar Young Turk movement had failed. In the nineteenth century, the Young Turks failed because the multinational character of the old Ottoman Empire rendered the appeal of being Turkish ineffective. Modern Turkish nationalists succeeded because the geographic limits of the new Turkish republic coincided with areas where people identified with being Turkish instead of Ottoman.

The new movement was led by a military hero named Ataturk (Mustafa Kemal). He was determined to break Turkey out of the backwardness of the Ottomans by creating a modern, secular Eastern European republic that could compete on equal terms with any country in the West. At the time, Ataturk's revolution was expected to be as significant as those of his contemporaries: Hitler, Mussolini, and Lenin. Sixty years after the founding of modern Turkey, Ataturk's reforms are not considered as revolutionary as they once were. Since the 1950s, Turkish nationalism has abandoned some of its more controversial themes. For example, Islam is a resurgent force in what was once considered to be a secular state. Nevertheless, as they have done for half a century, Turkish nationalists still turn away from the Middle East and look toward Europe for their future. We should remember that the central feature of Turkish nationalism has been the rejection of the failed institutions and solutions of the past in order to create an entirely new system.

In the 1990s, two opposing forces contend for power in Turkey. One, represented by the government establishment, the residents of the cities, and the university-educated elites, supports the original principles of the republic that Ataturk founded in 1923. They defend Western secularism, want to keep Turkey part of NATO, and wish to be admitted to the European Community. Others, including the Islamic traditionalists and conservative rural Turks, believe that the country has deserted a rich Middle Eastern heritage. These conservatives support efforts to control what they see as the excesses of modern Turkish society. They are active in attempts to regulate the public activities of women, which if successful would reverse the feminist gains made over a half century ago. Under their influence, more mosques are being constructed than at any time since the days of the Ottoman Empire. For the moment, conservatives are still a minority in Turkish politics.

Throughout the second half of the twentieth century, Turkish politics continually revolved around heated disputes between competing civilian forces that were often interrupted by military takeovers. After the passions of the moment cooled, the military would return to the barracks until the next time. During this period the military even removed Suleyman Demirel, the seven-time prime minister, from office on two occasions.

In spite of the uneven record of the past, there are now good prospects for democracy in Turkey. A stable political environment is essential if Turkey is to be accepted as a full partner in the economy of post–cold war Europe. That kind of political system appears to be evolving. After the death of Turquit Ozal in 1993, Suleyman Demirel, the Turkish Phoenix, was elected president by the Parliament. Tamsu Ciller was then selected to form a new government, succeeding Demirel as prime minister. She became the first woman in Turkish history to serve as the head of state. The 1996 elections forced moderate politicians to agree to form a coalition government in order to prevent conservative Islamic forces from taking power in Turkey. The fact that the politicians were able to overcome these crises and then proceed to form a new government in a democratic fashion reflected a growing maturity in Turkish politics.

The main stumbling block to the Turkish dream of obtaining full membership in the EC are the issues of Cyprus and the Kurds. Cyprus was invaded by Turkey following a Greek Cypriot overthrow backed by Athens in 1974. The Turkish military victory divided the island between Greek and Turkish Cypriots. The Greek government has threatened to oppose full EC membership for Turkey until the issue of Cyprus is resolved in a more equitable way for the Greeks living on the island.

The "dirty war" against the Kurds has been going on since 1992. Using Iraq and Iran for sanctuary, Kurds have often crossed the border to attack Turkish-controlled areas. These actions have provoked similar responses from the Turkish military. The Kurdish objective is first autonomy and then independence for Kurdistan. At times, this conflict has tied down half of the Turkish army. It is often used by the government to suppress the rights of the minorities in Turkey. Europeans opposed to Turkish entry into the EC point to these government actions as proof that Turkey does not deserve to be given full membership in the community.

Clearly, the geopolitical picture in the area has changed with the end of the cold war. Turkey is not as critical to Western interest as it once was. This new situation may also offer a new flexibility and independence to the Turks. Now Turkey has the opportunity to decide whether it will continue to follow the Western path taken by Ataturk or whether it will again turn toward the East. In the East, there is the lure of Iraq and Iran, once major Turkish trading partners. Perhaps more important for the future, there are also 60 million Turkish-speaking Moslems from the former Soviet Union looking to Turkey for leadership.

IRAN

Like the Ottomans, the Persian Empire (Iran) was an Islamic monarchy, except that Shiite Islam was the state religion. Iranian nationalism developed during Anglo-Russian interventions in Persia in the early days of the twentieth century. The history of nationalism in Iran can be divided into three periods: the reign of the Pahlavis, the Mossadeq crisis, and the Islamic Republic.

The first Pahlavi, Reza Shah, was an army officer who seized power in 1921 and had himself crowned king (Shah) in 1925. His rule lasted from 1925 to 1941. Reza Shah believed that a modern state, like Turkey, could be created in Iran. Although many proposed changes emulated those of Ataturk in Turkey, Iran was far less Westernized and change came slowly. Unlike Ataturk and Lenin, who destroyed the old to create a new system, Reza Shah wrapped himself in the traditions of the old Persian monarchy to establish his legitimacy. In the late 1930s, he indicated a sympathy for Adolph Hitler that provoked a Russian-British-American intervention in Iran once World War II began. Reza Shah was deposed, and with the approval of the Western powers, his young son, Mohammed Reza, was placed in power.

Mohammed Reza's reign was uneventful until the Iranian oil crisis of 1951. At that time, a popular nationalist leader, Mohammed Mossadeq, formed a political organization known as the National Front. He gained control of the government and then nationalized the British-owned Anglo-Iranian Oil Company. The Western oil powers responded by boycotting Iranian oil. Deprived of oil revenue by 1953, the Iranian economy was in such bad shape that the Shah used this crisis to attempt to have Mossadeq removed. The Shah's action failed and he was forced into exile in Switzerland. In one of the most interesting periods in modern history, supporters of the Shah were persuaded—it is now believed, with CIA help—to stage a counterrevolt.[13] Mossadeq's allies failed to respond effectively, and the Shah was returned to power within days. The downfall of Mossadeq ended the rule of one of the only truly popular, secular nationalist leaders in modern Iranian history. Returned to power, the Shah ruled in an increasingly arbitrary manner until he was forced into exile in 1979.

Totally reversing the two millenniums of Iranian monarchy, the Islamic Republic of Iran has represented, at the very least, a temporary victory for the religious nationalists over the secular nationalists of the 1950s. The leaders make effective use of the symbols of Shiite Islam to maintain their authority over the Iranian people. According to the rhetoric of the regime, this movement represents an attempt by Shiism to gain the leadership of the Islamic world. The progress of the Islamic revolutionary model developed by Iran is being watched with interest by many states of the Other World.

Even though many of the Western-trained Iranians who originally supported the downfall of the Shah were displaced by the triumph of the sectarians over the secularists, the Ayatollah Khomeini's successors have broad popular support. For the first time in this century, Iranians feel that they have wrested their future away from the neocolonial influence of the West.

Since the death of the Ayatollah Khomeini, his successors have attempted to keep the Islamic revolution on course while, at the same time, opening the door slightly to outside contacts. Since 1989, Hashimi Rafsanjani has served as president of Iran. During this period, his policies have sought to encourage economic contacts with Western Europe and Russia.

In 1994 the United States attempted to counter this policy by calling on the nations of the world to place an economic embargo on Iran until the Islamic state renounced terrorism. This policy was good politics in the United States but it failed to produce a positive response from the Europeans. The United States had little more success in Russia, where the Yeltsen government was threatened with the cutoff of U.S. aid over the sale of a nuclear reactor to the Iranians. Although the Russians agreed to modify their offer to Iran, the U.S. threat failed to halt the sale. At least in the short term, the Rafsanjani foreign policy was successful because most nations preferred trade with Iran over the restrictive dictates of U.S. foreign policy.

The real test for the long-term success of the Iranian revolution will depend on the ability of the Rafsanjani government to make measurable improvements in the lives of most Iranians. Until now, improvements have remained only promises. Unless some accommodations can be made to improve the living conditions of the average Iranian, the intensity of the Islamic revolution cannot be sustained. Although it is unlikely that Iran will return to the monarchy of the Pahlavis, it is likely that the regime's messianic message will fail in its goal to establish the Islamic republic as the dominant power in the Middle East.

EGYPT

Egyptian nationalism emerged as a reaction to Napoleon's invasion in 1798. The national movement is almost as old as the French Revolution. Experiencing both peaks and valleys during the nineteenth century, nationalists later championed the call to end the British occupation of Egypt that had begun in 1882. In the 1920s a middle-class anti-British political movement called the Wafd emerged to dominate Egyptian politics until the rise of Nasser in 1952.[14]

Probably no man in the history of the modern Middle East has successfully captured the hearts and minds of Other World peoples of all social classes and political philosophies as did Gamal Abdul Nasser. Espousing a militant nationalism of Arab socialism and social reform at home, Nasser also called for independence from foreign domination, opposition to Israel, and Arab unity abroad. He is best remembered by Middle Easterners for his successful challenges to the policies of the United States and the former colonial powers of Western Europe. It is important to note that Nasser's continuing contribution to Egyptian nationalism is symbolic and transcends specific successes or failures of his policies while he was the country's leader. Following Nasser's death in 1970, Anwar al-Sadat assumed control.

Anwar al-Sadat's 11-year rule over Egypt is extolled in the West as an example of what an enlightened Other World nationalist can accomplish. Sadat expelled the Russians in 1972, fought Israel to a standoff in 1973, then went to Jerusalem to begin a process that resulted in the 1979 peace agreement with Israel. Sadat's assassination in 1981 is still viewed in the West as a great setback to peace efforts in the region. Surprisingly, Egyptians rarely discuss the tenure of Sadat. In Egypt, he is considered to have frustrated the cause of Arab unity by stressing the separateness of Egypt and peace with Israel over the greater good of the Arab people. Sadat's virtual surrender of the Egyptian economy to Western investment raised new fears of a return to neocolonial status. The danger of an erosion of independence, whether direct or indirect, has become central to the thinking of many Egyptian nationalists who were opposed to Sadat.

The current president, Hosni Mubarak, has sought to develop a nationalism that steers a middle course between the economic excesses of Sadat and the political adventurism of Nasser. He has also worked hard to end Egypt's isolation in the Arab world. Expelled after the Camp David agreement, Egypt has been restored as a member of the Arab League and the league's headquarters has been returned to Cairo. The Egyptians continue to honor the peace agreement with Israel, have reestablished diplomatic relations with Russia, and remain the closest Arab ally of the United States. The thrust of all of these diplomatic efforts has been aimed at establishing Egypt as a bridge between competing states in the region.

Perhaps Egypt's most disturbing economic problem is corruption in the government. When President Mubarak assumed power, he promised that he would put an end to the corruption that had flourished under Anwar Sadat. There was great hope that through his leadership, conditions in Egypt would improve. Now that he is well into his third term as president, it is clear that the Egyptian government is as corrupt as ever. The standard of living for the average Egyptian continues to decline while the number of millionaires increases dramatically. According to the *Guardian* (a London newspaper), much of this wealth, in the midst of massive poverty, has come through influence peddling in the Mubarak administration.[15] The unfairness of this discrepancy of wealth has encouraged the growth of many Islamic groups dedicated to the goal of cleansing Egyptian society of corruption. The Mubarak response has been to clamp down on all opposition movements in Egypt, which has further increased opposition to his administration.

Of all the states of the Middle East, Egypt is the one that authorities speak of in the most pessimistic terms. Beset by a population explosion that is uncontrollable without using unacceptably draconian measures, no Egyptian government can hope to make significant improvements in the lives of the people in the foreseeable future. Out-of-control population growth renders the government impotent to deal with the problems of a worn-out economy, an inefficient bureaucracy, and a breakdown of almost all services. The question being asked by all who look at Egypt's problems is this: How long will the Egyptian masses wait before turning to more radical solutions to their problems? Since Egypt is the most populous Arab state, the direction that it takes will determine the future of much of the Middle East. Is time for Egypt growing short? Egypt's leaders have many problems and few solutions. The miracle is that Egypt continues to limp on, surviving each gloomy forecast.

THE ARABS

The political scientist Karl Deutsch once said, "A nation is a group of people united by a common dislike of their neighbors and a common misconception about their ethnic origins."[16] If one looks at the spirit of the nation from the perspective of the Arabs, it is clear that Deutsch's observation applies to the Middle East.

A Young Bicyclist Carries a Load of Chairs to Be Sold
in the Cairo Market
SOURCE: Joe Weatherby

Arab nationalism is often characterized as xenophobic, negative in international outlook, and dependent on a historical past that is often more myth than fact. Arabs are suspicious of others because of what they perceive to be more than 200 years of lies and deceit by the colonial powers. Throughout the nineteenth century and well into the twentieth, this pattern repeated itself with cynical regularity. For example, the British promised the Arabs independence during World War I, only to carve up the region into colonial mandates when the war was over. Arab nationalists from Gamal Nasser to Saddam Hussein have seen this event as a treacherous act, ensuring that the Arabs would remain a divided people who could be controlled by outsiders. Many Arab nationalists also see American support for the state of Israel as a fresh attempt to divide and dominate the Arab people.

The history that forms the basis of Arab nationalism is characterized by the gap between aspiration and reality. The aspiration is the reestablishment of a single, united Arab nation similar to that which existed during the early days of Mohammed. The reality is that this kind of unity has never existed. Even during its early days, the Islamic state was characterized by civil wars and assassinations. In modern times, the aspiration has been to free the Arab people from foreign domination. The reality has been a reliance on foreign influence, aid, and military support to accomplish Arab political goals. For example, Arab opposition to Israel caused nationalists to embrace almost any outside power that was perceived as being willing to aid in this effort. The reality of this approach has been to mortgage Arab sovereignty to external obligations. Finally, the aspiration that oil can be used to achieve Arab economic independence has clashed with the reality that Arab oil must be sold to the West for hard currency. Instead of unifying the Arabs, wealth generated by oil has divided rich and poor Arabs across the region.

Although Arab nationalism is a potent force, it has failed to meet the aspirations of those who seek the rebirth of a great, unified Arab nation.

ISRAEL

Israel may be described as a settler state with a European ideology transplanted into the Middle East. This impression may be less true today than it was in the past. Modern Israel is more conservative, militaristic, sectarian, and Middle Eastern than it once was. With U.S. financial aid more important than ever before, Israel reflects many of the same neocolonial fears and suspicions that are found in other Middle Eastern states.

Founded in Basel, Switzerland, in 1897, Zionism is a form of nationalism that calls for the establishment and maintenance of a Jewish state in Palestine. The specifics of this call have been modified to fit the changing needs of the movement. Today, Zionism generally means that the survival of the state of Israel must be guaranteed as a symbol of refuge for Jews everywhere, whether they choose to emigrate or not.

Over the years, two factions of nationalists emerged to contend for power. Those secular nationalists who were interested in the establishment of a modern state with viable borders were represented by the Israeli Labor Alignment. These nationalists included some of the great names of Israeli history—for example, David Ben Gurion, Golda Meir, and Abba Eban. They represented the ideas of the European founders of Israel, and their party alignments dominated the policies of Israel from the nation's founding until 1977.

In 1977, demographic changes in the Israeli population tilted politics in favor of non-European Jews. Continuing Palestinian hostilities combined with the new demographics to create conditions that brought a conservative coalition, called the Likud, to power. The Likud represented the second direction taken by the Zionists. Their view argued for the creation of a "Greater Israel" or a "Promised Land" that would include those portions of the Middle East that tradition held were promised by God to the ancient Hebrews. In recent years, non-European Jews supported the Likud as a way of protesting the "class" system perpetuated by the European- and American-dominated Labor party. Because many non-European Jews had experienced Arab domination, they also tended to support the hard-line policies of Likud vis-à-vis the Arabs.

A major change in the emigration policy of Russia, combined with a new restrictive immigration policy in the United States, sent large numbers of Jewish immigrants to Israel—in 1990, over 187,000 Soviet Jews. This was the highest number of immigrants since 1949 and reversed the situation in which more people were leaving than immigrating to the Jewish state.[17] Since that time, immigration from Russia has again declined. Baruch Gur, of the Jewish Agency, estimated that only about 50,000 Jews would arrive from Russia in 1994.[18] It would seem that immigration is directly related to the success of economic reforms in Russia. As conditions have gradually improved in the Russian cities, the number of people wishing to leave for Israel has declined.

At the present time, it is also unclear how long many of the immigrants can be persuaded to remain. After they have been furnished with passports, these new Israelis will be free to move to Europe and the United States. To hold onto the new arrivals, the Israeli government must do a better job than it has done in the past to create jobs, provide housing, and offer hope for a secure future.

In the 1992 elections, both the Likud and Labor blocs targeted these new immigrants as the variable in the Israeli political picture. Labor was able to broaden its base successfully by attracting the new arrivals in sufficient numbers to become the largest bloc in the parliament. The party campaigned on a promise to negoitate seriously with the Palestinians. Earlier, in 1990, the Likud had forged a coalition of religious and conservative parties, with irredentist claims on the West Bank and Gaza territories, to gain control of the parliament. In a post–1992 election interview, the then-losing Likud leader, Shamir, was quoted as saying that he would have "kept autonomy talks going for 10 years while [he] filled the West Bank with half a million Jewish settlers."[19]

After the 1992 election, the Israeli dilemma remained the same for Labor as it had been for Likud. Should Israel trade land for peace and risk the establishment of a Palestinian state, or should Israel attempt to hold onto everything captured during the 1967 war and face the possibility of an endless conflict with the Arabs? The Labor party opted to move Israel down the road toward peace. On September 13, 1993, Prime Minister Yitzhak Rabin signed an accord with the Palestine Liberation Organization that created an autonomous Palestinian entity in the Gaza Strip and the town of Jericho. On July 25, 1994, Rabin concluded an agreement with King Hussein of Jordan that ended a 46-year state of war between the two nations.

Since the conclusion of these agreements, the movement toward a larger settlement has been slow and erratic, overcoming attempts to derail the process by extremists on both sides. Until recently, Israeli authorities had largely ignored the threats made by Jewish extremists on the fringes of the land of Israel movement. They preferred to focus on the terrorist threat coming from Islamic fundamentalists. However, the November 4, 1995, assassination of the Israeli prime minister, Yitzhak Rabin, forced the government to face the reality of Jewish terrorism directed at stopping the peace process. This assassination made clear to all that there were extremists on both sides who were prepared to do almost anything to break up the momentum for further reconciliation between Jews and Arabs.

In spite of everything, the Labor party seemed to be directed toward achieving three policy objectives. They sought the expansion of a Palestinian entente in the occupied territories, the conclusion of a full peace treaty with Jordan, and the achievement of some kind of settlement for the Golan Heights with Syria. It was only by demonstrating to the Israeli people that peace with the Arabs was productive that the Labor party could remain in power. Whether these objectives could be achieved during a short period was problematical.

The terrorist bombings that occurred throughout Israel during 1996 caused a rise in popular support for the hard-line policies advocated against the Arabs by Likud. In analyzing the surprising Likud victory in the May 1996 elections, two conclusions may be drawn. First, after the terrorist attacks of February 1996, many Israelis did not trust the Arabs to honor their agreements. Second, Israelis were not ready to risk experiencing the real internal divisions that might occur if the Labor-backed peace agreements were fully implemented.

LOOKING AHEAD

> *Trust everybody, but cut the cards.*
> Finley Peter Dunne

As will be seen in the Flashpoints, many of the region's conflicts are indigenous and based on long-standing cultural and geographical factors. On the surface, each of these issues should stand alone. However, in the Middle East, the Arab-Israeli conflict dominates the politics of the region, and the failure of the parties to resolve this dispute has affected most of the other conflicts. The perception is left that the settlement of the Arab-Israeli problem is a precondition to the resolution of other important issues in the region.

What are the prospects for peace? Without a solution to the Arab-Israeli dispute, the old adage that "the more things change, the more they will remain the same" will continue. Two scenarios illustrate the difficulty in attempting to forecast the future for any political issue in the Middle East.

The Pessimistic Scenario

> *It is not the big armies that win battles; it is the good ones.*
> Maurice de Saxe, Marshal-General of France

Without a settlement to the Arab-Israeli dispute, those parties on both sides who prefer the status quo to peace can be expected to continue their present policies. The status quo benefits those Israeli factions who believe that any settlement will force Israel to make concessions in territory. Palestinians are fearful that the Arab states might be willing to sacrifice the Palestinian nation to regain territory previously lost to Israel. Many Arab leaders continue to use their dispute with Israel as an excuse to prepare for war abroad and to avoid reform at home.

If the deadlock continues, Arabs will accelerate the arms race to achieve qualitative military parity with the Israelis. This military development will be achieved at the expense of funds that could be made available for social development. The likely result of this scenario will be the continuation of Arab regimes that are volatile and unstable.

If the Israeli leadership encourages more Jewish settlement in the West Bank and Gaza, the Arabs will resist it with any means available. The continuation of the status quo means that there will be bloodshed on both sides. Because of the destructive capability of modern weaponry, there is always a chance that one of these sharp conflicts will escalate into a major war.

The Optimistic Scenario

> *God willing, there will be peace.*
> A Palestinian expression

The 1991 Persian Gulf war involved hundreds of thousands of American soldiers. In this conflict, the Arab-Israeli dispute was a secondary but important aspect. As Iraqi rockets slammed into Israeli cities, it became obvious to all that the issues in the Middle East were interrelated. This event shattered the complacency of those in America who had wished to avoid direct involvement in the affairs of the Middle East. Badly frightened at the prospect of a new Vietnam, many Americans became active in attempts to eliminate the conditions that could lead to a new American military involvement in the region. The result was that the United States applied pressure on all of the parties involved to force them to negotiate.

The end of the cold war also freed the hands of those leaders in the West who had used the policy of containing communism as a test for dealing with the governments in the Middle East. For the first time, there was agreement that it was in the interest of Russia, the United States, and the other Western powers to encourage a settlement between Arabs and Israelis. The major powers combined with a majority of other states in the world to encourage the parties of the region to talk seriously about peace. This new atmosphere made it possible for people living in the Middle East to hope for a period of peace and stability.

FLASHPOINTS _____

PALESTINE

For the better part of the twentieth century, a central feature of Middle Eastern politics has been the dispute between Jews and Arabs over the control of Palestine. Since 1948, the focus has been on opposition to the state of Israel. As a result of wars fought in 1948, 1956, 1967, 1973, and 1982, peripheral issues have emerged to obstruct movement concerning the future status of Palestine. Unresolved problems that are delaying progress on the main issue include a determination of the status of refugees displaced as a result of each of these wars; the future of Arab Jerusalem; and the status of the West Bank of the Jordan, the Golan Heights, and Gaza. Because there is so little trust, both sides have developed their own hidden agendas. Still, for the first time in many years, there is real hope that progress can be made in resolving some of these issues.

On September 13, 1995, the leader of the Palestine Liberation Organization (PLO), Yasser Arafat, signed an accord with Israel that created the first autonomous entente in Gaza and Jericho. Since that time, discussions aimed at enlarging the entente have moved slowly. A popular story illustrates the Palestinian frustration with the slow pace of peace. A car factory was built in the new entente. When the first car appeared, it had only one gear. When the customer asked why, the car dealer replied, "Why do you want more? Before you can shift into second, you will leave Palestine and be in Israel."

Time is now the enemy of peace. It is necessary for both the Palestinian and Israeli leaders to move rapidly to achieve visible results in their talks. If they fail in this objective, they are likely to be replaced by people less interested in a settlement.

The hard-liners fear that any compromise might prejudice discussion of the main issue, the future of Palestine. This impasse has existed between Arabs and Jews since 1948, when the state of Israel was created. It should be remembered that both sides can cite historical chapter and verse to support their respective positions. The central dispute remains because both Arab and Jewish hard-liners staunchly refuse to acknowledge that the other side's claim in Palestine has any legitimacy. To the outsider, this parochialism is the most frustrating aspect of the Palestinian dispute. The basic elements of the land in dispute are seen in figure 8.2.

THE PALESTINIANS

The Palestinians are an ancient people who trace their origins to the Philistines in the Bible. After the Arab conquest, their sense of national consciousness remained dormant until World War I, when they began again to speak of a Palestinian people. During the negotiations that preceded the creation of the state of Israel, serious proposals were also made in the UN for the creation of a Palestinian state. The UN proposal was rejected by the Arab side. Unfortunately, any further hope for the establishment of a state that would parallel the one created in Israel was lost with the Arab defeat in the 1948 war. Since that time, all the parties to the Arab-Israeli dispute have attempted to manipulate the aspirations of the Palestinians. The PLO claims to represent the interests of the Palestinian people. When the leadership of the PLO agreed to an autonomy agreement, they took a chance that measurable results could be achieved before the opposition to a limited agreement could grow. Many Palestinians, especially those exiled abroad, believed that the current agreement would never lead to Palestinian sovereignty. Furthermore, they charged that limited autonomy permanently surrendered the lands taken from the Palestinian people in 1948. The slow pace of events since the signing of the accord has strengthened the opposition to a settlement with Israel.

The decline of PLO fortunes since 1993 has resulted in the corresponding rise of the Islamic fundamentalist organization Hamas. Unlike the PLO, Hamas was opposed to any peace talks with Israel. By active participation in the Intifada, Hamas earned the respect of many Palestinians. Hamas is a "home grown" organization rising out of the occupied territories. Unlike the PLO, Hamas leaders were not intellectuals imported from the Palestinians living abroad. Furthermore, the Hamas opposition to Israel was clear and uncompromising. To a people forced to live under Israeli military occupation for over a quarter of a century, this hard line struck a responsive chord. Facing Hamas, moderate Palestinians were placed in a no-win position. When they moved to compromise with the Israelis and the West, they weakened their position with the Palestinians they claimed to repre-

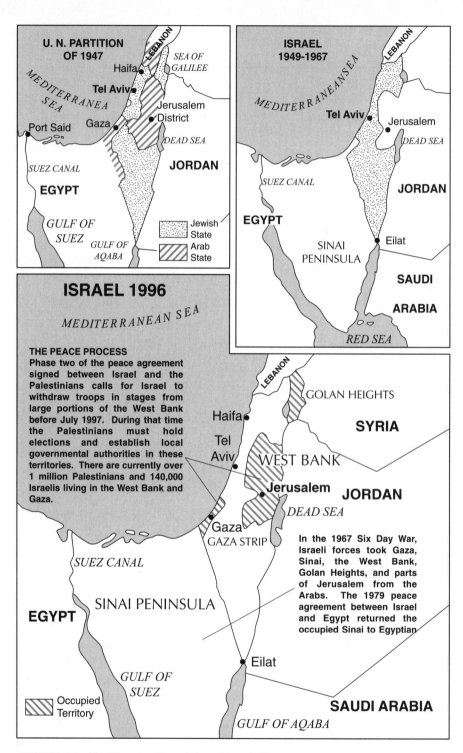

FIGURE 8.2 The Changing Boundaries of Israel. The boundaries of Israel have changed as a result of wars fought with Arab neighbors in 1948, 1956, 1967, and 1973.

sent. To the chagrin of both the PLO and the Israeli authorities, Hamas has been raised to the status of a major player in Palestinian politics.

For their part, the Palestinians have endured a political and social tragedy that colors their politics. The demise of the Soviet Union as the champion of the Palestinian cause has raised fear that a grand peace may be negotiated by the great powers at their expense. By their often violent actions, the Palestinians ensure that their cause will not be ignored. The result is a Palestinian movement that is a potent force everywhere in the Middle East.

THE INTIFADA (UPRISING)

As a result of victory in the 1967 war, Israel gained control of the West Bank and Gaza. Thus, Israel also became responsible for the administration of more than 1.7 million Palestinians. Israeli policy has encouraged Jewish settlement in these territories, which it calls Judea, Samaria, and Gaza, by using the military to control the opposition of the Palestinian majority. The Intifada represents the emergence of an active Palestinian opposition to the continuation of Israeli military rule.

Begun in 1987, the Intifada is a major change in the Palestinian movement, which before then had been controlled and represented by leaders living in exile. Palestinians in the occupied territories had tended to identify with the politics of Jordan. The early leaders of the Intifada were young, militant, and determined to end Israeli rule in the West Bank and Gaza. This uprising shifted Western attention away from the demands of the Palestinians in exile to focus on the necessity of reaching a settlement with those Palestinians who were living under Israeli occupation. The mass appeal of the Intifada undermined the traditional Palestinian leaders in exile by forcing thousands of people to make a visible commitment to the new, local leadership.

Although the violent images of Jews and Arabs confronting each other in the streets of the West Bank and Gaza have dominated television screens around the world, another story is emerging from the Intifada. The vast majority of the Palestinians living in the territories have been mobilized into a mass movement in resistance to Israeli military rule. The ability of the Palestinians to sustain this effort over an extended period of time has forced all parties to take their interests seriously.

Since the 1993 agreement was signed with Israel, the Intifada has moved into a stage of passive resistance to Israeli rule. However, the prospect of renewed violence remains a constant threat to the security of the occupied territories. If the autonomy agreement fails to bring improved conditions for most Palestinians, there could be another explosion like the one in 1987. Any attempts by the Israeli military to return to the harsh policies used in the past could trigger a serious conflict.

ARMENIA

The Armenians trace their history to the period preceding the fourth-century B.C. invasion of Anatolia by Alexander the Great. Armenia is believed to be the oldest Christian state. Since the time of the Romans, it has existed, like Afghanistan and Poland, as a small buffer state surrounded by powerful neighbors. Time after time, Armenians have suffered massacre, partition, and loss of independence. The most recent deprivation occurred during World War I, when it is said that the Ottomans massacred more than a half million Armenians on the pretext that they had sided with the Russians during the war. In the aftermath of World War I, an independent Armenia made up of portions of eastern Turkey and western Russia was proposed by the League of Nations. The revolution in Russia and the independence of Turkey caused this proposal to be stillborn. Today, only an Armenian republic located in the former Soviet Union remains to remind Armenians of a glorious past.

For over 70 years the former Soviet Union maintained tight control over the national aspirations of its people. However, the collapse of Soviet centralized power has revived a spirit of nationalism in the region. The 1988 dispute between Armenia and Azerbaijan over the status of Armenians living in the enclave of Nagorno-Karabakh has been difficult to resolve. In September 1991, Armenian nationalists made the situation worse by attempting to proclaim an independent republic in the enclave. If some of the Armenian nationalists living abroad are to be believed, a resurgent Armenia may also attempt to reassert its old claim to parts of eastern Turkey. Any aspiration to a return to Anatolia is certain to cause unrest in Turkey.

SIX NEW MUSLIM STATES

The end of the Soviet Union resulted in the emergence of six Muslim states. The newly independent states of Azerbaijan, Turkmenistan, Kazakhstan, Uzbekistan, Kyrgyzstan, and Tajikistan have a combined population of 50 million Muslims. Unlike Slavic Russia, which has cultural connections with Europe, the states surrounding the Caspian and Aral seas can be expected to look to the Muslim south and west for leadership.

This new development has the potential to reshape the political balance of power in the Middle East. Both the northern tier states of Turkey and Iran have moved aggressively into the vacuum left by the collapse of Soviet power, and Turkey has granted recognition to all six republics. Since most of these new states are Turkic-speaking, the Turks have a cultural advantage. Turkey is also a good potential outlet for trade with the six republics because of its close ties with Europe.

Iran has been successful in penetrating parts of the region. Iranian Azerbaijan is separated from former Soviet Azerbaijan by an artificial boundary established in 1813 after a war between the two states. The disadvantage of the Iranian thrust is that Shiism is practiced widely only in Azerbaijan, whereas the other five republics are staunchly Sunni.

With the end of the East-West struggle and the emergence of the United States as the region's most important outside power, Arab leaders who had backed the Russian side have now lost their power base. They, too, can be expected to court these non-Arab Muslims with the aim of creating a new Islamic bloc to counter the influence of the United States. The geopolitical implications of the struggle for 50 million Muslims in central Asia will be one of the major aspects of Middle Eastern politics throughout the decade of the 1990s.

KURDISTAN

Living on the borders of eastern Turkey, western Iran, northern Iraq, and Soviet Armenia, the Kurds are a significant problem in the northern tier. Although they number over 20 million, the Kurds have been unsuccessful in their attempts to create the independent state of Kurdistan. The states with large Kurdish populations, Turkey, Iran, and Iraq, will never agree to the creation of a Kurdish state out of their territories. Moreover, the Kurds have been used by these states as pawns in their own conflicts. For example, during the 1970s, anti-Iraqi Kurds were armed and financed by the Shah of Iran to further Iran's ambitions against Iraq. Still earlier, the Russians had supported Kurdish revolts in Iran to cause trouble for the Shah. During recent years, there have been low-intensity conflicts between Kurds and the authorities in Turkey, Iran, and Iraq.

The Kurdish dilemma is that for their dream of independence to be realized, the new state would have to encompass large portions of Syria, Iran, Iraq, and Turkey. Under these conditions, the creation of Kurdistan would destabilize the northern tier. All of the existing powers in the region oppose the creation of an independent Kurdistan.

In the unrest following the Iraqi defeat in the 1991 Persian Gulf war, Kurds failed in an attempt to break away from the government in Baghdad. Only Western military intervention prevented the Iraqi army from destroying much of the Kurdish population. Since that time Kurdish leaders have reduced their goals and now envision the eventual creation of an autonomous Kurdish region in northern Iraq. For the moment, it is in the Western interest to keep the Kurdish region alive as a way of putting pressure on Iraq. When the Western dispute with Iraq is resolved, the Kurds are likely to be abandoned again.

THE IRAQI DISPUTES

Iran.   If it is true, as the old saying goes, that "the bones of the Middle East were buried by the dogs of British imperialism," the Iraq-Iran dispute is a case in point. The border was created as the result of a nineteenth-century mediation by the British that favored the Ottomans over the Persians. The object of this effort was to keep Russia out of the Persian Gulf by giving control of the Shatt al-Arab river to the British-backed Ottomans. Although the Persians objected to the location of the border on the east bank of the river instead of the usually accepted main channel, it was not until 1975 that Iraq, the Ottoman's successor, agreed to use the navigable channel as the border. In return, the Shah of Iran agreed to stop aiding the Kurdish rebellion against Iraq. After the Shah's demise, Iraq unsuccessfully attempted to restore the old border by invading Iran in 1980. The result was one of the more terrible wars in modern history. When the fighting ended, the battle lines were in approximately the same location as the prewar border. To free troops for service in Kuwait in 1990, the Iraqi authorities conceded all of their major war gains to Iran.

Kuwait.   On August 2, 1990, the Iraqi army invaded Kuwait. This event was the latest in a series of disputes between Kuwait and Iraq going back for more than half a century. These disputes were raised by Iraq as challenges to the historical legitimacy of Kuwait.

The history of Kuwait can be traced to the eighteenth century, when the Al Sabah family gained control. This dynasty has remained in power since that time. During the nineteenth century both the Ottomans and the British attempted to influence the Al Sabahs. The Iraqi claims rest on the argument that the Al Sabahs recognized that Kuwait was part of the Ottoman Empire because it was nominally administered from the Iraqi city of Basra. The Iraqis argue that all of the Ottoman Empire that was administered from Basra should be part of Iraq. To them only British intervention during the early years of this century deprived Iraq of Kuwait. During the twentieth century, Kuwait was administered as an independent state under British protection. However, during this period both Saudi Arabia and Iraq claimed parts of its territory.

Although grounded in history, the latest dispute between Iraq and Kuwait was over oil. Because Kuwait controlled the third-largest reserves of crude oil in the world, it was able to influence the world price. The Iraqis charged that Kuwait violated agreements and dumped oil on the world market in order to harm Iraq. Iraq also disputed the Kuwaiti claims to an oil field on the border of the two countries. Finally, Iraq charged that Kuwait had failed to share its oil wealth with the poor Arab states.[20]

This dispute was complicated by the demographics of Kuwait. With the discovery of oil came thousands of foreign workers. Although denied full citizenship, these workers often prospered. By August 1990, there were more foreign workers in Kuwait than Kuwaitis. Many of these workers were employed by the state even though they were treated as second-class citizens. The 1990 invasion was welcomed by many of these "guest" workers because Iraq had promised that they would be given full citizenship by the new government.

The allied coalition forces routed the Iraqi army during the 1991 liberation of Kuwait. This victory invalidated most Iraqi claims. In the aftermath of the war, Kuwaiti authorities expelled large numbers of the foreign workers. By using these harsh methods, the authorities attempted to reduce the danger that guest workers might again threaten the stability of the regime.[21]

After years of UN-imposed economic sanctions, restrictions on oil sales, and international scrutiny of their every move, the Iraqi authorities remained defiant. They disputed the UN-imposed border settlement, they attempted to frustrate the work of the UN teams sent to destroy the Iraqi weapons of mass destruction, and they reasserted the Iraqi claim to Kuwait. Although these actions provoked occasional military responses, the Iraqi authorities gambled that their sustained pressure on the coalition would eventually force the UN forces to end their sanctions and withdraw from the Persian Gulf region.

Kuwait is a very rich, small nation located in a region noted for poverty. Arab nationalists charge that it has been used as an outpost of Western imperialism. Appealing to the poor of the Middle East, the Iraqis charge that the oil wealth of the Persian Gulf has been stolen from the Arab nations by Kuwait. To many, the massive military response mounted by the United States against the Iraqi invasion confirms the charge that Kuwait is still a colony of the West.

STRATEGIC WATERWAYS AND OIL PIPELINES

The Turkish Straits.   The Dardanelles and Bosporus are narrow straits, 1 to 4 miles wide, that dominate the Russian-controlled Black Sea. The straits have been a point of conflict between Russia and Turkey for centuries. The continued Turkish control of the Dardanelles and Bosporus is a source of irritation because it has frustrated repeated Russian attempts to gain easy access to the Mediterranean Sea. At the present time, Russian access to this area is governed by treaty. Should the Turks again attempt to block access they will provoke a major international incident.

The Suez Canal.   Opened in 1869, the canal, including the Great Bitter Lake and Lake Timsah, is 101 miles long. It serves as the only direct sea passage from the Mediterranean to the Indian Ocean. Much of the history of the modern Middle East has involved struggles for the control of this strategic waterway. Although the canal is at sea level and therefore requires no complicated, easily sabotaged system of locks, its location near unstable, hostile neighbors makes its access uncertain at times. For example, in the summer of 1984, an unknown terrorist organization was able to mine parts of the canal and the Red Sea to prevent ships from using the waterway. Because of its importance to Europe, threats to close the Suez Canal always raise the possibility of conflict.

The Persian (or Arab) Gulf.   The question over name implies a more serious conflict over control of the single most important waterway in the world. It is through the Persian Gulf (Arab Gulf) that two-thirds of the world's oil is exported. The conflict between Kuwait and Iraq raises the possibility of seizure of the Straits of Hormuz by an unfriendly power bent on shutting off oil shipments to the West. Because the United States is committed to keeping the oil flowing from the gulf, any closure will immediately provoke a great-power intervention, with all of its dangers.

Oil Pipelines.   One of the major problems associated with Middle Eastern oil is getting the product to the consumer. Pipelines are an efficient alternative to ships for the movement of petroleum products from the Persian Gulf and Saudi Arabia to Europe. For a number of years, some pipelines have connected Saudi Arabia with Lebanon and Israel, and others have linked Iraq with the Mediterranean through both Syria and Turkey. The chief problem of relying on pipelines is their vulnerability to sabotage during the periods of political instability that often occur in the lands they must cross. For example, the pipeline through Israel has been closed since 1948, and the pipeline from Iraq to the Mediterranean was closed by Syria for the duration of the Iran-Iraq war. Until the political situation in the Middle East changes, the potential of moving oil by pipeline will remain an unfulfilled dream.

CYPRUS

Although Greeks outnumber the Turks on Cyprus by a ratio of five to one, mainland Greeks have not formally controlled the island in modern history. From 1571 until 1878, the Ottomans ruled Cyprus as part of their empire. Power then shifted to the British, who stayed until independence was granted in 1960. Attempts were made to establish a Cypriot government that would guarantee a balance of power between Greeks and Turks on the island. This effort finally failed when Greek Cypriot nationalists attempted to move Cyprus into an association with Greece against the will of the Turkish minority. This move provoked the Turkish army's intervention and resulted in a forcible partition of the island in 1974.

During the intervention, 180,000 Greeks fled south and 80,000 Turks fled north. These mass population exchanges caused much bitterness. Since then an additional 60,000 mainland Turks have been resettled in the north by the Turkish government. The unilateral actions by Turkey have caused an open dispute between Greece and Turkey that still threatens the unity of Europe's southern flank.

OPEC AND THE POLITICS OF OIL

In 1901, a Western adventurer, William D'Arcy, received a concession to explore for oil in Iran. At almost the same time, an Armenian, C. S. Gulbenkian, obtained a similar concession in the Ottoman Empire. Less than 50 years later, these concessions had grown into a vast oil cartel controlled by seven Western companies: Exxon, Mobil, Standard Oil of California, Texaco, Gulf, British Petroleum, and Shell. Called the Seven Sisters, these companies gained a virtual monopoly on the production, refinement, and distribution of Middle Eastern oil.

Designed to present a united front when negotiating prices with the oil companies, the Organization of Petroleum Exporting Countries (OPEC) was organized in 1960 by Iraq, Saudi Arabia, Iran, Kuwait, and Venezuela. Subsequently, OPEC membership grew to include Qatar, Libya, Indonesia, Algeria, Nigeria, Ecuador, Gabon, and the United Arab Emirates.

The OPEC cartel was only marginally effective until the October 1973 Middle East war. At that time, the sale of petroleum products was linked by the Arab members of OPEC to the support for their cause against Israel. The selective withholding of oil caused an energy crisis in the West. During the next decade, OPEC oil rose from a pre-1973 price of around $3 a barrel to over $30 a barrel. This oil shock was difficult for the developed world, but it destroyed the hopes for many Other World states that were depending on low-cost energy to finance development. Ignoring 50 years of Western oil cartel exploitation, newspapers in Europe and the United States were filled with articles editorializing on the "evils" of OPEC. Today, more than 20 years after the first oil crisis in the 1970s, Western observers admit that although the economic impact of OPEC has been considerable, it is a political force in the Other World far out of proportion to its size.

In the mid-1980s, OPEC control of the petroleum market loosened. Some members failed to adhere to the cartel's price and production guidelines. The lack of discipline has combined with non-OPEC production increases and Western conservation measures first to stabilize and then to lower dramatically the world price of oil. As the price fell, states desperate to finance the high cost of development became suspicious of other states that exceeded their production quotas. The Iraqi charge that Kuwait cheated on oil production was one of the main reasons for the August 1990 invasion.

The market for oil is in the developed world. As in the days of colonialism, the developed countries will aggressively work to protect such essential resources. Political instability in the Middle East has forced the developed nations to seek alternative sources of energy. With the end of the cold war, there are interesting possibilities for importing oil from Russia. In the short term, there may be more difficulties in utilizing Russian oil sources than possibilities, but vast oil reserves exist in Siberia and the Russians will have to sell a portion on the open market if they have any hope of financing their economic development. If this possibility becomes a reality, it will have serious implications for every state in the region. Like Haiti with sugar and Brazil with rubber, Middle Eastern oil could become just another surplus commodity that is a victim of production elsewhere.[22]

THE 1994 CIVIL WAR IN YEMEN

To the surprise of many observers, former Marxist South Yemen and conservative North Yemen elected to merge and form one state on May 22, 1990. It was hoped that this action would end the years of tense relations between the two countries.

This stormy union lasted until the spring of 1994, when fighting between the rival military units broke out near the city of Sana. During that conflict, both parties conducted air attacks on the oil fields of the country. By mid-June, the northern forces had pushed to the outskirts of the southern capital of Aden. On July 7, the southern leaders went into exile, and the two-month-old civil war ended.

Although the government was able to restore quickly Yemen's oil production to prewar levels, many Western investors were badly frightened by the conflict. Major companies, including British Petroleum, announced plans to pull out of Yemen. The lesson to be learned here is that when there are many sources of oil outside of the Middle East, buyers may look to the development of more stable sources of petroleum elsewhere.

THE ALGERIAN DISPUTE

The rise of Islamic fundamentalism in Algeria has attracted the attention of the West. The problem originated when the secular nationalists, who had ruled Algeria since independence, prevented an Islamic party that appeared to have come to power after the 1992 elections from taking office. Although they had sought power democratically, the Islamic party's slogan had claimed that Muslims voting against them were voting against God. The secular nationalists charged that this kind of campaigning was unfair and justified cancellation of the election results, which provoked an unofficial civil war between the Muslim parties and the secular nationalists. This conflict has killed more than 20,000 people since 1992.

Why have the democratic powers, including the United States and the members of NATO, remained passive in the face of this antidemocratic action taken by the Algerian authorities? This ambivalence is compounded by a similar failure in dealing with the authoritarian rulers in Kuwait, Saudi Arabia, and Egypt. The answer is clear: Western leaders fear that a militant Islamic victory in Algeria can destabilize the friends of the West, not only in Algeria, but also in Morocco, Tunisia, and Egypt. They fear that the West will have to face a militant Islamic threat in North Africa similar to the one that Iran has presented to them in the Persian Gulf and eastern Mediterranean.

Furthermore, an Islamic victory in North Africa could cause a flight of thousands of Moroccan Algerians and Egyptians to the states of southern Europe already shaken by the dispute between Muslims and Christians in Bosnia. Europeans often cite the 1993 prediction by the political scientist Samuel Huntington, who warned that future conflicts in the world would not be over economics or ideology but would be cultural disputes like the current one in Algeria. Large numbers of Muslims moving into Spain, France, and Italy could cause serious internal tensions in those states.

If situations like the one in Algeria are to be effectively handled, the West must learn that Islam is no more monolithic than is Christianity. The Islamic movements in Iran, the West Bank, Egypt, Libya, and Algeria have little in common except broad general principles. They all support the idea of special roles for men and women, oppose secular nationalism imported from the West, reject Western cultural imperialism, and generally support a form of economic populism that aids the poor through the institution of the Mosque. There is little or no common political agenda that crosses state boundaries. It is a mistake for the West to assume that every Moslem in politics is trying to start another Iranian revolution.

Western leaders must learn to stick to the principles that they believe in regardless of who wins an election. To sacrifice support for the values of freedom and democracy abroad to achieve a short-term political goal will ultimately work against Western interests in the Other World. In the case of Algeria, this short-sighted action has actually strengthened popular support for the Islamic militants to the point that they could eventually become a threat to the security of southern Europe.

THE OIL FIRES OF KUWAIT: AN ENVIRONMENTAL DISASTER OF EPIC PROPORTIONS

Using a long-standing border dispute as a pretext, the armed forces of Iraq overran Kuwait on August 2, 1990. It was February 27, 1991, before Kuwait was finally liberated by the allied coalition forces. During the short, brutal Iraqi occupation of Kuwait, much of the physical infrastructure was destroyed or stolen. The Iraqi army looted the hotels, office buildings, apartments, and museums. They killed the animals in the Kuwait zoo. They stole, wrecked, or dismantled thousands of cars, trucks, and buses in Kuwait.

At the end of the hundred-hour allied attack that annihilated their army, the Iraqi leaders gave the order to destroy the oil fields of Kuwait. This order set in motion a series of events that was to create one of the greatest ecological disasters in human history, one that has had a negative effect on people living throughout the Gulf region. By the time they had finished their work, Iraqi engineers had blown up over 750 high-pressure oil wells. Of these, almost 650 were on fire when the allied forces arrived. The rest were throwing thousands of barrels of crude oil onto the surface of the desert. Smoke and ash climbed thousands of feet into the air, depositing their deadly cargo across large portions of the region. Lakes of crude oil spread out, polluting the desert for miles.

Fire-fighting experts were called into Kuwait from all over the world to deal with the problem. There were large contingents of firefighters from the United States, the United Kingdom, Canada, Russia, China, France, Iran, Hungary, Rumania, and Argentina. No one had ever faced an oil-field disaster of this size. First, there were the millions of Iraqi mines and unexploded allied shells that had to be cleared before fire fighting could begin. This task was completed by British and French explosive experts. Then there were the oil fires themselves. No two fires were alike: Some were in the middle of burning lakes, and others had exploded below the surface of the desert. To everyone's surprise, the multinational effort achieved rapid results. By September, 375 wells were under control. Although experts had predicted that the fire-fighting effort might take up to five years to complete, the last well was capped on November 6, 1992.

Almost immediately after liberation, the cleanup and assessment of the environmental damage was begun by Kuwait's environmental protection bodies. Their task was twofold: first, to get the wells back into production, and then to clean up the area. What they found was that most of the wells were either destroyed or damaged. Approximately 22 million barrels of crude oil were spilled on the surface of the desert in the form of lakes.

The experts were able to get oil production back to prewar levels within a year. They also recovered and recycled 19 million barrels of crude out of the desert oil lakes. What has remained has been more difficult to correct in a short time. Cleanup authorities estimate that every resident of Kuwait has suffered long-term damage from breathing polluted air and drinking contaminated groundwater. What remains from the oil lakes is a 6-foot thick, tarlike sludge that may cover as much as 10 percent of the Kuwaiti desert. The war destroyed much of the desert groundcover, causing the buildup of sand dunes in areas where they never existed and leading to increased sandstorms. Even the fish in some areas of the Persian Gulf may no longer be eaten.

The Kuwaiti authorities expect to spend billions of dollars before the cleanup is completed. New and as yet untried technologies are being employed in this effort. One of the most promising involves a joint effort betweeen the Kuwaitis and the Japanese to employ biological technology to treat the sludge from the old oil lakes. It is hoped that this approach will reduce the level of pollution that still exists in the desert areas. However, it will be many years before the air, land, and water can be restored to anything like the state they were in prior to August 1990. The question to be asked is this: What can humankind learn from the experience of the disaster in Kuwait? The answer is simple. Environmentally, we live in an interrelated world. Even in wartime, this geographical fact of life cannot be ignored. Whether through the use of nuclear or biological weapons, or simple explosives to blow up oil fields, humans have the potential to set in motion a chain of events that can have a negative impact on everyone.[23]

SUMMARY

Geographically, the Middle East and North Africa may be divided into three distinct regions: the plains of North Africa and Arabia, the Fertile Crescent, and the northern tier. The Middle East is an area of contrast, including some of the world's most famous deserts, mountain ranges, and rivers. Oil is the most important natural resource of the region. A scarcity of water limits agricultural development throughout most of the Middle East. The monotheistic religions Judaism, Christianity, and Islam have developed in the Middle East. Today, Islam is the professed religion of 90 percent of the population. Most political activity in this part of the Other World is affected by religion.

Nationalism is a second feature of Middle Eastern politics. Case studies in this chapter describe the various forms of nationalism that have developed in Turkey, Iran, Egypt, and Israel. A brief description of Arab nationalism is also included. These case studies illustrate the directions that nationalists have taken in this part of the Other World.

NOTES

1. Madeline Miller and J. Lane Miller, *Harpers Bible Dictionary* (New York: Harper & Row, 1973), p. 688.
2. Population sources: U.S. Department of State, *UN Statistical Yearbook*, and *UN Demographic Yearbook*.
3. For more information on the politics of water, see Adam Kelliher, "Thrust for Peace Is on Water," *Times* (London), August 3, 1991, p. 6.
4. Lawrence Ziring, *The Middle East Political Dictionary* (Santa Barbara, Cal.: ABC-CLIO Information Services, 1983), p. 415.
5. Lord Kinross, *The Ottoman Centuries* (New York: Morrow Quill, 1977), p. 85.
6. For more information on the Pentecostal Holiness Church, see Ed Housewright, "Faith on a Deadly Scale," *San Francisco Examiner*, March 12, 1995, p. A8.
7. The Ka'bah is a cubelike building located in the courtyard of the Great Mosque in Mecca. According to Muslim tradition, it was the first house of worship built by the prophet Abraham.

8. A. M. Khattab, *A Brief Introduction to Islam* (Perryberg, Oh.: Islamic Center of Greater Toledo, 1983), p. 5.

9. Mark Anderson, Robert Seibert, and Jon Wagner, *The Politics of Change in the Middle East: Sources of Conflict and Accommodation* (Englewood Cliffs, N.J.: Prentice Hall, 1993).

10. For more information on fundamentalist Islamic movements, see the Flashpoints on the Palestinians and on Algeria in this chapter.

11. For pre-1991 Gulf War petroleum export figures, see Richard Teitelbaum, "Where Do We Go from Here," *Fortune*, September 1990, p. 30.

12. Edward Mortimer and Michael Field, "Nationalism, the Steel of the Arab Soul," *Financial Times* (London), August 18/19, 1990, sect. 11.

13. Although never officially acknowledged by the U.S. government, there is little doubt about the CIA involvement in this episode. See Kermit Roosevelt, *Countercoup: The Struggle for the Control of Iran* (New York: McGraw-Hill, 1979), chaps. 11, 12, 13; and R. G. Grant, *MI 5, MI 6: Britain's Security and Secret Intelligence Services* (New York: Gallery Books, 1989), pp. 113–114.

14. Shortly after the end of World War I, nationalists formed the Egyptian Delegation (Wafd al-Misri) to pressure Great Britain for independence. This group eventually became the Wafd party.

15. David Hirst, "Poised between Control and Chaos," *Guardian* (London), February 11, 1995.

16. Mortimer and Field, "Nationalism."

17. "1990 Influx of Immigrants to Israel Largest Since 1949," *Los Angeles Times*, December 25, 1990, p. A21.

18. David Makovsky, "Rabin: If Russian aliya continues to drop, funding will be reassessed," *The Jerusalem Post*, April 29, 1994, p. 12.

19. Clyde Haberman, "Rabin Drops Call for Years Settlement Freeze," *International Herald Tribune* (London), July 1, 1992, p. 4.

20. This charge is countered by Kuwaiti officials who point out that during the last 20 years general assistance aid exceeded $17 billion, or 6 percent of the GNP of Kuwait. This percentage is many times greater than that of any other nation during this period. See Michael Kramer, "Toward a New Kuwait," *Time*, 136, 27 (December 24, 1990): 26–33.

21. For an account of the British-American activities during the 1991 Persian Gulf war, see John Witherow and Aidan Sullivan, *The Sunday Times: War in the Gulf* (London: Sidgwick & Jackson, 1991).

22. Theoretically, the new Siberian wells will enable oil production to be increased dramatically within the next few years. In spite of domestic needs, the Russians will have to export a large portion of their production for hard currency that will pay for the machines they need to modernize at home. For an account of joint energy ventures with the West in the former Soviet Union, see "Waiting for the Soviet Dust to Settle," *Dallas Morning News*, August 27, 1991, sect. D; and Elizabeth Shogren, "U.S.-Soviet Drilling Venture Untaps Siberian Black Gold," *Los Angeles Times*, October 13, 1991. For other accounts of competition for OPEC see Gregg Jones, "OPEC Says Rivals Are Acting Piggishly; Massive Output Hurts Prices Cartel Contends," *Dallas Morning News*, November 25, 1995, sect. F, p. 1; and Gregg Jones, "OPEC Nations Struggle with Waning Influence; Role Shifts as Group Turns More Diplomatic," *Dallas Morning News*, November 26, 1995, p. 1.

23. For an account of the status of the oil industry's recovery in Kuwait, see Peter Kemp, "No Smoke, but There Is Fire in the Market: Kuwait's Petroleum Industry," Special Report: Oil and Gas Industry Overview, *Middle East Economic Digest*, 38, 29 (July 22, 1994): 11 (ISSN 0047-7230).

FOR FURTHER READING

Badeau, John. *The Middle East Remembered*. Washington, D.C.: Middle East Institute, 1983.

Bar-Siman-Tov, Yaacov. *Israel and the Peace Process, 1977–1982: In Search of Legitimacy for Peace*. Albany, N.Y.: State University of New York, 1994.

Evron, Yair. *Israel's Nuclear Dilemma*. Ithaca, N.Y.: Cornell University Press, 1994.

Fernea, Elizabeth. *Guest of the Sheik: An Ethnography of an Iraqi Village*. Garden City, N.Y.: Anchor Books, 1965.

Fromkin, David. *A Peace to End All Peace: Creating the Modern Middle East 1914–1922*. New York: Henry Holt, 1989.

Hazelton, Fran, ed. *Iraq since the Gulf War: Prospects for Democracy*. London: Zed Books, 1994.

Hourani, Albert. *A History of the Arab Peoples*. Cambridge, Mass.: Belknap Press, 1991.

Kamen, Charles. *Little Common Ground: Arab Agriculture and Jewish Settlement in Palestine 1920–1948*. Pittsburgh: Pennsylvania University Press, 1991.

Lacey, Robert. *The Kingdom: Arabia and the House of Saud*. New York: Avon Books, 1981.

Mahler, Gregory. *Israel: Government and Politics in a Maturing State*. New York: Harcourt Brace Jovanovich, 1990.

Mango, Andrew. *Turkey: The Challenge of a New Role*. New York: Praeger, 1994.

The Middle East. 7th ed. Washington, D.C.: Congressional Quarterly, 1990.

Nutting, Anthony. *The Arabs: A Narrative History from Mohammed to the Present*. New York: Mentor Books, 1964.

Peretz, Don. *Intifada: The Palestinian Uprising*. Boulder, Col.: Westview Press, 1990.

Roskin, Michael, and Berry, Nicholas. *IR: The New World of International Relations*. chaps. 8, 9, and 14. Englewood Cliffs, N.J.: Prentice Hall, 1993.

Rubinstein, Alvin. *The Arab-Israeli Conflict: Perspectives*. 2nd ed. New York: HarperCollins, 1991.

Sahliyeh, Emile. *In Search of Leadership: West Bank Politics since 1967*. Washington, D.C.: Brookings Institution, 1988.

Shalev, Aryeh. *Israel and Syria: Peace and Security on the Golan*. Boulder, Col.: Westview Press, 1994.

Shipler, David. *Arab and Jew: Wounded Spirits in the Promised Land*. New York: Penguin Books, 1987.

Singerman, Diane. *Avenues of Participation: Family, Politics, and Networks in Urban Quarters of Cairo*. Princeton, N.J.: Princeton University Press, 1995.

Smith, Charles. *Palestine and the Arab-Israeli Conflict*. New York: St. Martin's Press, 1992.

Wright, Robin. *In the Name of God: The Khomeini Decade*. New York: Simon & Schuster, 1989.

Yapp, M. *The Near East since the First World War*. White Plains, N.Y.: Longman, 1991.

Zangeneh, Hamid, ed. *Islam, Iran and World Stability*. New York: St. Martin's Press, 1994.

CHAPTER 9

Prospects for the Future

Randal L. Cruikshanks and Earl D. Huff

If you aim at the stars, you will not lose your direction.
Proverb

In this concluding chapter, we will review the themes that were developed in the preceding chapters and discuss issues that need to be addressed by the global community. We will also assess the possible impact on the Other World of the momentous changes that are occurring in the global community. Finally, we will speculate on the future of the Other World as it enters the twenty-first century.

CROSSROADS 2000: THE OTHER WORLD IN THE TWENTY-FIRST CENTURY[1]

Three themes—which should be placed in the context of the policy decisions Other World countries must confront—emerge from the preceding chapters: (1) overcoming the effects of colonialism, (2) coping with population and food problems, and (3) managing conflict. A fourth—social issues such as race, gender, and religion—looms on the near horizon. The resolution of these issues requires peoples and governments to deal with their problems independently or to opt for cooperative efforts through regional and/or global organizations. Decisions will be made either by action or inaction, and no government can afford to adopt a fatalistic "what will be, will be" attitude. Clearly, the impact of these problems on the future of the Other World will be of major importance to us all.

The Legacy of Colonialism

The legacy of colonialism continues to frustrate the development efforts of Other World countries. When Britain, France, Germany, and other European powers granted independence to their former colonies, state boundaries were established, but no sense of national unity existed. The political institutions left behind were based on European models created for the convenience of the colonial rulers. The existing economic structures were geared to the exportation of goods needed by the mother country, not to internal and sustainable economic development.

Today, several decades after independence, most Other World countries still have inadequate infrastructures; low literacy rates; inadequate housing, education, and health facilities; and divisions along caste, tribal, ethnic, religious, and linguistic lines. Many have economies that were once ascending but now are in decline.

Other World countries responded to colonialism with nationalistic movements united to win independence from foreign exploiters. Sometimes these efforts came early and were successful without prolonged conflict, such as in much of Latin America. For others, the end of World War II marked the close of colonial occupation; foreign flags were lowered from colonial capitals and independence was declared. Still others have continued to fight wars of national liberation that persist today.

Nationalism is a double-edged sword. On the one hand, it can foster national unity by linking the people and culture to the state. On the other hand, it can promote differences between groups and lead to conflict over power and control, as in the former Yugoslavia during the 1990s. Nationalism is a social and psychological force, a development of unity and loyalty to the nation and state that cannot be simply proclaimed or stopped by a leader. Nationalism as it is understood in the West has yet to take firm root in many Other World countries, contributing to chronic political instability in much of Asia, Africa, and the Middle East.

The democratic processes of Western states are often unworkable in Other World countries, where the people remain fragmented, poorly educated, and more concerned about the daily requirements of living than the good of the state. In some cases, these processes are consciously rejected in favor of traditional, nonsecular approaches. In any case, many ex-colonies were ill prepared to continue where their colonial "masters" left off. When the British left India, a bureaucracy had been established that included many Indians. However, most other countries were not so lucky, having few if any educated and experienced nationals to assume leadership roles.

In parts of the Other World, the military is viewed as the only institution capable of maintaining public order and serving as a vehicle either for or against change. Although this belief conflicts with Western democratic tradition, the military is sometimes the only force with the technical training, organizational ability, and unity to govern. Furthermore, Other World peoples often view the military as both heroic and modern, whereas civilian society reflects the discredited values of a colonial heritage. For example, the military was used as a force for change by Nasser in Egypt and by the government of Turkey during the 1970s. The Other World is in a state of transition, development, and change at a pace that is unprecedented. Loyalty to existing states has yet to develop. Elsewhere, competing nationalistic movements feed on one another, threatening to disrupt society. A pattern has emerged that has been repeated in many Other World countries: Colonial status leads to nationalistic movements to repel the colonizers; independence follows, then a period of increasing internal instability that results in civil war; eventually, a government emerges to restore at least partial order, by force if necessary. Often the cycle is repeated. In recent decades, most civil wars have involved assistance from outside states and served as proxies in the global contest between the former Soviet Union and the United States. Resulting conditions were often detrimental to individual citizens if not to the survival of their governments.

The new states are striving for national development and acceptance in the international political and economic community. International governmental organizations such as the Organization of African Unity, the Association of Southeast Asian Nations, the Arab League, and the Economic Community of West African States were created to facilitate regional cooperation and mutual development. A major goal of these and other international organizations is to maximize the economic power of Other World countries as one means of lessening the economic effects of neocolonial practices and fragmentation.

Finally, although the future political organization of the Other World is unclear, the status quo is under attack. Present boundaries and political alignments are inadequate to meet the problems on the horizon in the coming century. Perhaps a rearrangement of priorities will lead to political organizations in the twenty-first century that would be totally unrecognizable to those observing this part of the world today. Only time will tell.

Food and Population

Perhaps the most formidable obstacle facing the Other World is population growth. The population explosion has many corollaries—the need for food, shelter, employment, and educational and health services. There are some hopeful signs that the rate of population growth in some Other World countries may be checked or lowered by the end of this century. However, in the poorest countries such optimism fails. Even with a lower birthrate, the population of Other World countries will continue to climb because there are so many young women of childbearing age.

The policy choice most Other World governments have to confront is whether to allow population growth to continue unabated and face the resulting social, economic, and political turmoil or to impose the types of population-planning programs discussed earlier. If governments are unable to lower birthrates through voluntary programs, more stringent interventions may occur, including forced abortions, infanticide, and the Chinese policy of one-child families.

The population explosion is a symptom of underdevelopment. As educational levels and economic development increase, population growth declines. Nevertheless, Other World food production must increase to meet the requirements of their people and generate needed revenue. This is a difficult task, especially for indebted countries, which often export food for hard currencies, leaving their own producers hungry. As one Brazilian said to the author, "Bakers' children go hungry in this country."

A corollary of the population problem in the Other World is the dramatic increase in the number of refugees and displaced persons over the past decade or so. It is true that some refugees are the result of war or other conflict, but many, such as those in Somalia, Ethiopia, or the Sudan, have sought food and refuge from drought or famine, either natural or man-made. Some, as in Bangladesh, have become refugees in their own country, and none has much basis for hope.

The food production problem in many Other World countries is not one of scarcity of land but rather unfavorable climate and the lack of water, resources, and technology to make the land productive. Primitive farming methods, particularly slash and burn, deplete the land's minerals and nutrients. Cutting wood for fuel or forests for pastures and overgrazing by domesticated animals rob the land of the groundcover needed to retain the rain, if it falls. Desertification increases. Such practices can be changed, but changes occur slowly if at all. Moreover, it is traditional and simply more profitable in some countries, such as Colombia or Myanmar (Burma), to grow marijuana, opium, or hashish rather than food crops.

One feature of the underdevelopment in the Other World is the absence of effective agricultural planning at any level. What agricultural planning does occur is done by government ministries that have little knowledge of the realities faced by peasants in the rural areas. The problem is to put expertise to practical use in the field. As one observer notes, "The ability of peasant farmers to learn how to use new technology is not in question. But the institutional apparatus for teaching them is in short supply throughout the developing world."[2] While countries are developing institutional means to bolster food production, they are also sending students to study modern agricultural techniques in the more developed countries.

What are the choices for these countries regarding food production? International assistance programs sponsored by the UN, the World Bank, and the U.S. Agency for International Development have proven successful in some instances. In central Java, Indonesia, malnutrition was high until the 1970s, when a new breed of goats was introduced that produces four times the amount of milk as the traditional breed. Fish farming was increased and the cultivation of fresh vegetables encouraged. In parts of Tanzania, new high-yield strains of rice are being sown, and in Sri Lanka the increased cultivation of soybeans and the development of new soy products have resulted in an increase in the daily consumption of calories and proteins.[3]

One of the most interesting developments of the 1980s was the green revolution—the explosion of food production capacity—in some Other World countries. Using chemical fertilizers and genetic engineering technology, such countries as India have been able to increase food *production* dramatically, to the extent that net production is theoretically capable of eventually supporting all of the food needs of that country's 900 million people. Unfortunately, this development left a sizable proportion of the population still undernourished. Why? It turns out that production is a necessary but insufficient condition for nutritional well-being. The new relative abundance of many foods is not enough; it is also necessary to integrate people into the money economy so that they can purchase goods. People at the subsistence level do not have surplus cash to participate in the marketplace. There is another problem. Even if there are food and consumers with cash to buy, there must also be an elaborate *infrastructure* that successfully sees goods from the point of production through storage and distribution to the point of sale. This requires warehouses; refrigeration; transportation, including roads, rails, or canals; and market outlets. Lacking these elements, there is often significant loss of otherwise consumable products, with consequent malnutrition and starvation. Although agricultural and other technologies have tremendous potential, other social, political, and economic factors also play a major role—a fact often overlooked by international aid agencies, whether public or private.

In addition to outside intervention by aid programs, Other World governments themselves will have to intervene with policies for managing agricultural land. If landowners who grow export crops are unwilling to convert to domestic food crops, governments will have to find ways to encourage this change. For example, village agricultural centers could be established where farmers can obtain supplies and expertise and share equipment to maximize production. Above all, farmers have to be convinced that changing their agricultural practices will raise their standard of living, as well as that of their neighbors.

It must be noted that there is considerable controversy about food aid. Food aid is a Band-Aid measure that satisfies the consciences of the donors and the immediate physical needs of the recipients but decisively does *not* provide permanent solutions. On the contrary, it can simply postpone the victims' agony unless there is a commitment to developing sustainable solutions that will accommodate the recipients long after the donors have moved on. Rightly or wrongly, this criticism was made of such efforts as Geldof's Live Aid rock festival in London in 1985. It was also a major consideration in the U.S.-led effort to aid Somalia in 1992, where local farmers could not sell food to people who could get it free from aid agencies just down the street.

Conflict

The twentieth century has taught many lessons, some of which have been learned better than others. Among the most important is that conflict is a fact of life; violence and war do not resolve it, and militarism is its most frequent corollary. The world must be collectively attentive to the fact that domestic and international conflict may intensify despite the euphoria of the post–cold war. Only the theaters of conflict have changed, along with the drastic decrease in the possibility of a confrontation between the West and the remnants of the former Soviet Union—at least for now.

Many conflicts that ushered in the twentieth century are just now in the process of being addressed, and others, long suppressed, are being unleashed. Two world wars only postponed the resolution of some major international conflicts, as did the post–World War II "balance of terror" between East and West. The dam broke in 1989–1990, severely burdening barely tested or trusted mechanisms of conflict management that were unready to assume the role that had been performed by war and nuclear stalemate.

Just as before the cold war, the world is now confronted with two options in approaching these conflicts: (1) cooperation within the framework of international institutions or (2) unilateral coercive (military) action within and between countries. The major powers seem to be gravitating toward the UN and other international bodies as centralized structures within which to confront politically and resolve old conflicts, but recent experience reveals that agreement on what course to take is difficult. Other World countries, however, may now be more prone to take matters into their own hands in both domestic and international or regional conflicts. Their problems, too, were checked by the East-West stalemate and are now being redefined in ways that appear decidedly disadvantageous from their perspective. Bolstered by inexperience, lack of interest by the major powers, and growing frustration, they will no longer be restrained.

Whereas the world was approaching the crossroads when this book first appeared in 1987, it is now in the intersection—and there are no traffic lights to regulate the gush of grievances thundering toward collision. For anyone, anywhere, to adopt a fatalistic attitude would be suicidal. Simply stated, the old political and economic world orders have collapsed, accompanied by such major transformations that one authority has referred to them as "sea changes."[4] This description includes but is not limited to an interesting paradox: As the United States and the states of the former U.S.S.R. literally destroy weapons, arms proliferation among Other World countries is increasing and now includes nuclear, biological, and chemical capabilities. Indeed, more than 40 countries may have nuclear weapons by the end of this century.

Social Issues

Changing conditions at the end of the twentieth century have started to affect social issues everywhere. What were formerly Western, value-based issues such as race, gender, religion, and population control are now becoming prominent in the Other World as well. These ideas may be Western-based, but they create tensions in the systems found in the Other World. There, many of these ideas are seen as Western-inspired threats to home, family, society, and religion. In the West, this opposition to rapid change is often linked to the loosely defined concept of family values. However, in the Other World, traditional elders often view these concepts as Western attempts to reimpose colonialism, divide peoples, and destroy religion through the importation of humanistic values. For instance, in many places the Western interest in Other World population control has been described as genocide.

With resistance to Western-inspired social planning linked to colonialism in areas stretching from Latin America through Egypt to India, it will be extremely difficult to make measurable change in the social practices of many Other World states in the foreseeable future.

DECISIONS 2000

There is a vast and growing agenda of issues that urgently needs to be addressed by the global community. Some concerns, such as those discussed above, are more applicable to the Other World, whereas others, such as restructuring the world order, affect everyone. Many problems require the cooperative efforts of all states if conditions are to improve and a more widely acceptable order is to be defined and maintained. This is the case with environmental issues and the economic relations within Other World states, as well as between them and the more industrialized world, which are addressed in the section on a new world order.

Environmental Issues

Environmental problems caused by the industrialized world have recently received considerable attention: the acid rain that is destroying forests and lakes in the United States, Canada, and central Europe; the hazards resulting from improper disposal of nuclear wastes; the pollution of the marine environment from supertanker oil spills and unprocessed sewage; and the exhaustion of finite resources such as oil, among other examples. The Other World has environmental problems that are equally devastating: overcrowded cities, lack of sanitation facilities, diseases spread by contaminated water supplies, and desertification resulting from poor land management and the cutting of trees for fuel and pasture. The environmental consequences are too damaging for such practices to continue. The world can be destroyed by the gradual disintegration of the Earth's ecosystem as well as by nuclear war. We can no longer ignore Barry Commoner's laws of ecology. His first law states, "Everything Is Connected to Everything Else"; his second, "Everything Must Go Somewhere."[5] The key question is whether we can continue to survive beyond the twenty-first century if present pollution and resource consumption continue.

Toxic Materials.   A vast amount of herbicides, insecticides, fungicides, and pesticides is used for agricultural purposes throughout the world. These poisons control weeds, encourage crop growth, and kill off unwanted insects. Unfortunately, they can also enter the food chain. The toxins are manufactured in industrialized states and exported to Other World countries. Although there are some positive consequences, their unregulated use represents a health hazard to agricultural workers and to all consumers who eat food products from the Other World. Some sprays are carcinogenic; some, including DDT, result in the premature death of small animals; and others, such as Agent Orange, which was used by the United States to defoliate the jungles in Vietnam in the 1960s and 1970s, are linked to birth defects in children and miscarriages in women.

The careless handling of even small amounts of radioactive material can have serious consequences. In late 1983, two employees at a hospital in Juarez, Mexico, took a core from a cancer therapy machine in the hospital's warehouse to sell for scrap. Unknown to them, a small hole in the core allowed the 6,000 pellets of radioactive cobalt-60 to spill into their pickup truck as well as into the scrap yard. The pellets became mixed with other junk, eventually being used by a foundry to make cast iron legs for tables in fast-food restaurants and some 6,000 tons of concrete reinforcing bars. Ultimately, and by accident, the radioactive products were discovered and destroyed, but not before they had been sold throughout Mexico and the United States. Prolonged exposure to such products can cause sterility and death.

In 1986, the near meltdown of the Soviet nuclear reactor in Chernobyl demonstrated to the whole world the dangers of technology that has been pressed beyond its limits in the rush to find alternative energy sources. American and other reactors have also had close calls, especially at Three-Mile Island, Pennsylvania. In 1990, the German government closed several Soviet-designed reactors in eastern Germany for safety reasons, but similar ones elsewhere continue to operate as those countries' *only* electrical energy supply.

Pollution.   Air, land, and water pollution are visible in all of the industrialized countries, and efforts made to counteract the environmental effects have met with varying degrees of success. Paradoxically, in many Other World cities, air pollution is often regarded as an indication of economic strength. Factories that belch flumes of smoke into the air represent employment opportunities, economic self-sufficiency, and less dependence on Western economies. Much of the water pollution in the Other World can be traced to poor or nonexistent sewage disposal and to the chemicals in fertilizers that collect in lakes and underground water supplies.

Rainforests.   The tropical forests in countries near the Equator are essential to the health of the world's ecosystem. The rainforests, in conjunction with green plants growing on land and on the oceans' surface, act as a natural cleansing system by removing from the atmosphere carbon dioxide produced by the combustion of fossil fuels. Over the last 50 years, many rainforests have been cut down or severely reduced in size. Over half the world's remaining tropical rainforests are now in the Amazon region of Brazil. Some are also found in central Africa, but the forests in West Africa, southern Africa, the Caribbean, North America, and some parts of India are largely gone. In the Amazon alone, some 50 million acres of rainforests, an area about the size of the state of Nebraska, are lost *annually* to logging, the clearing of jungles for farm and grazing land, slash-and-burn agricultural practices, and population resettlement policies that promise impoverished urban refugees newly cleared farmland in the jungles if they will relocate.

As the rainforests are cut back, there is a resulting increase of carbon dioxide in the atmosphere, which scientists fear will result in a gradual warming of the Earth's climate. This greenhouse effect could cause some melting of the polar ice caps, a reduction of regional rainfall, and a change in growing seasons. The rainforests are a combination of a vast variety of trees and undergrowth. When the hardwood trees are cut down for export or simply burned, the undergrowth dies and the rain washes the topsoil away. The resulting erosion makes it unlikely that new growth can survive in place of the old.

The reduction of the rainforests is understandably a concern to environmentalists, particularly those in the industrialized world, where few rainforests still exist. However, in the Other World, the rainforests are considered an untapped source of wealth. As Brazil's foreign debt increases, harvesting hardwoods in the Amazon could be a means of repaying loans through wood exports. Presently, most hardwoods are burned for lack of a market or access to markets. There is a political aspect to this practice as well, as one observer noted: "In many tropical

Loss of Rainforest. This area in the Amazon rainforest has been logged off in preparation for rice planting.

SOURCE: Domingo/Lenderts

countries where the few have a lot and the many hardly anything, the rainforest is a political asset. The wealthy and powerful abhor land reform—so why not shunt the land-hungry poor into that great green forest, especially if expenses will be underwritten by some international nonprofit lending institution?"[6] This reference to international nonprofit institutions includes the World Bank, which has provided funds to the Indonesian government to relocate residents of overcrowded Java and Madura to sparsely populated islands. Some rainforests have to be cleared for the new settlements, and a new economy dependent on the further reduction of the wooded areas is created. Much of the hardwood cut in Indonesia is exported to Japan and ultimately sent to the United States as stereo cabinets and other furniture.

Environmental Trends

There is growing international concern about the global environment. In June 1972, the first UN Conference on the Global Environment was held in Stockholm, Sweden. Some 1,200 delegates from 113 countries and 400 international agencies participated, although delegates from the Soviet bloc boycotted the meeting because of a dispute over whether representatives from East Germany would be allowed voting privileges. At the end of the 11-day program, the delegates adopted a 109-point action plan and a "Declaration on the Human Environment." Both were subsequently officially recognized when the UN General Assembly established the UN Environmental Program to act as a prime force and clearinghouse to coordinate multinational efforts to resolve environmental problems.

Since then, other conferences on the international environment have been held, and countries have set up their own agencies for environmental protection. However, some countries have been concerned that environmental controls might inhibit their economic development, and international protective measures continue to be favored. If international efforts are to be successful, the industrialized countries must help finance them. In 1972, $100 million was pledged, although actual contributions to the UN Environmental Program were significantly less, mainly because of inflation and other domestic economic problems in the industrialized states.

In spite of its reduced budget, the UN Environmental Program is monitoring changing environmental conditions and recommending feasible plans to help countries enact sound environmental policies. Meanwhile, internal environmental movements in Other World countries are gaining strength. Costa Rica has more land under protected status than any other country in Latin America and "debt swapping" schemes in which protection of forest is promised in return for relief from international debt. In Kenya, two nongovernmental organizations planted more trees in a two-year period than the government had in the previous five. In Indonesia, environmental organizations have put pressure on the government to reduce water pollution, regulate mining operations, and reevaluate the wisdom of overcutting hardwood forests.[7] In short, there are critical environmental decisions to be made the world over as the close of the twentieth century approaches.

The most recent effort to address questions about the global environment was held in Rio de Janeiro in June 1992. The UN Conference on Environment and Development, dubbed the Earth Summit, brought together world leaders to establish acceptable trade-offs among environmental protection, the Other World's need to develop, and the industrialized countries' need to maintain growth and jobs. It was also hoped that the Convention on Biological Diversity would be signed in order to forestall species extinction—the disappearance of more of the planet's animal and plant species. Only the United States refused to sign because of serious questions about the treaty's provision for sovereign rights over genetic resources.

TOWARD A NEW WORLD ORDER

The world of the 1990s is a dramatically different place than it was when the first edition of this book was published in 1987. The intervening years have witnessed events that few could have predicted. First in Eastern Europe and then in the U.S.S.R. itself, the collapse of communism produced a surge toward democracy and free-market economic systems there and elsewhere. Faced with increasing demands for national autonomy and a steady erosion of their power, conservative Soviet communists launched an abortive coup in August 1991. Their action discredited their party, strengthened their reform-minded opponents, and hastened the demise of the state they had hoped to preserve. Today, the remnants of that state are being subjected to numerous disruptive changes as the dormant forces of religion, nationalism, and ethnicity reemerge and interact with the economic and political changes begun by former Soviet President Gorbachev and, later, more vigorously pursued by Russian President Boris Yeltsin and others. Before its demise, the U.S.S.R. had become a land of economic retrenchment within its borders, accompanied by a reduction of commitments beyond. For the moment, these processes seem to be continuing. However, the world cannot now view these events with a sense of detachment. In an interdependent world, events affecting Russia, the Ukraine, Chechnya, and other segments of the former Soviet Union offer both opportunity and danger for people throughout the world.

In China, it has become apparent that the aging leaders of the Communist party are unwilling to match their economic reforms with political reforms. In June 1989, demands by students and workers for greater democracy were eventually met with a determined and ruthless suppression by elements of the People's Liberation Army (PLA) in Tiananmen Square. That action was followed by similar acts of suppression throughout China and by a continuing campaign against "bourgeois democracy." Internally, China remains a rigidly authoritarian state determined to take from the outside world only those things that contribute to its economic development and to resist the importation of the political beliefs and practices that have accompanied such development elsewhere. China's pragmatic leaders realized that the resumption of its traditional role of leadership in Asia and the strengthening of its claim to such a position in the larger world community required the restoration of the political and economic ties that were damaged, at least temporarily, by its actions in 1989. Thus it engaged in many international activities ranging from the hosting of the 1990 Asian Games and numerous international meetings to diplomatic efforts, such as mending its sometimes tattered relations with neighboring states like Russia and Vietnam.

Throughout the 1990s, such efforts appeared to bear fruit as internal order prevailed, foreign investment strengthened, and China's gross domestic product resumed its double-digit rate of growth. Perhaps typical is a statement by Israel's first ambassador to China, Zev Sofott, made a few months after the two states established diplomatic relations in 1992: "China is a big trade partner and its import value topped more than $60 billion dollars last year. We would like to have a small part of that value."[8] Israel was by no means alone in wanting "some of that value." After trying to alter China's human rights performance by threatening to end its most-favored-nation (MFN) trading status, President Clinton reversed his position and agreed that the two issues would no longer be linked. By the middle of the decade, China again seemed assured of a major role in world affairs, both economically and politically.

In the West, the European states continued their movement toward economic and political integration with the ratification of the Maastricht Treaty (1992), creating the European Union (EU), and the removal of all trade barriers between members. In addition, the EU now has a united Germany as its major economic force. The apparent success of the EC has encouraged many of the former Soviet satellite states to seek a greater role in the economic integration of Europe. Also searching for a role in the common "European home" are the economically and politically troubled states of the former Soviet Union itself. Beyond Europe, the

United States is also trying to adjust to changing conditions by seeking a greater political role for NATO in the increasing ties between Eastern and Western Europe and by fashioning a free-trade agreement with Canada and Mexico (NAFTA) in 1993. Elsewhere, similar regional trading blocks are taking form in the Other World—for example, the 1992 formation of a free-trade zone by the ASEAN states and the Asia Pacific Economic Cooperation forum (APEC).

These changes have contributed to a new if fitful spirit of cooperation between East and West to a degree unimaginable a few years ago. Former Soviet President Gorbachev spoke of "new political thinking" in seeking accommodation with the West and access to its economy and technology. Former President Bush spoke of a "new world order" to replace confrontation with cooperation as former antagonists jointly use their power and influence to settle international problems. As this decade began, it seemed that after over 40 years of immobilization by cold war politics, the concept of collective security might at last fulfill the order-building role it was assigned by UN founders. However, there are forces afoot that are jeopardizing this progress and could plunge the world into a new era of conflict, both "hot" and "cold."

Alternatives to the Old World Order

Certainly, the momentous changes noted above will affect the Other World. Indeed, given such massive changes in the "first" and "second" worlds, the term *Third World* is perhaps even less valid now than it was a few years ago. Many of the people living in the less developed regions have long regarded it as an arrogant label devised by the developed states to relegate the people and problems of the less developed countries to inferior status. Today, segments of the East and West seem to be merging into a single developed world, which may interact collectively with the less developed Other World. Although the precise nature and impact of these interactions are still unclear, recent events in Afghanistan, Europe, Cambodia, Nicaragua, Panama, the Persian Gulf, and Palestine may provide some instructive and perhaps disquieting hints.

In each of these regional conflicts, past tendencies of both East and West to seek a political advantage were replaced by a high degree of cooperation in the search for solutions. In each instance their efforts were supported by several Other World states. If this is to be taken as evidence of the emergence of a new world order, what will be its probable nature? One possibility is that in this new era of multipolarity, the great powers will move toward a role that great powers traditionally played in world affairs. It was described nearly half a century ago by former British diplomat Sir Harold Nicholson:

> It was assumed that the Great Powers were greater than the Small Powers, since they possessed a more extended range of interests, wider responsibilities, and, above all, more money and more guns. . . . Throughout this period the Small Powers were assessed according to their effect upon the relations between the Great Powers: there was seldom any idea that their interests, their opinions, still less their votes, could affect a policy agreed upon. . . .[9]

Simply put, such a world order assumes that although all sovereign states are legally equal, those that possess greater power have a greater responsibility to maintain the international political and economic system than do lesser powers. To carry out these responsibilities, the great powers jointly construct and enforce the international system, at times even acting as "police," either unilaterally or in concert with other great powers.

Great-power efforts to bring pressure on the belligerents in Afghanistan, Cambodia, and the Middle East, and to a lesser degree, Bosnia, may represent movement toward this model. Should such a model prevail, a few great powers, like the United States, Japan, Russia, China, and the EU, might assume the responsibility for maintaining order throughout the Other World. Such a "condominium of power" has been condemned in the past. Most notably perhaps, China has often warned against great-power hegemony in which major powers impose their solutions to world problems. However, China seems to be increasingly willing to accept such leadership when it is included among those great powers. Certainly there is a degree of haughtiness in an order that arrogates to a few states such global responsibilities. Still, as the twentieth century began, such an arrangement would not have been regarded by most states as unreasonable or unusual. It is not altogether impossible that the same attitudes may prevail as the century ends.

A somewhat less arbitrary scenario would see East and West cooperating within the UN framework to promote international cooperation through the rule of law. As noted above, conditions may now allow the UN Security Council to function in the manner envisioned by its founders. The UN response to the 1990 invasion of Kuwait by Iraq may be an indication that such a world order is at least beginning to emerge. At the instigation of the United States, the Security Council quickly condemned the invasion and provided for sanctions against the offending state. With the United States again providing the leadership, several states sent military forces to the region to deal with what former Secretary of State James Baker called the first international crisis of the post–cold war era. A few months later the Security Council approved the use of military force by member states to restore Kuwait's independence. Significantly, the forces sent to the gulf remained under the command of their own governments. Although no Soviet units were included in the military force confronting Iraq, the Soviets joined in the demand for the withdrawal of Iraqi troops from Kuwait and the restoration of its sovereignty. They also suggested that the Soviet military might participate in a military action if it were conducted under direct UN command. The EC, China, and Japan joined in the condemnation of the Iraqi action and in varying degrees supported the UN sanctions. With few exceptions, Other World states joined the developed states in supporting the UN sanctions against Iraq. On the surface, at least, collective security seemed to be working.

In spite of such general support, there is some question about whether the condominium-of-power model or the rule-of-law model better describes the effort to confront Iraq. Although most actions were sanctioned by votes in the UN Security Council, the United States clearly took the initiative and provided the bulk of the force and influence that sustained them. It also seemed to view itself as the prime arbiter of its actions. Similarly, other states militarily involved in the region jealously guarded their sovereign right to command their armed forces, thereby complicating collective efforts through the UN. A case can be made that the Other World states that most actively supported the effort felt directly threatened by Iraq's actions; were heavily dependent on the United States, like Egypt; or had their own anti-Saddam Hussein agenda, like Syria. Of the great powers, only the Soviet Union wanted its forces, had they been provided, to be part of a UN-directed military effort.

Perhaps a better illustration of the rule-of-law model came later in the decade with the conflicts in Bosnia and other segments of the former Yugoslavia. In those conflicts, the various military forces sent to serve as "peacekeepers" *did* serve under the direct control of the United Nations. Under indecisive and divided UN leadership, no state or combination of states (e.g., the EU or NATO) stepped forward to shoulder the responsibility of implementing the UN resolutions as the United States had done in the Persian Gulf crisis. The result in Bosnia was paralysis, leading to a U.S.-spearheaded NATO intervention beginning in late 1995.

In short, one may question whether the Persian Gulf crisis or the crisis in Bosnia provides a better illustration of the application of the rule of law in international affairs. If, as seems likely, Bosnia is the better example, there seems to be serious reason to doubt whether that model will prevail unless such enforcement is vigorously led by a major power or a group of such powers. In such a situation, the difference between the two models we have discussed becomes rather slight and the outlook for an effective UN is remote.

There is, of course, another possibility. In an age when the United States and the former Soviet Union no longer compete with each other for influence in the Other World, major powers may simply ignore that region unless there is a direct threat to their interests. This course could seem especially attractive to the successors to the U.S.S.R., torn as they are by internal dissention and economic difficulties. Although under considerably less stress, the United States no longer possesses the economic preeminence on which its worldwide influence once depended. Although Japan and the EU are active economically, neither seems avidly interested in greater political or military involvement in Other World problems. China sees itself as a part of the Other World and seems likely to continue its effort to play a leading role there. However, it also appreciates its role as a major player on the larger world stage. If its actions in the conflicts discussed above are any indication of its future intentions, it seems likely that China will tend to cooperate with other great powers, at least in the short term. If so, Other World states may indeed receive considerably less attention from the developed states. One positive result would be that Other World states would no longer serve as arenas for proxy conflicts between East and West. However, in the absence of East-West competition, the already small transfer of wealth from the developed world to the Other World may diminish even further.

States are all too often motivated by national interest alone. However, it may be hoped that this attitude will not always prevail. It is possible that the developed states may use some of their post–cold war "peace dividend" for an increased effort to solve the many problems that confront the Other World.

Unfortunately, there is little evidence now to suggest that this course will occur, as there is little or no political constituency in the developed states to promote it. Local interests, of course, do have such constituencies—for example, the various interests in the United States that scurried about for a share of the expected peace dividend as tensions began to ease between East and West.

Indeed, tendencies in the developed world seem to be toward greater concern with its own interests and less involvement in the problems of the Other World. To overcome a massive government deficit, the U.S. Congress made large cuts in foreign aid to Other World states in 1995. As internal problems divert the attention of the former Soviet states from foreign involvements outside Europe, the EU seems intent on a more protectionist course. To the West, the culturally similar nations of Eastern Europe may be seen as a safer and more familiar terrain for investment. In the relatively less developed states of Eastern Europe there are populations whose education, experience, and training are such that investments may be more quickly recouped as those states are slowly integrated economically, culturally, and politically with Western Europe.

Should a new world order emerge in which the UN and the rule of law achieve greater acceptance worldwide, habits of cooperation might develop that could eventually lead to greater joint efforts by the developed states to address the problems of the Other World. However, it is difficult to envision such changes occurring by the end of this century.

NEW INTERNATIONAL RELATIONSHIPS

If the world community is to manage a large and growing number of conflicts, new economic and political relationships must be fashioned. Existing institutions, such as the UN, that can be used to resolve international disputes must be strengthened; new credible and sustainable structures and processes must be created, particularly at the national and regional levels, and all countries must develop the habit of resolving international and domestic conflicts within those frameworks. Unless this task can be accomplished sooner rather than later, the twenty-first century could be a most unpleasant experience for us all.

New Economic Relationships

As noted, the Other World's disadvantageous economic relationship with the industrialized states has contributed to a massive international debt, now approaching $2 *trillion*.[10] The disadvantage to emerging states is especially evident in the international trade market: The industrialized states and their multinational corporations control some 80 percent of the global economy. Other World states lack the capital, industrial capacity, technology, and infrastructure to compete with the industrialized countries, which have been honing their economic might for over a century. Because of the need for hard currencies, Other World countries are forced to use their cheap labor to produce goods for export rather than tailor their economies for domestic consumption. This condition means that most

Other World countries are almost totally dependent on trade revenues in an international market over which they have little control. To compound the problem, the industrialized states, to protect their economic interests, can increase tariff barriers and impose quotas limiting the amount of goods imported. The question that the industrialized world has to address is this: What economic concessions is it willing to make to help Other World states achieve their economic independence?

In the 1960s, many Other World countries urged the UN to take a positive step toward the economic rejuvenation of their segment of the world. In the 1970s, the movement for a New International Economic Order (NIEO) took root. Its agenda called for (1) more aid for the Other World from the wealthy states, (2) dispersal of funds through multilateral agencies such as the World Bank instead of country-by-country aid, (3) an increased voice for Other World representatives in the World Bank and IMF, (4) a restructuring or cancellation of debts owed to the industrialized states, (5) some domestic control over multinational corporations, and (6) special trade privileges for Other World countries with the industrialized states.[11] The NIEO advocates argued that Western states must accept responsibility for the economic inequalities in the Other World since they were responsible for the exploitation that came with colonization. Moreover, they argued, it is the Western countries that continue to reap profits because of their control over international pricing mechanisms and neocolonial practices. The Soviet bloc countries supported NIEO demands but maintained that they should apply only to the Western economies since the Soviet Union and its allies were not part of the colonial experience.

In the 1980s, the General Agreement on Tariffs and Trade (GATT) supplanted both the UN Conference on Trade and Development (UNCTAD) and the NIEO as the principal mechanism of all international economic activity, including MFN status. The NIEO's influence diminished proportionately. Although it is still uncertain whether the Other World will benefit from this change, the GATT did have policymaking authority that the NIEO never had. The GATT was succeeded by the new World Trade Organization (WTO) in January 1995. While it has a more extensive range of agreements, including intellectual property rights, it has no power to enforce.

A new approach was taken by the South Commission, whose report, *The Challenge to the South*, was issued in 1990. It emphasizes the need for cooperation among Other World states and asserts that "responsibility for the development of the South lies in the South, and in the hands of the peoples of the South."[12] Clearly both cooperation and understanding will be needed from the northern, industrialized countries, although the report represents a major departure from the earlier notion that development of the Other World was the responsibility, indeed the duty, of the North. It does not, however, provide for any institutional framework.

Major change will be forthcoming in the international economic order during the next decade as Other World countries become more organized and interconnected with the world's economy. Some Western states did recognize the NIEO demand for lower tariffs on Other World imports, although many did not.

Conventional wisdom suggests that the natural resources of the Other World and its cheap supply of labor are vital to the industrialized states. However, some observers believe there is a permanent oversupply of foodstuffs, raw materials, and even labor in the Other World that will lead to their suppliers' "uncoupling" from industrialized economies.[13] Some Other World countries may form cartels like OPEC to control production and prices. The Other World voice in international institutions will not achieve all of the NIEO goals by the year 2000 or even soon afterward. However, such actions seem certain to conflict with the interests of emerging trade blocs like the EU and NAFTA, and efforts continue to provide more substance to the Pacific Rim and to an expanded American economic community without trade barriers (North, Central, and South America—from Canada to Tierra del Fuego). Perhaps NAFTA is just the beginning.

New Political Relationships

It is indisputable that the cold war is over and its two former poles, or blocs, are no longer capable of maintaining or returning to the old order. At this writing, the United States is clearly the world's dominant military power and police force. However, in every other way, the world is now more multipolar than at any time in the last half century, and there is no permanent political or institutional structure to support it. It is precisely the absence of the cold war structure that presents the greatest challenge. What will take its place? A revitalized, reorganized, and strengthened UN? New or revitalized and strengthened regional or international political and economic organizations? Or simply a free-for-all? In 1990, Stanley Hoffmann proposed

> not a world government for which states and peoples are unprepared (and that the managers of the business civilization would not like), but a new experiment in polycentric steering, in which the three major economic powers—plus the Soviet Union . . . and perhaps China—would form a central steering group, and in which regional powers would play comparable roles in their areas.[14]

In this or any other prospective world political structure, there are numerous relevant issues. Among them are power, force, economics, and people—large numbers of people taking to the streets to engage in direct political action.

Power.   As anyone who has studied politics and international relations knows, power is a difficult concept to grasp and define. It is very clear that power is taking on a whole new dimension, at least internationally, in the post–cold war era. Alvin Toffler, the futurist, has suggested that above all, power is based on knowledge—that even military and economic power are now predicated on knowledge and technology. This is a far cry from the prewar and cold war eras, when international power was defined in terms of nuclear megatons, strength of society and economy, size, and capability and mobility of armies. The United States and the Soviet Union excelled in those power capabilities, as defined in traditional terms, and actually were at *military* parity by the time the Berlin Wall collapsed; both had the ability to "overkill" each other's populations many times over. Perhaps it was a sign of things to come that all that military power had helped neither superpower in Vietnam or Afghanistan, and none was unleashed by either side as the U.S.S.R. and communism collapsed. How power is distributed and balanced will be a major issue in constituting any future structure.

Force.   Perhaps the greatest lesson of the twentieth century is that force and the threat of force, military or otherwise, domestic or international, resolves nothing. It can postpone problems, as it has for much of this century, but it cannot eliminate or resolve them. If it is accepted that force is of surprisingly little use as a long-term tool of domestic and foreign policy, it is quite remarkable that there are no structures, institutions, processes, and traditions to take the place of force on any but a short-term basis. Sadly, there are still people in power the world over who think force works—for example, the actions orchestrated by Serbian President Milosevic, Bosnian leader Karadjic, and Boris Yeltsin in Chechnya. Although it may seem to work in the short term, one of the lessons of history in general, and this century in particular, is that force does not work in the long term and creates wounds that take long years, if not forever, to heal.

Economics.   It has always been difficult to disentangle politics and economics at either the domestic or international level. However, it has never been more difficult than it is now, as the nature of state power is redefined and the global economic community takes on a life and inertia of its own. The economic friction and potential battle between the United States, Japan, and China is only one example of the future conflicts that will dominate as the world enters the twenty-first century. In all such cases, the question is this: Who and what will call the shots? Traditional sovereign states? Boards of directors of multinational corporations, isolated from public scrutiny and control? Centralized international, regional, or global organizations?

People.   A word on people power is important in light of events in the Philippines, China, Eastern Europe, South Africa, and elsewhere. It cannot and should not be underestimated, as actual events in the past several years demonstrate. Nobody can ever forget the bravery of the young man who stopped a column of tanks from proceeding toward Tiananmen Square in Beijing; or the people of Leipzig who confronted the once formidable East German Army, thereby risking the "Chinese solution" (massacre); or the Sowetans (South Africa), West Bank Palestinians, Romanians, and others. However, given the mixed achievements in these examples, the risks are high and the prospects for success are by no means certain and should not be overestimated.

In a related vein, people the world over continue to demand public services such as education and medical care. They may be expected to react when such services are threatened by political or economic disarray or by government budget cuts. For example, some voters in Eastern Europe and the former Soviet republics have freely elected communists to public office, no doubt in response to major disruptions in their lives resulting from the shock of free-market reforms.

Such actions also provide evidence that the social democratic variation of Marxism is still very much alive even though Stalinism, or monolithic, dictatorial communism, is largely a thing of the past.

CONCLUSION

The world has changed drastically during the half century since World War II, a war that saw the first use of atomic weapons. The UN was born out of that destruction, with the goal of preventing another such catastrophe. Although much has occurred since 1945 and much more will take place before the new century, the global community now has the capacity to self-destruct or peacefully coexist.

The UN Charter was signed by 51 states in 1945. Today, there are approximately 185 members.[15] The expanded membership reflects an international environment that has grown more politically complex and which now has an even greater potential for violent conflict than half a century ago. At the same time, breakthroughs in communications, transportation, and other technologies have shrunk the world immeasurably, making personal contact easier, more frequent, and almost instantaneous.

Some relationships do not change with time. The inequalities in standards of living persist and are even expanding in many areas of the Other World. Students of the world's condition can note many cruel paradoxes. Medical advances have prolonged the lives of millions, yet tens of thousands die each year from starvation and diseases that accompany malnutrition. There is more widespread awareness now of the fragile nature of the Earth's environment than ever before, although there are now more ways of damaging that environment than ever before. Industrial and technological developments have freed many workers from the drudgery of assembly-line production, yet many more will face a lifetime of illiteracy, poverty, and marginal employment at best.

The status of the world's states will change over the next half century. Some will gain more international prestige; others will see their standing diminish; and some, like Czechoslovakia, will disappear. One hundred years ago, England ruled the seas and governed an empire that extended to every corner of the earth. Today, only the faded remnants of that power remain. The United States will continue to be an international power in the years ahead, even though that power may be redefined. It is unlikely that the Other World will be a cohesive force in the near future, although some states such as China, India, and Brazil are pursuing more prominent leadership roles.

A gloomy scenario for the world in the next century cannot be easily dismissed, based on human actions of the past, although the world and its peoples have demonstrated a remarkable capacity to survive the adversity of natural and human-made disasters.[16] However, a fatalistic outlook that might have been appropriate before is no longer. This is the dawning of a new, exciting, and dangerous age. Increased cross-cultural understanding has helped us to grasp our future—a future that does not belong to the Other World or to the First or Second World. The future belongs to all of us; it belongs to the world. The only question is whether we are collectively up to the tasks before us. Shall we survive, perish, or prevail?

NOTES

1. This section depends heavily on material from the same segment of the first edition, written by John H. Culver.
2. Pierre Crosson, "Agricultural Land: Will There Be Enough?" *Environment*, 26 (September 1984): 43.
3. Elaine M. Murphy, *Food and Population: A Global Concern* (Washington, D.C.: Population Reference Bureau, 1984), p. 8.
4. Miles Kahler, "The International Political Economy," *Foreign Affairs*, 69 (Fall 1990): 139.
5. Barry Commoner, "The Ecosphere," in *Global Resources*, ed. Martin I. Glassner (New York: Praeger, 1983), pp. 24–25.
6. Peter T. White, "Rain Forests," *National Geographic*, 163 (January 1983): 46.
7. Norman Myers, "Third World: Mixed News on the Environment," *Environment*, 25 (June 1983): 44–45.
8. *Beijing Review*, 55 (May 18–24, 1992): 10.
9. A. Harold Nicholson, "The Old Diplomacy," in *Crisis and Continuity in World Politics*, 2nd ed., ed. George A. Lanyi and Wilson C. McWilliams (New York: Random House, 1973), p. 361. Originally published in Harold Nicholson, *The Evolution of Diplomatic Method* (New York: Macmillan, 1954), pp. 99–107.
10. World Bank, *World Debt Tables* (Washington, D.C.: World Bank, 1994), p. 25.
11. James Lee Ray, *Global Politics*, 6th ed. (Boston: Houghton Mifflin, 1995), pp. 294–296.
12. South Commission, *The Challenge to the South: The Report of the South Commission* (New York: Oxford University Press, 1990).
13. See Peter Drucker, "The Changed World Economy," *Foreign Affairs*, 64 (Spring 1986): 768–777; and Peter Drucker, *The New Realities* (New York: Harper & Row, 1989).
14. Stanley Hoffmann, "A New World and Its Troubles," *Foreign Affairs*, 69 (Fall 1990): 120.
15. This number is approximate because Czechoslovakia, East and West Germany, North and South Yemen, North and South Korea, Yugoslavia, the Baltic states, and others have changed their UN status and membership as a result of post–cold war realignments.
16. For a chilling forecast, see Robert D. Kaplan, "The Coming Anarchy," *Atlantic Monthly*, 273, 2 (February 1994): 44–76.

FOR FURTHER READING

Berger, Peter L. *Pyramids of Sacrifice: Political Ethics and Social Change*. New York: Anchor Books, 1976.
Brown, Lester, ed. *State of the World, 1994. A Worldwatch Institute Report on Progress toward a Sustainable Society*. 2nd ed. New York: Norton, 1995.
De Soto, Hernando. *The Other Path*. New York: Harper & Row, 1989.
Galli, Rosemary, ed. *Rethinking the Third World*. New York: Crane Russak, 1992.
Gillis, Malcolm; Perkins, Dwight H.; Roemer, Michael; and Snodgrass, Donald. *Economics of Development*. 3rd ed. New York and London: Norton, 1992.
Hauchler, I., and Kennedy, P. M., eds. *The Almanac of Development and Peace*. New York: Random House, 1993.

Hughes, Barry B. *World Futures*. Baltimore: Johns Hopkins University Press, 1985.

Kegley, Charles W., and Wittkopf, Eugene R., eds. *The Future of American Foreign Policy*. 2nd ed. New York: St. Martin's Press, 1994; Kegley, Charles W., and Raymond, G. A. *A Multipolar Peace? Great Power Politics in the 21st Century*. New York: St. Martin's Press, 1994.

Kennedy, Paul. *Preparing for the 21st Century*. New York: Random House, 1993.

Manor, James, ed. *Rethinking Third World Politics*. London and White Plains, N.Y.: Longman, 1991.

Mittelman, James H. *Out from Underdevelopment*. New York: St. Martin's Press, 1988.

Randall, Vicky, and Theobald, R. *Political Change and Underdevelopment*. Durham, N.C.: Duke University Press, 1985.

Thurow, Lester. *Head to Head: The Coming Economic Battle among Japan, Europe, and America*. New York: Warner Books, 1993.

Wright, Robin, and McManus, Doyle. *Flashpoints: Promise and Peril in a New World*. New York: Knopf, 1991.

Index

Abacha, General Sani, 183
Afghanistan coup d'état, 216-217
Africa
    colonialism, 159-164
    economic and natural resources, 151,
        169-172
    environment, 151, 186-187
    ethnic groups, 156, 176-177, 180-181
    famine, 154, 182
    geography, 151-154
    government, 164-166
    history, 154-164
    International Monetary Fund, 171, 172
    international relations, 168-169
    irredentism, 159
    Islam, 156, 158
    land mines, 184, 185
    migration, 182-183
    military, 151, 183, 184
    nationalism, 162-164
    political parties, 186
    population growth, 151, 157, 187
    races, 154-156
    religions, 156, 158
    Roman Catholic Church, 156
    United Nations, 176, 179, 182, 185
    World Bank, 171-172, 177, 185
African National Congress, 78, 172, 174
Afrikaners, 172
AIDS, 177, 179-180
Algeria, 24, 33, 230, 231, 232, 233, 245,
    267

Allende, Salvador, 76
Alliance for Progress, 118
Andeau Free Trade Association, 86
Angola, 178-179
Apartheid, 173-174
Appropriate technology, 53
Arab League (also League of Arab States), 90
Arafat, Yasser, 258
Argentina, 137
Arias, Oscar, 121
Arias Peace Plan, 121-122
Aristide, Jean-Bertrand, 146-148
Arms proliferation, 278
Aryan Invasion, 196
Asia
    culture, 195
    geography, 190-194
    history and government, 196-200
    politics, 190
    religion, 195
Asia Pacific Economic Cooperation
        Conference (APEC), 86, 284
Asian Economic Growth, 219-220
Association of Southeast Asian Nations
        (ASEAN), 214-215, 224, 284
Asunción, Treaty of, 136
Aswan High Dam, 33, 232, 236
Ataturk, 249
Aung San Suu Kyi, 214
Authoritarian government, 118
Ayodhya, 209
Aztecs, 108

Baena Soares, Joao, 121
Banana Republics, 117
Bandung Conference, 210
Barre, Mohammed Siad, 181–182
Batista, Fulgencio, 132
Belgian Congo, 185
Bharatiya Jamata Party, 209
Bhutto, Benazir, 210–211
Bretton Woods Agreements, 56
British East India Company, 196
Bolivar, Simon, 114
Bonaparte, Napoleon, 252
Buthelezi, Chief Gatsha, 164, 174, 175

Cabildo, 112
Calles, Plutarco, 124
Cambodian Conflict, 212–213, 217
Cambodian Peoples Party, 214
Capitalism, 4, 51, 55, 61
Cardenas, Cuauhtemoc, 125
Cardenas, Lazaro, 125
Caribbean Commonwealth, 136
Carraza, Venustiano, 123
Castro, Fidel, 132–135
Castro, Raul, 132
Cote d'Ivoire, 166
Caudillo, 117
Central Intelligence Agency (CIA), 133
Ceuta, 31, 32
Chamorro, Violeta, 121
Chechen Republic, 26
Child labor, 41
Chinese border disputes, 217–218
Chinese leadership, 218–219
Ch'ing Dynasty, 198
Chou En-lai. *See* Zhou Enlai
Christianity, 23, 227, 238
Chung-Kuo, 192
Ciller, Tamsu, 250
Civil strife, 78
Cocoyoc Declaration, 50
Collective security, 86
Collor de Mello, Fernando, 130
Colon, Cristobal, 108
Colonialism, 59, 244–246, 273
Commonwealth of Independent States, 86
Communist China, 198
Communist Party of China, 202
Comte, Auguste, 123
Condominium of power, 285
Conflict, 7–10, 17, 73
    general, 277–278
    strategies of, 77
    unresolved, 82

Confucianism, 198
Congo Free State, 162
Conquistadores, 24, 108
Consensus, 74
Contadora peace initiative, 121
Continuum of Conflict, 75
Costa Rica, 121
Coup d'état, 79
Cristero rebellion, 111
Criollo, 112
Cuba, 131–135
Culture, 15, 18, 20

Debt swapping, 282
de Klerk, Frederick W., 174
Democratic, 4
Deng Xiaoping (Teng Hsiao-ping), 218
Dependence, 10
Dependency Theory, 7, 61, 118, 130
Desert Storm, 86. *See also* Gulf War
Development, 50–71
Diaz, Porfirio, 123
Dimirel, Suleyman, 250
Dom Pedro I, 115
Dominican Intervention, 120

East Asia, 197–199, 200
Ecological standards, 42
Economic Community of West African
    States (ECOWAS), 89
Egypt, 28, 33, 40, 227, 229, 244, 252–253,
    265
Elegant, Robert S., 190
Endara, Guillermo, 141
Eritrea, 180, 181
Escobar, Pablo, 139
Ethiopia, 180–181
European Community (EC). *See* European
    Union (EU)
European Union (EU), 86, 89, 283, 289. *See
    also* Treaty of Maastricht (1992)

Falkland Islands, 29, 30, 119
Ferdinand, King of Aragon, 111
Five Principles, 207
Food, 275–277
Foreign Aid, 47
Four Little Dragons, 219
Four Modernizations, 203
Fourth World, 58
Frontline state, 92
Fujimori, Alberto, 121

Gandhi, Indira, 207–208

Gandhi, Mohandas, 196, 205-206
Garcia Perez, Alan, 122
General Agreement on Tariffs and Trade
    (GATT), 56, 288. *See also* World
    Trade Organization (WTO)
Germany, 24-26, 35
Ghana, 163, 172
Gibraltar, 29-30
Global Village, 7
Goulart, Joao, 128
Green Revolution, 57, 59-60, 276
Government, 62
Group of 77, 90
Guerrilla, 114
Guinea, 163
Gulf War, 6, 88, 209, 286. *See also* Desert
    Storm

Haiti, 28, 114, 120, 146-148
Hamas, 82, 259
Han Dynasty, 197
Harrison, Paul, 59
Hay, John, 140
Hegemony, 56
Hidalgo y Costilla, Padre Miguel, 114
Hobbes, Thomas, 62
Hong Kong, 30
Horn of Africa, 180-182
Huntington, Samuel, 65

Incas, 108
Income, 13, 14
India, 59-60
Indian National Congress, 196-197
Indus Civilization, 196
Inflation, 11
Inkatha, 174
Inter-American Treaty of Reciprocal
    Assistance (RIO Treaty), 119
International Bank for Reconstruction and
    Development, 56. *See also* World
    Bank
International conflict, 87
International Court of Justice (ICJ), 94
International Governmental Organization
    (IGO), 89
International Monetary Fund (IMF), 56, 63,
    129, 288
International Organizations
    regional, 89
    functional, 90
Intifada (Uprising), 78
Iraq, 64, 227, 231, 234, 235, 246, 247, 263
Isabella, Queen of Castile, 111

Islamic fundamentalism, 221
Islamic law, 211
Israel, 31, 38, 235, 236-237, 255-257, 258,
    259, 260
Italy, 24, 25
Iturbide, Agustin, 115

Japan, 25
Jiang Zemin, 218
Jordan, 236, 246, 256
Judaism, 227, 234, 237, 270
Junta, 79

Kashmir, 209, 220
Kennedy, John F., 150
Kenya, 157
Keynes, John Maynard, 51-52
Khmer Rouge, 212-213, 217
Kurds, 263
Kuwait, 227, 247, 264, 268-270

La Frontera, 44, 45, 46
Lake Nasser, 236
Lake Victoria, 186
Latin America, 105-149
    conflict resolution, 119-121
    development, 117-118
    economics, 116-118
    geography, 108-110
Latin American Free Trade Association
    (LAFTA), 89
Lebanon, 24, 231, 234, 235, 245
Leys, Colin, 64
Liberation Theology, 111
Lin Piao, 202
Lisbon (Portugal), 115
Lop Nor Region, 200

Machado, Gerardo, 132
Machiavelli, Niccolo, 63
Macmillan, Harold, 150
Mafaus, Nagib, 42
Mahan, Alfred Thayer, 140
Manchu Dynasty, 198
Mandela, Nelson, 92, 174, 175, 184, 185
Mao Zedong (Mao Tse-tung), 201-202
Maquiladores, 43, 44
Marx, Karl, 51, 54, 190, 194
Marxism, 5
Mayas, 108
Mengistu, Haile Mariam, 180, 181
Mercantilism, 61, 114
Mercosur, 86, 89
Mexico, 60, 123-126

Mexico (*continued*)
    peso collapse, 35
Mobutu, Sese Seko, 168, 185
Modernization, 11–12
Monroe Doctrine, 105, 116
Morocco, 24, 29, 232, 237
Most-favored-nation states (MFN), 283
Mozambique, 184–185
Mubarak, Hosni, 253
Mugabe, Robert, 177
Multinational corporations, 64, 69–70, 89,
    93, 95
Muslims, 111

Namibia, 164, 178
Narcotics, 138–140
Nasser, Gammal Abdul, 252
Nationalism, 22, 39, 40, 229, 237, 247–257,
    261, 274
Nationalist China, 198. *See also* Republic of
    China (Taiwan)
Nehru, Jawaharlal, 205–207
Neocolonialism, 22, 34–39, 59, 61, 117
Neo imperialism, 46
Neves, Tancredo, 129
New International Economic Order (NIEO),
    90, 288
New World Order, 64, 69
Nicholson, Sir Harold, 284
Nigeria, 183–184
Nixon, Richard, 207
North American Free Trade Agreement,
    (NAFTA) 60–61, 86, 89, 136,
    143–145, 284
North American Free Trade Association, 44
North Atlantic Treaty Organization (NATO),
    81, 85, 284, 286
Nyerere, Julius, 52, 164

Obregon, Alvaro, 124
Oil pipelines, 265
Oman, 234, 237
Opium War, 198
Organization of African Unity (OAU), 91,
    167
Organization of American States (OAS), 89,
    91, 119–123
Organization for Economic Cooperation and
    Development (OECD), 57
Organization of Islamic Conference (OIC),
    89
Organization of Non-Aligned States, 90
Organization of Petroleum Exporting
    Countries (OPEC), 90, 266

Oriental carpets, 41–42
Other world, 4
Ottomans, 32, 33, 243–249, 262
Ozal, Turquit, 250

Palestine Liberation Organization (PLO), 79,
    259
Palestinians, 247, 256, 259, 261
Pan Africanism, 166–168
Panama, 140–141
Panchsheel. *See* Five Principles
Paracel Islands, 218
Paraguay, 126
Peninsulares, 112
People power, 290
Pérez de Cuellar, Javier, 122, 123
Peron, Juan, 117
Peru, 119
Petrella, Riccardo, 64
Philippines, 25
Pinochet, Augusto, 119
Platt Amendment, 131
Pol Pot, 212–213, 217
Political culture, 74
Political economy, 55
Political institutions, 74
Political process, 74
Politics, 55, 62, 73
Pollution, 280
Population, 3, 12, 14, 17, 59, 275, 277
Poverty, 12–14, 16
Power, 62
Privitization, 64
Protests, 77
Punjab, 209

Qaddafi, Muammar al-, 28, 39

Rabin, Yizhak, 256
Rafsanjani, Hashimi, 252
Rain forests, 280
Reagan, Ronald, 121
Red Guards, 202
Refugees, 275
Republic of China (Taiwan), 200
Revolution, 80
Roosevelt corollary, 116
Roosevelt, Franklin D., 131
Roosevelt, Theodore, 116
Royalist Party (Funcinpec), 213
Rule of law, 285
Rwanda, 64, 175–177

Sadat, Anwar, 252
Sahara, 231, 154
Sahel, 154
Salinas de Gortari, Carlos, 125
Sandinistas, 121
Santa Ana, Antonio Lopez de, 115
Sarney, Jose, 129
Saro-Wiwa, Ken, 183–184
Saudi Arabia, 227, 232–233, 246–247, 266
Schmacher, E. F., 65
Sea change, 278
Selassie, Haile, 180
Self-determination, 212
Serbian Republic (former Yugoslavia), 76
Shiite Muslims, 211
Shining Path (Sendero Luminoso), 81, 122
Sihanouk, Noro Dom, 213
Soccer War, 110
Socialist, 6
Somalia, 64, 181–182
South Africa, 167, 172–175, 187
South Asia, 175, 196–197, 205–212
Southeast Asia, 200, 212–215
Southeast Asia Collective Defense Treaty, 210
Southern Africa Development Community
        Conference (SADCC), 167–168
Soviet Union, 26, 38, 40, 261, 262
Spratly Islands, 218
Strikes, 77
Structural Adjustment Programs, 63
Subsistence, 16, 19
Sudan, 180
Suez Canal, 265
Sunni Muslims, 211
Sustainable Development, 53, 70–71
Syria, 234, 243, 256

Taiwan, 198, 200
Take-off theory, 51–52
Taliban, 211, 217
Tamil separatists, 222–223
Teleology, 51
Teng Hsiao-ping (Deng Xiao-ping), 202
Teng-Hui, Lee, 223
Tenochtitlan, 110
Terrorism, 80
Third World, 4
Thrasymachus, 51, 66–67

Tiananmen Square, 83, 283
Tiananmen Square Massacre, 204–205
Toffler, Alvin, 65
Tordesillis, Treaty of, 24
Torrijos, Omar, 140
Totalitarian temptation, 80
Toxic materials, 279
Transnational organizations, 89
Transnationalism. *See* New World Order
Treaty of Maastricht (1992), 283. *See also*
        European Union (EU)
Tunisia, 24, 229, 233, 246
Turkey, 227, 235, 246, 262, 249–250
Turkish Straits, 265

United Nations (UN), 6–10, 16, 18, 20–21,
        81, 89
    Charter, 92, 291
    General Assembly, 94
    International Court of Justice, 94
    Security Council, 92
    United Nations Conference on Trade and
        Development, 90, 288
    United Nations Protection Force, 81
    Universal Organization, 92
United States, 44, 47, 227, 229, 232, 235
Uruguay, 118

Vargas, Getulio, 117, 127–128
Villa, Francisco "Pancho," 124

Wallerstein, Immanuel, 55–56
Warsaw Pact, 85
Women, 14, 18, 19
World Bank, 14, 56, 288
World Trade Organization (WTO), 288

Xiao-ping, Deng. *See* Teng Hsiao-ping

Yemen, 234, 267

Zaire, 168, 185–186
Zapata, Emiliano, 123
Zapista, Army of National Liberation (EZLN),
        126, 141
Zhou Enlai, 201, 207
Zimbabwa, 172, 177–178
Zionism, 255

About the Authors

JOSEPH N. WEATHERBY

Joseph N. Weatherby has been a professor of political science at California Polytechnic State University since 1968. He has held a joint professorship in the Douglas MacArthur Academy at Howard Payne University, Texas, since 1993. In 1977 he was an invited visiting scholar at Wolfson College, The University of Cambridge, England. He has been awarded a summer Fulbright to the Middle East and an *NEH* Fellowship in Middle East Studies at The University of Michigan. At Cal Poly, he has chaired the academic senate and received the university's outstanding teaching award. He holds B.A. and M.A. degrees from Baylor University, a foreign trade degree from The American Graduate School for International Management, Arizona, and a Ph.D. in political science and Middle East Studies from The University of Utah.

RANDAL L. CRUIKSHANKS

Randal L. Cruikshanks has been a professor of political science at California Polytechnic State University since 1972. He served as an officer in the United States Army in Germany and has held appointments at The University of New Mexico, The University of Kent, Canterbury, England, and The University of Maryland. He was awarded a summer Fulbright to Brazil and has spent time in China, Africa, and Russia. He served as department chair of the political science department at Cal Poly and holds a B.A. degree from The University of California, Berkeley, and M.A. and Ph.D. degrees from The University of Oregon in international and comparative politics.

EMMIT B. EVANS, JR.

Emmit B. Evans has been a faculty member in the political science department at California Polytechnic State University since 1990. He has conducted research in Kenya, Mexico, and at the Scripps Institution of Oceanography and was the executive director of a rural community development organization in the southwestern United States for 10 years. His teaching and research interests are in the areas of comparative development administration, world food politics, and contemporary global issues. He is a former Peace Corps volunteer, having served in East Africa. He earned a Ph.D. degree in political science from The University of California, Berkeley.

REGINALD GOODEN

Reginald Gooden was born in Camaguey, Cuba, and spent his early years in Cuba and Panama. He has taught classes in inter-American relations and political philosophy at California Polytechnic State University since 1970. At Cal Poly he has chaired the academic senate. He has also served on The California State University Chancellor's Advisory Committee on General Education. He has been a member of the California State Academic Senate for the last 10 years. He did his undergraduate work at U.C.L.A. and earned his Ph.D. degree in political science from the University of California, Santa Barbara.

EARL D. HUFF

Earl Huff received his Ph.D. degree from the University of Idaho in 1970. He has travelled extensively in Asia, the Middle East, and elsewhere. Dr. Huff was the recipient of two Fulbright awards to study in Beirut, Lebanon, and in New Delhi, India. In the United Kingdom, he was awarded a Fulbright teaching position and also was an invited visiting scholar at Cambridge University. Although his primary academic interest is in the areas of U.S. foreign policy and Asian politics, he has also coauthored a very successful American government textbook.

RICHARD KRANZDORF

Richard Kranzdorf has been a professor of political science at California Polytechnic State University since 1971. His specialties are African politics and environmental politics. He received a summer Fulbright to Pakistan and a second one to Poland and Hungary. Among the courses Dr. Kranzdorf currently teaches are: Introduction to International Relations, Politics of Global Survival, Contemporary Global Political Issues, Politics of Developing Areas, and African Politics. He is a former Peace Corps volunteer, having served in West Africa. He earned a B.A. degree from The University of Pennsylvania and a Ph.D. in political science from The University of California, Los Angeles.

DIANNE LONG

Dianne Long teaches political science and public administration at California Polytechnic State University in San Luis Obispo, California, where she has been a member of the faculty since 1982. Her teaching and research interests center on public policy and administration. A former Peace Corps volunteer in Central Africa, Dr. Long continues her writings on the nature of Third World peoples and politics. As a contributor to two chapters in *The Other World*, she brings to the text a perspective on issues affecting women, environmental change, and technological adaption. She holds a Master of Public Administration degree and a Ph.D. degree in political science from Michigan State University. She served as chair of the political science department at Cal Poly and as administrator of the Master's of Public Administration program at Michigan State University.